World Politics and International Law

Duke Press Policy Studies

World Politics and International Law

Francis Anthony Boyle

Duke University Press   Durham 1985

© 1985 Duke University Press
All rights reserved
Printed in the United States of America
Library of Congress Cataloging in Publication Data
Boyle, Francis Anthony, 1950–
World politics and international law.
Bibliography: p.
Includes index.
1. International law. 2. International relations.
3. United States—Foreign relations—1945–
4. World politics—1945–   . I. Title.
JX3110.B58W67 1985   341   85-4374
ISBN 0-8223-0609-3
ISBN 0-8223-0655-7 (pbk.)

FOR ELIZABETH AND VIRGINIA

Contents

This book by Professor Francis A. Boyle tries to bridge the gap between international lawyers and those political scientists who write about international politics. In the first part, the author discusses the influence of Professor Morgenthau's realist school on the current thinking of political scientists and the abandonment of this school by its originator in the last years of his life. The author concludes that the best way to test the validity of different approaches is to discuss various international crises in the light of contrasting theories and to analyze each situation from both the legal and political points of view. In particular, he tries to ascertain to what extent vital national interests could be accommodated within an international legal framework, or could require a distortion of international rules in order to achieve national objectives.

In the second part, the author dissects the Entebbe raid, where Israeli forces rescued a group of hostages being detained by hijackers at a Ugandan airport. His analysis shows the deficiencies of the international system in dealing with such a complex issue, where several contradictory principles of international law could be applied and were defended by various protagonists.

The third part starts with a parallel problem—the Iranian hostages crisis, where a group of U.S. officials found themselves in an unprecedented situation of being captured by a band of students. A critical analysis of the handling of this problem by the Carter Administration is followed by vignettes of other crises faced by that Administration and by its successor, the Reagan Administration. This part is less analytical and more prescriptive. The author is no longer satisfied with pointing out what went wrong; instead, he departs from the usual hands-off policy of political scientists and tries to indicate how much better each situation could have been handled if the decision makers had been paying more attention to international law and international organizations. The theme is slowly developed that in the long run national interest is better served not by practicing power politics and relying on the use or threat of force but by strengthening those international institutions that can provide a neutral environment for first slowing down a crisis and then finding an equitable solution acceptable to most of the parties in conflict.

The value of this book lies primarily in giving the reader a real insight into several important issues of today that are familiar to most people only from newspaper headlines and television news. While not everybody can agree with all his criticisms of the mistakes of various governments, there is an honest attempt by the author to present issues impartially and to let the blame fall where it may. Being both an international lawyer and a political scientist, the author has had the advantage of combining the methodology of these two social sciences into a rich tapestry with some startling shades and tones.

We are living in an era in which we need to reconsider our premises and to reappraise our values. This book can help us in this process.

> Louis B. Sohn
> Woodruff Professor of International Law,
> University of Georgia School of Law, and
> Bemis Professor of International Law, Emeritus,
> Harvard Law School

Acknowledgments

It has been my great privilege and distinct pleasure to have studied with the most gifted group of teachers and scholars ever assembled at one university: Richard Baxter, Harold Berman, Abram Chayes, C. Clyde Ferguson, Jr., Roger Fisher, Paul Freund, Lon Fuller, Stanley Hoffmann, Robert Jervis, Edward L. Keenan, Jr., John D. Montgomery, Richard Pipes, Judith Shklar, Louis Sohn, Henry Steiner, Adam Ulam, Roberto Unger, Detlev Vagts, and Michael Walzer. I would also like to express my gratitude to Anthony D'Amato, Richard Falk, Leo Gross, Richard Lewontin, Alfred Rubin, and Burns Weston. For all the knowledge they and many others have imparted to me over the years, I am truly grateful. For all this essay lacks, I alone am responsible.

This book is dedicated to the memory of my international relations teacher, Hans Morgenthau. In a day when young men and women were seeking to comprehend the meaning of that great tragedy which befell our generation, he enlightened us with the fire of his own spirit. May his fire burn within our hearts forever.

F. A. B.

November 7, 1984

Part One

*The Schism between International
Legal Studies and International
Political Science*

I

The "Irrelevance" of International Law and Organizations

The Problem

From the moment of its creation as an intellectual discipline in the aftermath of the Second World War, international political science has maintained that international law and organizations are essentially irrelevant to a proper understanding of international politics and consequently are irrelevant to the progressive development of international political theory. Historically this discipline has repudiated both the descriptive validity and the prescriptive worth of international legal considerations for that sector of international relations dealing with matters of "vital national interest" or of "high international politics." Now, after nearly four decades during which these assumptions have determined the basic course of thought about international relations in the United States of America, it is high time for someone who is both a political scientist and an international lawyer to reexamine them.

Perhaps the foremost example of the tenacity of this belief can be found in the collection of essays written in honor of Professor Leo Gross of the Fletcher School of Law and Diplomacy entitled *The Relevance of International Law* (1971), which was edited by two former colleagues, Professors Karl Deutsch and Stanley Hoffmann of the Harvard Government Department.[1] The reputed purpose of the book was to analyze the relevance of international law to the problems of war and peace, to the challenge Third World countries present to the stability of the international system, to the growth of international organizations, and to the consequent evolution of "world order." Yet a lead essay by Hoffmann strove mightily to refute what was supposed to be the book's main proposition, namely, that international law and organizations were indeed relevant to international politics and thus to international political science.[2]

There and elsewhere Hoffmann attributed responsibility for this situation to the alleged fact that contemporary international affairs manifest a "revolutionary" and "heterogeneous" nature as opposed to a "moderate" and "homogeneous" one due to a variety of political, economic, cultural, demographic, and scientific factors.[3] Such factors include dissolution of the classical balance of power, worldwide revolutionary insurgency, infinitely destructive nuclear weapons systems, the relentless power of nationalistic fervor, division of the world into hostile ideological camps, uncurbed exponential population growth, and unremitting technological and industrial innovation. These elements were said to interact synergistically to create an international political environment irremediably inhospitable to the application, growth, and well-being of international law. The irrelevance of international law and organizations would persist until the world returned to the conditions of relatively simple placidity that supposedly characterized its formative period. In other words, international law and organizations would not become relevant to international politics in the foreseeable or even distant future.[4]

Another variant on the same theme maintains that there exists a mélange of inherently debilitating characteristics so fundamental to legal education and training, to the processes of legal reasoning, to the practice of law, and to the legal profession as a whole that they seriously impede if not prevent a lawyer *qua* lawyer from ever becoming a decent let alone consummate statesman. To enumerate just a few:

1. The narrow-minded development of legal principles through the inductive technique of analogical reasoning
2. The piecemeal accumulation of such principles into a consequentially formalistic doctrine of little practical utility
3. The disregard of crucial facts in search for the broad principle, or vice versa
4. The rigidity of legal analysis and methodology
5. The stubborn insistence upon rules, agreements, and expectations when circumstances have been materially altered so as to render them obsolete or useless
6. The play-it-by-the-book attitude and innate conservatism this fosters
7. The stifling of intuition, creativity, and initiative, and, worst of all
8. A preference for manipulation of a given set of rules within an established game rather than the creation of a new game with an entirely different set of rules.

These alleged constituents of the legal mind are postulated to be thoroughly inadequate to achieve success and may even be counterproductive when brought to bear upon international political problems. For by definition solutions to the latter are said to require freedom and agility in thought and analysis, imagination, flexibility, a high tolerance for risk taking, and adroitness at rule making, rule breaking, and game invention. In comparison to international political scientists, such qualities are lacking or are at least intolerably deficient in the international legal profession.

In essence, this critique reduces itself to the dubious proposition that lawyers are not by nature opportunistic and unprincipled enough to function well in an international political arena where Machiavellian power politics and raison d'état are the order of the day.[5] Henry Kissinger's classic exposition of this thesis has become standard textbook reading for introductory courses in international political science,[6] where for over a generation students have been successfully indoctrinated to disbelieve the utility of international law and organizations for the conduct of international relations. It is apparent, however, that Kissinger spent only one year (1954–55) as a special student at the Harvard Law School and never practiced law for a big corporate law firm.[7] From his "realist" perspective, Kissinger's deep admiration for Dean Acheson as one of the great American secretaries of state is an anomaly achieved in spite of, rather than because of, the latter's professional origins as a lawyer.[8] To an international lawyer, however, the reason for Acheson's superlative performance in foreign affairs is intuitively obvious. As Professor Harold Berman of the Harvard Law School once said to this author: "Anyone who can become a senior partner at Covington & Burling must *a fortiori* be a superb realist!"[9]

As Qualified

Admittedly, in affirming the irrelevance of international law and organizations, political scientists do not intend to imply that considerations relating to them play absolutely no important part in the conduct of international relations by the world's governments. Political scientists are astute enough to recognize that international law is pervasive in both its presence and its effects throughout the international system. It directly regulates or else indirectly seeks to influence (whether successfully or not will be examined below) the entire course of international relations, from the most seemingly insignificant of matters, all the way along the continuum of international political importance to the macrocosmic questions of war or peace, and life or death for peoples, states, and civilizations.

Within this scheme of things, it is also undeniable that international organizations play a significant role. International organizations, from the smallest to the United Nations itself, are tangible manifestations of the effective operation of international law. International organizations come into existence, grow, prosper, and serve mankind because their respective founding states sign multilateral treaties that become their constitutional documents, and subsequent members accede to the principles of law enunciated therein. International organizations are the products of international law.

International political scientists are willing to concede these basic points. Indeed, a separate school of international political science has developed out of this concession—the so-called functional-integrationist approach to international relations. This approach was best exemplified by Ernst Haas's definitive study of the International Labor Organization in *Beyond the Nation-State* (1964).[10] The title of Haas' work epitomized the essence of the functional-integrationist position. Through the elaboration of a complicated international, supranational, subnational, and interpersonal network of political, economic, cultural, and educational relationships, the international community would gradually, almost ineluctably, be drawn closer together to the point where international organizations could take over the most significant functions presently performed by governments of nation states. Eventually the nation state as known today would, to use Engels' descriptive terminology, "wither away" because it would prove superfluous to any type of metafunctional activity. It would be replaced altogether as the fundamental unit of global political organization by a centralized world government or reduced to the status of a semi-sovereign constituent unit in a federal or confederal world state analogous to the position occupied by the states of the American Union under the Constitution or the Articles of Confederation. Predictably, international law is destined to play a central role in this metamorphosis of an international community into a transnational or universal society.[11]

Forced by their functional-integrationist colleagues to concede the relevance of international law and organizations to measures requiring cooperation in international relations, international political scientists refocused their intellectual assault by restricting their critique to matters of serious dispute between nations. Therefore, when international political scientists assert the irrelevance of international law and organizations, they are not concerned with the vast multitude of relatively inconsequential international relations governed by the international legal order. Instead, they refer to that portion of international relations which, they claim, escapes the effective control of international law and organizations altogether—conflict over matters of "vital national interest" and "high international politics." Needless to say, these are terms of art whose essence, like beauty, resides within the eye of the beholder.[12]

In the opinion of most political scientists, international law might indeed be pertinent to, if not determinative of, the microcosmic elements of international relations. But such relevance, when multiplied by the minimal importance of these matters, becomes, overall, inconsequential when compared to the irrelevance of international law and organizations to conflicts involving vital national interests. International law is therefore irrelevant to those matters which count the most, or more forcefully, to those matters which count for everything, in international relations.

Political Realism

This denial of the relevance of international law and organizations to "high" international politics is not characteristic of any one or more schools of international political science, but is endemic to most of the profession. The genesis of modern international political science is attributable to an extreme negative reaction to the so-called legalist-moralist or utopian approach to international affairs, said to have influenced the conduct of international relations by the United States and the other Western democracies during the period between the First and Second World Wars. International political science originated from this "realist" or power-politics-oriented school of international relations. Its best exemplars were the writings of scholars such as Edward Hallett Carr[13] and Hans Morgenthau,[14] and the careers and publications of statesmen like Dean Acheson,[15] George Kennan,[16] and later Henry Kissinger.[17]

In the realist view of international relations, international law and organizations totally lack any intrinsic significance within the utilitarian calculus of international political decision making.[18] International law, morality, ethics, ideology and even knowledge itself are mere components in the power equation, devoid of non-instrumental significance or prescriptive worth, subject to compulsory service as tools of power when deemed necessary for the vital interests of state.[19] There are no barriers to the acquisitive nature of the nation state beyond its own inherent limitations and those constraints imposed upon it by the international political milieu. Consequently, the analysis of international relations must concentrate exclusively upon the dynamics of power politics and the machinations of that metaphysical entity known as the "balance of power." Considerations of international law do not and should not intrude into such areas. Or, if they do intrude, it should be only for the instrumental purpose of serving as a source for the manufacture of ad hoc or ex post facto justifications for decisions taken on the basis of antinomian factors such as Machiavellian power politics and national self-interest.

The reasons responsible for the realists' extremely negative perception of international law and organizations are more the product of metaphysical speculation than solid empirical research. The nations of the world are theorized to survive precariously in the Hobbesist state of nature, where life is "solitary, poor, nasty, brutish, and short."[20] Here there exists no law or justice, no conception of right or wrong, no morality, but only a struggle for survival in a state of war by every state and against every state.[21] The acquisition of power and aggrandizement at the expense of other states in a quest for unattainable absolute national security is the fundamental right, the fundamental law, and the fundamental fact of international politics.[22] Sheer physical survival in a Machiavellian world of power politics, raison d'état, totalitarianism, and nuclear weapons must be the litmus test for the validity of man's political, philosophical, moral, and legal presuppositions.

Statesmen, it is argued, who disobey the "iron law"[23] of power politics at the behest of international law and organizations invite destruction at the hands of aggressors and thereby facilitate the destruction of third parties which, in today's interdependent world, cannot realistically hope to remain neutral in a serious conflict between great powers. Historically, the realists assert, whenever statesmen have in good faith interjected determinative considerations of international law into attempted solutions for the monumental problems of international politics, the probability that violence, war, defeat, death, and destruction would ensue was magnitudinally increased. For the realists the primary case in point was said to be President Woodrow Wilson's approach to international affairs after the outbreak of the First World War.

The Realist Critique of "Legalism-Moralism"

On January 8, 1918, President Wilson delivered an address to a joint session of Congress in which he set forth the war aims and peace terms of the U.S. government for ending the Great War.[24] This was the speech that contained the fabled Fourteen Points, the last one of which laid the cornerstone for the League of Nations, the ill-fated predecessor to the

United Nations. In that speech Wilson emphatically decreed the death of Machiavellian power politics and all its essential accouterments for the postwar world: the balance of power, secret diplomacy, trade barriers, armament races, and the denial of self-determination. The system of power politics, based upon an outmoded and dangerous set of interconnected principles for the conduct of international relations, had resulted in such cataclysmic consequences that it had to be replaced completely by a system consisting of antithetical operational dynamics: international organizations and law, collective security, open diplomacy, free trade, freedom of the seas, arms reduction and disarmament, and national self-determination. A new era of world history was to dawn with the League of Nations, and the old world of power politics was to be left behind as an evolutionary stage of barbarism in the human condition to which, like Rousseau's state of nature,[25] mankind would never return.

Unfortunately, the world of power politics returned two decades later, and the political realists laid the blame for World War II on the doorstep of Wilson and those Western statesmen who adopted his allegedly "legalist-moralist" approach to the conduct of international relations during the interwar period.[26] According to the realists, the leaders of the Western democracies had neglected, condemned, and repudiated the techniques of power politics in favor of an anti-power politics approach to international relations. Instead, the exact opposite should have been done. The Treaty of Versailles and especially its first part, the Covenant of the League of Nations, were not really the perfect incarnations of truth, justice, peace, and righteousness as they were said to be by the leaders of the Allied and Associated Powers.[27] Rather these were mere instrumentalities of power politics designed by the victorious nations of the First World War to secure and perpetuate, with the maximum possible degree of legal and institutional coercion, the favorable political, economic, and military status quo following the armistices ending the Great War. This treaty was imposed *vi et armis* in contravention of Wilson's express promises given to induce surrender. If the peoples of the world believed anything else, they had been sorely deluded by the ideological rhetoric deceptively manipulated by their leaders to fan the flames of patriotic fervor in order to hasten the prosecution of the war to its successful conclusion.

If the victors of Versailles intended to keep their ill-gotten gains, they had to be willing to employ military force against a revanchist Germany whenever the latter attempted to resist the terms of the so-called peace. But the Western democracies lacked the requisite Nietzschean will to power. Instead of fighting to preserve their hegemony, they preferred to trust in their own illusions. They put their faith into such meaningless pronouncements as Wilson's Fourteen Points, the Kellogg-Briand Pact,[28] and its corollary, the Stimson Doctrine;[29] into the ineffectual organs of the League of Nations—the Council, the Assembly, and the Permanent Court of International Justice; into vapid and useless legalist-moralist doctrines such as neutrality, disarmament, and arbitration; into the codification of international law and the formulation of a definition of aggression. Perhaps most egregiously of all, they actually believed in the existence of a benevolent world public opinion that would will the world on its path toward peace.

These chimera were exploded when a powerful and resurgent Germany, under the leadership of a demonic yet brilliant tyrant, together with like-minded allies in Italy and Japan, challenged the status quo of Versailles with the might of their armies.[30] International law was a farcical joke to the Axis powers. The only way to stop them was through the prodigious exercise of that lone medium they understood and appreciated most—sheer, naked, brutal force, stripped of all pretensions to anything but outright conquest. Hence the need for their unconditional defeat and the demand for their unconditional surrender.

It was too bad for the lives of millions of people that the Western democracies' infatuation with international law and organizations meant the world had to learn this lesson the hard way, after the mistakes of Manchuria, Ethiopia, the Rhineland, Spain, Austria, Czechoslovakia, and Poland. If Western statesmen had been attentive to the historical imperatives of power politics, and not fascinated by the seductive allurements of international law and organizations, World War II might never have happened. Or else it would have occurred in the middle 1930s when the devastation could have been minor in comparison to what it was in actuality. They could have fought the war on their own terms and at the time of their own choice, not those of their natural adversaries. The Western democracies had only themselves to blame for World War II.

Political realists delight in bandying about that hackneyed quotation from George Santayana: "Those who cannot remember the past are condemned to repeat it."[31] Consequently, the political realists argued, faced with a Communist threat in the aftermath of World War II, the United States had to repudiate its deeply ingrained legalist-moralist approach to international relations in favor of pure Machiavellian power politics in order to survive its confrontation with the Soviet Union.[32] In the political milieu of the Cold War, the Western democracies could not repeat the same near-fatal mistake they had made after the termination of World War I if they wished to avoid a suicidal third world war—reliance upon the fictitious and fatuous strength of international law and organizations to preserve world peace. Hence, the realists' justification for the necessity of the Marshall Plan, the Truman Doctrine, the policy of containment, the Berlin airlift, U.S. intervention in Korea, and the creation of the North Atlantic Treaty Organization (NATO). These elements of postwar American foreign policy were quite properly founded upon pure calculations of national self-interest and power politics.

Hans Morgenthau

The definitive exposition of a modern theory of political realism appears in Hans Morgenthau's *Politics among Nations: The Struggle for Power and Peace* (1948). This work set the discipline of international political science on its feet and has remained its greatest classic. The book was written with the power, brilliance, and analytical insight of an international lawyer who had been profoundly disillusioned by the experience of World War II. Little sympathy remained for international law and organizations precisely because they had been tragically repudiated by history itself.[33]

Hans Morgenthau passed away in New York City on July 19, 1980, at the age of seventy-six. It is the general consensus of his political science colleagues that Morgenthau was the most brilliant analyst of international relations to have taught and written in the post–World War II era. And yet he was by training and temperament an international lawyer. Morgenthau was born in Coburg, Germany, on February 17, 1904, and took his early degrees in law at the Universities of Munich and Frankfurt. He was admitted to the bar in 1927 and practiced law for three years. He then became assistant to the law faculty at the University of Frankfurt and acting president of the Labor Law Court at Frankfurt. He went to teach at the University of Geneva in 1932, and when Hitler came to power in Germany the next year, Morgenthau decided not to return home. He then became professor of international law at the Institute of International and Economic Studies in Madrid (1935–36); instructor of government at Brooklyn College (1937–39); assistant professor of law, history, and political science at the University of Kansas (1939–43) and a member of the Missouri Bar; associate professor of political science, then professor, and finally Albert A. Michelson Distinguished Service Professor at the University of Chicago. He later became Leonard Davis Distinguished Professor at the City College of New York and University Professor at the New School for Social Research.[34]

Shortly after the outbreak of World War II, Hans Morgenthau wrote one of the most intellectually stimulating articles ever published in the *American Journal of International Law*, "Positivism, Functionalism, and International Law" (1940).[35] According to Morgenthau, by the late 1930s positivist international legal studies had reached a point where it partook of the worst elements of medieval scholasticism. The discipline had become so detached from the reality of its surrounding historical conditions that it lived in its own metaphysical world of delusions where theory had long ago replaced fact as the ultimate raison d'être. A positivist approach to international law had to be replaced by a "functionalist" analysis that would first explain and then attempt to narrow the gap that exists between law and politics in the realm of international relations. A functionalist analysis would discard all tenets of international legal positivism that prevent an understanding of those undeniably multifaceted relationships between social forces and international law. By means of functionalism the theory of public international law must and could be rejoined with its social context in order to survive and have meaning in a postwar world organized around the twin principles of power politics and national interest. Functionalism must undertake this task and revitalize international legal studies for the future.

Unfortunately, Morgenthau never wrote that follow-up article with his proposed methodology for devising a functionalist analysis of international law. By the time the horrors of World War II were fully revealed, he and others like him had become thoroughly disillusioned over the chances of international law and organizations ever playing a meaningful role in the regulation of international conflict. Instead of developing a functionalist jurisprudence of international law, Morgenthau and his colleagues founded the "realist" or power politics school of international political science, which essentially denied the relevance of international law and organizations to matters of "vital national interest" or of "high international politics." The decisive break between international political science and international legal studies dates from this point and still exists today.

At the time of its publication, *Politics among Nations* read like a "declaration of war"[36] against the alleged legalist-moralist approach to international relations. It railed against those who sought to interject the least infinitesimal particle of utopian or non-power elements into the analysis of international relations or into the calculations of international political decision makers in any fashion even reminiscent of a value judgment. Of course Morgenthau did not write upon a tabula rasa. He was deeply influenced by Edward Hallet Carr's classic work *The Twenty Years' Crisis, 1919–1939* (1939).[37] Therein Carr appointed himself as founder of the anti-utopian school of international affairs. Carr argued that during the interwar period, the techniques of power politics had been neglected, and worse yet, condemned and repudiated by the Western democracies in favor of a non-power-oriented or anti-power politics approach to international politics. Carr held this denigration of power politics responsible to a great extent for the predicament of the world as of 1939. Although written from this realist perspective, the book did strive to achieve an uneasy synthesis of elements from both the utopian movement and its realist critique. Carr argued that even though the first and foremost duty of the statesman was to pragmatism and expedience, he could still be moral as well. Statesmen could have their proverbial cake and eat it too, so long as they followed Carr's recipe.

Morgenthau completely rejected any theoretical synthesis between power and non-power elements. Instead, he took up realist theory where Carr had left it a decade before and carried it to its logical and most extreme conclusions. When reading any one of the five editions of his *Politics among Nations*, spanning over a quarter of a century, one is struck by the methodically ruthless vitality of Morgenthau's attack upon the legalist-moralist approach to international relations. Both the substance and the spirit of the book distinctly remind the reader of Machiavelli's *The Prince*. For what Machiavelli did to the Christian ethos in politics, Morgenthau did to legalism-moralism in the study of international relations.

After Morgenthau's initial declaration of war, there ensued a pitched battle between the political realists and their alleged legalist-moralist adversaries. The former were assisted in this intellectual struggle by a Cold War with the Soviet Union that suddenly became "hot" in Korea in 1950. This seemed to demonstrate the validity of the realist analogy of the Communist threat to its fascist predecessor. The Korean War destroyed any residual enthusiasm on the part of international political scientists for international law and organizations. Hence by 1954 Morgenthau was able to declare that the battle against legalism-moralism had been won, and all that remained to be done was for the realist school to consolidate its position.[38] The split between international legal studies and international political science was complete. In the estimation of most international political scientists, the realists had thoroughly discredited a legal positivist approach to the study and practice of international relations. However, this process of disparagement did not stop there.

The Subsequent Development of International Political Science

For just as political realism represented an extreme negative reaction against international law and organizations, the subsequent intellectual history of international political science can be interpreted to consist of a series of ideological chain reactions precipitated by the theories of the realist school.[39] Yet except for the early functional integrationists and the later "regime theorists," these succeeding schools consciously or unconsciously accepted the validity of the realist thesis that international law and organizations are essentially irrelevant to international politics.

The realists were followed by advocates of a decision-making approach to international relations.[40] The latter attacked the realists for their failure to consider the microcosmic units and factors of analysis in international political decision making common to all nation states. This defect was said to have proceeded ineluctably from realism's almost exclusive preoccupation with the macrocosmic movements of the entire international system.

Next came the systems theorists, who strove to refocus the concentration of the discipline upon the broad systemic movements of international affairs through the utilization of an analytical methodology and terminology that was self-proclaimedly more rigorous, theoretical, value free, and therefore supposedly more scientific and useful than that applied by the realists.[41] The systems theorists were in turn followed by the behavioralists, who once again broke down the units of analysis to the level of small decision-making groups and even focused on the human mind in order to examine their respective operational dynamics and impact upon the processes of foreign policy decision making.[42]

The game theorists employed a mathematically based methodological technique derived from pure economic theory to develop intricate and subtle decision-making solutions to well-defined problems with limited potential applicability to international politics.[43] In a similar vein, theorists of strategic studies explored the hypothetical dynamics of a future world war in order to extrapolate in reverse the essential elements of successful war-preventive or at least war-ameliorative foreign affairs and defense policies.[44] Then there emerged the organizational theorists and those who proposed a bureaucratic politics approach to the interpretation of foreign policy decision making and execution by governments.[45] Only quite recently and with a so far limited degree of impact have proponents of "regime theory" emphasized the crucial importance of analyzing the status of and evolution in international legal rules and institutions for cultivating a proper comprehension of both short-term developments and long-range movements in international relations.[46] And even they have yet to grapple directly with the difficult issue of either proving or disproving the relevance of international law and organizations to conflicts between states over matters involving "vital national interests" or "high international politics."

There are now as many theories of international political science as there are international political scientists. It has become a truism to state that international political science is a field in search of a "paradigm." But although the proponents of these respective theories differ among themselves in a plethora of ways, for the most part they nevertheless wholeheartedly embrace the realists' general disavowal of the utility of international law and organizations to the study and practice of international relations. International political science as a discipline is realist by birth and continued persuasion because of its solemn affirmation of the irrelevance of international law and organizations to international politics.

Today very few professors of international political science possess even a rudimentary training in international law and organizations, let alone teach, write, or comment favorably about them. Departments of political science have phased out courses in international law and organizations, and even place obstacles in the paths of those few advanced graduate students who seek such specialized training at law schools. Near total ignorance of and disregard for international law and organizations is rampant among the current and the future generations of international political scientists. Mention of international legal considerations in a discussion with them about "high international politics" will be met by snickers and smirks, if not outright disbelief and hostile opposition. A residue of animosity remains from the original repudiation of international law and organizations by the founders of the realist school and permeates all levels of the profession. Even the students of the students of the original realists are ready, willing, and able to refight the theoretical battles that their grand-teachers had already supposedly won over a generation ago, by simply regurgitating chapter and verse from *Politics among Nations*.

Most unfortunately, this evolutionary differentiation of international political science from international legal studies has been transmuted from the academic classroom into the real world of international political decision making. To a great extent the heuristic success of modern political realism has been responsible for the increasingly hard-nosed Machiavellian fashion in which American foreign policy has been designed and executed since the Korean War. An entire generation of American foreign policy and defense decision makers has been weaned on *Politics among Nations*; they believe that international relations is nothing more than a Thucydidean jungle where the strong do what they will and the weak suffer what they must. Yet the height of tragic irony occurred when this Machiavellian approach to international relations reached its apotheosis in the Vietnam War, and none other than Hans Morgenthau led the forces of intellectual opposition to America's continued involvement. The ruthless application of Machiavellian power politics by the U.S. government during the Vietnam War compelled the eminently humane Morgenthau into undertaking a major reexamination of the utility of political realism for ensuring the continued survival of mankind in a thermonuclear age. As a direct result of this process, toward the end of his life Morgenthau soundly repudiated power politics in order to embrace once again international law and organizations.[47] But Morgenthau's monumental realist legacy still remains to haunt the future of both international political science and American foreign policy. The memoirs of recent American statesmen such as Richard Nixon, Henry Kissinger, Zbigniew Brzezinski and Alexander Haig, Jr., demonstrate that Machiavellianism still remains the predominant mode of thought about international relations among the members of today's U.S. foreign affairs and defense decision-making establishment.

2

The Real Origins of International Legal Positivism

The Myth of "Legalism-Moralism"

When modern political realists ritually incant George Santayana's time-worn aphorism to support the validity of their proposition that international law and organizations are essentially irrelevant to conflicts between states over matters of vital national interest, they overlook the fact that those who misinterpret the past are just as likely to repeat it. For contrary to the general assumptions universally held by contemporary international political scientists, throughout the twentieth century there has never existed some monolithic entity commonly, though mistakenly, known as the American "legalist-moralist" approach to international relations. This is because the modern "legal positivist" approach to international relations was purposefully designed and carefully constructed by American international lawyers around the turn of the twentieth century in order to function in a manner diametrically opposed to a "moralistic" attitude toward international law and politics.

Indeed, the American legal positivist approach to international relations did not even begin with Woodrow Wilson's moralizing, but rather was born well before the outbreak of World War I. These historical oversights have led international political scientists into committing the grievous analytical error of confusing "positivist" international legal studies with the pursuit of Wilsonian international morality in order to create some phantasmagorical legalist-moralist straw man warranting condemnation for the Machiavellian "sins of princes" supposed by the realists.[48] From the perspective of any good international legal positivist, the very notion of there existing some legalist-moralist approach to international relations represents a bald-faced contradiction in basic terms.

This self-conscious differentiation of law from morality by turn-of-the-century American international lawyers was explicitly intended to surmount the objections of John Austin, who denied the existence of international law as real "law" and maintained instead that international law represented nothing more significant than the "rules of positive morality."[49] In the late nineteenth and early twentieth centuries, American international lawyers were vigorously engaged in the task of sharply distinguishing a "scientific" or "positivist" approach to the study of international law from its natural law heritage and proclivities stemming from Hugo Grotius, whose work *De Jure Belli ac Pacis* (1625) was generally regarded as the start of international legal studies. These founding international legal positivists wanted to at last definitively repudiate those elements of their Grotian education that preached international morality under the guise of international law, which in turn was piously represented as the incarnation of natural law. In their collective opinion international legal studies had to step irrevocably forward into the twentieth century by developing an actual science of public international law based upon a positivist approach that was antithetical to the content and methodology of outmoded natural law and natural right theories. Continued reliance upon such amorphous concepts by the international legal profession gratuitously provided ammunition for philosophical assault to Austin's omnipresent protégés.

At the outset of the twentieth century the classic "paradigm"[50] for international legal positivism, which still dominates the profession after seventy-five years, was expounded in the second volume of the *American Journal of International Law* by the renowned Lassa Oppenheim, Whewell Professor of International Law at Cambridge University, in his seminal article "The Science of International Law: Its Task and Method" (1908).[51] According to Oppenheim, a "positive" method required that its foundation be built upon the extant and recognized rules of international law as set forth in the customary practice of states and in the formal conventions concluded between them, instead of upon philosophical speculations about some nonexistent law of nature. The former facts of international life must never be distorted by the latter hypotheses about what international law "ought" to be. A true international legal positivist must perform seven tasks in order to promote the "science" of public international law: (1) exposition of existing rules of law, (2) historical research, (3) criticism of existing law, (4) preparation of codifications, (5) maintenance of the distinction between old customary and new conventional law, (6) fostering of international arbitration, and (7) popularization of public international law, since public opinion can indeed influence governments in its favor.

This positivist method did not preach that international law should never concern itself with the promotion of moral values. Rather, it was premised upon the forthrightly admitted assumption that international legal positivism, as opposed to the Grotian natural law tradition, constituted the superior means to progress toward the Aristotelian "final cause" of international legal studies — preservation of peace among nations to the greatest degree possible under the given historical circumstances. Positivist international legal analysis was more likely to facilitate successful interstate agreement upon current and proposed rules of international behavior than was interminable disputation over the dogma of Grotian natural law morality, whose reputed tenets invariably masked national interests and national prejudices. International legal positivism could, therefore, better serve to diminish the inevitable friction and ameliorate the unavoidable conflict between states in their conduct of international relations.

At this time in world history, war, imperial conquest, and the threat and use of force were accepted facts of international life to which the rules of public international law were quite readily accommodated.[52] The purpose of international law was not as yet perceived to be the outlawry of these manifestations of interstate violence, but more simply to reduce their incidence, mitigate their fury, and limit their scope so as to protect neutrals and prevent the development of a worldwide conflagration. International law was never viewed as a transcendent end unto itself but only as a means to achieve the ultimate goal of peace in the human condition.[53] The institution of a more just arrangement in the relationships among states would further the maintenance of world peace and thus contribute to the promotion of all human values.

The International Legal Positivist Critique of Austin

From the perspective of the turn-of-the-century international legal positivists, Austin committed a serious methodological error when he mistakenly assumed that international law functioned in a manner similar to that of municipal law. At the time there was a clear-cut distinction between the two systems, since the former was essentially one of customary law while, by contrast, the latter was characterized primarily as one of statutory law. Obviously, the operational features of each system should be fundamentally different. An analyst cannot profitably evaluate the effectiveness of international law by means of standards and techniques derived from and applicable to municipal legal systems. This early legal positivist critique of Austin has been restated in the literature of contemporary international political science, which addresses the so-called level-of-analysis problem, pointing out that the functional dynamics of international relations in comparison to domestic affairs are so basically dissimilar that they cannot properly support the construction of useful comparative analogues.[54]

According to early international legal positivists, Austin's position that international law was not really law but only positive international morality also misperceived the essence of the "sanction" behind obedience to municipal law, regarding it as coercion and punishment by some absolute Hobbesist sovereign instead of, more appropriately, the effective influence of domestic public opinion. Without considering the power of public opinion, the phenomenon of customary law on either level of analysis, whether international or municipal (such as Anglo-American common law), could not be accounted for except, perhaps, by the fictive maxim that what the sovereign permits he also commands. Since there existed no Hobbesist sovereign in international relations, these positivists believed that customary international law bound states because they were deemed to have consented to be bound by the general customs and usage of international intercourse embodied in its rules.

For the positivists the ultimate sanction behind international law was public opinion, which, of course, included the irresistibly compelling factors of public fear of war, and its converse, public pressure to resort to war. Likewise, this explicit or implicit consent of states to be bound by international law bound their respective citizens as well. International law was incorporated into their domestic legal orders so that citizens were bound by its rules in their mutual relations with each other and foreigners.[55] In the positivist opinion the efflorescence of a community of such internally and externally law-abiding nations by means of a constantly increasing degree of interaction and interdependence throughout the world could create a truly global public opinion that would serve as the ultimate sanction for international law.[56]

Explained in somewhat more tangible terms, to these positivists the real sanction behind international law was the exclusion of a state violating its principles from the benefits accruing to it from coordinate regulation of its relationships with other states and international agencies with respect to vital concerns of its national interest. The task of the "new diplomacy" incumbent upon international legal positivists was to establish a framework for cooperation among nations in which substantial advantages could be obtained by joint state action that would not otherwise be realized by states acting in isolation. This web of international legal ties would eventually become so strong that no state could consider disrupting it by resorting to war; or, in the unfortunate event that war remained a quasi-permanent feature of the international system, many of these legal and institutional patterns of relations could persist to survive and function despite the outbreak of violent hostilities.[57] The demands of international intercourse had already required the provision of limited powers of competence and action, not subject to the veto of any one state, to international administrative organs such as the Universal Postal Union. Although nations were exceedingly reluctant to give such organs more power, it was in this direction, these positivists argued, that the future development of international relations would best proceed toward the achievement of world peace.[58]

At some point in the distant future a world federal state could come into existence, organized according to the functional model of the United States of America, whereby the nations of the world would each accept a semi-sovereign status analogous to that of states in the Union.[59] Presumably, a world federal law would thereafter govern the relations between states. This would require the creation of some form of world government with sufficient legislative, judicial, and executive power to promulgate, adjudicate, and, if necessary, enforce international law against recalcitrant states in a manner that would not precipitate global warfare. This could be accomplished because punishment of the culprit would be accepted as legitimate by all other participants, since each state had already consented to be so governed.[60]

Thus, these early international legal positivists explicitly embraced the classic Machiavellian dichotomy between the "is" (effectual truth) and the "ought to be" (imaginary truth) of world affairs,[61] and chose to classify international law into the former category and Grotian natural law morality into the latter. This categorization of law as an effectual truth instead of an imaginary truth received tacit support from Machiavelli himself.[62] To an international legal positivist the effectiveness of any system of law, whether on the domestic or international level of analysis, had to depend upon the existence of some source of underlying power, whether military, political, economic, or ideological in nature. So when realist international political scientists castigated international legal positivists over the latter's supposed ignorance of or disregard for the realities of power, the realists simply demonstrated their complete unawareness of the legalists' Machiavellian and Hobbesist premises.

The American Legal Positivist Approach to
International Relations

Around the turn of the twentieth century, the mainstream attitude of
American international lawyers towards the actual and potential role of
international law and organizations in world politics was not at all naive,
idealistic, or utopian. It was acutely realistic and relatively sophisticated
in its comprehension of the dynamic interrelationship between power
and law in international affairs. These early American international legal
positivists were not men who shrank from advocating the forceful exercise of American power around the globe, whether as teachers, scholars,
and polemicists or, as many of them were, government officials, diplomats, and statesmen. If anything, as a group they were all too prone to
encourage and support the United States government in the planning
and execution of its imperialistic endeavors by elaborating arguments
and rationalizations in favor of such policies, which they then formulated
in terms of the rules of international law and the requirements of maintaining international peace and security. At the very beginning of this
century, Americans in general demonstrated a marked tendency to believe
international law to consist of whatever the immediate satisfaction of
their national self-interests necessitated,[63] and in this regard American
international lawyers were not essentially different from their intensely
nationalistic compatriots. Apart from a few notable expressions of regret,
chagrin, or dissent, as a group American international lawyers mounted
no systematic or even significant criticism of the overall conduct of U.S.
imperialist foreign policy from the perspective of those supposedly trained
in and sensitive to the requirements and needs of a truly international
legal order.

During this era, there was a large-scale cooptation of the skills of
American international lawyers by the U.S. Department of State because
of their critical relevance to the management of the complex difficulties
resulting from the conduct of an American foreign policy that was
simultaneously striving to reconcile the inexorable demands of a newly
launched imperialism with the tenacious pull of a traditionally deep-
seated isolationism. American international lawyers, operating from
within the foreign policy establishment, brought their unique perspective on international relations directly to bear upon the policy formulation process. In fact, it was during the interim between the Spanish-
American War and World War I that American international lawyers
exercised a more profound influence upon the formation of American
foreign policy than they have as a group at any time before or since.

For example, of the eight U.S. Secretaries of State who held office from 1898 until 1920 (viz., John Sherman, William Rufus Day, John Hay, Elihu Root, Robert Bacon, Philander Chase Knox, William Jennings Bryan, and Robert Lansing), only Bacon was not a lawyer.[64] Furthermore, Elihu Root, his longstanding international law advisor James Brown Scott, and Robert Lansing were all founding members of the American Society of International Law and its *American Journal of International Law*, both of which under their direction became the driving forces behind the development of American international legal positivism before World War I. It is to that historical period, therefore, not the interim between the two world wars, that this study must turn in order to delineate the paradigmatic elements of the classic American "legal positivist" approach to international relations.

International Legal Positivism as a Reaction to the
Spanish-American War

The single most formative event in the development of a distinctively legal positivist approach to international relations in the United States was the 1907 publication of the first volume of the *American Journal of International Law*, the first periodical devoted exclusively to international law in the English-speaking world.[65] American scholars and practitioners of international law thereby created a central forum in which to articulate an essentially legal positivist analysis of international relations that was purposefully intended to be different from the respective approaches taken by proponents of natural law theory and political scientists.[66] The birth of both the American Society of International Law and its journal can, in significant part, be attributed to the experience of the United States during its war with Spain in 1898. The exhilarating feeling of sudden and decisive victory in the Spanish-American War stimulated within all sectors of the country an increased awareness of international affairs and generated a felt need within the American international law community for an organization and a publication in which to express its concatenating attitudes towards the legal dimension of America's new and far-flung international relations.[67]

Of course, prior to that brief encounter, the United States had not been totally dormant within the cocoon of isolationism spun by Washington's farewell address and the Monroe Doctrine.[68] The country had engaged in at least two formal international wars with significant hemispheric consequences: the War of 1812 and the Mexican-American War of 1846. The former can be broadly interpreted as an attempt by the new government to consolidate its recently won independence from Great Britain. The latter was an imperialist enterprise designed to seize most of what is today the southwestern section of the United States in an effort to fulfill the country's so-called "manifest destiny" of complete continental expansion.[69] The numerous expeditions against the American Indians could also fit neatly within the category of continual imperialist expansion, though some early legal positivists disingenuously argued that since Indian territorial occupation was not entitled to any respect, their subjugation did not qualify as an act of imperialism.[70] Yet, the net effect of these disputes upon their contemporaneous global political environments was relatively insignificant when compared to the astounding ramifications for the United States and the world at large ensuing from the Spanish-American War of 1898.

The decrepit Spanish Empire was almost instantaneously dissolved, and the United States assumed its imperial mantle in Cuba, Puerto Rico, Guam, and the Philippines.[71] Acquisition of the former two colonial territories situated the United States in the heart of the Caribbean where it could control the gateway to the isthmus of Central America. From there it was an almost inevitable imperial step to American intervention into Colombia in order to instigate and secure the independence of Panama for the purpose of facilitating construction of a canal;[72] to promulgation of the Roosevelt Corollary to the Monroe Doctrine in order to justify U.S. economic receivership for the Dominican Republic, Honduras, Nicaragua, and Haiti;[73] and to repeated military intervention into and occupation of Cuba pursuant to the Platt Amendment.[74] These developments paved the way for the subsequent history of persistent imperialist interventions by the United States into the affairs of Central American and Caribbean countries that has chronically plagued U.S. foreign policy toward the region adjoining the Panama Canal for the past three-quarters of a century.

On the other side of the world, the decision to take over the Philippines propelled the United States directly into the affairs of the Orient and therefore indirectly into the European balance of power system, since the major powers of Europe had already staked out their respective colonial claims in the Far East.[75] American efforts to preserve and extend its geopolitcal and economic position in that region of the world, especially the maintenance of its so-called Open Door policy in regard to China, ultimately set the stage for serious and prolonged friction with Japan that culminated forty years later with the latter's sneak attack on Pearl Harbor and thus America's entry into World War II.

In the pre–World War I era of international relations the major philosophical dilemma confronting American international lawyers was the reconciliation of this new U.S. course of world imperialism commenced by the Spanish-American War with the traditional ideals of American foreign policy based upon the inalienable rights of the individual, the self-determination of peoples, the sovereign equality and independence of states, non-interventionism, respect for international law, and the peaceful settlement of international disputes. Within the American international law community, there did exist a minority anti-imperialist sentiment which espoused the "neutralization" of U.S. colonial territories along the lines of Belgium in order to remove them from the extant zone of international contention.[76] But the majority legal positivist viewpoint accepted American imperialism, like war, as an irreversible fact of international life that must be dealt with on its own terms.[77] In their opinion, imperialism could nevertheless be reconciled with American ideals through recognition of the imperative that the true purpose of American imperial policy, unlike that of Europe, must not be territorial aggrandizement and economic enrichment, but ultimately achievement of the American dream of freedom, independence, dignity, and equality for all the peoples living within the current American imperial domain.[78] These milieus objectives could be secured in a manner consistent with America's expansive definition of its national security interests by pursuing a foreign policy that actively promoted international law and international organizations.

International Legal Positivism as a Rejection of Participation in the European Balance of Power System

Near the turn of the century, American analysis of European politics transpired through the conceptual prism of the "balance of power"—a phenomenon perceived to be the operative determinant of international relations between the states of the Old World. By contrast, the United States was still believed to occupy the fortunate position of "splendid isolation" vis-à-vis the machinations of Machiavellian power politics on the Continent that it had held throughout the nineteenth century by virtue of the British navy.[79] Admittedly, the European balance of power system had by now extended its tentacles to worldwide dimensions by including within its grasp the decaying Ottoman Empire,[80] Africa,[81] the Near East, Central Asia,[82] India, Southeast Asia, China, Japan, and the Pacific. Only the Monroe Doctrine and the Roosevelt Corollary had prevented Europe from reasserting its stranglehold over Latin America, and, despite Europe's presence in the Far East, the American-sponsored policy of maintaining an "Open Door" to the exploitation of China could somehow magically keep the balance of power for that region in equilibrium. The rest of the world was duly consigned to the unhappy fate of becoming the arena for intense rivalry and periodic conflict over territory between the major imperial powers of Europe and Japan. In this worldwide struggle for colonies, the rules of international law had little applicability except to the extent that they accorded some semblance of legitimacy and order to the process of imperial subjugation by recognizing the existence of formal legal statuses known as "protectorates" or "condominiums," inter alia, over conquered territory whereby the exclusive or hegemonial position of one or more imperial powers could be definitively acquiesced in by its cohorts.[83] Yet, even in respect to the process of colonial conquest, the formation of new international institutions for the peaceful settlement of interstate disputes could play a decisive role in providing useful forums for the amelioration of imperial rivalries among the great powers that were, on their merits alone, not worth starting a general systemic war over.

Despite strident advocacy in favor of a resolutely interventionist American foreign policy throughout the Western Hemisphere in the aftermath of the Spanish-American War, for the most part American international lawyers did not believe the United States should radically depart from the sage advice of Washington's farewell address by actively engaging itself in the European balance of power system. The United States had both the luxury and the duty to abstain from choosing sides between the contending alliance systems in Europe because such a choice could easily precipitate America into war over another state's interests. Especially with the disintegration of the Ottoman Empire and the revival of the Balkan question by the Austrian annexation of Bosnia and Herzegovina in 1908, it seemed that a monumental struggle between Russia and Austria-Hungary and their respective allies over Serbia was in the offing for the not-too-distant future.[84] In the event of a general war in Europe, isolationism would ensure that the United States did not jeopardize its newly won possessions in the Far East and its hegemonial position over Latin America, while the international laws of neutrality would permit American merchants to profit handsomely from increased trade with both sets of belligerents.

Acceptance by American international lawyers of this generally held prescription for isolationism in peace and neutrality in war vis-à-vis the European balance of power system did not, however, prompt them to espouse inaction by the United States government in the diplomacy of world politics.[85] To the contrary, in the legal positivist opinion it was vitally necessary for the United States to pursue a foreign policy that actively promoted international law and international organizations to the members of the world community for the express purpose of preventing a general systemic war that originated among the European powers but could readily pull in America, as happened in 1812. This task could be accomplished by an American foreign policy that sought to produce a fundamental transformation in the modus operandi of the European balance of power system from the constant threat and use of force to reliance, instead, upon new rules of international law and new institutions for the peaceful settlement of international disputes.

The United States occupied the ideal diplomatic position to spearhead such a war prevention program on behalf of Europe precisely because America had maintained intact its traditional isolationism from great power politics that did not directly concern its own interests. America's pristine detachment from the European great powers could reduce the latter's respective nationalistic suspicions that inevitably accompany and often defeat major diplomatic initiatives from their outset. America could most safely and effectively protect both itself and the world at large from the scourge of future battles by striving to reform the historical condition of Europe from war to peace. By preserving its distance America would have the perspective for leadership in the development of international law and international organizations. It would be the height of folly for America to abandon this high moral ground in order to grasp and wield the dangerous weapons of power politics by becoming an actual member of the European balance of power system.

3

The Achievements of International
Legal Positivism

The International Legal Positivist War Prevention
Program for World Politics

The United States' response to the European balance of power system was a fundamental commitment to isolationism in peace and neutrality in war. By comparison, the pre–World War I American legal positivist approach to international relations seemed activist and globalist. If anything, American international lawyers moved considerably farther and faster down the road of internationalism than their isolationist colleagues in the U.S. government because of their sincere belief in America's overarching need to seize the initiative in formulating a war prevention program for the great powers of Europe on the basis of international law and organizations. As it took shape and matured over twenty years, the elements of the American legal positivist approach to international relations during its classical period from 1898 to 1917 came to consist of attaining the following concrete objectives: (1) the creation of a general system for the obligatory arbitration of disputes between states; (2) the establishment of an international court of justice; (3) the codification of important areas of customary international law into positive treaty form; (4) arms reduction, but only after, not before, the relaxation of international tensions by means of these and other legalist techniques and institutions; and (5) the institutionalization of the practice of convoking periodic conferences of all states in the recognized international community.[86] In addition, a subsidiary element of this American legal positivist program was to strengthen the well-established international legal institution of neutrality and the humanitarian laws of armed conflict in order to further isolate the bulk of the international community, especially the United States, from some future war that still might erupt between the great powers of Europe despite the enactment of these preventive legalist devices. American international lawyers prudently hedged their country's bets on the likelihood of a general systemic war occurring in Europe.

Theoretically, these five steps were to be achieved in an approximately sequential fashion, since each stage was to some extent dependent upon fulfillment of the prior goal. But in practice, all these legal positivist objectives were pursued in a roughly simultaneous manner because of their highly interdependent and mutually supportive nature. Realization of the fifth stage would have represented the first step toward the creation of a rudimentary form of a world legislature which, when conjoined with an effective world court, would have constituted two-thirds of the branches required for the institution of a world government patterned along the lines of the legislative, judicial, and executive departments of the U.S. federal government.[87] Nevertheless, until after the outbreak of the Great War in 1914, the mainstream of the American international legal community did not devote much time, effort, or resources to promoting the idea of founding some executive "league to enforce the peace," equipped with an effective international police force and necessarily accompanied by some degree of progressive disarmament by the great powers.[88] To be sure, such a visionary goal was endorsed by some American international lawyers as a desirable destination for the long-term evolution of international relations.[89] Yet at the time there seemed to exist a general consensus among international legal positivists that such a scheme must not be allowed to detract from the immediate realization of the far more practicable agenda outlined above. Moreover, there was absolutely no desire or intention on the part of these intensely nationalistic early twentieth-century American international lawyers to surrender any degree of U.S. "sovereignty" to some type of supranational organization.[90]

Though admittedly far-reaching, this American war prevention program based on international law and organizations seemed to stand more than a plausible chance for eventual success because of the relative homogeneity of the system of international relations in the pre–World War I era, at least in comparison to the endemic heterogeneity so characteristic of the post–World War II period.[91] Publicists and statesmen of this earlier epoch actually thought in terms of the existence of a real international community of states.[92] Basically this world community consisted of the countries of Europe, North America, South and Central America, the Ottoman Empire,[93] and Japan.[94] The rest of the world was viewed essentially as an arena for intense colonial competition among the great powers that rendered even more vital the institution of the foregoing mechanisms in order to attenuate and manage the inevitable imperial conflicts. All of these nations participated in the same system of international political and economic relations and were subject to the same corpus of European public international law. All of the major actors except Japan shared a similar cultural heritage—the Old Testament, Greece, Rome, medieval Christendom, Renaissance and Reformation, the European Enlightenment, the Industrial Revolution, the French Revolution and Napoleonic Wars, and the tradition of a "concert" of European powers determining matters of world politics by mutual consent and negotiated agreement throughout the nineteenth century. The American legal positivist war prevention program for international relations intended to build upon this solid foundation of cooperation, shared experiences, cultural similarities, and interdependent national interests to create an even more stable and secure world order for the twentieth century and the dawn of mankind's next millenium. It was definitely not a pipedream, but a practical program that could successfully be implemented in the not-too-distant future by means of vigorous American leadership designed to bring forth a reasonable degree of enlightened self-interest on the part of the great powers of Europe.

A System for the Obligatory Arbitration of International Disputes

Secretary of State John Hay instructed the American delegation to the First Hague Peace Conference of 1899 to propose a plan for the foundation of a permanent international tribunal organized along the lines of the United States Supreme Court,[95] which would be endowed with the competence to decide all questions of disagreement between states, except those related to political independence or territorial integrity.[96] But there proved to be little support among the conference participants for the conclusion of a general multilateral pact calling for the obligatory arbitration of all disputes, let alone politically significant disputes, between states.[97] Germany adamantly opposed the conclusion of a general multilateral pact calling for the obligatory arbitration of even a limited number of certain categories of disputes possessed of relatively inconsequential political significance.[98] Consequently, the First Hague Peace Conference had to content itself with the establishment of the purely voluntary system of arbitration known as the Permanent Court of Arbitration (PCA) which, among other procedures, was instituted by its

1899 Convention for the Pacific Settlement of International Disputes.[99] The Permanent Court was (and still is) not a real "court" of arbitration, but only a list of distinguished jurists appointed by the contracting powers to the convention from which parties to a dispute that cannot be settled by means of diplomacy could, if they so desire, choose an arbitrator or panel of arbitrators to settle the dispute in accordance with a fixed set of procedural rules.

Although a general pact for the obligatory arbitration of some disputes was defeated at the First Hague Peace Conference, article 19 of the 1899 Convention sought to encourage obligatory arbitration by reserving the right of contracting powers to conclude general or special treaties of obligatory arbitration among themselves. Although article 19 did not seem to possess much significance at the time of its adoption, between 1899 and 1908 some seventy-seven arbitration treaties were concluded by the various countries of the world, and all but twelve provided for some sort of reference to the Permanent Court.[100] Such references were generally subject to reservations concerning certain categories of disputes, typically excluding from arbitration matters involving a state's independence, vital interests, honor, sovereignty, or the rights of non-contracting parties.[101]

By the time of the Second Hague Peace Conference in 1907, Germany had dropped its objection to the principle of obligatory arbitration, but then insisted that the proper approach should be the negotiation of a series of bilateral arbitration treaties between interested states instead of the conclusion of a general multilateral pact.[102] Consequently, the Second Hague Peace Conference had to content itself with the adoption of a unanimous declaration that merely accepted the principle of obligatory arbitration and declared that differences "relating to the interpretation and application of international conventional stipulations are susceptible of being submitted to obligatory arbitration without any restriction."[103] Nevertheless, the wording of this 1907 declaration on obligatory arbitration was chosen specifically to enable those nations favoring compulsory arbitration to conclude special treaties on the subject among themselves outside the framework of the Hague Conferences.[104] Pursuant to this recommendation, U.S. Secretary of State Elihu Root promptly negotiated a series of twenty-five general arbitration treaties on behalf of the United States, all of which were ratified by the Senate,[105] and twenty-two of which eventually entered into force.[106]

Prior to the outbreak of the First World War, several major international disputes were submitted to the Permanent Court of Arbitration at The Hague, and the U.S. government played the lead role of midwife in bringing this institution to life. From the perspective of maintaining international peace and security, the most significant of the Hague Court's arbitrations proved to be the *Venezuela Preferential Case* (Germany, Great Britain, and Italy vs. Venezuela et al.)[107] and the *Casablanca Case* (France vs. Germany).[108] Pressure by President Roosevelt to refer part of the former controversy surrounding Venezuela's default on its public debts to arbitration before the Permanent Court and the rest of the dispute to mixed commissions contributed to the successful termination of ongoing military hostilities conducted by Germany, Italy, and Great Britain in an effort to forcefully collect on their respective nationals' monetary claims against the Venezuelan government.[109] Their action threatened to draw the United States of America directly into the conflict in order to protect Venezuela from this anticipatory breach of the Monroe Doctrine.

Likewise, because the Casablanca incident of 1908 was universally considered to have concerned the honor of France and Germany, given the militaristic tenor of the times, its non-resolution by means of the Hague Court might have easily resulted in hostilities between the parties.[110] This conflict could have rapidly escalated into a general systemic war in Europe because of their respective memberships in competing alliance systems. Thus, despite its congenital defects, the Hague Permanent Court of Arbitration contributed to the termination of one concerted military operation and to the prevention of one war. History must judge it to have been a phenomenal success and recognize the positive role played by international law and organizations in the amelioration of the generally violent conditions of world politics prior to World War I.

The Foundation of an International Court of Justice

Following in the footsteps of the unsuccessful American plan for a world court originally introduced at the First Hague Peace Conference, the U.S. delegation travelled to the Second Hague Peace Conference of 1907, instructed by Secretary of State Elihu Root to propose the formation of an actual international court of justice that was intended to be judicial in nature and function, as opposed to the arbitral proceedings of the Permanent Court of Arbitration.[111] When it finally emerged from the proceedings of the Second Hague Peace Conference, the American plan for creating an international court of justice called for the institution of a "Court of Arbitral Justice" (CAJ) consisting of an as yet unspecified number of judges appointed in an as yet unspecified manner for a term of twelve years.[112] The CAJ was not designed to replace but rather to coexist with the PCA, so that states would remain free to choose between the two institutions. Nevertheless, the implication was clear that states would quickly grow to prefer adjudication over arbitration since the former institution supposedly more nearly coincided with their vital national security interests in creating a more effective system for the peaceful settlement of international disputes.

The primary obstacle to the actual establishment of the Court of Arbitral Justice at the Second Hague Peace Conference proved to be an unbreakable deadlock over the manner of selecting judges for the court. Specifically, the smaller states, and especially those from Latin America, opposed the institution of a system for the selection of CAJ judges among themselves on a rotational basis, while the great powers would each be accorded the right to always have one of their respective appointees sitting on the CAJ.[113] The net result was that the Second Hague Peace Conference could only content itself with a recommendation that the signatory powers adopt an annexed Draft Convention Relative to the Institution of a Court of Arbitral Justice "as soon as an agreement shall have been reached upon the selection of judges and the constitution of the court."[114]

Nevertheless, the Draft Convention Relative to the Institution of a Court of Arbitral Justice recommended for adoption by the Second Hague Peace Conference did set forth an institutional plan that ultimately represented a crucial intermediate stage in the evolution of international dispute settlement tribunals from the relatively primitive 1899 Permanent Court of Arbitration to the far more sophisticated 1921 Permanent Court of International Justice (PCIJ), the immediate predecessor to the modern International Court of Justice. In the opinion of James Brown Scott, an American international legal scholar who was intimately involved in the preparation of both the 1907 CAJ Draft Convention and the 1921 PCIJ Statute, the latter "was to most intents and purposes similar to, if not identical with, the draft of 1907."[115]

The Codification of Customary International Law

At the turn of the century, it was generally supposed that any viable scheme for the creation of some international court of justice required the contemporaneous codification of international law, because states would be less willing to submit their disputes to judicial resolution so long as the European system of public international law remained primarily one of customary instead of conventional law.[116] The codification of customary international law was also necessitated by the fact that a majority of judges on any international court would undoubtedly be trained in the European Continental tradition, which varied significantly from the Anglo-American heritage in numerous important respects. This unavoidable arrangement ran a significant risk that the minority of judges from Anglo-American common law countries might be consistently outvoted in court decisions attempting to settle disputed principles of customary international law. Without preexisting codifications for the various subjects of customary international law, the anticipated principle of majority rule on any international court might predetermine the inevitable demise of the distinctively Anglo-American practice. This phenomenon could produce a subtle transformation in the international political, economic, and military status quo to the substantial benefit of Continental states at the direct expense of the United States and Great Britain. The progressive codification of customary international law was therefore essential to mitigate the consequences of such an imbalance in the composition of any international court, and thus to encourage the evolution of institutions for the peaceful settlement of international disputes from the relatively primitive stage of arbitration to the supposedly more advanced and effective level of adjudication.

Some of these theoretical and practical problems concerning the codification of international law and its crucial importance for the promotion of international adjudication are illustrated by reference to the unfortunate history of the aborted International Prize Court project commenced at the Second Hague Peace Conference by Great Britain and Germany with the active support of the United States government.[117] At that time one of the principal achievements of the Second Hague Peace Conference was deemed to have been its adoption of the Convention Relative to the Creation of an International Prize Court (IPC).[118] The Prize Court was intended to be a permanent standing tribunal consisting of fifteen judges appointed by the contracting powers for a term of six years, with judges appointed by the eight great naval powers (Germany, U.S.A., Austria-Hungary, Great Britain, France, Italy, Japan, and Russia) "always summoned to sit" on the Court, and the other seven positions rotating among judges appointed by the remaining signatories according to their maritime interests, though during wartime each belligerent would be represented by an appointee.

The Prize Court would adjudicate appeals from decisions by the national prize courts of belligerent captors of neutral and enemy property; it would apply the intricate and unsettled or hotly disputed rules of international law in time of maritime warfare. Formation of the Prize Court was intended to eliminate a chief cause for serious friction between neutrals and belligerents that might impel the former to enter the war in order to prosecute their rights against the latter, as the United States had done against Great Britain in the War of 1812. The IPC was designed to restrict the scope of an ongoing war through the techniques, principles, and institutions of international law.

Pursuant to article 7 of its Convention, in the absence of a treaty, the Prize Court was to apply "the rules of international law," and if no generally recognized rule existed, the Court was ordered to give judgment in accordance with "the general principles of justice and equity." Due to the composition of the Court, the Anglo-American judges would be in a minority and therefore the United States and Great Britain ran the substantial risk that the Anglo-American viewpoint on certain aspects of the law of prize would be replaced by the Continental tradition. Hence, Great Britain adamantly insisted that the international law of prize be codified into positive treaty form before it ratified any Prize Court Convention.[119]

Consequently, Great Britain summoned a conference of representatives of the major maritime powers of the world (Germany, U.S.A., Austria-Hungary, Spain, France, Great Britain, Italy, Japan, Netherlands, and Russia) to meet in London towards the end of 1908 in order to determine what were the generally recognized principles of international law referred to in article 7 of the Prize Court Convention.[120] This meeting resulted in the 1909 Declaration of London Concerning the Laws of Naval War.[121] The Declaration of London built upon the foundations established by an informal compromise on the codification of maritime warfare that had been worked out but not adopted at the Second Hague Peace Conference.[122]

The Prize Court Convention, an Additional Protocol and the Declaration of London all received the advice and consent of the United States Senate.[123] This approval was readily obtained because a functioning International Prize Court would greatly benefit a state such as the United States, which anticipated being neutral in the event of another general war in Europe. But the American government was unwilling to deposit its instrument of ratification without the cooperation of Great Britain. This was never forthcoming because the British preferred to consider certain provisions and lacunae in the Declaration with reference to their potential bearing upon some future naval war with Germany instead of on their merits alone as a reasonable amalgam of compromises between competing Anglo-American and Continental practices concerning the doctrines of blockade, contraband, continuous voyage, the destruction of prizes, unneutral service, etc.[124] Hence the Naval Prize Bill of 1911, purporting to amend English law relative to naval prizes of war so as to enable British participation in the International Prize Court Convention, passed in the British House of Commons, but failed in the House of Lords because of public opposition.[125] Since there was no point in proceeding with either the International Prize Court or the Declaration of London without the world's greatest naval power, neither project subsequently came into effect of its own accord.

Nevertheless, a preliminary provision to the Declaration of London stated that the signatory powers agreed that the rules set forth therein "correspond in substance with the generally recognized principles of international law."[126] This provision created the potential for belligerents in some future naval war to apply the rules enunciated in the Declaration by virtue of their generally recognized status as declaratory of customary international law on the conduct of maritime warfare. Thus the United States government revised its naval war code in 1912 to correspond with the Delcaration of London.[127] Likewise, in 1913 the British Admiralty espoused the Declaration of London as the heart of its new naval prize manual.[128] With such weighty imprimaturs, it was not surprising that at the beginning of the First World War the Declaration of London was generally considered to have constituted the most authoritative enunciation of the laws of war at sea as they stood in 1914.[129]

Arms Limitation, Disarmament, and New Procedures for the Peaceful Settlement of International Disputes

ARMS LIMITATION AND DISARMAMENT

The First Hague Peace Conference proved totally incapable of adopting any substantive measures concerning the overall limitation or reduction of armaments.[130] Instead, the conference had to content itself with the adoption of a unanimous resolution in favor of restricting military budgets[131] and of two *voeux* that governments examine the possibility of an agreement respecting the employment of new types and calibers of rifles and naval guns,[132] and an agreement limiting armed forces on land and sea and war budgets.[133] These meager results confirmed the conventional wisdom espoused by the majority of the American international legal community that serious proposals for arms limitation and disarmament would only succeed as conditions subsequent, not precedent, to the relaxation of international tensions by means of new rules of international law and new institutions for the peaceful settlement of international disputes.[134] To that end, of course, the First Hague Conference proffered its Convention for the Pacific Settlement of International Disputes, which instituted the Permanent Court of Arbitration and other novel procedures for this purpose.

Although the Russian government attempted to exclude the limitation of armaments from the agenda of the Second Hague Peace Conference so as not to impede its arms buildup in the aftermath of defeat during the Russo-Japanese War of 1904–05, Great Britain and the United States, inter alia, insisted that the matter be considered.[135] Nevertheless, the Second Hague Peace Conference likewise failed to adopt any substantive measure concerning the overall limitation of armaments.[136] Upon the motion of Great Britain and with the support of the United States, it simply confirmed the resolution of the 1899 conference in regard to the limitation of military burdens and declared that it would be "highly desirable" for governments once again to seriously examine this question.[137] The international community would make no significant progress in regard to the limitation of armaments until after World War I, when the U.S. government undertook the initiative to convene a conference of the Principal Allied and Associated Powers (Great Britain, France, Italy, Japan, and the U.S.) on the subject of the limitation of armaments to be held at Washington, D.C. toward the end of 1921.[138]

GOOD OFFICES AND MEDIATION

In addition to the creation of the Permanent Court of Arbitration, the 1899 Convention for the Pacific Settlement of International Disputes established the modern right of third parties to offer their good offices and mediation to two states in conflict in order to achieve a pacific settlement of the dispute without the latter being able to regard this as an unfriendly act of intervention.[139] These Hague provisions for the peaceful settlement of international disputes were to bear fruit when President Theodore Roosevelt offered his good offices and mediation to Russia and Japan during their war of 1904–05.[140] Thereafter, representatives of both belligerents met in the United States, and on September 5, 1905, concluded the so-called Peace of Portsmouth, terminating the war on terms favorable to Japan, the military victor.[141] For the success of his initiative, Roosevelt was awarded the Nobel Peace Prize for 1906.[142]

INTERNATIONAL COMMISSIONS OF INQUIRY

Title III of the 1899 Convention for the Pacific Settlement of International Disputes[143] created a voluntary procedure for the formation of an international commission of inquiry to investigate, ascertain, and report upon international differences involving neither honor nor vital interests and arising from disputed points of fact that could not be settled by means of diplomacy. The theory behind the procedure was that once the facts had been impartially ascertained, authenticated, and communicated to the parties in dispute, a pacific settlement of the conflict on the basis of the commission's report should be readily forthcoming. In its very first test case, at the suggestion of France, an international commission of inquiry was successfully employed to resolve the Dogger Bank controversy between Great Britain and Russia, which arose out of the Russo-Japanese War.[144] Non-resolution of this dispute could have easily resulted in a very serious conflict, if not war, between the parties.[145] The successful resolution of the Dogger Bank incident by an international commission of inquiry demonstrated to the entire international community that even disputes between states concerning their honor and vital interests could be subjected to some procedure for peaceful settlement.[146] Hence, two new procedures instituted by the First Hague Peace Conference for the peaceful settlement of international differences proved their usefulness during the Russo-Japanese War.

CONVENTION ON THE OPENING OF HOSTILITIES

Another procedural innovation concerning international disputes that was instituted by the Second Hague Peace Conference was the 1907 Convention Relative to the Opening of Hostilities.[147] The contracting parties agreed that hostilities between them would not begin without explicit notice either in the form of a reasoned declaration of war or of an ultimatum with a conditional declaration of war. The state of war must be made known to neutral powers without delay and was not effective in regard to them for purposes of the laws of neutrality until they received notice or if it was clearly established that they knew in fact of the state of war.

Proposals at the conference to fix a mandatory interval between delivery of the declaration or ultimatum and the commencement of hostilities failed.[148] Hence the Convention essentially left each signatory free to fix whatever interval was best suited to its own interests, even though tactically the interval could be so short as to take the enemy by surprise. Nevertheless, hope was expressed that the Convention might create an opportunity for third states to offer their good offices or mediation to the parties in dispute, or to convince the latter to submit the matter for decision by the Permanent Court of Arbitration, in order to forestall the outbreak of war.[149] Up to the time of this Convention, a declaration of war or an ultimatum that preceded the opening of hostilities was the exception, not the rule, of international belligerent practice.[150] By contrast, at the outset of the First World War, most of the major belligerents dutifully complied in good faith with the terms of this 1907 treaty.[151]

THE PORTER CONVENTION

The final mechanism for the peaceful settlement of international disputes instituted by the Second Hague Peace Conference was the Convention Respecting the Limitation of the Employment of Force for the Recovery of Contract Debts.[152] This treaty is commonly referred to as the "Porter Convention" in honor of General Horace Porter, U.S. delegate to the 1907 conference who proposed it on behalf of the American government and labored so strenuously to obtain its adoption.[153] Pursuant to its terms, the contracting powers agreed not to have recourse to armed force for the recovery of "contract debts"[154] claimed from the government of one country by the government of another country on behalf of its nationals. However, this undertaking was rendered expressly inapplicable when the debtor state refused or neglected to reply to an offer of arbitration, or, after accepting the offer, prevented the arbitration from proceeding, or, after the arbitration, failed to submit to the award.

The implication was clear that in the event the debtor state was unwilling to adhere to the terms of the arbitral procedure, the creditor state would retain whatever freedom of action it allegedly possessed under customary international law to use force in order to collect on the debts. Despite this loophole, subsequent history has proven the Porter Convention to have been a phenomenal success. It virtually put an end to the generally tolerated practice of stronger (invariably European) creditor states threatening or using military force in order to collect upon contract debts owed to their nationals by weaker (typically Latin American or Caribbean) debtor states. The Porter Convention was claimed to have been a great victory for U.S. foreign policy because the conclusion of a multilateral pact essentially designed to protect Latin American states from European intervention was interpreted to amount to an implicit recognition by all parties of the validity of the Monroe Doctrine as partially incarnated into this new principle of public international law.[155]

THE THIRD HAGUE PEACE CONFERENCE

The fifth and final element of the American legal positivist war prevention program for world politics during the 1898–1917 period was the institution of some mechanism for the periodic convocation of peace conferences among the nations of the international community for the purpose of completing, perfecting, and advancing the work of the First and Second Hague Peace Conferences. The First Hague Peace Conference had been convoked upon the initiative of Tsar Nicholas II of Russia. Several provisions of its Final Act contemplated a subsequent conference in order to deal with a variety of unresolved issues, but nothing specific was said concerning who had the right to initiate its convocation or when this should be done.

The outbreak of the war between Japan and Russia over Manchuria in 1904 rendered it politically unfeasible for the tsar to assume the initiative in calling for the convocation of a second conference. Consequently, upon the original initiative of U.S. President Theodore Roosevelt,[156] the Second Hague Peace Conference commenced its deliberations on June 15, 1907,[157] and signed its Final Act and Conventions on October 18, 1907. Among the latter was a recommendation that the holding of a third peace conference should take place within a period of time similar to that which had elapsed since the first conference (i.e., eight years, or 1915), on a date to be set by joint agreement among the powers.[158] The Final Act also stated that it would be desirable that a preliminary committee be charged by the governments about two years before the probable date of the meeting (i.e., in 1913) with the duty of collecting various propositions to be considered by the conference, to prepare a program for it, and to determine the mode of organization and the procedure for the third conference.[159] The language of the Second Hague Peace Conference's Final Act concerning a third conference was specific enough to indicate that any state represented at the First or Second Hague Peace Conferences could undertake the initiative to convene the Third Hague Peace Conference, thus implicitly repudiating any putative claims that Russia possessed the exclusive right of priority to do so.[160] The U.S. delegation was in the vanguard of the movement to terminate the tsar's proprietary interest in calling for the convocation of future Hague Peace Conferences.[161]

In June 1912, President Woodrow Wilson appointed a governmental advisory committee to consider proposals for a program for the third peace conference.[162] Following its deliberations, on January 31, 1914, Secretary of State William Jennings Bryan dispatched an identical circular note to the diplomatic officers of the United States accredited to the governments which took part in the Second Hague Peace Conference suggesting that the latter entrust the duties of the International Preparatory Committee for a Third Peace Conference to the Administrative Council of the Permanent Court of Arbitration at The Hague (which consisted of the Netherlands Minister of Foreign Affairs and the diplomatic representatives of the contracting powers accredited to The Hague) and that the third conference be held in 1915.[163] In light of the various responses received from some of the powers, Bryan issued a follow-up circular note on June 22, revising his prior proposal by suggesting that the Third Peace Conference meet at The Hague in June, 1916, and that the duties of the International Preparatory Committee be entrusted to a committee to be selected from among the members of the Permanent Court of Arbitration's Administrative Council by themselves.[164] Shortly thereafter, on June 26, 1914, the Netherlands government invited the contracting powers that had participated in the Second Hague Peace Conference to name one member of a preparatory committee to meet in 1915 to consider the questions to be brought before the Third Peace Conference.[165] Two days later, Archduke Francis Ferdinand of Austria-Hungary and his wife were assassinated at Sarajevo by a Serbian nationalist, thus precipitating World War I.[166]

This simultaneity of developments indicates the surprise and suddenness by which the First World War descended upon the great powers of Europe.[167] The 1919 Paris Peace Conference to end the war had to serve in default of the never-realized Third Hague Peace Conference.[168] Yet the longstanding American legal positivist objective of establishing some means for the periodic convocation of peace conferences among all nations of the international community was finally achieved and, indeed, far exceeded by the establishment of the League of Nations.

4

International Legal Positivism after the Outbreak of World War I

Refutation of the Realist Critique of Early International Legal Positivism

Today, in the post–World War II era, with the enlightened but uninspiring benefit of historical hindsight, it would be easy, yet simplistic, for political realists to argue that pre–World War I American international lawyers *qua* statesmen should have foreseen that the worldwide interests of the newly imperial United States demanded its active participation in the European balance of power system after 1898; that America had succeeded to the geopolitical position of Great Britain by effectively becoming the "holder" of a worldwide balance of power radiating from and around Europe; that the primary obligation of the holder of the balance was the willingness to abandon its "splendid isolation" when necessary in order to "restore" the balance if it was threatened or disrupted; that the moment had come for the United States to countermand its traditional policies of isolationism in peace and neutrality in war by allying itself with the two other major Western democracies, France and Great Britain,[169] in time to forestall the development of a general war in Europe; and, finally, that immediately after the outbreak of the European war in 1914, the United States should have forthwith thrown in its lot with the Allied Powers.[170]

In retrospect, contemporary political analysts are certainly entitled to raise the general question whether the First World War decisively proved that the war prevention program of the American legal positivists was an abysmal failure, predicated upon naive, idealistic, and utopian assumptions concerning the inherent utility of international law and international organizations. Yet before this question can be properly answered, it is necessary to consider a different set of questions drawn from an antithetical historical perspective. What if Germany had not objected to the principle of obligatory arbitration at the First Hague Peace Conference, or to the conclusion of a multilateral obligatory arbitration treaty at the Second? What if the Latin American states had not opposed the formation of the Court of Arbitral Justice at the Second Hague Peace Conference over the issue of its composition, which did not impede adoption of the plan for the International Prize Court? What if the House of Lords had not rejected the Declaration of London and the International Prize Court in 1911? What if the nations of the world had proceeded on schedule in 1913 to enter into preliminary preparations for the convocation of the Third Hague Peace Conference in 1915? Would there have been a First World War in 1914 if any one or more of these international legal positivist developments had occurred prior thereto?

The historical record will substantiate the proposition that with just a little more support from a few obstreperous actors at key moments in time, the elements of the pre–World War I American legal positivist war prevention program for world politics could have fallen into place soon enough to create a reformed structure of international relations in which conditions propitious for the outbreak of a general systemic war in Europe could have been substantially ameliorated. There is absolutely no evidence that the American legal positivist approach to international relations was responsible for the eruption of the war to any extent, and it would be difficult to maintain that the adoption of any one or more of these legalist schemes for improving international law and promoting international organizations would have rendered World War I more likely to have occurred. Since the veracity of this proposition is self-evident, one should immediately become skeptical of the claim by modern political realists that this same American international legal positivism was somehow responsible for the outbreak of World War II.

The breakdown of world order in 1914 was definitely not caused by international law and international organizations, or by a legal positivist foreign policy pursued by the United States government. Rather, a good historical argument could be made that the First World War occurred in substantial part because there was too little, and certainly not too much, international law and organizations. When the Great War among the European powers finally broke out, it occurred in spite of, not because of, America's perspicacious efforts to prevent, forestall, and ultimately confine a feared global conflagration through prophylactic implementation of its legal positivist approach to international relations.

American Neutrality Toward the Great War

Since the subject of neutrality was not on the agenda of the First Hague Peace Conference, it did not adopt any conventions on the laws of neutrality per se but rather just a *voeu* to the effect that the next conference should consider the question of the rights and duties of neutrals in warfare. [171] Pursuant to that wish, the Second Hague Peace Conference adopted the Convention Respecting the Rights and Duties of Neutral Powers and Persons in Case of War on Land [172] and the Convention Respecting the Rights and Duties of Neutral Powers in Naval War. [173] In addition, the 1907 Convention Relative to the Laying of Submarine Mines [174] was primarily designed to protect neutral shipping, and the 1907 Convention Relative to Certain Restrictions on the Exercise of the Right of Capture in Maritime War contained protections for neutral postal correspondence. [175] When the Great War in Europe erupted in the summer of 1914, the United States was a party to these four Hague Conventions.

On the domestic level, extant U.S. neutrality legislation dated back to the first Neutrality Act of June 5, 1794. [176] Although it expired after two years, it was renewed in 1797 for two more years [177] and was eventually made permanent with amendments by an Act of April 20, 1818. [178] The President was authorized to employ the land or naval forces or the militia for the purpose of carrying out the provisions of the 1818 Act, or to compel any foreign ship to depart from the United States when so required by the laws of nations or treaty obligations. Some of the fundamental proscriptions of U.S. domestic neutrality legislation and practice, together with principles drawn from the pathbreaking 1871 Treaty of Washington between the United States and Great Britain that settled the famous "*Alabama* Claims," were eventually to find their way into the two major 1907 Hague neutrality conventions governing land and sea warfare. [179]

A joint resolution of Congress approved by the president on March 4, 1915, was designed to better enforce and maintain U.S. neutrality by authorizing him to direct customs collectors to withhold clearance from any vessel that he had reasonable cause to believe to be about to carry certain materials and men to ships of a belligerent nation in violation of U.S. obligations as a neutral state. [180] It was thought that the 1818 Act, together with this 1915 joint resolution, were all that was necessary to bring the United States government into full compliance with its international legal obligations of neutrality at the start of the war. [181] This was not surprising since the U.S. government had historically played a leading role in the development of the international laws of neutrality by obtaining general acceptance of its policy pronouncements on such matters from the countries of Europe throughout the late eighteenth, nineteenth, and early twentieth centuries.[182] As the ferocity of the European conflict intensified, however, by 1916 the U.S. government felt the need to pass additional legislation in order to better protect its neutrality from the ravages of the war.[183] Somewhat ironically, these proposed amendments were eventually enacted into law after the United States had abandoned its neutrality and entered the war on the side of the Allied Powers.[184]

Taken as a whole, the international and domestic laws of neutrality were designed to operate in a system of international relations where war was considered to be an inescapable fact of international life, and yet in which the outbreak of war between even major actors did not automatically precipitate a total systemic war among all global powers. According to the laws of neutrality, the conduct of hostilities by a belligerent was supposed to disrupt the ordinary routine of international intercourse between a neutral and the belligerent's enemy to the minimal extent required by the dictates of military necessity.[185] Such arrangements were intended to permit the neutral power to stay out of the conflict, while at the same time they allowed its nationals to take advantage of international commerce and intercourse with all belligerents.

The political and strategic dimensions of the international laws of neutrality were complicated by the fact that they operated upon the basis of a legal fiction concerning the neutral government's reputed lack of responsibility for what were intrinsically non-neutral acts committed by its citizenry against a belligerent during wartime. Generally a belligerent state could not hold a neutral government accountable for the private activities undertaken by the neutral's citizens even if they worked directly to the detriment of the belligerent's wartime security interests. The laws of neutrality were essentially predicated upon Lockean assumptions concerning the nature of government and its proper relationship to the citizen: The political functions of government must impinge upon the private affairs of the citizen to the least extent possible, especially in the economic realm where the right to private property and its pursuit were deemed fundamental.[186] Hence, the primary duty of a neutral government was to maintain strict impartiality in its governmental relations with all belligerents. Yet the laws of neutrality specifically denied that the neutral government had any obligation to guarantee that its nationals conduct their affairs with belligerents in a similar fashion or, indeed, in accordance with any but the most rudimentary set of rules.

For example, according to the 1907 Hague Convention Respecting the Rights and Duties of Neutral Powers in Naval War, belligerents were bound to respect the sovereign rights of neutral powers and to abstain, in neutral territory or neutral waters, from any act which would, if knowingly permitted by any power, constitute a violation of neutrality (art. 1); any act of hostility committed by belligerent warships in the territorial waters of a neutral power was deemed to constitute a violation of neutrality and was strictly forbidden (art. 2). In return, a neutral government could not supply warships, ammunition, or war materials of any kind to a belligerent under any circumstances (art. 6). However, this did not mean that the neutral government had any obligation to prevent its nationals from participating in the export or transit for the use of either belligerent, of arms, ammunitions, or, in general, of anything which could be of use to any army or fleet (art. 7). Any conditions, restrictions, or prohibitions made by the neutral power in regard to the admission into its ports, roadsteads, or territorial waters of belligerent warships or of their prizes, however, had to apply equally to the two belligerents. Contraband of war shipped by neutral nationals to a belligerent was properly subject to capture and confiscation by the offended belligerent. Yet even these latter actions had to be undertaken by the belligerent in accordance with the laws of war at sea and the international law of prize.

The U.S. Decision to Enter the War on the Side of the Allied Powers

Without the recognition of a status such as "neutrality" by international law and politics, non-belligerents would be virtually compelled by circumstances to choose up sides in a war so as to maintain economic relations with at least one set of belligerents. In theory, the neutral state had an economic disincentive to participate in the war because it could greatly prosper from only moderately restricted international trade, since all belligerents would be in desperate need to purchase goods from its nationals. Conversely, a belligerent would, supposedly, not act to violate the neutral's rights and those of its nationals in order to keep the neutral from entering the war on the side of its enemy. Another legalist theory speculated that since the number and strength of neutral states in a future war would be proportionately greater than those of belligerents, the community of neutral states could impose obedience to the laws of neutrality upon the belligerents. [187]

In practice, however, these theories were undercut by the fact that each neutral's normal international trading patterns invariably worked to the greater advantage of one set of belligerents during the war.[188] So the disadvantaged belligerent had to engage in a complicated cost-benefit analysis over whether the greater harm was the continued sufferance of this strategic disadvantage in trade or its termination through outright destruction of the neutral commerce with consequent risk that the neutral power would eventually enter the war against it. Also, instead of acting as part of some international community of neutrals, each neutral state constantly assessed the relative advantages and disadvantages of maintaining its own neutrality as opposed to belligerency on one side or the other in accordance with quite selfish calculations of its vital national security interests. Unless guaranteed by treaty, the violation of one neutral's rights did not obligate another neutral to declare war or even to undertake measures of retorsion against the violator.

GERMANY'S VIOLATION OF THE INTERNATIONAL LAWS OF NEUTRALITY

The United States did not enter the First World War in order to defend the international laws of neutrality in the abstract. This was evidenced by its failure to consider the German invasion of either neutral Belgium or neutral Luxembourg as a casus belli. It was only when Germany's gross and repeated violations of American citizens' neutral rights of trade and intercourse with Great Britain seriously interfered with their ability to engage in international commerce and resulted in the large-scale destruction of American lives and property that the United States government invoked the sacred cause of the international laws of neutrality as one of the primary justifications for its intervention into the war on the side of the Allied Powers.[189]

Generally, the American international legal positivist community approved of this attitude of strict and impartial neutrality taken by the United States government at the start of the European war.[190] Yet as international lawyers they could reach no other conclusion but that Germany and Austria-Hungary must assume full legal responsibility for the outbreak of the war.[191] In their opinion, the German invasions of neutral Belgium[192] and of neutral Luxembourg,[193] in explicit violation of international treaties, represented completely reprehensible behavior for which there was no valid excuse.[194] Deserving special opprobrium in the eyes of American international lawyers was the August 4, 1914 speech by German Chancellor Bethmann-Hollweg to the Reichstag publicly admitting the German invasions of neutral Belgium and Luxembourg to be in violation of international law but arguing that Germany was "in a state of necessity, and necessity knows no law."[195] Later that same day he uttered his notorious statement to the British ambassador that the 1838 treaty guaranteeing the neutrality of Belgium was a "scrap of paper."[196]

The need to uphold the rules of international law made it crystal clear to American international lawyers on which side they should personally stand on the war, even if their government remained formally neutral. As far as they were concerned, these egregious violations of international law by Germany made continued American neutrality towards the war a highly dubious proposition.[197] Such legal positivist perceptions would exert a profound impact upon the evolution of the U.S. government's neutrality policy into a stance of "benevolent neutrality" in favor of the Allies and against the Central Powers.[198]

This tendency was accelerated when, in an ominous portent of U.S. entry into the war, William Jennings Bryan resigned as secretary of state on June 8, 1915, in strong disagreement with President Wilson's pursuit of a hard-line approach toward Germany over the sinking of the British passenger ship *Lusitania* with a heavy loss of American lives.[199] He was replaced as secretary of state by Robert Lansing, previously counselor of the State Department and a founding member of the American Society of International Law.[200] Bryan would have preferred that Wilson propose to Germany the creation of an international commission of investigation to settle the dispute, and furthermore that the U.S. government warn against, if not prevent, American citizens from travelling on belligerent vessels or with cargoes of ammunition even though they might have the perfect right to do so under the international laws of neutrality. Instead of following his advice, Wilson chose to reiterate a previous American demand for an official disavowal of the *Lusitania* sinking and other illegal sinkings of merchant ships by German submarines, for the payment of reparations, and for assurances by the German government that it would prevent the recurrence of similar gross violations of the humanitarian principles of sea warfare by its submarines.[201] In Bryan's opinion, Wilson's insistence upon Germany adhering to the punctilio of the international laws of neutrality could only propel the United States into Europe's war.

As the intensity of the war heightened and the Allies imposed their stranglehold over commerce shipped from the United States to the continent of Europe,[202] the Central Powers took the position that the American government was under an obligation to take affirmative measures to rectify the developing imbalance of trade in arms, munitions, and supplies that U.S. nationals were successfully transporting to the Allies but not to them. Both the United States government and the American international legal community were quite emphatic in their rejection of this complaint. If one belligerent was militarily unable to secure the safe passage of neutral commerce to its shores because of the misfortunes of war, that was its problem, not that of the neutral government, which possessed the perfect right under international law to permit its citizens to continue trading with the militarily more powerful belligerent.[203] For a neutral government to discriminate in favor of the weaker belligerent in order to compensate for the military imbalance would constitute an unneutral act that could precipitate a declaration of war upon it by the stronger belligerent. Moreover, legalists argued that even if the neutral government were to embargo all trade in contraband of war by its citizens with both sets of belligerents, this affirmative departure from the normal rules of neutral practice during the course of an ongoing war could compromise its neutrality.[204]

GERMANY'S VIOLATION OF THE INTERNATIONAL LAWS OF MARITIME WARFARE

It was generally believed within the United States that both the quality and quantity of violations of international law committed by the Allied Powers were of a nature and purpose materially different from and far less heinous than those perpetrated by the Central Powers (i.e., destruction of property vs. destruction of life and property).[205] Of decisive impact upon American public opinion and governmental decision-making processes was Germany's wanton and indiscriminate destruction of innocent human life (American, neutral, and enemy civilian) by institution of its policy of "unrestricted" submarine warfare against merchant vessels and passenger ships.[206] This policy commenced with Germany's imposition of a "war zone" in the waters surrounding England and Ireland, including the entire English Channel, on February 4, 1915, by which Germany did not as yet assert any intention to destroy neutral ships, but did warn of the serious dangers the latter might encounter by traversing the proscribed seas.[207] It culminated two years later with the announcement by the German government that from February 1, 1917, all sea traffic, including neutral ships, would be stopped with every available weapon and without further notice in designated blockade zones around Great Britain, France, Italy and in the eastern Mediterranean.[208] Such behavior was in express violation of several provisions of the unratified Declaration of London[209] that were generally considered not only to state the customary international laws of maritime warfare but, moreover, to embody rudimentary norms of humanitarian conduct by any civilized nation.[210]

Tactically, German submarine warfare could only partially compensate for the preponderant surface naval supremacy fielded by Great Britain and her allies, who were then quite successfully imposing an economic embargo on neutral commerce destined for Germany and her allies. It was extremely dangerous for a submarine to forego the security afforded by undetected submersion in order to surface and comply with the rules for interdiction of enemy or neutral merchant vessels suspected of transporting contraband that were applicable to surface warships, as set forth in the Declaration of London. It had become standard British practice to arm its merchant vessels with defensive weapons sufficient to destroy a thin-hulled submarine should it surface,[211] and also to fly neutral flags on British merchant vessels in order to deceive an enemy submarine commander.[212] Under these circumstances, application of the international laws of maritime warfare as specified in the Declaration of London to the conduct of hostilities by submarines would in effect have essentially precluded submarine warfare for most practical purposes, and thus have provided Great Britain and her allies with a virtually uninterrupted stream of military and commercial products purchased from merchants in neutral states, most particularly the United States, for the duration of the war.

Legally, of course, the German government justified its imposition of the war zone decree as a legitimate measure of retaliation for the undoubtedly grievous and repeated British violations of the Declaration of London and generally recognized rules of international law, both of which Germany alleged it had been strictly obeying.[213] In addition, Germany complained that the neutral powers had been either unable or unwilling to exert enough pressure upon Great Britain in order to secure its compliance with customary and conventional laws of maritime warfare and neutrality in order to guarantee the continuation of their nationals' recognized right to trade with Germany and her allies.[214] The neutral states' collective failure to effectively prosecute their rights against Great Britain or, in the alternative, their refusal to at least diminish proportionately the free flow of weapons, munitions, and supplies to England by their own merchants, worked to the substantial military and economic detriment of Germany.

Notwithstanding the validity of some of these German objections, as far as American public and governmental opinion was concerned, if the submarine could not be effectively utilized without violating international law, then Germany must jettison the submarine, not the international laws of maritime warfare and neutrality.[215] Germany's persistent refusal to relent and its consequent sinking of merchant ships with indiscriminate and large-scale loss of innocent human life directly precipitated the U.S. decision to intervene into the war against Germany[216] and later Austria-Hungary,[217] which had endorsed the German practices. As President Woodrow Wilson phrased it in his April 2, 1917 request to a joint session of Congress for a declaration of war against Germany:[218] "The present German submarine warfare against commerce is a warfare against mankind."[219]

The Wilsonian Hybrid of "Legalism-Moralism"

The U.S. government's insistence upon the international legal right of its citizens to trade with the Allies no matter how unequal the military situation would play a significant part in the decision by the Central Powers to pursue their policy of waging "unrestricted submarine warfare" in order to destroy this vital neutral commerce irrespective of the international laws of neutrality and maritime warfare. And the U.S. government would eventually respond by entering the war in order to secure those rights of its nationals and thus uphold the international laws of neutrality and armed conflict. Hence, consistent with its "legal positivist" approach to international relations, the U.S. government did not enter the First World War for some nebulous reason such as "upholding" or "restoring" the European balance of power system. Instead, America abandoned its neutrality to support the Allies for the very "realistic" purpose of redressing these egregious violations of its most fundamental rights under international law committed by the Central Powers.

That was exactly how the European system of public international law was supposed to operate before the foundation of the League of Nations. Resort to warfare by one state against another was universally considered to constitute the ultimate sanction for the transgressor's gross and repeated violations of the victim's international legal rights. The United States ultimately fought in the Great War precisely in order to vindicate the customary and conventional international laws of maritime warfare and neutrality.[220] America's decision to abandon its neutrality and enter the war on the side of the Allied Powers ineluctably spelled defeat for the Central Powers. This proved to be the definitive and most effective "sanction" for Germany's wanton attempt to destroy the entirety of the international legal order extant as of 1914.

Of course coupled with this legal positivist justification for entering the war came Wilson's political rationalization and propagandistic moralization that by abandoning its neutrality America thereby joined a great universal moral crusade on behalf of the forces of good (i.e., democracy) arrayed against the forces of evil (i.e., autocracy).[221] Autocratic governments were necessarily presumed to be inevitably warlike by nature, and democratic governments inherently peaceful. Therefore the peace of the entire international community required the utter destruction of autocracy throughout the world and its replacement by democratic forms of government everywhere. In the words of President Woodrow Wilson: "The world must be made safe for democracy."[222]

In his April 2, 1917 address to a joint session of Congress, Wilson (who was both a lawyer and a political scientist) attempted to fuse the classic American legal positivist approach to international relations with these newly invented "moralistic" elements in order to bolster his request for a congressional declaration of war against Germany. Nevertheless, Wilson's purported fusion violated the cardinal tenet of the founders of the American legal positivist approach to international relations that all such considerations of moralizing should be excluded from the "science" of positivist international legal studies.[223] The moralistic elements of Wilsonianism were completely incompatible with the U.S. international legal positivism that had been developed during the 1898–1917 period by the American international law community in their scholarly writings and in their formulation of U.S. foreign policy at the Department of State. As classically defined and articulated American "legalism" was totally antithetical to Wilson's moralizing about the inherent superiority of democratic forms of government. Both at the time and in retrospect, therefore, the pre–World War I American international law community would most appropriately be categorized as staunch "legal realists" who would have been proud to bear such an appellation had it been in vogue then. The very idea that post–World War II international political scientists universally fail (or refuse) to discriminate between their "positivist" endeavors and Wilson's grotesque hybrid of "legalism-moralism" would have astounded, perplexed, and appalled these quintessentially "realist" international lawyers.

International Legal Positivism and the League of Nations

The incongruous suppositions underlying the international laws of neutrality could not withstand the rigors of twentieth century "total warfare" with its all-encompassing political, military, economic, and propagandistic dimensions. World War I demonstrated the abject failure of the international laws of neutrality to perform their intended purpose of constricting the radius of the war. This tragic experience led many American international lawyers to the unavoidable conclusion that in the postwar world the international community had to abandon neutrality as a viable concept of international law and politics and instead create a system of international relations in which some international organization would be formally charged with the task of enforcing international law against recalcitrant nations.[224]

Henceforth, the international legal rights of one state must be treated as rights pertaining to all states. National security could no longer be a matter of individual concern, but rather a collective responsibility shared by the entire international community organized together. Although the pre–World War I American international legal community did not expend much effort promoting the idea of creating some executive "international police power," the experience of the First World War and the failure of the international laws of neutrality to protect the United States from the scourge of war induced many of them to support the foundation of the League to Enforce Peace, which ultimately metamorphosed into the League of Nations.[225]

In the opinion of many (though certainly not all) American international lawyers, the United States government must at last definitively repudiate its traditional policies of isolationism in peace and neutrality in war in order to become a formal participant in the new postwar worldwide balance of power system. Admittedly, this balance had been wrought by brute military force. Yet its continued existence could nevertheless be legitimized, if not sanctified, by the adoption and effective enforcement of the principles of international law set forth in the Covenant of the League of Nations. America's vital national security interests, on the one hand, and its professed philosophical and moral ideals, on the other, could most successfully be reconciled, and indeed would coincide and reinforce each other, by means of U.S. membership in the League.

Despite this majority sentiment, however, the question of whether or not the United States should join the League and, if so, upon what terms, provoked a sharp and irreparable divergence of viewpoints among the members of the American international law community. A vocal minority opposed U.S. membership in the League precisely because this step would represent a decisive repudiation of America's classic position of isolationism in peace and neutrality in war vis-à-vis the European balance of power system that had served American national security interests so well since Washington's farewell address and the Monroe Doctrine. Other international lawyers argued that whatever the merits of continued American isolationism, the League of Nations as currently proposed was fatally defective because article 10 of the Covenant guaranteed the preservation of an essentially unjust status quo in favor of France and against Germany that was not entitled to U.S. support during peace or war. Elihu Root and James Brown Scott took the intermediate position that the United States should join the League but enter a reservation as to article 10.[226]

Whatever the merits of the dispute, however, the fight over the ratification of the Treaty of Versailles split the American international law community into a pro-League majority and an influential anti-League minority. From this point in time on, it was no longer possible to speak about the existence of one relatively homogeneous American international law community. And yet despite their differences over the advisability of the United States joining the League, during the subsequent interwar period, American international lawyers remained intrinsically and almost uniformly "positivist" in their orientation towards the relationship between international law and politics. Hence, in regard to the World Court, the overwhelming majority of the American international legal community was united in its enthusiastic support for U.S. participation in the Permanent Court of International Justice even if America did not join the League.

International Legal Positivism and the Advent of World War II

Of course, the United States government never joined the League of Nations and never became a party to the Statute of the Permanent Court of International Justice (PCIJ) because of strident opposition to both organizations consistently mounted by isolationist members of the U.S. Senate. Even the technical separation of the Court from the League by the device of adopting a Protocol of Signature for the PCIJ Statute that permitted non-League members to ratify the latter without joining the League was insufficient to induce the Senate into giving its advice and consent to the Protocol on terms that could prove acceptable to its contracting parties. But to the extent that U.S. non-participation in the work of the League of Nations and the Permanent Court of International Justice vitiated the effectiveness of these organizations, and to the extent that their institutional inefficacy can accurately be said to have contributed to the development of historical conditions ripe for the eruption of World War II, responsibility for this situation must be placed squarely upon the shoulders of the isolationist members of the U.S. Senate and their supporters.

The foundation of the League of Nations and of the Permanent Court of International Justice was the direct result, if not the ultimate consummation, of the pre–World War I American legal positivist approach to international relations. Both before and after the First World War, American international lawyers had astutely led the way in promoting support for the creation of these organizations and their immediate predecessors among the states of the international community. It was certainly not their fault that after the Great War the U.S. Senate chose to repudiate fundamental elements of the American legal positivist war prevention program for world politics that U.S. international lawyers had meticulously planned and vigorously championed since the time of the First Hague Peace Conference.

During the period between World War I and World War II, it was America's innate isolationist tendencies, going all the way back to Washington's farewell address and the Monroe Doctrine, that reasserted themselves and triumphed over America's relatively more recent international-ist foreign policies promoting international law and organizations. Thus, the American legal positivist approach to international relations, classi-cally defined and articulated from 1898 to 1917, cannot fairly be held responsible for either the First or the Second World War. If anything, both world wars occurred in spite of, and not because of, the best efforts by the American international legal community to prevent them through the creation of new rules of international law and new institutions for the peaceful settlement of international disputes. If the habitually obstruc-tionist U.S. Senate had implemented those constituent elements of the American international law community's 1898–1917 war prevention program for world politics by giving its advice and consent to the Treaty of Versailles and the PCIJ Protocol of Signature, there is perhaps a strong possibility that the Second World War might never have occurred.

U.S. membership in the World Court and some "league to enforce the peace" under the aegis of the United Nations Organization would occur only after and as a direct result of the tragic experience of World War II. During this war there developed a profound realization of the extreme dangers of continued American isolationism and, furthermore, of the essential wisdom of the pre–World War I American legal positivist approach to international relations, which convinced the U.S. govern-ment of the compelling need for it to sponsor and join the United Nations. When the U.S. Senate grudgingly accepted the compulsory jurisdiction of the International Court of Justice in 1946, the pre–World War I American legal positivist approach to international relations finally attained its fullest fruition.[227] Ever since then these products of Ameri-can international legal positivism have substantially contributed to the maintenance of international peace and security and to the prevention of a suicidal third world war.[228]

International Legal Positivism and the Future of
American Foreign Policy

In 1898 the United States purposefully chose to emulate the imperial
countries of the Old World by setting out to become a major global
power by performing a series of naked acts of military, political, and
economic expansion. Since that time it has struggled to come to grips
with the irreversible consequences of those fateful decisions which directly
contradicted several of the most fundamental normative principles upon
which America was supposed to be founded. During this imperialist era
of its history, the improvement of international law and the promotion of
international organizations have usually provided the United States with
the means for reconciling the idealism of American values and aspirations with the realism of world politics and historical conditions. The
U.S. government's resolute dedication to pursuit of this classic legal
positivist approach to international relations has proven to be critical for
the preservation of America's internal psychic equilibrium, which in turn
has historically proven to be a necessary precondition for the successful
advancement of its global position.

Both well before and immediately after World War I, as well as
immediately after World War II, the United States established an excellent track record for pioneering innovative rules of international law and
novel institutions for the peaceful settlement of international disputes.
Drastic departures from the 1898–1917 tradition of American legal
positivist diplomacy in order to follow instead a foreign policy based
essentially upon strict isolationism after the First World War or, under
the influence of the modern political realists, upon Machiavellian power
politics after the Korean War, have only produced a series of unmitigated
disasters for the United States government both at home and abroad. The
primary lesson to be learned from the history of American foreign policy
during the twentieth century is that the United States must grow to
possess a little more courage and foresight and a little less selfishness
and fear when it comes to the advancement of international law
and organizations as impediments to the development of a nuclear
Armageddon.

In contrast, the current American foreign policy decision-making
establishment's reliance upon the Machiavellian teachings of the modern
political realists, which are derived from a completely erroneous interpretation of twentieth-century U.S. diplomatic history, will ineluctably
produce such a terrible day of reckoning. Since modern political realism
represents nothing more sophisticated than a superficially rationalized

Machiavellianism updated to the historical conditions of the twentieth-century nation-state system, its continued pursuit by the nations of today's world will only create the self-fulfilling prophecy of global nuclear warfare. This is because the philosophy of power politics was basically constructed by men who lived in times of all-out warfare for the express purpose of fighting for survival (e.g., Thucydides, Machiavelli, Hobbes, and Morgenthau). In peacetime, however, the pursuit of power politics by governments will simply bring about that very war in which the principles of power politics were designed to operate successfully. So long as statesmen actually believe that only Machiavellian power politics matter in international relations, then so it might very well be until the nuclear destruction of mankind.

The escape from this apparent dilemma is the realization that power politics is not some "iron law" of history, as Hans Morgenthau called it many years ago, but only a complicated set of philosophical premises and an elaborate psychological justification for pursuing a policy of gratuitous violence that is factually inaccurate as a description of political events under all historical conditions except those of absolute warfare. One purpose of this book is to develop a philosophy of international relations on the basis of international law and organizations that is designed to preserve and extend world peace, while at the same time to protect the vital national security interests of states. The rules of international law and the procedures of international organizations for the peaceful settlement of disputes cannot serve as a general panacea for all the problems of contemporary international relations. But they do point one direction out of the rotting morass of Machiavellian power politics that has engulfed the American foreign policy decision-making establishment for over a generation.

5

Functionalism as a Substitute for Positivism

The Problem with International Legal Positivism Today

In many respects, the turn-of-the-century American legal positivist approach to international relations constituted a genuine precursor of the contemporary "functional integrationist" school of post–World War II international political science. Yet, in the former's attempt to overcome the Hobbesist doctrine that since the will of the sovereign is the source of all law, where there is no sovereign there is no law, early international legal positivism succumbed to another variant of the same fiction: the notion of sovereign consent as the sole basis for determining legitimacy in international relations. At the start of the twentieth century, reliance upon the concept of sovereign consent as manifested in customary and conventional international law was useful to international legal positivists to combat the Austinian denial of international law as real law because, theoretically, sovereign consent was a tangible factor whose presence could presumably be determined by objective criteria. Positivism's requirement of sovereign consent would thus avoid allegations of preaching Grotian natural law morality under the name of public international law. Nevertheless, stubborn insistence on sovereign consent to the exclusion of all other principles for legitimization has created a stark predicament for international legal positivism toward the end of the twentieth century.

Today, the nations of the world are striving to cope with the progressive evolution of a system of international relations that needs to move beyond the principle of sovereign consent, which provides each state with an inherent veto power over the creation of new rules, to its replacement by the principle of consensus, based upon reciprocal expectations of state behavior. There is nothing sacrosanct about sovereign consent as the basic legitimizing principle of international law and politics. Such notions derive from the social contract theorists such as Hobbes, Locke, and Rousseau, who postulated citizen consent to be the essential basis for political legitimacy in order to undercut the legitimizing role of the medieval Christian Church in Western political philosophy. This is another instance where the aforementioned "level-of-analysis" problem occurs. Within the system of municipal affairs, the principle of citizen consent may still operate in the desired fashion, but within the system of international relations sovereign consent has rapidly proven to be increasingly unworkable.

Post–World War II international legal positivists are thus not totally blameless for the development of the schism between international political science and international legal studies. Some remain oblivious to what has happened. The better ones are aware of the problem, but either do not know what to do about it, or else do not believe anything should be done: Let the political scientists hoist themselves with their own petard!

Having fallen into profound despair over their collective failure to turn the mainstream of American foreign policy from Machiavellianism toward its proper "legalist" course, contemporary public international lawyers have developed a highly formalistic and exclusively technical international legal positivist approach to international relations. Now the purpose of the modern positivist's scholarly life lies in the mechanistic determination of the legality or illegality of a proposed or completed course of state conduct in accordance with the punctilious terms of public international law. Extraneous considerations such as the relevance of this sacerdotal rite to international politics must not taint the purity of the legal analysis. Today's positivists treat illegality as if it were a sin deserving of punishment and damnation. By implication, the international legal positivists hold the keys to eternal salvation in their anointed hands. Like Socrates and Christ, they seem to preach that it is better to die good than to live evil. Yet the first alternative is a very real possibility for the entire human race in a thermonuclear age. No wonder international political scientists have been exasperated by public international lawyers.

Even some of those few international lawyers who do become actively involved in the public debate over the great issues of American foreign policy and world affairs seem to be impelled like lemmings by some mysterious force that drives them into the deadly embrace of their philosophical adversaries where they disavow their heritage by espousing Machiavellianism. There they try to outdo the political realists by proving how tough they really can be. The international lawyer who converts to political realism is the most vehement, articulate, knowledgeable, and effective advocate of the proposition that international law and organizations are irrelevant to international politics. Hans Morgenthau was the leading case in point.

All too often the current members of the American international legal community have wittingly or unwittingly served as mouthpieces for the Machiavellian foreign policies of the U.S. government by means of manufacturing legal arguments as ad hoc or ex post facto justifications for decisions taken on the grounds of power politics and national self-interest. Their fascination with the possibility of someday wielding governmental power has seduced American international lawyers into becoming apologists for its profligate use, rather than teachers of its proper exercise in international relations. In the process, both the vital national security interests of the United States and the strength of the international legal order have grievously suffered. Historically the cause of neither one has been advanced by the base subservience of American international lawyers to the Machiavellian policy pronouncements issued by the White House, the Departments of State and Defense, and the Central Intelligence Agency.

On the one hand, public international lawyers must appreciate the importance of reestablishing a working relationship with international political scientists. They must take upon themselves the burden of proving to the latter profession the functional relevance of international law and organizations to "high international politics" and conflicts over "vital national interests." In return, international political scientists must be fair and open-minded enough to reexamine some of the most fundamental assumptions underlying their discipline. Otherwise both groups will continue to pursue those objectives they share in common—international peace, security, prosperity, human dignity, and social justice—in profound isolation from each other or, worse yet, the two groups will pursue their common objectives while working at cross-purposes to one another. They will rarely benefit from the wisdom, counsel, experience, and direct assistance of their opposite numbers. Both academic disciplines can only continue to suffer grievously from the prolongation of this unwarranted schism within the community of international relations scholarship. Conversely, the analysis of international relations can only be enhanced by a reintegration of international legal studies with international political science.

In what direction does a solution to this problem lie? Quite obviously, it does not entail the further refinement of international legal positivism, even assuming this could be done. Nor must it lie in the proliferation of yet another pseudo-paradigmatic approach to international politics within the discipline of international political science. As Hans Morgenthau was reported to have said about a methodological seminar for international political scientists held at Princeton University: "All these people constantly sharpening their tools—but when are they ever going to cut something?" The necessary tools are already at hand. It is time to select those which are appropriate and put them to work. "Functionalism" was a key concept in Hans Morgenthau's transition from international lawyer to political realist and thus in the divorce of international political science from international legal studies. Consequently, a path toward reunification of the two disciplines lies in the direction of developing a functionalist jurisprudence of the relationship between international law and politics.

Rejection of McDougal-Lasswell Jurisprudence

At first glance, a primary vehicle for the accomplishment of this objective might seem to be the further elaboration of the human value-oriented jurisprudence of international law developed by Myers McDougal, Harold Lasswell, and their associates at the Yale Law School during the past quarter century. This is because it originated out of a solid social science background and has so far represented the first and only full-scale theoretical attempt in either discipline to marry international legal studies with the social sciences. It would appear that McDougal-Lasswell jurisprudence could easily be reconciled with the principles and methodology of international political science, or at least it seems more easily reconcilable than modern international legal positivism.

Historically, however, this has not proven to be the case. Indeed a somewhat skeptical observer could readily conclude that international legal positivism, McDougal-Lasswell jurisprudence, and international political science have little in common with each other today except for the fact that all three are concerned with topics of an international nature. McDougal-Lasswell jurisprudence has been and will remain unsuitable for the purpose of achieving the reunification of international legal studies with international political science. This unsuitability is attributable to several fundamental reasons flowing from the respective philosophical premises underlying all three approaches to international relations.

In their seminal article published in the 1959 edition of the *American*

Journal of International Law, "The Identification and Appraisal of Diverse Systems of Public Order," McDougal and Lasswell essentially repudiated the international legal positivist "paradigm" set forth by Oppenheim over half a century before in the pages of that same journal.[229] Instead, they called for a complete reevaluation of the "doctrines and operations having the name of international law" in light of the "contribution that they make to the realization of human dignity in theory and fact." The positivist myth that international law was truly "universal" simply permitted totalitarian dictators in the Soviet bloc to manipulate the concepts of international law for the purpose of "advancing toward an imposed universalization of the totalitarian form of public order." The task which they set for themselves and their associates would be to develop a non-positivist social science methodology that would enable them to conceptualize, analyze, and explain international law for the ultimate purpose of creating a "universal order of human dignity":

> . . . We shall outline a map of the undertaking that we have in mind and in whose execution we invite all like-minded scholars to participate. . . .
>
> The map we recommend begins with (a) orienting ourselves in world social process, (b) identifying within this, a process distinctively specialized to power, (c) characterizing as the legal process those decisions that are at once authoritative and controlling, and (d) defining as the public order those features of the whole social process which receive protection by the legal process. From this map we proceed to (e) outline our commitment to the realization of a universal system of public order consistent and compatible with human dignity, (f) analyze the intellectual tasks that confront the scholar who accepts this overriding goal, (g) indicate some of the specific questions that arise in the consideration of any system of public order, and (h) refer to the scholarly procedures by which the task of inquiry can be executed on a satisfactory scale of depth and coverage.[230]

The degree of contrast between the tasks McDougal-Lasswell promulgated for discharge by their international law associates, on the one hand, and those Oppenheim prescribed some fifty years earlier for fulfillment by his international legal positivists, on the other, could not have been more pronounced.

OBJECTIONS TO MCDOUGAL-LASSWELL'S
EXPLICIT ADOPTION OF ANY VALUE-ORIENTATION

The first and foremost objection to utilizing McDougal-Lasswell jurisprudence for the purpose of bridging the chasm between international political science and international legal studies is the fact that its explicit adoption of any value-orientation is unacceptable to both international political scientists and international legal positivists.[231] Some theoretical bridge attempting to span the gap between two disciplines must rely for its support upon the paradigmatic requirements of each. McDougal-Lasswell jurisprudence fails to do so for either.

From the perspective of the international political scientists, McDougal-Lasswell jurisprudence fails to rigorously differentiate the Machiavellian "is" from the Platonic "ought to be" of international politics and law. The establishment and preservation of this analytical distinction is axiomatic to modern political philosophy and, *a fortiori*, to international political science. Without it, McDougal-Lasswell jurisprudence cannot serve as the starting point for the development of what must at least purport to be a "scientific" theory of the relationship between law and politics in the international system.

The international legal positivists raise a similar objection. To them, McDougal-Lasswell jurisprudence appears to be nothing more than an atavistic return to the promotion of Grotian natural law concepts dressed up in the jargon of mid-twentieth-century social science. Oppenheim and his colleagues struggled valiantly and successfully to extricate international legal studies from this morass. They set the discipline upon its proper and "scientific" course of international legal positivism. Their heirs will not allow the study of international law to be seduced by natural law in the guise of social science terminology.

OBJECTIONS TO THE MCDOUGAL-LASSWELL PREFERENCE
FOR LOCKEAN LIBERAL VALUES

Even if these interrelated objections to the self-professed value-orientation of McDougal-Lasswell jurisprudence could somehow be overcome, the universality of its value system would still remain seriously suspect. This is because McDougal-Lasswell jurisprudence is inextricably rooted in the Western liberal tradition of natural right[232] that was so eloquently and definitively stated by John Locke in his *Second Treatise of Government*.[233] Indeed, the objectionable features of the natural law structure of McDougal-Lasswell jurisprudence are the inexorable result of this Lockean natural right foundation.

In his classic work Locke revised and expanded upon Thomas Hobbes' analysis of power politics found in the *Leviathan*, and transformed it into the Anglo-American liberal philosophy of government, law, freedom, and rights as it exists today. In effect, Locke rendered Hobbesism eminently palatable to Anglo-American sensibilities. Yet Hobbes and his theory of power politics still remain at the heart of the modern liberal tradition.

Like Hobbes, Locke postulated the existence of a natural man who possessed natural rights and lived in a state of nature where he is governed by natural laws. These laws are the product of human reason flowing from man's natural desire for self-preservation and well-being. The Lockean state of nature, however, is not tantamount to a Hobbesist state of war by every man against every man. Although Lockean men are, by nature, selfish, they are eminently reasonable and empathetic beings. Therefore, the Lockean state of nature is essentially a state of peace.

Man creates civil society for the express purpose of better protecting and promoting his "property," a term Locke defined to include life, liberty, and estate—that famous Lockean trilogy which Jefferson transmogrified into the "Life, Liberty and the Pursuit of Happiness" of the American Declaration of Independence. Locke theorized that the institution of private property existed antecedent to and independent of civil society. His first proposition was that every man has property in his own person. By mixing the property of his own person with the elements of nature through his own labor, man can rightfully lay claim to the products resulting therefrom as his own possessions. This was the essence of Locke's labor theory of value, which constitutes the core of a modern theory of capitalism.

Civil society is only one step removed from the state of nature. Human nature remains essentially selfish in both milieus. Man is primarily concerned with the advancement of his own self-interest in each condition. Therefore, whether in the state of nature or in civil society, man owes no affirmative obligation toward his fellow men to improve their situation in life.

Within civil society man must be free to do whatever he wants so long as he does not infringe upon the right of his fellow men to do the same. It is the purpose of government to determine by law the limits of one man's freedom of action in relation to that of his fellow citizens in the event of conflict. But within these limited restrictions man must remain free to pursue his own self-interest and happiness as he sees fit. And this is especially true in the economic sphere of activities.

From Hobbesism Locke developed a theory of limited government and, as a corollary thereto, a right of revolution when the sovereign transgresses those limitations placed upon his power. The sovereign cannot be absolute because he is a party to the social contract and thus subject to the laws of civil society. The citizens can enter into a state of war against a tyrannical sovereign because he is an aggressor, yet do so without precipitating a Hobbesist state of nature/war among themselves.

This is because the Lockean social contract can survive the dissolution of the government brought about by revolution.

MCDOUGAL-LASSWELL VERSUS ROUSSEAU, BENTHAM, MARX

Despite the predilections of McDougal-Lasswell jurisprudence, Lockean Hobbesism did not prove to be the definitive word on modern constitutional theory. An alternative philosophy starts with the premise that there is no such thing as a natural man with natural rights living in a state of nature and ruled by natural law. Rights are not natural, inalienable, or inviolable. Rights cannot be treated as an abstract Platonic form, but can only be considered meaningful within the context of civil society.

Man is a social creature entirely dependent upon civil society for his physical survival, moral development, and personal happiness. Therefore, man's enjoyment of rights must be conditioned upon the performance of positive duties, not simply upon the mere abstention from negative harm. The primary purpose of government is to advance the common interest for the betterment of all. An individual must often forego the pursuit of his own self-interest for the good of others. Ideally, a citizen will achieve the fulfillment of his own desires through realization of the common good. If a citizen is unwilling to act towards this end voluntarily, however, the laws of civil society must force him to be altruistic. Failure by a citizen to discharge his social duties not only justifies but usually requires a deprivation of his rights. For the rights of man are ultimately conditioned upon the purpose of the state.

The seminal source for this theory of government and its relationship to the individual can be found in the writings of Jean-Jacques Rousseau and Jeremy Bentham, and from there it percolated into Marxist philosophy. Rousseau explained his theory in terms of the concept of the "general will"; Bentham, by the principle of "utility."[234] Yet the two philosophies are functionally similar in establishing the priority of social duty over individual right. Marx adopted Benthamite utilitarian principles and put them to the service of one segment of the Rousseauian general will, the proletariat.[235] In a communist society rights are thus determined in accordance with calculations of utility designed to enhance the condition of the proletariat.

HUMAN RIGHTS VERSUS CAPITALISM

Locke, on the one hand, and Rousseau, Bentham, and Marx, on the other, represent the philosophical archetypes for the debate over the proper relationship between fundamental human rights and the requirements of social and state obligation currently raging between First World countries ("capitalist" and "democratic") and Third World countries ("developing" and "authoritarian"), the latter of which are supported by Second World countries ("communist" and "totalitarian"). The fundamental issue is whether or not human rights exist prior to and independent from the needs of civil society, especially in the area of economic development.

Due to its philosophical presuppositions, McDougal-Lasswell jurisprudence has irreversibly chosen sides in this debate in favor of the Lockean liberal position.[236] McDougal-Lasswell jurisprudence postulates capitalism to be the preferred economic system for the realization of its conception of a world public order promoting fundamental human rights.[237] Underlying McDougal-Lasswell jurisprudence on human rights is the assumption that it is legitimate to discriminate in terms of wealth for reasons relevant to merit or capability. Yet implementation of this precept would violate the fundamental canon of communism: "From each according to his ability, to each according to his needs!"[238]

From a Marxist perspective, by conceptualizing man in terms of property Locke reduced man to a form of property. Locke's "chattelization" of the human being becomes the philosophical explanation for the exploitation of the proletariat by the bourgeoisie and for the fundamental alienation of all human beings within capitalist society. Locke is nothing more than an apologist for capitalism; his theory of human rights, an ideology to legitimatize and perpetuate capitalist exploitation. From a Marxist perspective, the same could be said for McDougal-Lasswell jurisprudence.

MCDOUGAL-LASSWELL'S IMPRIMATUR ON AMERICAN FOREIGN POLICY

A similar line of analysis can account for the oft-repeated criticism of McDougal-Lasswell jurisprudence when it is applied to determine the propriety of specific instances of state conduct in international politics. Namely, it possesses an uncanny ability to justify in pseudo-legal terms whatever course of behavior the U.S. government deems expedient to its national self-interest under the particular historical conditions.[239] Since Lockean liberal values serve as the starting point for the value-oriented analysis of McDougal-Lasswell jurisprudence, and because the U.S. government is founded upon essentially Lockean principles (for example, the Declaration of Independence, the Constitution, and the Bill of Rights), it becomes a simple exercise in circular reasoning to legitimate whatever America does in its relations with other nations simply because America does it.

For these reasons Lockean liberal values, especially because of their central emphasis upon the sanctity of private property, cannot serve as the basis for the formation of a system of world public order encompassing countries, peoples, and civilizations espousing fundamentally different if not antithetically opposed sets of values. Indeed, insistence upon the primacy of Lockean liberal values by the U.S. government in its conduct of foreign affairs can easily lead to international conflict or world disorder. A paradigmatic example of this phenomenon was the Reagan administration's shortsighted rejection of the U.N. Law of the Sea Treaty on July 9, 1982, essentially because it did not provide U.S. multinational corporations with an almost unfettered right to exploit the resources of the deep seabed in whatever manner they saw fit.

So even if international relations scholars set out to construct a value-oriented jurisprudence of international relations, McDougal-Lasswell should still not be the point of departure. Moreover, the counterargument that at least the methodology, as opposed to the substance, of McDougal-Lasswell jurisprudence is essentially value-free and therefore can be profitably employed by proponents of diametrically opposed value systems is intrinsically suspect and ultimately unconvincing. Such claims sound remarkably similar to the prideful boasts uttered by that ancient master of sophism and teacher of sophists, Protagoras, who in the Platonic dialogue of that name was vanquished by the true philosophy of Socrates.[240] The international legal profession needs no more sophists than it already has.

The International Crises and the Role of Law *Series*

In contrast to McDougal-Lasswell jurisprudence, the series of five books published under the auspices of the American Society of International Law from 1974 to 1978 entitled *International Crises and the Role of Law*, constituted a first step in the proper direction toward reestablishing the relevance of international law and organizations to international politics, and thus in developing a functionalist jurisprudence of international relations that could reintegrate international legal studies with international political science.[241] Yet that project did not go far enough. In that series, the case studies performed the invaluable first task of assembling the historical data into a set of descriptive statements establishing the role that international law and organizations played during the respective crises. This author would like to suggest the utility of engaging in at least four additional stages of analysis.

First, for each case study, an effort must be made to deduce from the

historical descriptive statements a set of theoretical propositions about
the role international law and organizations played in relation to the
crisis at hand. To be specific:

> *Descriptive statement.* During the Cuban missile crisis, among the vari-
> ous alternative courses of conduct considered by the United States
> government (viz., invasion, surgical airstrike, blockade, "quarantine"),
> it chose to implement a "quarantine" of Cuba with the endorsement of
> the Organization of American States.
>
> *Theoretical proposition.* During time of international crisis, a govern-
> ment will respond at the outset with that viable option it perceives to
> be the least violative of the international legal order.

This theoretical proposition gives rise to a host of interesting and important questions. Does it hold true for "totalitarian" governments as well as
for "democratic" governments? What if the original "least violative"
response fails? Does the approval of a "least violative" but arguably
illegal response by an international organization adversely affect its ability to participate in the effective management of future international
crises?

Such questions cannot be answered solely by reference to the Cuban
missile crisis. The theoretical proposition can only serve as the starting
point for further investigation of these issues in regard to other international crises. Without the derivation of such theoretical propositions,
however, there is no meaningful way to connect the lessons of one case
study with those of any other.

If, but only if, a set of theoretical propositions concerning the role of
international law and organizations in each particular crisis has been
formulated, it would then be possible to enter upon the next stage of the
analytical process. This more complicated step would consist of synthesiz-
ing the theoretical propositions drawn from each case study into one
theoretical model for the role of international law and organizations in
time of international crisis. The usefulness of that model would be a
function of the number, quality, and diversity of the individual case
studies upon which it is based. Yet the initial construction of such a
theoretical model would permit the generation of additional case studies
undertaken in reference to it and thereby permit the further perfection of
the model.

Although guided by a common purpose, the individual case studies
comprising the *International Crises and the Role of Law* series do not share a
mutual framework for analysis. Nor has this shortcoming been remedied
by relating the conclusions of one study to those of another in a rigorous

methodological fashion. The development of a theoretical model for the role of international law and organizations in international crises will solve both of these interrelated problems.

With the accumulation of such interrelated case studies, the derivation of theoretical propositions therefrom, and the latter's consequent addition to the theoretical model, researchers should eventually feel confident enough with the model to formulate and test some predictive hypotheses regarding the role of international law and organizations in time of international crisis. These predictive hypotheses could be verified by reference to future international crises or to past international crises that have yet to be researched. As pointed out by Thomas Kuhn, one of the best and most assured methodologies for proving the validity of a theoretical model is the formulation, testing, and verification of predictive hypotheses logically derived from it.[242]

Further perfection of the model in this manner would make it possible to suggest some tentative prescriptive statements about how historical conditions could be altered so as to optimize the role of international law and organizations in time of international crisis. Recommendations could be made concerning the promulgation of new international law, the improvement of international organizations, or the alteration of national or international decision-making procedures and institutions in order to better cope with international crises. Here the speculations of academic theory enter the domain of political reality, and the general admonition by Hans Morgenthau to all theorists is applicable: "In the world of the intellectual, ideas meet with ideas, and anything goes that is presented cleverly and with assurance. In the political world, ideas meet with facts, which make mincemeat of the wrong ideas and throw the ideas into the ashcan of history."[243]

Even then, the performance of this final task of formulating prescriptive statements assumes that international law and organizations do indeed have a positive role to play in the prevention, management, and resolution of international crises. This contention is denied by international political scientists who, for the most part, would assert the essential irrelevance of international law and organizations to international crises because the latter involve conflicts of "vital national interest" and are the stuff of "high international politics." The interconnected set of assumptions underlying the respective positions of public international lawyers and international political scientists on this point needs to be exposed, tested, proved, disproved, or improved by the facts of history itself. Rhetoric alone on either side will not suffice to do the job. The *International Crises and the Role of Law* series took the first invaluable step in that direction. It is in this direction that a solution to the problem of the alleged "irrelevance" of international law and organizations lies. Hopefully, it is also by movement in this direction that the reintegration of international legal studies and international political science can occur.

Hans Morgenthau's Volte-Face

In May of 1978, Hans Morgenthau delivered a stunning presentation before Stanley Hoffmann's Seminar on American Foreign Policy at the Center for International Affairs of Harvard University. Although the talk was all too brief, its theoretical implications for international political science, international legal studies, and international politics were profound. Morgenthau's basic thesis was that in a world of nuclear weapons systems developed to the current level of technical expertise, where the instantaneous destruction of mankind is imminently possible, power politics as the guiding principle for the conduct of international relations has become fatally defective and could ultimately result in the destruction of the human race through precipitation of a suicidal third world war. Morgenthau proceeded to delineate what he believed to be the only possible solution to this overarching dilemma of the international political system as it approaches the twenty-first century: formation of a world government.

He did not go into specific details about the process of its creation from the present nation-state system. Nor did he outline its preferred configuration once formed. He did not comment upon the utility of the proposals set forth by Grenville Clark and Louis Sohn in their great classic *World Peace Through World Law* for the creation of a "World Disarmament and World Development Organization."[244] He did suggest, however, that the United Nations Organization could serve as one possible starting point for the gradual formation of a world government.

To be sure, this process would take a long time, and Morgenthau refused to give an estimate of its probable period of gestation. He did not even utter a prediction as to whether the creation of a world government was historically possible at this stage of human evolution. He simply stated that world government has become an historical imperative.

As a stage penultimate to and facilitative of a world government, however, the nations of the world must, for the immediate future, participate in the creation of a plethora of functionally related international organizations in order to cope with the subjects of primary concern to international relations. The development of a large number of specialized international organizations could eventually lead, through a process of gradual integration, to the formation of a world government. Here Morgenthau joined the camp of his functional-integrationist colleagues, perhaps much to their surprise or chagrin.

Needless to say, those in the audience familiar with his work were thunderstruck by what appeared to be a thoroughgoing repudiation of the fundamental principles Morgenthau had successfully advocated on behalf of both himself and international political science for the past thirty years. In an attempt to make certain that such was his intention, this author asked him a series of three interrelated questions. Morgenthau's startling answers need no explanation. To paraphrase the content of the discussion:

> Q: Since international organizations and world government now seem to be the key to the future of mankind and since both are and will be the products of international law, does this not mean that international law and therefore international lawyers are relevant and indeed essential to the future of international relations?
>
> A: Well, of course international law must play an important role in the creation of international organizations and the formation of a world government. But I do not know if I would go so far as to include international lawyers within this category of what is essential. [Jokingly.]
>
> Q: Then, with all due respect, I am somewhat perplexed and at a loss as to how I should understand what you are saying. You come here today and tell us that it is vital for the future of mankind to create a world government through the progressive development of international organizations which, you have admitted, requires a central role for international law. And I do not see how you can realistically exclude international lawyers from that process. Have you not come full circle?
>
> That is to say: You started out many years ago as a young man, trained in the law, teaching international law and publishing in the field. Then along came the Second World War, and you and a group of disenchanted international lawyers broke away from the discipline and established international political science as a separate and independent discipline, based upon essentially anti-legalist or legal nihilist premises—those of power politics and what you called "political realism." For thirty years you stridently argued this position against all comers, whether international lawyers or other international political scientists. Now you come here and tell us that you have changed your mind; that it is necessary for us all to

turn to world government, international organizations, international law and, by implication, international lawyers simply in order to survive into the next century. Have you not returned to the point where you started over fifty years ago?

A: As is oftentimes the case, Francis, you are perfectly correct. But that just goes to show that you can learn something new in thirty years. [Jokingly.]

Q: In other words, you have come out precisely where Professor Louis Sohn of the Harvard Law School has been for the past thirty years?

A: Sohn and I might start from different principles, but we have arrived at the same conclusion.

Those familiar with the work of both men could not have been more surprised by Morgenthau's breathtaking answers. In the post–World War II study of international relations it had always been assumed that there existed a spectrum of viewpoints ranging from the extreme realism of Hans Morgenthau, on the one side, to the extreme idealism of Louis Sohn, on the other, and with everyone else falling on the line somewhere in between. Morgenthau himself had turned that line into a circle. By his own hands he had joined the two endpoints.

International political scientists and public international lawyers may agree or disagree with Morgenthau's conclusions. But the significant fact is that the very founder of the school propounding the irrelevance of international law and organizations changed his mind on the subject. We should all take note of this development and give Morgenthau's reversal of opinion serious consideration. Are international law and organizations relevant or irrelevant to international politics? Is there any justification for the continuance of the schism between international political science and international legal studies? These are weighty questions for all international political scientists and public international lawyers to ponder. The answers should be forthcoming if we can only bring ourselves to work together toward their solution. The time to start is now.

Conclusion

On November 10, 1979, shortly after the seizure of U.S. diplomats in Teheran, this author visited with Hans Morgenthau at his home in Manhattan. It proved to be our last conversation before his death on July 19, 1980. At the end of the discussion, I asked him what he thought about the future of international relations. He replied:

> Future, what future? I am extremely pessimistic. In my opinion the world is moving ineluctably towards a third world war—a strategic nuclear war. I do not believe that anything can be done to prevent it. The international system is simply too unstable to survive for long. The SALT II Treaty is important for the present, but over the long haul it cannot stop the momentum. Fortunately, I do not believe that I will live to see that day. But I am afraid you might.
>
> Of course I am in a very pessimistic mood today, so perhaps you should come back at another time and ask me that question again. [Jokingly.]

Unfortunately, those who teach and practice international relations will no longer have the benefit of Morgenthau's penetrating insight to guide us through the turbulent years ahead.

Somewhat serendipitously the late George Kistiakowsky made the same prediction some three months later before an audience at Harvard University:

> I think that with the kind of political leaders we have in the world . . . nuclear weapons will proliferate. . . . I personally think that the likelihood for an initial use of nuclear warheads is really quite great between now and the end of this century, which is only twenty years hence. My own estimate, since I am almost eighty years old, [is that] I will probably die from some other cause. But looking around at all these young people [in the audience], I am sorry to say I think a lot of you may die from nuclear war.[245]

To the same effect have been subsequent public statements by George Kennan[246] and Hyman Rickover,[247] among others. Indeed, like Morgenthau, the arch-realist Kennan explicitly endorsed the Clark-Sohn proposals as a constructive alternative to global nuclear destruction.

It is imperative that we undertake a committed and concerted effort to disprove Hans Morgenthau's final prediction on the cataclysmic demise of international affairs. For us to gainsay or ignore the distinct possibility, if not the preponderant probability, of a global nuclear war is to engage in that classic psychoanalytical defense mechanism known as "denial."[248] Far better to think about the unthinkable and try to come to grips with it, than to deny strategic nuclear reality and allow the unthinkable to destroy us. Perhaps a nuclear war cannot be prevented, but at least we must attempt to do so.

If a third world war does occur, it is less probable that it will result from an outright Warsaw Pact invasion of Western Europe coupled with a preemptive Soviet nuclear attack upon the United States, than from the deterioration of an international crisis between the two nuclear superpowers over a peripheral area (e.g., Cuba, Berlin) or a crisis between regional surrogates that escalates into direct superpower confrontation (e.g., President Nixon's nuclear alert during the Yom Kippur War). The immediate question will then become whether the crisis can be managed by the participants. If not, the actors will find themselves placed on a ladder of escalation in which temptation will lead to the employment of conventional military forces, then battlefield or theater nuclear weapons, and finally strategic nuclear forces. As demonstrated by Graham Allison's definitive study of the Cuban missile crisis in *Essence of Decision* (1971), once set in motion an international crisis generates an incredible momentum of its own that is extremely difficult for even intelligent, rational, informed, and well-intentioned crisis management decision makers to control and terminate. Understanding the nature of international crises and the means whereby they can be prevented and controlled by international law and organizations provides one invaluable starting point for guaranteeing the future of human civilization.

How this can be done will be demonstrated in the second part of this book. Drawing upon Hans Morgenthau's sketchy description of "functionalism" set forth in his seminal 1940 article, this author will attempt to construct a functionalist analysis of the relationship between international law and politics in time of international crisis when at least one of the participants perceived its vital national security interests to be at stake. Part Two will establish why and how considerations of international law and organizations are of critical relevance to real world crisis management decision makers. As part of this process, Part Two will also develop a general methodological framework that should permit both public international lawyers and international political scientists, jointly and severally, to bring to bear their respective tools of expertise upon the analysis of other instances of "high international politics" or conflicts over "vital national interests." Hopefully by means of this device, the schism between international legal studies and international political science can begin to be healed.

Part Two

*International Law in Time of Crisis
from the Entebbe Raid
to the Hostages Convention*

6

A *Functionalist Analysis of International
Law and Politics*

The Facts

On June 24, 1976, Air France flight 139 from Tel Aviv to Paris was hijacked by three men and a woman who identified themselves as members of the Popular Front for the Liberation of Palestine, approximately eight minutes after a scheduled stop in Athens, where they had boarded the plane.[1] The jet was then flown to Benghazi, Libya, for refueling.[2] After the release of a pregnant woman at Benghazi, the Airbus continued on to Entebbe airport in Uganda, where it landed at 3:00 A.M. on June 28.[3] Nine hours later, passengers disembarked and were transferred to a seldom-used airport terminal.[4]

The hijackers demanded the release of 53 imprisoned "freedom fighters" (forty held in Israel, with the rest scattered among France, Switzerland, Kenya, and West Germany) by the afternoon of July 1 in exchange for the safe return of the 241 passengers and twelve crew members of the hijacked plane.[5] Otherwise, they threatened to kill all the hostages.[6] On June 30, the hijackers released forty-seven non-Israeli women and children.[7] Shortly before the expiration of the July 1 deadline, Israel agreed to negotiate.[8] The hijackers subsequently released another 101 captives, keeping only Israelis, those believed to be Jewish, and the Airbus crew.[9] The deadline was extended to July 4.[10]

At 11:30 P.M. on Saturday, July 3, the Israeli Defense Forces conducted a military raid that rescued the hostages.[11] During the ensuing battle, three captives, one Israeli soldier, at least twenty Ugandan soldiers, and all of the hijackers were killed.[12] One other hostage, Dora Bloch, who held dual British and Israeli nationality, died in Uganda, though not in the raid. She had been hospitalized in Kampala prior to the time of the raid after she began to choke on a piece of meat that had lodged in her throat while eating. She was left behind, and later killed on Idi Amin's orders.[13]

The purpose of Part Two is to develop a set of theoretical propositions concerning the various roles played by international law and organizations in time of crisis from a "functionalist" as opposed to the traditional legal positivist approach to international relations. It focuses upon the Entebbe incident not as an end in itself but as a vehicle for the elaboration of a common analytical framework applicable to the phenomenon of international crisis in general. This study follows in the path blazed by the *International Crises and the Role of Law* series published under the auspices of the American Society of International Law.[14] Yet it strives to advance that endeavor one evolutionary stage beyond its genesis. In that series, case studies of various international crises performed the invaluable first task of assembling historical data into a series of descriptive statements concerning the roles of international law and international organizations during these crises. In Part One of this book, however, I have suggested the utility of engaging in at least four additional stages of analysis.

In the second stage, a set of theoretical propositions must be derived from the descriptive historical statements about the functions which international law and organizations played in relation to the crisis at hand. This process of abstraction makes possible the third stage of analysis: construction of a general theoretical model for the functions of international law and organizations in time of crisis through synthesis of the particular sets of theoretical propositions. Fourth, the model can be improved by the formulation and testing of predictive hypotheses about the functions of international law and organizations in time of future international crises. Fifth, tentative prescriptive recommendations can be offered concerning the promulgation of new international law, the improvement of international organizations, and the alteration of national or international decision-making procedures and institutions in order better to cope with international crises.

Two Paradigmatic Questions

FOR THE INTERNATIONAL LAWYER

If the reader is an international lawyer, the odds are fairly good that he will start reading Part Two with the following question in the forefront of his mind: Was the Israeli raid at Entebbe a violation of international law? Obsessive preoccupation with the determination of legality or illegality is characteristic of a modern legal positivist approach to international law and international politics.[15] The issue of legality is important, but all too often this becomes the first, last, and only question today's international lawyers ask themselves or are even interested in answers for. Part Two will suggest to the public international lawyer an array of equally important questions that should be of concern to him as well. Part Two will not specifically answer the question of the legality of the Entebbe raid in positivist terms. Yet it will adduce the arguments on both sides of the issue and offer a tentative formulation as to how that question could be answered from a functionalist perspective.

FOR THE INTERNATIONAL POLITICAL SCIENTIST

If the reader is an international political scientist, he will not be terribly worried about the legality or illegality of the Entebbe raid. His opening question, rather, will be something along the following lines: Would the government of Israel have refrained from launching the raid at Entebbe if it had determined that such action violated international law? In other words, would any state sacrifice its perceived vital national interests on the altar of international legality? Supposing the negative, is international law really relevant in any meaningful sense to international crises?

International political scientists, and even many public international lawyers, do generally suppose the negative, and in a certain sense they are correct in that conclusion, but not for the reasons generally assumed. During an international crisis, states rarely, if ever, sacrifice their vital national interests for considerations of international law or vice versa because, in situations of apparent conflict between the two, governmental decision makers commence to define or redefine their vital national interests to include considerations of international law; conversely, they define or redefine international law to take account of their vital national interests. Invariably, decision makers engage in both processes simultaneously. In this fashion, vital national interests are tailored to the demands of international law and vice versa. An initially perceived gap between the two is narrowed from both sides to a point of at least plausible argument concerning its nonexistence.

This process of dialectical interaction between vital national interests and international law during and following a crisis exerts a strong force toward reconciliatory modification upon each. If a similar crisis occurs again in the future, the experience of the first crisis will have already altered the contours of the international system so as to render the second dispute more manageable. Or, a similar crisis might not even erupt again because a body of international law, procedures, or institutions were developed in the aftermath of the first crisis specifically for the purpose of preventing such problems in the future. Likewise, vital national interests will have become altered in the wake of a crisis in order to make recurrence of such a crisis less likely. In such instances, international law, international organizations, and vital national interests work hand-in-hand to prevent the recurrence of crises and thereby maintain the stability of the international system for all its members, including those unaffected by the first crisis.

From the perspective of an international lawyer trained in the "realist" or power politics approach to international relations, these observations are not at all surprising. When analyzed in accordance with the Aristotelian doctrine of the mean, the principles of international law possess an intrinsic core of rationality that creates a workable path between human nature and social convention critical to continued survival.[16] International law articulates those rules which the actors in the international system have found to be indispensable for international life. And that which is essential to international life becomes enshrined in the rules of international law.

States create the rules of international law for the express purpose of serving and advancing their respective national interests. States do not adopt useless, impractical, or dangerous rules to regulate their relations in the first place. Therefore, the requirements of international law should substantially, albeit imperfectly, coincide with the dictates of vital national interests and vice versa. Even in a time of severe international crisis, adherence to the rules of international law usually proves to be in a state's best interest anyway.

Here the writings of the late Professor Lon Fuller of the Harvard Law School become apposite.[17] His work indicates that any system of law is most properly understood as creating a facilitative framework of rules that permits and enhances the quality of interaction among its participants. Law must not simply be interpreted in its Hobbesist legal positivist sense as the making, breaking, and enforcement of rules.[18] Any system of law, even an imperfect one, usually proves to be more beneficial and, therefore, preferable to each participant than the existence of no legal rules at all. This argument has been developed at length by the Harvard political scientist Thomas Schelling through the application of game theory to conflict situations.[19] The reason why two cars approaching each other on a narrow mountain road obey the rules of the road by each driving on its right-hand side supplies an excellent analogy as to why states will follow international law in time of crisis.[20]

This line of argument is not intended to dispose of the international political scientist's question by ignoring it. It is impossible to prove that a government would have taken a hypothetical course of action if it had evaluated the surrounding circumstances and arrived at a conclusion diametrically opposed to the one it did in fact reach: Would Israel have launched the Entebbe raid if it had determined the raid violated international law, when in fact it determined the exact opposite? An analyst must be content with establishing the reasons why a government did undertake a particular course of conduct, and not allow hypothetical answers to speculative questions to undercut the significance of the lessons taught by historical facts themselves. Part Two will demonstrate that one important reason for the Israeli government's decision to launch the Entebbe operation was its bona fide belief that the raid was consistent with the requirements of international law. Therefore, the political scientist's conjecture that Israel would have launched the raid anyway, even if the government had believed that it was illegal, becomes immaterial to the analysis.

The Need for a New Approach

These two archetypal questions of international legal positivism and international political science (was the action legal? what difference does it make?) share in common an either/or view of the universe: either legal or illegal; either vital national interest or international law. Real life and historical fact are rarely so clear-cut, so susceptible to such dogmatic assertions and the automatic derivation of conclusions therefrom. Part Two eschews the either/or approach for a dialectical interpretation. It focuses upon the dynamic interaction of law and politics during one particular incident of contemporary international affairs charged with the atmosphere of an international crisis. This dialectical approach to the study of international law and international politics does not detract from the integrity of either. It simply demonstrates that it is a logical and historical fallacy to believe that law and politics are essentially independent of each other. In the realm of international relations, they are so highly interdependent as to be almost indistinguishable. International politics is and becomes international law, while international law is and becomes international politics.

It must be the joint and several task of public international lawyers and international political scientists to elucidate the dynamics of interaction between international law and politics in a time of crisis. This essay will provide both groups with a common framework of analysis that is acceptable to the scientific, philosophical, and methodological foundations of each. It will permit both groups to bring to bear their respective expertise upon these potentially cataclysmic problems of contemporary international affairs. This essay will contribute to the development of a more synthesized, multidimensional, and holistic understanding of the nature of international crises and the means by which they can be prevented or controlled. In the process, this functionalist analysis of Entebbe will also demonstrate how and why international law and organizations are critical to conflicts between states over matters of "vital national interest." It will thus refute the conventional political realist hypothesis that both are essentially irrelevant to "high international politics."

The Five Functions of International Law and Organizations During an International Crisis

Part Two falls within the second of the five stages of analysis mentioned above. The purpose of this section, therefore, is the derivation of theoretical propositions concerning the roles of international law and organizations in a particular international crisis. The facts of the Entebbe raid are not recounted (stage one) except to the extent necessary to facilitate the progress of the discussion.[21] The construction of a general model for the role of international law in time of crisis (stage three) is not attempted, since the theoretical propositions to be derived from the Entebbe incident will necessarily be limited to the facts of that case, and similar propositions derived from other case studies have yet to be produced. Nor, consequently, can Part Two formulate predictive hypotheses or prescriptive recommendations (stages four and five) concerning the functions of international law and organizations in future international crises.

This part of the essay will, however, generate a set of theoretical propositions concerning the roles or functions international law and organizations played or failed to play during the Entebbe crisis. In order to reduce this task to manageable proportions, I shall delineate five functions of international law and organizations in the context of the Entebbe incident and relate the theoretical propositions to them. In sequential order and shorthand form they will be called (1) definition, (2) decision, (3) adjudication, (4) resolution, and (5) redefinition.

To be specific: The first function that international law performed during Entebbe was the *definition* of the international behavioral standards applicable to the crisis in the perceptions of all the actors involved. Next, international law served as an important element of *decision* in the

Israeli governmental crisis management proceedings. The third function of international law in the Entebbe crisis was *adjudication* of the outstanding dispute between Israel and Uganda before the United Nations Security Council. This adjudication prepared the way for the fourth function of international law and organizations in regard to Entebbe— *resolution* of the crisis by the Security Council. The fifth and last function consisted of a *redefinition* of international behavioral standards to go beyond those existing prior to the outbreak of the crisis. Entebbe generated the momentum necessary to propel an inchoate international consensus against the taking of hostages into the concrete form of a special U.N. committee for the drafting of an international convention to prevent this phenomenon. Its subsequently adopted United Nations Hostages Convention now codifies the elements of the Entebbe debate consensus and thereby attempts to remedy those problems of international law and international politics exposed by Entebbe.

This list of five functions is not intended to be exhaustive. Yet it should allow the Entebbe crisis to be understood as one paradigmatic manifestation of the dialectical interaction between international law and international politics that begins with the concatenation of a set of preexisting conditions into a chain of events whose effects are still progressing in a cognizable fashion throughout international relations today. A functionalist analysis of international law and politics in time of crisis will reveal the dynamic processes by which the entire international system proceeds to cope with a crisis in order to survive.

The Function of Definition Performed by International Law

The first function that international law performed in the Entebbe crisis was the definition of the situation for all the actors involved. Even before the hijacking of the Air France plane that led to the Entebbe raid, international law had already established standards of behavior that were continually relevant to the facts of the crisis during its various stages of development. These rules of law provided a fountainhead for the generation of conceptions of legality or illegality, right or wrong, just or unjust, through which the actors perceived the unfolding of events. The rules thus shaped the perceptions that conditioned the decision makers' responses to the crisis. There was, at all times, a dynamic interaction between initial conduct, its evaluation in accordance with perceived standards of behavior, and responsive conduct.

Drawing upon the teachings of the behavioralist school of international political science,[22] a functionalist analysis of international law deemphasizes the traditional positivist concern with whether a particular rule or set of rules was legally binding in a formal sense upon one or more of the parties to the crisis. What becomes critically important instead are the perceptions about rules held by the decision makers themselves. A rule that might not be technically binding may still become relevant to the decision-making process in a variety of ways. For example, neither state X nor state Y might be parties to treaty A, but decision makers in X could nevertheless perceive Y's behavior as deficient in light of the standards enunciated within A. In a court of law, X would not have the *jus standi* (i.e., "standing") to raise a claim against Y under A per se, although X might argue that A is merely declaratory of customary international law or else has been transformed into customary international law through the accumulation of state practice, the passage of time, the development of an international *opinio juris* (i.e., a belief that it is binding), and a general acceptance of the practice by states.[23] In the realm of governmental decision making, however, and especially during time of international crisis, due to the force of circumstances, crisis management decision makers demonstrate a marked tendency to blur, obscure, or ignore the precise distinctions intrinsic to such formalistic legal technicalities. In their minds principles *de lege ferenda* (i.e., "law coming into being") can readily be treated as *lex lata* (i.e., "fixed law"). From that point these perceptions are quickly translated into political and military action.

THE DEFINITIONAL CONTEXT OF THE ENTEBBE HIJACKING
AND HOSTAGE TAKING

Hijacking. Provisions of the Tokyo Convention on Offenses and Certain Other Acts Committed on Board Aircraft of September 14, 1963,[24] were relevant to the Entebbe hijacking by way of analogy, although not technically binding upon Israel and Uganda in relation to each other at the time, since the former was a party while the latter was not. Article 11 of the Tokyo Convention obligates the state of landing to take all appropriate measures to restore control of an unlawfully seized aircraft to its commander, to permit the passengers and crew to continue their journey as soon as practicable, and to return the aircraft and cargo to those entitled to possession. It has been argued that irrespective of the Tokyo Convention, these provisions are declaratory of principles of customary international law binding upon parties and non-parties alike.[25] Article 13 of the Tokyo Convention also requires the state of landing to take into custody an alleged hijacker, but the state of landing is not required to choose between prosecution or extradition of the alleged hijacker.

At the time of the Entebbe crisis both Israel and Uganda were parties to the Hague Convention for the Suppression of Unlawful Seizure of Aircraft of December 16, 1970.[26] Article 4 thereof required Uganda to take such measures as were necessary to establish its jurisdiction over the hijackers. Under article 6, Uganda was required to take the hijackers and their accomplices into custody. Article 7 obligated Uganda either to extradite the offenders or to submit their case to its competent authorities for purpose of prosecution. Though the Hague Convention does not specifically require that the hijackers actually be prosecuted, article 7 required Ugandan authorities to make the decision whether to prosecute as they would for an ordinary offense of a serious nature under domestic law. By the terms of article 9, Uganda had to take all appropriate measures to restore control of the aircraft to its lawful commander, to facilitate the continuation of the journey of the passengers and crew as soon as practicable, and to return without delay the aircraft and cargo to its rightful owners. These were positive norms of international law directly binding upon Uganda which created undisputed obligations in its relations with Israel.[27]

The act of unlawful seizure of aircraft would usually include the act of unlawful interference with an aircraft, as defined by article 1 of the Montreal Convention to Discourage Acts of Violence Against Civil Aviation of September 23, 1971.[28] So, the obligations of that convention were brought into play as well. Article 5 requires a contracting state to establish its jurisdiction over the offense; article 6, to take an offender into custody; article 7, to extradite the offender, or else to submit the case to the state's own competent authorities for prosecution; article 10, to facilitate the continuation of the journey of the passengers and crew as soon as practicable, and without delay to return the aircraft and cargo to those lawfully entitled to possession. Although Israel was a party to the Montreal Convention at the time of the crisis, Uganda was not. Nevertheless, its provisions were relevant to Entebbe by way of analogy. Arguably, these principles were generally declaratory of customary international law on this subject.[29]

Piracy. The Entebbe situation also presented an analogy to the international crime of piracy as defined by article 15 of the 1958 Geneva Convention on the High Seas.[30] To be sure, this hijacking did not fit within the formal definition of the term "piracy" as set out in the convention, since the action was neither (1) undertaken for private ends, nor (2) directed by one plane against another, and (3) it occurred over Greece and therefore was within the territorial jurisdiction of a state. Yet the analogy was there to be seized upon and used to define the context of the crisis.[31]

Hostage Taking. Finally, the Entebbe hijacking also bears an analogy to the principle of international law forbidding the taking of civilian hostages during times of armed conflict. Article 34 of the Fourth Geneva Convention of August 12, 1949, explicitly prohibits the taking of civilians as hostages during times of international armed conflict.[32] Article 147 defines this offense to be a "grave breach" of the convention warranting the imposition of severe penal sanctions.[33] Moreover, article 146 of the Fourth Geneva Convention requires a contracting party to search for persons who have committed "grave breaches" and either bring them before its own courts or else hand such persons over for trial to another concerned party.[34] Article 3, common to all four of the 1949 Geneva Conventions, prohibits the taking of hostages with respect to persons having no active part in hostilities in cases of armed conflict not of an international character.[35] Of course, none of the four Geneva Conventions was directly applicable to the Entebbe hostages situation because it did not occur during international or civil war. But, if the taking of civilian hostages is prohibited in times of both international and civil war, then *a fortiori* it is or should be forbidden during peacetime as well. This principle should hold true even during so-called wars of national liberation. Nevertheless, these latter two points had not been codified into positive treaty law by the time of the Entebbe crisis. Entebbe would generate the momentum necessary to close the last loophole on hostage taking in the coverage of international law.[36]

State Responsibility. Taken together, these sources of international law established basic standards for state behavior and responsibility for incidents of international civil aviation hijacking and transnational hostage taking. A state's failure to live up to the spirit of these sources and to follow, at least in a general fashion, the shared pronouncements contained in them, could only sharpen the perceived incongruity between its action and the fundamental requisites of international deportment. Uganda's outright violation of the terms of the Hague Convention necessarily contributed to the attitude of Israeli governmental decision makers that Uganda's behavior was inexcusable under even the most rudimentary standards of international law and politics. As will be demonstrated herein, these perceptions exerted a profound influence upon the Israeli decision to launch the raid at Entebbe.

THE DEFINITIONAL CONTEXT OF THE ENTEBBE RAID

An entire catalogue of well-known principles, strictures, and doctrines of public international law are directly applicable to the military operation at Entebbe itself, or, indeed, to any contemporary use or threat of force in international relations. Relevant treaty law includes the U.N. Charter's article $2(3)^{37}$ and article $33(1)^{38}$ obligations for the peaceful settlement of disputes; the article $2(4)^{39}$ prohibition on the threat or use of force; and the article 51^{40} right of individual or collective self-defense. Related to the right of self-defense are its two fundamental requirements for the "proportionality"[41] and the "necessity" of the forceful response to the threat. Furthermore, as definitively stated by Secretary of State Daniel Webster in the famous case of *The Caroline*, "anticipatory" self-defense might be justified when the "necessity of that self-defence is instant, overwhelming, and leaving no choice of means, and no moment for deliberation."[42]

In addition to treaty provisions, principles of customary international law also operate in this area. They include the doctrines of intervention, protection, and self-help.[43] These three doctrines were, however, unanimously rejected by the International Court of Justice in the seminal *Corfu Channel Case* (United Kingdom v. Albania)[44] as being totally incompatible with the proper conduct of international relations in the post–World War II era.[45] Even more significantly, the Court repudiated these three doctrines without explicitly relying upon the U.N. Charter because Albania was not yet a party while Great Britain was. Hence, the Court's holding on this point can be construed to constitute an authoritative declaration of the requirements of customary international law binding all members of the international community irrespective of the Charter. A *fortiori*, therefore, when both parties to an international crisis are U.N. members, such as Israel and Uganda at Entebbe, articles 2(3), 2(4), and 33 absolutely prohibit any threat or use of force that is not specifically justified by the article 51 right of individual or collective self-defense.

Nevertheless, the facts of the *Corfu Channel Case*, unlike those of Entebbe, did not involve an imminent threat to human life. A dissenting opinion by Judge Azavedo[46] and an individual opinion by Judge Alvarez[47] recognized the right of a state to intervene and use force in another state in the event of an "emergency" or in "exceptional circumstances," respectively. The Entebbe hostage-taking crisis might very well have fit within these putative exceptions to the universal prohibition against the use of force across state lines.

Finally, three seminal General Assembly resolutions have a distinct bearing on this issue: the Declaration on the Inadmissibility of Intervention in the Domestic Affairs of States and the Protection of Their Independence and Sovereignty,[48] the Declaration on Principles of International Law Concerning Friendly Relations and Cooperation among States in Accordance with the Charter of the United Nations,[49] and the

Definition of Aggression.[50] Considered together, these three resolutions can be interpreted to stand for the general proposition that, in the emphatic opinion of the members of the U.N. General Assembly, non-consensual military intervention by one state into the territorial domain of another state is prohibited for any reason whatsoever. Hence the Israeli raid at Entebbe could quite possibly be classified as a "breach of the peace" or an "act of aggression" within the meaning and purpose of U.N. Charter article 39 interpreted by reference to these resolutions.[51]

The Need for a Functionalist Analysis of These Rules

The purpose of this essay is not to analyze the problems inherent within these principles (e.g., what precisely does the article 51 language "armed attack" require?); their interrelationships with each other (e.g., do intervention, protection, and self-help survive under the regime of Charter article 51?); and then to apply them as defined, explicated, or clarified to the facts of the Entebbe crisis, thereby rendering a decision as to the legality or illegality of the raid. That task has already been quite competently discharged in numerous articles on the Entebbe raid, so it would be superfluous to replicate that line of analysis here.[52] This route towards examination of the Entebbe crisis is characteristic of a legal positivist approach to the subject of international law in time of crisis. Whatever its value for other problems of international relations, a legal positivist approach to a particular international crisis or to the phenomenon of international crisis in general amounts to an essentially sterile exercise which is not very productive for the improvement of crisis management procedures or for the promotion of international law and organizations. After all, there are only so many ways in which the concepts enumerated above can be juggled, and when they all come down at the end of an article, their configuration often represents, or at least neatly coincides with, the instinctive, preconceived value judgments of the writer/juggler concerning the "right" or "wrong" of the parties to the crisis.

In this fashion international legal positivism and, unfortunately by way of association, public international law as well, are almost ineluctably transformed into vehicles for the expression of personal opinion or, worse yet, disfigured into tools for political purposes: i.e., the legitimization of conduct by one party to an international dispute with the simultaneous castigation of its adversary. Because of international legal positivism's obsessive concentration with rendering adjudications of right or wrong, it possesses an inherent propensity for such instrumental use within the utilitarian calculus of international affairs. When viewed from

a positivist perspective, international law quite readily and almost ineluctably serves as a primary source for the manufacture of ad hoc or ex post
facto justifications for governmental decisions taken on the basis of non-
legal factors such as national interest, power politics, and economic gain.

This positivist tendency toward self-serving use of international legal
principles lies at the heart of the international political science critique
of international law as basically irrelevant to both international crises and
the major problems of contemporary international politics. International
political scientists unquestioningly accept a legal positivist approach to
international law as the paradigmatic methodology of international legal
studies. They seem unconsciously to equate public international law
with international legal positivism. In their minds, this positivist methodology becomes indistinguishable from the substantive significance of
international law itself. Failure on their part to perceive the fundamental
distinction between the substance and the methodology is understandable, however, since international legal positivism is in fact the predominant mode of thinking about international law within the discipline of
international legal studies. International political scientists are therefore
oftentimes just as positivistic as some public international lawyers in
their comprehension of the international legal order. Nevertheless, the
former should not be faulted too seriously for taking the latter at their
collective word that the methodology of international legal positivism is
pari materia with international legal studies.

By accepting the primacy of a legal positivist approach to international law, international political scientists and, *a fortiori*, many public
international lawyers are inevitably led to the conclusion that international law is essentially irrelevant to international crisis. Here both
groups of academics commit the same analytical mistake for identical
reasons: Just because international legal positivism might be irrelevant
to international crisis, it does not logically follow that international
law and organizations are irrelevant as well. The peculiarities and shortcomings of this particular methodology must not be vicariously attributed
to the principles, institutions, and procedures of public international
law itself.

Instead of rejecting the relevance of international law and organizations to international crises, what should be done is to denigrate the
utility of an international legal positivist approach to the study of
international crises and to replace it with a functionalist approach. For
when analyzed from a functionalist perspective, international law and
organizations become not simply relevant but in fact critical to the
development of an international crisis. The next chapter will explore how

the definitional framework of positive legal rules described above entered into the decision-making process of the Israeli government during the Entebbe crisis and, once there, how considerations of international law and organizations thereby impacted upon, influenced, channelled, and indeed, determined the course of decisions actually taken, and thus the outcome of events. Subsequent chapters in Part Two will continue to focus upon the functions international law and organizations played both in the immediate aftermath of the Entebbe crisis and throughout its long-term chain of events. This functionalist approach to the problem will establish both why and how international law was relevant during the Entebbe crisis. Such information is far more useful to understanding future international crises and the means whereby they can be prevented and controlled than an international legal positivist's simplistic determination of right or wrong.

7

The Function of Decision Performed by
International Law and Organizations

Formation and Composition of the Crisis Management Team

After defining the situation for the actors involved, the next function performed by international law during the Entebbe crisis was to serve as an element in the Israeli government's decision-making processes. According to its formal practice, the Israeli Labor government dealt with international crises by the formation of a crisis management team consisting of a small number of key cabinet ministers and their chief assistants.[53] The ultimate decisions were then discussed and made under the guiding influence of the prime minister and transmitted to the full cabinet for debate and approval.

Immediately upon receipt of the information that the Air France plane had been hijacked with a large number of Israeli nationals aboard, Prime Minister Rabin directed his head of bureau to convene a special meeting of five ministers of the government:[54] Peres (Defense), Allon (Foreign Affairs), Yaakobi (Transportation), Zadok (Justice), and Galili (minister without portfolio).[55] The team was formed on a functional basis and worked on the principle of a highly compartmentalized division of labor.[56] Peres was in charge of the design and execution of the military operation. Allon handled the foreign affairs aspects of the crisis. Yaakobi was designated to supervise bringing the situation to the attention of the International Civil Aviation Organization (ICAO) and the International Federation of Airline Pilots Associations (IFALPA), as well as to explain the decisions of the government to the public, especially its initial stance of non-negotiation with the hijackers. Galili participated as confidant to the prime minister.

Even at this formative stage of the decision-making process, it is significant that the minister of justice was included in the team. Yaakobi later said that the minister of justice was routinely included in crisis management teams dealing with international problems in order to present the legal aspects of the crisis to the other members for their consideration. For example, the minister of justice would give the members of the team opinions on the progress of the negotiations and any advisements under relevant international law.[57] Furthermore, Yaakobi stated that Zadok was supposed to and did in fact provide his opinion on the legality of the military operation. In Yaakobi's view it was necessary for the minister of justice to be in the group because considerations of legality are important to Israeli public opinion and to public opinion abroad, particularly Israel's friends among the Western democracies.

The routine inclusion of the minister of justice in Israeli international crisis management teams was especially significant when compared with American practice. In the United States, this would be equivalent to formally including the attorney general in crisis management decision-making teams for the express purpose of rendering legal opinions throughout the process of decision. Instead, that task is delegated to the secretary of state with the assistance of the legal adviser and his office.[58] In effect, the secretary of state must consider and balance both the political and the legal aspects of the situation. This practice risks subordination, or at least diminution, of legal considerations to the foreign policy dimension of the crisis. Worse yet, legal arguments might be manufactured as ad hoc or ex post facto justifications for decisions taken on the grounds of national interest and power politics in express violation of international law. Because current U.S. practice does not routinely provide for independent institutional representation of international legal considerations at the highest echelon of crisis management decision making, these risks are real ones indeed.[59] The legal adviser is simply not bureaucratically situated to insist on respect for international law during a crisis.

By including the Israeli minister of justice in the crisis management team, it became possible to interject legal considerations directly into the entire course of the decision-making process. Justice had a voice and a vote equal to that of Defense and Foreign Affairs. Unlike the American practice, this allowed for direct, equal, and independent institutional access to the highest echelon of the crisis management decision-making process. The legal aspects of the crisis did not risk dilution by the foreign policy dimension in a stage penultimate to their presentation before the determinative body. Of course, once the legal aspects were presented they had to compete in the marketplace of ideas drawn from other perspectives. But the significant factor was that those legal ideas were presented, and on an independent basis, in the first place. The bureaucratic politics school of international political science emphasized exactly how important such institutional representation is for the furtherance of the particular interests of a bureaucracy.[60] During the Entebbe crisis, international law had its own personal advocate.

Zadok's background gave every indication that he would serve as an effective advocate for international law within the Entebbe decision-making process.[61] He had been minister of justice since 1974, and before that, minister of commerce and industry from 1965 to 1966. A graduate of Jerusalem Law School, he joined the Hagana and Jewish Settlement Police, and fought with the Israeli Defense Forces in the War of Independence. He was deputy attorney general from 1949 to 1952, lecturer in law at Tel Aviv Law School from 1953 to 1961, and among other positions had been chairman of the key Knesset Foreign Affairs and Defense Committee and member of the Knesset Constitutional, Legal, and Judicial Committee. This most impressive biography, together with his powerful legislative and bureaucratic connections gave Zadok's opinions no less weight than those of Peres and Allon. Zadok could use this considerable influence to ensure that Israel protected its vital national security interests at stake in Uganda in a manner compatible with his perception of the requirements of public international law.

Early Decisions

This conclusion that Zadok's influence was considerable is supported by examination of the first set of decisions taken at the initial meeting of the ministerial crisis management team.[62] Not surprisingly, several of these were legal in nature. The first decision was to contact the French government to express the official Israeli position that France, as owner of Air France, had ultimate legal responsibility for the safety of all passengers and was obliged to do everything in its power to secure the release of all passengers without discrimination, particularly against Israeli nationals or dual nationals. Second, the team decided that the minister of transportation (Yaakobi) should urgently approach the president of ICAO to demand vigorous action for the release of all passengers. Third, it was decided that the managing director of the Israeli airline, El Al, should pressure the president of IFALPA for the same purpose.

Other decisions in the early stage of the crisis also had a legal character. Professor Shlomo Avineri, the director general of the Foreign Ministry[63] and a political scientist by profession,[64] suggested to Foreign Minister Allon that Chaim Herzog, then Israel's ambassador to the United Nations, be utilized.[65] Allon accordingly instructed Herzog to talk to Secretary General Kurt Waldheim and secure his personal intervention in an effort to obtain the safe release of all hostages.[66] According to Yaakobi, the crisis management team did not take this U.N. approach seriously because of the constant attacks upon Israel in the U.N. throughout the preceding several years: "But," Yaakobi reasoned, "if it could help in some way, why not?"[67]

From their intelligence sources the crisis team knew that Amin was cooperating with the hijackers.[68] When asked about allegations later made by Herzog in the Security Council debate that Amin knew about the entire hijacking plan beforehand,[69] Yaakobi said he believed on the basis of Israeli intelligence sources that Amin did not know about the escapade until very shortly before the plane was to land at Entebbe. Most probably Amin learned of the plane's imminent arrival through the Palestine Liberation Organization (PLO) representatives in Kampala, who contacted him after they had been informed by phone by representatives of the Popular Front for the Liberation of Palestine (PFLP) in Mogadishu, Somalia that the plane was coming to Uganda.[70] The hijackers did have a map on board with a route plotted to Uganda,[71] but Yaakobi did not believe this indicated that Amin had prior knowledge of the hijacking.

The Israeli government had dealt with Amin before, so the decision team felt they knew his nature well enough. Yaakobi characterized Amin as crazy, but talented, wild, with good intuitions, and clever, but totally unpredictable. After a period of close cooperation between the two governments, Amin broke diplomatic relations in 1972 because Israel had refused to provide him with bombers able to hit Dar-es-Salaam, the capital of Tanzania.[72] He then installed the PLO in the private residence of the Israeli ambassador in Kampala,[73] and thoroughly associated himself with the hardline anti-Israel policy of that organization.[74] These experiences with Amin led the decision team to expect the worst from him and, consequently, to explore the possibility of a military solution from the immediate outset of the crisis.[75]

These shared perceptions on the need for military intervention were strengthened by the behavior of France. Yaakobi was highly critical of the role the French government played throughout the entire affair. In his opinion, the French were reluctant to help Israel because of France's desire to minimize its involvement in a dispute concerning the Palestinian cause. Presumably this reluctance was the product of a reorientation of French foreign policy towards a more favorable pro-Arab stance after the 1967 Six Day War.[76] France needed to guarantee its oil supplies by not unduly offending Arab pro-Palestinian sentiments. Therefore, according to Yaakobi, the French government informed Israel that any effort on its part that was more than just an appeal to Amin would be counterproductive. Yet France did appeal to the Ugandan government for the safe release of the hostages.[77]

Yaakobi stated that Zadok told the crisis management team that under international law, France had complete responsibility as the owner of the plane to secure the release of all passengers. This legal conclusion had a definite impact upon the decision makers' perception of French reluctance to act and further narrowed their assessment of available options.[78] If France was shirking its international legal duties, if the U.N. was paralyzed and largely ineffective, if Uganda was actively assisting the hijackers, Israel would have to take the matter into its own hands to save the lives of its nationals. This conclusion became crystal clear when all of the non-Israeli hostages were voluntarily released by the hijackers and flown to safety.[79]

Narrowing the Options

At a meeting of the Security and Foreign Affairs Committee of the Knesset, Prime Minister Rabin and Director General Avineri stated that Israel was not going to ask for formal Security Council intervention pursuant to article 35 of the Charter[80] because Israel did not want to appear willing to relieve France of ultimate responsibility for the fate of the hostages.[81] But a perceived French reluctance to fulfill its duties under international law was not the only reason Israel decided not to go to the Security Council, which was in session at that time on another matter (whose significance will be discussed below). For the decision had been essentially made to go ahead with the raid; and, as Israeli Foreign Minister Allon explained when he specifically requested French Foreign Minister Sauvagnargues not to bring the matter to the attention of the Security Council on his own accord, this "would only complicate matters."[82] Yaakobi said that the judgment of the crisis management team was that if the matter went to the Security Council, a resolution would be passed calling upon the hijackers to release the hostages and, in addition, calling upon all states not to take any type of military action or use force in any way. The crisis management team feared that Israeli disobedience of a Security Council resolution would have had an adverse impact upon Israeli public opinion and upon international public opinion, especially among those sectors in the West upon which Israel traditionally relied for support, whereas the hijackers would not obey a U.N. Security Council resolution in any event. Thus, an Israeli or French approach to the Security Council offered Israel no benefits and would at least add significantly to the political costs of a rescue operation and would likely limit Israel's freedom to pursue a unilateral military solution to the problem. Since the decision to intervene unilaterally if possible had already been made, a request for U.N. intervention would have been counterproductive.

To be sure, Yaakobi said that Israel would have launched the raid even in the face of an explicit Security Council resolution calling upon states not to take military action. Moreover, Yaakobi asserted that Israel would launch a similar rescue operation in another country in the future, if necessary and feasible, irrespective of the praise or condemnation of its allies, and, *a fortiori*, irrespective of U.N. opinion. As Yaakobi put it: "On this Israel must stand alone for its own survival."

These are speculative answers, however, to hypothetical questions. They do not provide a definitive answer to the question of whether the decision-making team would have launched the raid in the face of an explicit determination by Minister of Justice Zadok that it would be illegal under such a prohibitory Security Council resolution or otherwise. Rather, the facts of the Entebbe case indicate that even in its failure to go to the Security Council, Israel pursued a course of conduct which minimized the force of any allegations that it had violated international law.

The Israeli crisis management team had three basic alternatives before it: (1) not to launch the raid at all, (2) to launch the raid without any prior referral to the Security Council, (3) to bring the matter to the attention of the Security Council and risk having to launch the raid while the debate was in progress or after passage of an anticipated Security Council resolution prohibiting the use of force. Of these three alternatives, the second was the least objectionable, whether viewed from a legal, moral, or political perspective.

Concerning the first option, intelligence sources indicated that the hijackers were planning to execute one or more hostages on Sunday, July 4, to demonstrate their determination to secure release of their imprisoned comrades.[83] Originally there was a strong sentiment against negotiations with the hijackers among the members of the crisis management team.[84] But Israel had negotiated under such circumstances before,[85] and as the crisis unfolded the decision was made to announce that Israel was willing to reverse its traditional policy and enter negotiations for the release of the hostages.[86] According to Yaakobi, the offer to negotiate was sincere, but it was also intended to stall for time in order or prepare for a raid.

Permitting the risk of imminent death for the hostages when a raid was possible was viewed as a completely unacceptable alternative to the decision makers. Yaakobi stated that the most important shared common denominator within the operative assumptions of the members of the crisis management team was survival. The physical survival of approximately one hundred Israeli nationals or dual nationals was perceived to be at stake and, with them, the very ability of the state of Israel to ensure its own existence. The spirit of the state of Israel was not to surrender its survival or jeopardize its existence in any way. So the first option was discarded once a viable military plan was formulated.

The third option would have opened Israel to charges of bad faith and illegality. If Israel or France (with Israel's approval) had brought the matter to the attention of the Security Council, and Israel had then gone ahead and launched the raid while the debate was in progress, Israel would have found it difficult to avoid the charges that it was obligated by such reference to await the outcome of the debate in the Security Council before acting and that its precipitous unilateral action had prevented the Security Council from attempting to achieve a peaceful settlement of the dispute, and thus had violated U.N. Charter articles 2(3), 2(4), and 33. Of course, to launch the raid in the face of a specific Security Council prohibition against the use of force would have amounted to a more serious violation of Israel's obligation under article 25 of the Charter to carry out the decisions of the Security Council.[87] Option three would also have undercut the article 51 self-defense argument that Israel needed to overcome any alleged violation of article 2(4). The third option entailed the risk that the Security Council either would have been in the process of acting or would already have acted when Israel launched the raid, making it difficult to substantiate any Israeli claim to exercise a unilateral right of individual self-defense.

The second option was the most appealing of the three. To be sure, Israel could be left open to the charge that it had violated its Charter obligation to seek a peaceful settlement of its dispute with Uganda before the Security Council. But Israel was pursuing a peaceful settlement of this dispute on all other fronts, including negotiations with the hijackers. A gesture to the Security Council would, in all probability, have been futile, and perhaps have occasioned delay in the rescue operation at the expense of the hostages' lives. Option two would also allow Israel to make a solid claim that the raid was a legitimate exercise of its right of self-defense pursuant to article 51 of the Charter, and the legitimacy of this claim could then be tested at the Security Council, but at a time when one hundred human lives were no longer in jeopardy.

In effect, the Israeli governmental decision-making team found itself engaged in the classic dilemma of choosing the least among several evils.[88] If successful, option two would preserve human life in a manner that was arguably consistent with the standards of international law. It would certainly not have been the expression of disdain and contempt for the Security Council nor the flagrant breach of international law risked by option three. And it did not, like option one, surrender the lives of the hostages to the good will of the hijackers and Idi Amin. The second option was the least destructive of the human, moral, legal, and political values at stake in Uganda. By choosing option two, Israel operated in accordance with the standards of international law to the best of its ability under these unique historical circumstances.

The Decision to Intervene

When it came down to that final meeting of the ministerial crisis management team which would make or break the decision to launch a raid, Defense Minister Peres, in charge of developing the plan for military intervention, believed that three out of the six members of the team — Yaakobi, Allon, and himself — would support intervention at any cost or risk. Peres needed one more vote to gain a majority, and for that he tried to convince Minister of Justice Zadok to agree to a raid. Zadok had already resolved any questions about the legality of such an operation in its favor. Upon the approach of Peres before the meeting, Zadok was reported to have said: "The question isn't what Zionism and our sovereignty can expect if we don't rescue the hostages. The question is whether there is a plan for a military rescue — one with a high probability of success."[89] Peres responded affirmatively and Zadok nodded. Although Zadok did not promise to support the plan, he allowed Peres to believe that he was leaning in this direction.

According to Yaakobi, at that fateful team meeting, when Zadok's turn to speak on the proposed raid came, he got up and stated that in his opinion there were no international legal obstacles to a military operation. Apparently Zadok had checked this matter with the attorney general of Israel and his legal advisers.[90] Yaakobi stated that Zadok's opinion was sufficient as far as he and his colleagues were concerned. In Yaakobi's view, this was Zadok's job; the members of the crisis management team had enough confidence in his legal ability to trust him completely. The team then voted to approve the raid. Next, Zadok suggested that the

Ministerial Defense Committee be convened to formally authorize the launching of the raid. There, eighteen ministers, including Zadok, voted unanimously in favor of the military operation.[91]

The Raid

The execution of the raid itself was handled exclusively by the military with little, if any, input from other sources. According to Yaakobi, the team had rejected as impractical the chief of staff's proposal made on the second day of the crisis to intervene and take the hostages out by car to Kenya. The sentiment on the team was that until the military was able to devise a fully detailed plan that looked as if it could work, there was no point in launching the raid and further endangering the lives of the hostages. An enormous amount of intelligence work was performed by El Al, the Mossad, and the Ministry of Foreign Affairs, and unless all these details could be collected and a viable plan formulated out of them, the team would not give its approval to a raid.[92]

Yaakobi said that the raid was to be executed so as to minimize the risk for the hostages as much as possible. Therefore, the crisis team decided to employ only the minimum amount of force necessary to effect the rescue. Israel had no reason or desire to fight or punish the Ugandan army even though its soldiers were assisting the hijackers in detaining the hostages. Orders were given to Israeli troops to scare Ugandan soldiers away if possible and to keep Ugandan casualties to the minimum extent consistent with accomplishing the mission.[93] On the other hand, orders were given to kill all hijackers on sight.[94] According to Yaakobi, all the hijackers were killed and Israeli forces took none back to Israel for interrogation.[95]

Concerning the destruction of the Ugandan MIG planes at Entebbe hangers,[96] Yaakobi stated that although the reason given in public for this action was to prevent the pursuit of the rescue planes by the MIGs, the primary reason for their destruction was to serve as a penalty upon the Ugandan government for involving itself with the hijackers to the degree it had. The members of the crisis management team felt that Uganda had to pay some price for what it had done. So the MIGs were destroyed and, with them, the bulwark of the Ugandan air force was obliterated. Thus, the destruction of the MIGs was not "necessary" to the success of the rescue mission. Yet this one instance of purposeful illegality does not detract from the generally high degree of respect paid to considerations of international law and organizations by the Israeli crisis management team in its design and execution of the Entebbe raid.

The Easy Case?

At this juncture, an international political scientist might interject that the *decision* stage of this analytical framework proves little of any consequence: Israel is the "easy case" because it is a Western liberal democracy which, by definition, can be expected to conform with the requirements of the Western view of international law in its conduct of foreign affairs. The validity of that objection, however, depends upon one's perspective.

Today there exist a substantial number of Arab, African, Asian, and communist states which definitively repudiate the notion that Israel possesses even a rudimentary commitment to upholding the fundamental principles of international law. To these nations Israel is a militaristic, aggressive, and expansionist state that has consistently violated the most sacred principles of international law and politics in pursuit of a comprehensive policy of conquest, subjugation, and intimidation throughout the Middle East. From this perspective, the 1956 War; the continued occupation of the West Bank, Gaza Strip, and the Golan Heights; the establishment of Israeli settlements in the occupied territories; the annexations of Arab East Jerusalem and the Golan Heights; the repressive treatment of the Palestinian people tantamount to genocide and denial of their right to national self-determination; continued military intervention into Lebanon and ultimately occupation of its sovereign territory by Israeli troops; the acquisition of a nuclear weapons capability; and the bombing of an Iraqi nuclear reactor are all examples of Israel's total disregard for the basic principles of international law.

On many of these complaints, Third World and Second World states have been joined in their condemnation of Israel by the latter's erstwhile friends among the so-called Western liberal democracies of the First World and even, occasionally, by Israel's nominal ally, the United States. On some of these issues, Israel has stood alone in a seemingly willful refusal to adhere to even the most basic requirements of international law in its relations with other states and peoples. The list of abuses is so extensive and universally held that Israel has gradually become a pariah state within the international community, a status it shares with the apartheid regime of South Africa.

From an Arab perspective, Israel would definitely not be the "easy case" for proving the theoretical proposition that considerations of international law and organizations do in fact play a crucial role in governmental decision-making processes during times of international crisis. Instead, Israel would constitute the "worst case" possible under any circumstances. Therefore, establishing the validity of this proposition for Israeli crisis management decision making should be the "acid test" for its general applicability. Thus, from an Arab perspective, if even Israel pays heed to international law and organizations during a crisis, then any state must do so, since no other state appears to be so fundamentally lawless in its conduct of foreign affairs.

In January of 1977, this author delivered an oral version of Part Two before the faculty of a distinguished school of international relations. Afterwards a professor of apparent Arab origin approached me with the following comment:

> In my opinion, Mr. Boyle, you have conclusively proved your thesis that international law is relevant to serious international crises. This is because you have chosen to examine the hardest case possible—Israel. You did indeed demonstrate that a government as essentially lawless as Israel actually paid attention to international law in a crisis such as this. You could have chosen an easier case. But the fact that you did not makes your results all that more significant.

8

The Function of Adjudication as Performed
by the U.N. Security Council

The third function of international law in the Entebbe crisis was adjudi-cation of the outstanding dispute between Israel and Uganda. The imme-diate crisis was over. The mode of its termination, however, had trans-formed the dispute between Israel and Uganda from a single-issue problem concerning state responsibility for hijacked hostages into a more complicated problem concerning the legitimacy of a responsive, non-consensual, foreign military intervention launched to rectify an alleged failure in the discharge of state responsibility. The Israeli government believed that its behavior had comported with the conditions required for a legitimate exercise of its right to self-defense under international law. It expected the reasonability of this belief to be tested in debate, and in essence "adjudicated" under international law by the appropriate international institutions. Nevertheless, Israel was certain that its actions were defensible. Meanwhile, international law had already progressively narrowed the contours of this dispute to manageable proportions. And, as will be demonstrated in the next chapter, the success of this adjudica-tory process would ultimately facilitate the resolution of the crisis. To properly understand this adjudicatory role of international law and orga-nizations in time of crisis, it is crucial to clarify what was, and, even more importantly, what was not, at issue in this phase of the Entebbe dispute.

What Forum?

Even prior to the Entebbe raid itself, international law had already established the primary forum for adjudication of disputes involving the maintenance of international peace and security: the U.N. Security Council. Consequently, there was no problem of creating or choosing an appropriate forum for adjudication of the dispute; there was no question about the competence of the Security Council to deal with this crisis; and no state questioned the right of the parties to the dispute to bring it to the attention of the Security Council pursuant to article 35 of the Charter. Once the matter had been submitted to the Security Council, all interested parties (except the PLO/PFLP, for reasons that will be explained below) appeared and presented their claims and counterclaims during the course of the debate. The parties expected the dispute to be brought to the Security Council, and they wanted this opportunity to present their respective cases before that body in its capacity as the so-called "court" of world public opinion.

Had there been forum problems relating to the existence, competence, or procedure for adjudication, they would have been major obstructions to the adjudication and consequent resolution of the outstanding dispute between Uganda and Israel, and thus might have precipitated another immediate confrontation between the two countries and their respective supporters. Instead, they had already been anticipated and disposed of by the U.N. Charter.

THE OAU

The first institutional adjudication of the Entebbe dispute was by the Organization of African Unity (OAU), of which Uganda was a member. On July 2, five days after the crisis began, Amin travelled to Mauritius to open the thirteenth session of the OAU's Assembly of Heads of State and Government and to hand over the chairmanship of the Organization to the prime minister of that country.[97] For this reason, the hijackers extended the original deadline for compliance with their demands from Thursday, July 1, to Sunday, July 4. It was the extension of that deadline which gave Israel the necessary time to prepare and launch a raid with a reasonable chance of success.[98] Surprisingly, therefore, a consideration of international law (i.e., respect for the OAU) entered into the decision-making process of the hijackers themselves, and exercised a decisive impact upon the outcome of events. Such respect for the OAU by the PLO/PFLP hijackers/hostage takers is explainable by the fact that in 1974 the OAU had adopted a resolution in which it declared its full support for the PLO as the sole legitimate representative of the Palestinian people.[99]

In a unanimous resolution adopted by the Assembly of the Heads of State and Government, the OAU condemned the Israeli raid at Entebbe as a violation of Uganda's sovereignty.[100] It charged its new chairman, together with Guinea and Egypt, to support Uganda in submission of its case to the U.N. Security Council. This action was undertaken in accordance with article VIII of the OAU Charter which gives the Assembly the power to "discuss matters of common concern to Africa with a view to coordinating and harmonizing the general policy of the Organization."[101]

AN INSIGHT INTO FIGHTING THE WAR
AGAINST INTERNATIONAL TERRORISM

Admittedly, the assertion of the preceding section that the PLO/PFLP hijackers/hostage takers actually manifested some degree of basic respect for considerations of international law and organizations challenges the generally held assumption that putative transnational "terrorists" possess absolutely no respect for any legal-moral value principle. This author submits that such an assumption is misleading, if not clearly erroneous. It is more logical to assume that a politically motivated hijacker or hostage taker possesses an internal normative value structure which is just as (if not more) clearly defined and highly refined as that of the ordinary citizen, let alone that of the common criminal. After all, neither one of the latter two types is ordinarily prepared to die for what he believes in.

The real problem, therefore, is not that the transnational "terrorist" completely lacks values, but only that his values are antithetical to those of his adversaries. If political "terrorists" are presumed to have no values, then the most appropriate way to deal with them is to treat them as outlaws and kill them whenever feasible. If, on the other hand, political "terrorists" are presumed to have values, the proper way to deal with them is through the process of negotiation. Negotiation is more likely to change their value structure than destruction, which will simply reinforce it and encourage another cycle of violence.

From this perspective, it makes little practical sense to treat a member of a recognized national liberation movement who has allegedly committed an act of "international terrorism" as if he were a common criminal. Such classification would not serve the traditionally recognized purposes of the various domestic systems of criminal justice administration prevalent in most states of today's world: viz., retribution, general or specific deterrence, reformation, and rehabilitation. To attempt to include national liberation fighters within the reach of the ordinary criminal law simply distorts the fiber and ultimately weakens the integrity of the criminal justice system itself.

As demonstrated by the situation in Northern Ireland, the prolongation of this process will inevitably destroy the set of procedural protections created by any system of criminal justice administration pursuant to the basic requirement of "due process of law." This will in turn redound to the severe detriment of the civil rights and civil liberties of the entire citizenry. Treating recognized national liberation fighters as common criminals only subverts the rule of law in the domestic political order and thus eventually undermines the democratic forms of constitutional government that are so vitally dependent upon it.

A better approach to the problem of "fighting the war against international terrorism" would be to take recognized national liberation fighters at their collective word, and therefore to treat them as privileged combatants under the laws of war and the international laws of humanitarian armed conflict. In other words, they would be treated analogously to soldiers fighting in an international armed conflict. Hence, when a national liberation fighter is captured after attacking a legitimate military target, he would not be punished, but instead treated as a prisoner of war and interned as such for the duration of the conflict. In Northern Ireland and the Middle East, the duration of such internment would probably be for quite some time.

Similarly, when a national liberation fighter is captured after attacking innocent civilians, he would still be treated as a prisoner of war, but would be prosecuted for the commission of war crimes. If found guilty, he would be punished as a war criminal, not a common criminal. Under generally recognized principles of international law, the former status warrants the imposition of extremely severe penalties upon the perpetrator, up to and including death. Treatment of national liberation fighters who have violated the international laws of humanitarian armed conflict as war criminals instead of common criminals would bring home to themselves, their movements, and the world at large the unique nature of the gravity and heinousness of their crimes.

Furthermore, the classification of members of recognized national liberation movements as privileged combatants in accordance with and subject to the rules of international law would provide their respective organizations (e.g., PLO, IRA, SWAPO) with an enormous political incentive to concentrate their violent attacks exclusively upon legitimate military targets capable of defending themselves, much to the benefit of the innocent civilian population. Conversely, obstinate refusal by the concerned governments to accord such treatment to national liberation fighters creates no incentive for the latter's respective organizations to distinguish attacks upon the civilian population from those upon military targets, exactly because their fighters will be punished as common criminals no matter whom they attack. For the purpose of promoting respect for the fundamental human rights of their own citizenry, it makes far more sense for governments to treat national liberation fighters analogously to soldiers than to common criminals. To the extent that concerned governments refuse to do so for political reasons or propaganda purposes, they must assume a considerable amount of indirect responsibility for the horrible violence that is inflicted upon their civilian populations by national liberation movements.

THE SECURITY COUNCIL

The OAU's resolution condemning Israel set the stage for consideration of the Entebbe dispute by the U.N. Security Council. Unlike the OAU, however, the Security Council has the "primary responsibility" for the maintenance of international peace and security.[102] Any adjudication of the merits of the dispute between Israel and Uganda by the Security Council would not be subject to the criticism leveled at the OAU that it proceeded ex parte and merely manifested regional prejudice in favor of a member against a non-member. The chairman of the OAU registered the Organization's complaint in a letter[103] to the president of the Security Council in accordance with the right of U.N. members to bring any dispute or any situation which might lead to international friction or give rise to a dispute to the attention of the Security Council under article 35(1) of the Charter. The OAU chairman's letter charged that the unprecedented "aggression" by Israel against Uganda constituted a danger not only to Uganda and Africa but to international peace and security as well.[104]

What Dispute?

The matter was inscribed on the Security Council agenda as "Complaint by the Prime Minister of Mauritius, current chairman of the OAU, of the 'act of agression' by Israel against the Republic of Uganda."[105] The United States and Israel's other sympathizers on the Council did their collective best to broaden the terms of the debate to also include consideration of the issue of international hijacking and terrorism.[106] This was part of an effort to place the question of Israeli legal responsibility for the raid squarely within the overall context of a campaign of repeated military attacks against Israel by the PLO and its member organizations.

This effort to broaden the scope of the debate was strenuously resisted during the Security Council Entebbe debates by those countries lining up for the condemnation of Israel.[107] Eventually two draft resolutions reflecting these opposed positions were introduced.[108] A three-power draft resolution sponsored by Benin, Libya, and Tanzania would have had the Security Council condemn Israel's flagrant violation of Uganda's sovereignty and territorial integrity, and demand that Israel meet the just claims of Uganda for full compensation for the destruction inflicted.[109] A two-power draft resolution introduced by the United States and the United Kingdom would have had the Security Council condemn hijacking and all other acts which threaten the lives of passengers and crews and the safety of international civil aviation, and call upon all states to take every necessary measure to prevent and punish all such terrorist acts.[110] Under the U.S.-U.K. draft resolution, the Council would have also deplored the tragic loss of human life which had resulted from the hijacking of the French aircraft, reaffirmed the need to respect the sovereignty and territorial integrity of all states in accordance with the U.N. Charter and international law, and enjoined the international community to give the highest priority to consideration of further means of assuring the safety and reliability of international civil aviation.[111]

The African draft resolution would have placed guilt squarely upon the shoulders of Israel, while the U.S.-U.K. draft resolution would have avoided an explicit adjudication of either Israeli or Ugandan guilt or innocence. By implication, however, the adoption of the U.S.-U.K. resolution would have absolved Israel from any alleged violations of international law committed during the raid. The Security Council met five times on Entebbe between July 9 and July 14.[112] The three-power African draft resolution was not pressed to a vote because it seemed obvious that even if it obtained the nine votes necessary for adoption, at least the United States would veto it.[113] The U.S.-U.K. draft resolution was actually brought to a vote, but failed to be adopted because it lacked the requisite majority.[114] The final vote was six in favor (France, Italy, Japan, Sweden, United Kingdom, United States) to none against, with two abstentions (Panama and Romania).[115] Seven delegations (Benin, China, Guyana, Libya, Pakistan, U.S.S.R., and Tanzania) did not participate in the vote on the two-power draft resolution,[116] ostensibly because it was not representative of the item which was inscribed on the agenda as an "act of aggression" by Israel against Uganda.[117] During the debates, however, both the abstainers and the non-participators in this vote had argued against the legality of the Israeli raid under the U.N. Charter and general principles of public international law.[118]

Why Proceed Any Further?

Viewed from a legal positivist perspective, this seemingly inconclusive result of the Security Council Entebbe debates and vote would suggest that international law and organizations are indeed irrelevant to the phenomenon of international crisis. After all, had not the Security Council proven its inability to deal with this international crisis by its failure to adopt any resolution on the Entebbe incident? Is this failure not typical of the operation of that body, charged by the international legal order with the "primary responsibility" for the maintenance of international peace and security, and therefore characteristic of international law and organizations in general? Does not the Entebbe experience in the Security Council demonstrate the utter futility of the United Nations and public international law when it comes to the management of international crises? Both an international legal positivist and an international political scientist might answer these questions in the affirmative and end Part Two on these fairly negative points.

On the other hand, a functionalist analysis of international law in time of crisis would look behind and beyond the non-adoption of a Security Council resolution on Entebbe in order to determine the true meaning and significance of this outcome. Mere failure to adopt a formal resolution on the Entebbe incident does not mean that the Security Council debates and vote lacked substantive significance and were therefore essentially irrelevant to this international crisis. In Security Council practice, what is not said in the form of an adopted resolution is oftentimes just as important as what is expressed in this manner. A careful analysis of the content of the Entebbe debates can reveal the nature and extent of an underlying consensus among Security Council members on fundamental principles deemed so basic as to require no formal enunciation or imprimatur. Delineation of the elements of this consensus sheds light upon the true meaning of the seemingly indeterminate outcome of the Security Council Entebbe vote. In order to accomplish this, it is necessary to examine both the arguments that were made and the arguments that were not made by each side in the debates. Such a line of analysis will allow derivation from the Security Council proceedings of the real "lessons of Entebbe" for future instances of international crisis akin to it.

What Arguments?

POTENTIAL ARGUMENTS

There are at least six different types of arguments that can be made in regard to the rules of public international law, or, for that matter, the rules of any legal system. Here, they will be classified as arguments over the (1) existence of rules, (2) reference for rules, (3) inclusivity of rules,

(4) priority among rules, (5) interpretation of rules, and (6) application of rules to facts. Of course, a seventh related type of argument does not involve dispute over the nature of rules per se, but is concerned with the determination of the actual historical facts to which the rules should be applied.

These seven categories of potential arguments are listed in an approximately descending order of magnitude, ranked according to the degree of complexity posed to the parties in dispute. As a general proposition, it will be assumed that a higher order argument can contain one or more arguments of a lower order as well. For example, an argument concerning priority among rules (4) may include arguments concerning their interpretation (5). Thus, it will prove more useful to analyze the higher order argument first and then to proceed sequentially through the lower order arguments, than to do the reverse. There is not much point in arguing over (4) the priority among or (5) the interpretation of rules when the parties to a crisis do not recognize (1) the existence of any set of rules regulating their mutual relations in the first place. This sevenfold classification scheme will make it possible to identify and categorize what arguments were made and what arguments were not made in the Security Council debates on Entebbe, and thus permit the derivation of some ultimate meaning from the debates and subsequent vote.

Existence. An argument over the existence of rules concerns the question of whether the parties to a crisis believe that any standards of behavior exist to govern their interrelationships. If not, the parties will deem themselves free to do whatever they please in regard to each other, without interference by the international system through international law or international organizations. In time of international crisis, a problem of this nature is well-nigh insoluble. Indeed, it was this very issue of existence that precipitated the Entebbe crisis in the first place.

The Palestine Liberation Organization (PLO) is the umbrella organization for what is called a "national struggle for the liberation of Palestine" from the state of Israel.[119] The PLO includes within its structure the Popular Front for the Liberation of Palestine (PFLP),[120] whose members were responsible for the Entebbe hijacking.[121] The PLO's constitutional document, the Palestinian National Charter of 1968, explicitly calls for the destruction of the state of Israel and its replacement by a secular Palestinian state on the territory of what was once the League of Nations' Mandate for Palestine awarded to Great Britain at the end of World War I.[122] Article 10 of the National Charter proclaims that "commando action constitutes the nucleus of the Palestinian popular liberation war."[123] The Entebbe hijacking was merely one incident comprising the war of national liberation that the PLO/PFLP was and still is waging against Israel.

Israel and the PLO have placed themselves into a classical Hobbesist state of nature in regard to each other,[124] which, by definition, is tantamount to a state of war.[125] Here, there exists no right or wrong, no justice or injustice, no morality or immorality.[126] Rather, life is "solitary, poor, nasty, brutish, and short."[127] The survival of each is deemed to necessitate the physical annihilation of the adversary. Neither side can perceive the existence of any rules in its war with the other; or, if for some reason they did, extant rules would give way to the dictates of survival and necessity. It is predictable that until each side is willing to recognize the right of the other to exist in accordance with an established system of rules, little if any progress can be made toward a resolution of their fundamental dispute. An international crisis or series of crises is the expected outcome from such a monumental struggle for existence between two peoples.

Reference. Assuming that an argument over the existence of rules is not at stake and that the parties to a crisis at least implicitly acknowlege that they are not free to do as they please to one another, the problem of reference comes into focus: Do the parties refer to the same locus or to different sources for the derivation of standards of behavior that they believe are applicable to the crisis? Potential sources of reference for rules are, inter alia, law, morality, utility, justice, fairness, equity, ideology, and religion. For example, the Israeli government of former Prime Minister Menachem Begin publicly claimed the right to settle the West Bank of the Jordan River not primarily under principles of public international law, but under God's grant of "Judea and Samaria" to the Jewish people in the Old Testament.[128] A dispute concerning the locus of reference for relevant rules would prove to be extremely difficult to solve during the course of an international crisis. It could well serve as the direct cause for a future crisis or else as a condition for the prolonged deterioration of a situation into a crisis. The dispute over the alleged right to establish Jewish settlements on the West Bank is such an example.[129]

Inclusivity. If there is agreement upon the existence of rules and upon their source of reference, the next problem in degree of difficulty is inclusivity: Is a particular rule, whose validity is asserted or denied by one of the parties to a crisis, to be included within the referent set of rules? For example, in regard to the Israeli raid at Entebbe, do the customary principles of intervention, protection, and self-help survive in their own right as rules of public international law under the regime of the United Nations Charter and despite the *Corfu Channel Case?*

Priority. Priority among rules is likely to be the next source of conflict in time of international crisis. Even if a principle is deemed to be included within the referent set of rules acknowledged to exist by the parties to a crisis, argument over the order of priority within the referent set between that principle and other, conflicting principles is probable. For example, assuming that the principles of intervention, protection, and self-help persist to some extent, what is the order of priority between them, on the one hand, and the U.N. Charter article 2(4) prohibition on the threat or use of force? Can these three principles of customary international law be given priority over article 2(4) as elements of the "inherent right" of individual self-defense recognized by article 51 of the Charter?

It is clear from the text of article 51 that the right of self-defense was intended to take precedence over the article 2(4) prohibition. But to reach this conclusion it is necessary to interpret the meaning of article 51. Thus, arguments concerning the priority and the interpretation of rules, although logically distinct, may be functionally almost inseparable. Because they so readily coalesce with each other, arguments over priority and interpretation of rules could quite appropriately have been denominated, respectively, arguments over (1) the interpretation of rules as they are related to each other and (2) the interpretation of rules in isolation from each other. Nevertheless, this distinction will be drawn and maintained in the aforementioned terms.

Interpretation. Once an order of priority among rules is established, it is still necessary, prior to application, to interpret the precise meaning of a rule. For example, article 51 of the U.N. Charter allows a state to use force in self-defense if an "armed attack" occurs against the defending state. Was there an "armed attack" by Uganda against Israel at Entebbe or vice versa? Is an "armed attack" a sufficient but not the exclusive condition for an exercise of the right to self-defense?[130] Are the principles of intervention, protection, and self-help not precluded under article 51 even in the absence of an "armed attack"?

Application. Arguments over the application of undisputed and unambiguous international legal rules to the facts of particular cases must be considered next. In the Entebbe crisis, for example, there arose several important questions of applicability: Had Israel fulfilled its obligation under U.N. Charter articles 2(3) and 33 for the peaceful settlement of its dispute with Uganda before it resorted to the use of force at Entebbe? Was the Israeli raid at Entebbe "necessary" under the test of the *Caroline* case? Was it "proportional" to the threat presented to the lives of the hostages? Extensive factual material related to these three issues regarding the application of rules has already been presented and analyzed above. The reader is free to draw his or her own conclusions on these legal positivist points.

The facts. One final source of dispute between parties to an international crisis is over the facts of the situation itself. For example, did the Ugandan government actually do all that it could under the circumstances to secure the safe release of the Israeli hostages held at Entebbe? Or did it in fact actively assist the PFLP hijackers in the commission of their deeds? Once again, factual material relating to these questions has been set out above. It remains to be established how these seven types of potential arguments were actually developed, or why they were not presented, in the Security Council Entebbe debates by Israel, Uganda, and their respective partisans and antagonists.

ACTUAL ARGUMENTS

Consensus on Israel's right to exist. It is striking to observe the high degree of underlying consensus that existed among the participants in the Security Council Entebbe debates to the effect that this was not the time nor were these the appropriate circumstances to raise the general question of the right of Israel to exist as a state. Consequently, no arguments were presented in the debates directly focusing on that issue. To be sure, Israel's Ambassador Herzog chose to view the Entebbe incident as part of a continued attack upon Israel's existence, [131] and Libya castigated Israel for its alleged violation of Palestinian national rights. [132] But there was no outright attack upon Israel's right to exist. That there were only a few oblique and tangential references indicating that this might have been a contested issue of contemporary international relations seemed somewhat remarkable at the time. [133]

A variant on the same theme would have begun with an argument that Uganda was entitled to assist the PFLP hijackers at Entebbe because this operation was part of the PLO's legitimate war of national liberation against Israel. This position could have been premised upon the assertion that such assistance was permitted by the "seek and receive support" language of the Declaration on Principles of International Law Concerning Friendly Relations and Cooperation among States in Accordance with the Charter of the United Nations, [134] which was incorporated into article 7 of the Definition of Aggression. [135] Thus, Ugandan assistance to the PFLP at Entebbe would have been consistent with or at least not in violation of the requirements of international law. Yet not one participant in the Entebbe debates made that argument. It would have opened up the issue of Israel's existence from another direction. Quite apparently, no one wanted to do that.

It is also significant that a representative of the PLO was not invited to participate in the Security Council Entebbe debates. The very presence of a PLO representative in front of Ambassador Herzog would have dramatically raised the question of existence. Conversely, his absence tends to indicate that the members of the Council deemed such a confrontation to be neither necessary nor desirable under the circumstances.

This purposeful failure to raise the issue of the right of Israel to exist as a state during the Entebbe debates becomes even more remarkable in light of the fact that from the outset of the crisis, the Security Council was in session on the question of the exercise by the Palestinian people of their inalienable rights.[136] On June 29, 1976, the United States vetoed a draft resolution which would have had the Council affirm the inalienable rights of the Palestinian people to self-determination, including the right of return and the right to national independence and sovereignty in Palestine, in accordance with the United Nations Charter.[137] Both the United States and the four abstainers from the vote (France, Italy, Sweden, and the United Kingdom) refused to support the draft resolution because it did not recognize the right of Israel to live within secure and recognized boundaries.[138] A representative of the PLO was invited to participate in the debate[139] with the same rights of participation as those conferred upon a U.N. member under rule 37 of the Council's Provisional Rules of Procedure.[140] In this context, the right of Israel to exist was called into question directly. Yet there was no spillover effect on this issue from the Palestinian debates to the Entebbe debates, which commenced immediately afterward on July 9.[141]

Consensus on the illegality of aerial hijacking and hostage taking and on state responsibility in such crises. Nor did the problem of reference for rules come into play during the Security Council Entebbe debates. All participants were in basic agreement that the appropriate source for derivation of relevant rules was the United Nations Charter and the extant body of public international law. Here, too, there existed a remarkable degree of underlying consensus on what constituted acts inconsistent with the requirements of international law: (1) engagement in a war of national liberation was not a sufficient justification for specific instances of hijacking in international civil aviation by so-called freedom fighters; (2) fighting a war of national liberation would not justify the detention of hijacked hostages; consequently, and *a fortiori* (3) a state could not provide assistance to alleged freedom fighters in such enterprises. To the contrary, when considered collectively, the participants in the Entebbe debates: (1) condemned acts by anyone that would disrupt international civil aviation, (2) opposed the detention of hijacked hostages, and (3) asserted that states are under an obligation to refrain from participation in such activities and should take effective measures to prevent their occurrence and to secure the release of hostages in the event that a hijacked plane lands within their territorial jurisdiction.

On these points Uganda merely argued, and Israel emphatically denied, that it had indeed lived up to these recognized standards of international behavior at Entebbe. [142] By entering into negotiations with the hijackers, Amin had successfully obtained the release of the non-Israeli nationals and, by implication, had he been given more time, could have secured the release of the remaining hostages. [143] Naturally, Israel had good cause to disbelieve these factual assertions. The more important point, however, is that the disagreement between Israel and Uganda in this regard was confined to the comparatively simple dispute over facts, whereas the principles of law involved were never contested. By arguing that it had done everything in its power to secure the release of Israeli hostages, Uganda implicitly admitted the existence of its obligation to do so in the first place. [144]

Contention over these factual matters became the essence of the dispute between Uganda and Israel. The higher-order arguments over the application, interpretation, priority, and inclusivity of international legal rules were subordinated to this most easily manageable and resolved issue among the seven potential sources of contention between parties to an international crisis. And, of course, the two highest-order arguments over the existence and source of reference for rules never arose in the first place.

Moreover, the members of the Security Council evidently perceived that Uganda was not telling the truth about the facts, and this must have affected the Africans' decision to withdraw their draft resolution condemning Israel. The shocking disappearance and then suspected death of Dora Bloch must have had a similarly chastening effect upon even the most virulently anti-Israeli participants in the debate. Probably for these reasons, the Israeli antagonists sought to limit the Security Council debate to the legality of the Israeli raid at Entebbe without reference to Ugandan conduct. Since Uganda could only lose on the facts of the case, it was necessary for them to concentrate exclusively upon the assertion of an absolute prohibition under international law against non-consensual military intervention by a state into the territory of another. Israel's opponents essentially had to argue that the Israeli raid at Entebbe could not be justified even if Amin had been an accomplice to the hijackers and hostage takers.

Consensus on the illegality of foreign military intervention. No participant in the Security Council Entebbe debates argued that standards of behavior simply did not exist concerning non-consensual foreign military intervention in international relations.[145] All parties essentially agreed that military intervention by one state into the territorial domain of another ordinarily is illegal. By founding its defense in the Security Council squarely upon the right of individual self-defense in international law, Israel implicitly admitted that it was not free to do whatever it wanted to Uganda. Once again, a primary issue in the Security Council debates was not presented in a posture that would have turned upon the existence or nonexistence of any legal rules at all. The Israeli decision to kill the Entebbe hijackers but to spare Ugandan soldiers as much as possible was consistent with this interpretation. Israel was waging a war of existence against the PLO/PFLP, not Uganda.

Not only did all parties agree that relevant standards of behavior existed, but they also agreed that those rules were to be derived from public international law. For example, Israel did not argue that its right to intervene at Entebbe must be determined in accordance with the laws of the Old Testament. The delegate representing Amin's Islamic regime did not rely upon the Koran or the Sharia to justify Uganda's position during the Security Council debates. Rather, by not making arguments based upon religious law, both sides implicitly agreed that the authoritative source of reference for the derivation of applicable rules must be to the principles of public international law. Consequently, this aspect of the Entebbe crisis did not require adjudication of the comparatively difficult problem concerning disputed sources of reference for rules.

This was not a foregone conclusion. During the Entebbe crisis management proceedings of the Israeli government, the Ashkenazi Chief Rabbi informed Prime Minister Rabin through an aide that the *Halacha* (a compendium of legal precedents in the Jewish religious tradition) would permit the exchange of "terrorists" for hostages. He cited Moses Maimonides and Deuteronomy in support of this proposition. At almost the same time, the Sephardic Chief Rabbi notified the government that he had reached a similar legal conclusion.[146]

Those who doubt the power of religious law in Israel easily forget that the ostensible cause for Prime Minister Rabin's dissolution of the Knesset, which was followed by loss of the consequent elections to Menachem Begin, was the ouster of the National Religious Party from the Labor coalition government because its members failed to support Rabin on a no-confidence motion introduced by another religious bloc, the United Torah Front, over charges that Rabin had desecrated the Jewish Sabbath by holding a welcome ceremony in the late afternoon of Friday, December 10, 1976, for three F-15 fighter jets obtained from the United States. The ceremony was alleged to have continued past sundown, the start of the Sabbath. [147]

Dissent concerning exceptions to the rule. When it came to the general prohibition on non-consensual foreign military intervention in international law, Israel merely argued, and Uganda emphatically denied, (1) that there were exceptions to this rule and (2) that these exceptions encompassed the facts of the Entebbe incident. Uganda and its protagonists argued that non-consensual foreign military intervention by one state within the territorial domain of another is forbidden for any reason whatsoever. [148] In other words, the article 2(4) prohibition of the U.N. Charter is absolute. A prima facie breach could not, therefore, be justified on the ground that it was not directed against the territorial integrity or political independence of the target state, or for the reason that it was consistent with the purposes of the United Nations (e.g., "humanitarian" intervention). [149] Under this interpretation, article 2(4) precludes military intervention by a state to protect its nationals abroad from even a gross deprivation of their fundamental human rights by the host state.

Implicit in the Ugandan position were a number of subsidiary arguments: that the principles of intervention, protection, and self-help are not included within the body of public international law (an argument over [3] the inclusivity of rules); that these principles do not survive under the regime of the Charter as elements of the article 51 right to self-defense and therefore cannot take precedence over the article 2(4) prohibition (arguments over [4] the priority among and [5] the interpretation of rules); that there must be an actual "armed attack" by one state against another for the article 51 right of self-defense to come into play (i.e., [5] interpretation of rules); that it was Israel which had perpetrated an article 51 "armed attack" against Uganda, and not vice versa (i.e., [5] interpretation of rules and [6] application of rules to facts); that the Israeli raid at Entebbe was neither "necessary" nor "proportional" under the circumstances (i.e., [6] application of rules to facts); and, finally, that Israel had violated its Charter obligation to attempt a peaceful settlement of its dispute with Uganda (i.e., [6] application of rules to facts). Of course, Israel took a diametrically opposed position on all these points. Yet the disagreement over these matters raised only the relatively simple questions of inclusivity, priority, interpretation, and application of rules. Nowhere did the arguments venture into the more difficult and perhaps irresolvable issues over the existence of rules or their source of reference.

These lower order rule arguments, as well as the dispute over the actual facts themselves, were not serious enough to dilute the high degree of underlying consensus among the participants in the debates over the following points: (1) that hijacking in international civil aviation is illegal; (2) that the detention of hijacked hostages is illegal; (3) that states have a responsibility to refrain from participation in such activities and, where possible, to prevent or thwart their occurrence or continuation; and finally (4) that the general prohibition on non-consensual foreign military intervention is a fundamental principle of international law and international politics. The elements of dissent among the participants in the Security Council Entebbe debates, therefore, proved to be both legally and politically insignificant when compared to these elements of consensus.

Adjudication as a Prelude to Resolution

From the perspective of a functionalist analysis of international law in time of crisis, the categories of potential arguments that were not made in the Security Council Entebbe debates proved to be more important than the types of arguments actually given. The contentions presented in the Security Council were all lower-order arguments, and the dispute itself was reduced to three lower-order components. Foremost was the dispute over the actual facts themselves, the lowest order of the seven potential sources of disagreement. Second was the disagreement over a strict, absolutist interpretation of the general principle of military non-intervention into the territorial domain of another state. Third were arguments of subsidiary importance centered around related lower-order problems of inclusivity, priority, interpretation, and application. The reason why the debates were conducted at such a low level of intensity was that there already existed a general consensus among the participants that the higher-order issues should not be raised in regard to Entebbe, that most of the lower-order issues were not subject to dispute, and that the few open-ended lower-order issues were not all that significant in the face of agreement on the more fundamental principles of international law and politics at stake.

Arguments not made in the Security Council were those of the two highest orders, concerning the existence of rules and the source of reference for rules. If the dispute between Israel and Uganda had involved either one of these higher-order arguments, the participants in the debates might never have achieved any consensus on the four fundamental principles of international law and politics set out above. Such lack of consensus might very well have rendered stillborn the momentous suggestion made by the delegate from the Federal Republic of Germany during the course of the Entebbe debates that consideration be given by the next session of the U.N. General Assembly to preparation of a convention against the taking of hostages.[150] Conversely, the existence of a Security Council consensus upon these essential points paved the way for the appointment of an ad hoc committee on the drafting of a hostages convention by the General Assembly in December of 1976[151] and for the eventual adoption by the General Assembly of the committee's draft hostages convention in December of 1979.[152]

What Result?

THE MEANING OF THE ENTEBBE VOTE

From a functionalist perspective, the seemingly indeterminate outcome of the Entebbe debates and vote in the Security Council can indeed be viewed as constituting an effective adjudication of the dispute between Israel and Uganda. Israeli government spokesmen argued that given the bias of the United Nations Organization against Israel, the Security Council's failure to adopt a resolution condemning or even critical of the Entebbe raid must be interpreted as tacit recognition that the rescue operation at least did not violate public international law.[153] Moreover, in statements made directly after the vote on the U.S.-U.K. draft resolution, Mr. Bennett, speaking on behalf of the U.S. government, took "considerable satisfaction" in that not one member of the Security Council "could bring itself to vote against such a balanced draft resolution."[154] The implication of his statement was that in the opinion of at least the U.S. government, the Security Council had fully vindicated the Israeli position on Entebbe.

This argument draws additional credence from the African failure to press their three-power draft resolution to a vote. If the African countries really intended to express their strong disapproval of the raid at Entebbe and to avoid an expected Israeli claim that the Council's failure to condemn was tantamount to implicit approval, they could have brought the resolution to a vote, and forced the United States (if not Great Britain and France as well) to veto the resolution. According to the Tanzanian ambassador who announced the decision not to press the African resolution to a vote, this action was taken because of the confrontations which had been exhibited in the Security Council and in light of the Council's seeming determination to ignore Africa's legitimate complaint.[155]

But these considerations do not appear sufficient to account for their retreat on the Entebbe votes. For example, African countries have not been deterred by the threat of a U.S. veto on matters concerning South Africa. In that context, they have persisted to the point of eliciting the veto precisely in order to embarrass South Africa and the vetoers, as well as to put themselves firmly on record as virulently opposed to that regime.[156] A forced U.S. veto of a resolution condemning Israel for the Entebbe raid could have caused significant embarrassment to both countries in the eyes of a substantial number of Third World states. Veto of the resolution by the United States would have added to Uganda's credibility and could have been denounced as part of the continuing "zionist-imperialist-racist" conspiratorial plot fomented by Israel, the United States, and, for good measure, South Africa. A fairly large number of propaganda points could have been scored by the African countries by simply pressing their draft resolution to a vote and a veto. Simultaneously, the Israeli claim to a victory in the Security Council because of the latter's non-adoption of a formal resolution on Entebbe would have been sharply undercut.

It is likely that the African draft resolution was not brought to a formal vote as a result of an honest disbelief of the Ugandan factual position on Entebbe, the negative if not deprecatory attitude that many African leaders held toward Amin, and a feeling that Amin had received a well-deserved comeuppance from Israel. After an initial period of euphoria throughout Africa over Amin's humiliating expulsion of the United Kingdom's influence from Uganda, Amin's buffoonery on the international scene and his systematic repression and massacre of opponents at home led African leaders to consider him a serious embarrassment to their collective stature.[157] Even the Soviet Union thought he had gone too far when he suggested the erection of a monument in tribute to Adolph Hitler for his policy of exterminating the Jewish people.[158] More serious, at least from an African perspective, were his bellicose pronouncements directed toward his immediate neighbors: the Sudan, Kenya, and Tanzania.[159] It was Israel's refusal to provide Amin with bombers capable of striking Dar-es-Salaam which led him to break diplomatic relations with Israel in 1972. Amin's later precipitous invasion of Tanzania ultimately led to his overthrow by a combination of President Julius Nyerere's armed forces and Ugandan rebels in April of 1979.[160]

Moreover, there was a strong collective sentiment that Amin had simply gone too far in formally associating an African government with the activities of the PLO/PFLP hijackers/hostage takers. Granted, Arab-

African states such as Libya and Algeria had provided assistance to the PLO in such cases before. But no state, let alone a Black African state, had ever gone so far as to actively aid, abet, and identify itself with a specific hijacking/hostage-taking incident to the extent Amin had at Entebbe.[161] All states in the region had a stake in the preservation of the safety and freedom of international civil aviation, and none could afford to have Africa become known as a safe haven for hijackers and hostage takers. From the other side of the Entebbe dispute, therefore, African national interests were not sacrificed but advanced during the adjudication of the Entebbe raid under international law by the Security Council.

The Third World generally believed that PLO hijackings and hostage takings had lost their utility and were probably even counterproductive to securing the formal recognition of international legitimacy for the organization, especially by those countries in the West which alone could bring real pressure to bear on Israel. The PLO had more to gain at the conference table than in the cockpit. The period after Entebbe was to witness a marked decline in the number of such spectacular hijacking and hostage-taking operations by the PLO and its splinter groups. To be sure, the PLO still launched military raids from Lebanon and elsewhere into Israel proper and the occupied territories. But with the encouragement of Arab states, the PLO seemed to enter a new, evolutionary phase in which the military war against Israel took second place to a diplomatic offensive.[162]

THE LESSONS OF ENTEBBE

A succinct statement of the "lessons of Entebbe" distilled from the Security Council's treatment of this entire complex of events surrounding the crisis would be something along the following lines: Given the current imperfections in the development of international law and its enforcement by international organizations, including the Security Council, it would be unwise for that body, as the representative of the international community, to condemn Israel for its raid at Entebbe. As indicated by the debates over the raid, however, failure to condemn Israel does not mean that the Security Council approves of military intervention by one sovereign nation into the territorial domain of another. Nor does the Security Council thereby condone in any way international hijacking or hostage taking perpetrated for whatever reason. The international community will continue to strive, through the United Nations Organization and otherwise, to create an international system in which neither alleged acts of international terrorism nor counteractive military intervention will be necessary, and therefore to create a system of international relations in which both types of conduct will be unequivocally illegitimate, effectively repressed if they occur, and ultimately condemned and punished. Until that day, the Security Council can only examine the facts of each case as they are presented. It must judge them in light of the historical conditions of international relations and the current evolutionary stage of international law and organizations. The Entebbe crisis is symptomatic of deficiencies in both that can, must, and will be remedied in time and with a modicum of international cooperation by all interested parties.

9

The Function of Resolution as Performed by the U.N. Security Council

Public international law's third function, *adjudication* of the dispute among parties to a crisis, merges imperceptibly into the fourth function, here denominated as *resolution* of the outstanding dispute between the parties. Amin had threatened to take retaliatory action against Israel for the Entebbe rescue operation.[163] This threat raised the specter of continuing the crisis in their relations into the indefinite future at considerable cost to themselves and to the peace and stability of this highly volatile region surrounding the horn of Africa. Yet the institutions and procedures of international law played a critical role in forestalling Amin's threat to retaliate for Entebbe. International law resolved the Entebbe crisis, not necessarily to the complete satisfaction of either Uganda or Israel, but in the sense that it provided the means for the interruption and termination of the cycle of force and counterforce that had developed between the two states. The rules of international law and the vital national interests of all concerned states coincided and reinforced each other during the urgent effort to find a peaceful resolution of the Entebbe crisis at the U.N. Security Council.

Uganda's Submission to the Security Council

Certainly retaliation is not a legitimate exercise of the right to self-defense.[164] Beyond this positivist point, however, is the more significant functionalist observation that by its voluntary participation in the submission of the dispute to the Security Council, Uganda substantially undercut both its putative right and whatever limited ability it possessed to retaliate against Israel for Entebbe. In going to the Security Council,

Uganda effectively committed itself, both legally and politically, to abide by the Council decision, whatever that might be. Military retaliation was no longer a viable option.

Of course, a leader as brutal and repressive as Amin could not really have been expected to care too much about the niceties of international legal procedure. He must have had very definite, self-interested reasons for submitting the Entebbe crisis to the Security Council. For if Amin was really serious about his threat to retaliate, he would not have permitted the dispute to be brought to the attention of the Security Council in the first place. Non-submission would have preserved intact at least an alleged right to act unilaterally against Israel. A similar rationale underlay the Israeli decision not to bring the hijacking/hostages phase of the Entebbe crisis to the Security Council. In both of these stages in the development of the Entebbe crisis, the respective parties resorted to the Security Council only to the extent they believed it was both possible and desirable for that body to devise a peaceful resolution of the dispute.

Despite the threat of retaliation, it was in Amin's self-interest to achieve a peaceful resolution of the Entebbe crisis under the auspices of the Security Council. Amin was trapped by his threat of retaliation. He had to make it, but it was too dangerous to carry out. The internal stability of his regime was never great in the first place. Assured Israeli counter-retaliation would have destabilized the domestic situation even further, perhaps to the point of Amin's violent deposition, which had already been attempted several times.[165] Amin had to terminate the crisis immediately and not retaliate, but termination had to occur in a manner that would salvage whatever prestige his regime retained after the raid. Debates in the Security Council would satisfy these twin criteria. They would shift the focus of attention from the manifest military disaster at Entebbe airport to abstract arguments over legal principles in New York. Even if Uganda could not win the war of words in the Security Council, a seemingly inconclusive result would permit Amin to claim vindication and victory by virtue of majoritarian rhetoric alone. Submission of the dispute to the Security Council provided Amin with a face-saving and peaceful alternative response to the humiliation he had suffered at Entebbe. Without the Security Council as an outlet to express rage and receive some semblance of legitimizing support, however, Amin might have felt impelled by circumstances to make good on the threat to retaliate simply in order to shore up his internal power position.

Security Council Non-Action Consecrates the Status Quo

A peaceful resolution of the Entebbe crisis was obtained in the Security Council even though it did not adopt a positive resolution formally disposing of the matter. Non-action was a form of action itself. By default, the non-adoption of a resolution by the Security Council automatically established the political and military situation existing after the raid as the legal status quo, and the prohibition of Charter article 2(4) immediately operated to protect this status quo. Uganda could not plausibly retaliate pursuant to any alleged right of individual self-defense under article 51 without a new, separate, and independent breach of article 2(4) by another Israeli threat or use of force. Yet Israel neither threatened nor undertook further retaliatory measures against Uganda for what it had done at Entebbe. The Security Council's non-action thus effectively ensured that the cycle of violence would cease at the Entebbe airport.

Of course Uganda could have retaliated against Israel for Entebbe after the conclusion of the Security Council debates. But to use force without a plausible claim for legal authority to do so adds significantly to the political and military costs already involved. These additional costs can also serve to increase the number and strength of other factors deterring a contemplated course of violent conduct. [166] After voluntarily submitting the dispute to the Security Council, it would have been extremely costly for Uganda to have countermanded the Council's collective decision not to disturb the legal status quo existing after the Entebbe raid.

The Entebbe crisis demonstrates that the Security Council can attempt to resolve an international crisis in one of two ways: actively through the passage of a formal resolution embodying the terms of a new or existing status quo; or by non-adoption of any resolution, which under certain circumstances can implicitly approve of the existing order as the legal status quo. Neither action nor non-action would prevent the Security Council from mandating a change of the status quo in the future. Nor would these possible results prevent an injured party from pursuing other peaceful methods for adjusting the status quo. For example, the state could demand compensation for its injuries. But the threat or use of force is no longer a legitimate technique for alteration of this status quo. And in the absence of such peaceful change, the temporary status quo established in time of international crisis becomes permanent.

The Security Council, Peace, and the Status Quo

The Entebbe experience indicates quite clearly that one of the most important functions of the Security Council during an international crisis is to establish, whether actively or passively, a legal status quo which, by definition, attaches serious political and military consequences to its disruption. Indeed, an international legal positivist or an international political scientist might argue that the primary purpose of the Security Council should be to break a chain of violent interaction among states through the consecration of any status quo at some point in a cycle of violence irrespective of the merits of the original dispute. They would thus reason that, for the sake of maintaining the stability of the entire international system, the Security Council's formal creation and active preservation of some status quo during an international crisis is preferable to continued violence.

As illustrated by the Entebbe crisis, however, the chief problem with this line of analysis is that the status quo approved by the Security Council's non-adoption of a resolution was not out of line with the merits of the dispute between Israel and Uganda as adjudicated by the Council. Since Council members essentially agreed that Israel should not be held at fault for the Entebbe raid, it was both proper and convenient for them to do nothing further and thus allow the postraid status quo to become permanent. The equities of the situation had been fairly well adjusted by the aura of plausible legality produced by the design, execution, and success of the raid itself.

To preserve world peace, the Security Council can always attempt to establish a legal status quo at some point during a cycle of violent interaction between states without regard to the merits of the fundamental dispute that precipitated the crisis. To do so, the Council might have to sacrifice the interests and values of at least one party to the crisis for the perceived benefit of all other members of the international system derived from the maintenance of peace. But when there exists a significant discrepancy between such a Security Council decision and what any disputant perceives to be moral, just, fair, equitable, or ordained by God or history, the Security Council would have to be ready to enforce its status quo by the threat or use of force or other coercive measures. Such Security Council decisions constitute the utilitarian calculation par excellence. Yet, just as John Stuart Mill pointed out that justice must be the highest form of utility,[167] so too there exists a practical limit as to how far an imposed peace can depart from the values at stake in an international crisis and still remain effective. International law and organizations must always maintain their contact with international political reality in order to work at all.

The Security Council Is Not a Hobbesist Sovereign

In regard to this general observation drawn from the Entebbe crisis, consider the almost universal criticism of the United Nations put forth by international political scientists, some international legal positivists, and many government decision makers in First World states, to the effect that the Security Council cannot effectively enforce its decisions upon recalcitrant state members which repeatedly commit gross violations of fundamental principles of international law. Of course this objection assumes that the Security Council was really designed to do so in the first place, and furthermore that this function still remains the most important task for the Organization as a whole to perform. In the aftermath of the ascent to independence of an enormous number of formerly colonized territories, a substantial majority of the U.N. membership now collectively believe that the Organization's primary emphasis should shift from the maintenance of international peace and security to the promotion of economic development and social welfare for the world community.

Putting this latter issue aside, however, the former critique of the Security Council's effectiveness basically represents a reincarnated version of the Hobbesist doctrinal thesis that if the will of the sovereign cannot be enforced, then there is no law: The United Nations cannot enforce the peace within the so-called commonwealth of nations and therefore states must still remain in the Hobbesist state of nature/war in their relations with each other. Since the Security Council cannot effectively enforce international law, then international law, even if it might exist in name, is essentially irrelevant to violent state conflicts over matters of vital national interest. These assertions, however, overlook or ignore a significant number of instances in which U.N. peacekeeping operations have played a critical role in preserving some semblance of peace in the world during the post–World War II era: e.g., UNEF I & II, UNFICYP, ONUC, UNDOF, UNIFIL, etc. Hence the real problem does not seem to be that the U.N. Security Council cannot effectuate its will, but rather that it does not formulate a united "will" on every crisis presented to it.

CHARTER ARTICLE 2(4) AND THE LEAGUE OF NATIONS COVENANT

Article 2(4) of the U.N. Charter sought to terminate the Hobbesist state of nature/war among the members of the Organization with the following words: "All Members shall refrain in their international relations from the threat or use of force against the territorial integrity or political independence of any state, or in any other manner inconsistent with the Purposes of the United Nations." Article 2(4) closed the loophole left open in the League of Nations Covenant by articles 11(1), 12(1), 13(4), 15(6), and 16(1), wherein states retained a legal right to resort to war upon the fulfillment of certain conditions. [168] At that time "war" had a technical legal meaning which, although disputed, encompassed a spectrum of violent action far narrower than "force." The seriousness of this gap in coverage by the Covenant became evident in the Sino-Japanese hostilities over Manchuria beginning in 1931, when neither party formally declared "war" upon the other as part of an ultimately unsuccessful effort to circumvent the establishment of jurisdiction over the dispute by the Council of the League.[169] Changing the trigger word from "war" in the League Covenant to "force" in the U.N. Charter counteracted such a maneuver and, more generally, provided the Council of the new Organization with prima facie competence to become involved at a much lower threshhold of violence, when presumably the situation would be far more susceptible to peaceful resolution than during a full-scale war.

CHARTER ARTICLE 51 AND THE KELLOGG-BRIAND PACT

The U.N. Charter article 2(4) prohibition on the threat or use of force, however, was made subject to the "inherent right" of individual or collective self-defense recognized by article 51. The official French version of the Charter refers to self-defense as a *droit naturel*,[170] which provides a better indication of the Hobbesist origins and connotations of this doctrine even in a document as supposedly enlightened as the U.N. Charter. Article 51 of the Charter closed a gaping procedural loophole left open in the coverage of international law by the Kellogg-Briand Pact of 1928, which in turn purported to close in part the aforementioned "war" loophole left open in the League Covenant.

By the terms of the Kellogg-Briand Pact the states of the extant international community agreed to renounce war as an instrument of national policy.[171] However, during the negotiation of the Pact, the parties made it quite clear that they reserved to themselves the right to resort to war in self-defense in accordance with their own determination of the necessity to do so.[172] These reservations belie the standard interpretation of the Kellogg-Briand Pact as a naive, utopian dream, that was somehow indicative of the "legalist-moralist" manner in which the Western democracies foolishly conducted foreign policy during the interwar period. What the governments gave away with one hand in the text of the treaty for public consumption, the foreign offices took back with the other hand in the form of reservations for actual practice. If anything, these interwar governments should be faulted for being somewhat too Machiavellian in the art of statecraft for the manner in which they concluded the Kellogg-Briand Pact.

In contrast, pursuant to article 51 of the Charter a state preserves its "inherent right" of individual or collective self-defense, but only "until the Security Council has taken the measures necessary to maintain international peace and security." Under the regime of the Charter, therefore, the Security Council, not the state itself, becomes the final arbiter of the legitimacy of actions allegedly taken in self-defense. The implication is clear that the continued threat or use of force by a member state inconsistent with such Security Council "measures" violates article 51, the article 2(4) prohibition, as well as the article 25 obligation to "carry out" the decisions of the Security Council.

CHARTER ARTICLES 24(1), 2(6), 2(7), 43
AND THE SECURITY COUNCIL'S
MONOPOLY OF VIOLENCE

Article 24(1) of the U.N. Charter endows the Security Council with the "primary responsibility for the maintenance of international peace and security." Nevertheless, even if a state is not a member of the U.N. civil society and therefore, from a Hobbesist perspective, still exists in a state of nature/war in relation to U.N. members, pursuant to Charter article 2(6) the Security Council is not authorized to act coercively against non-members unless disruption of international peace and security is threatened or occurs. [173] This restriction represents a significant moderation of the Hobbesist conception of international relations as a state of unmitigated warfare.

Charter article 2(7) permits the Security Council to intervene in matters essentially within the domestic jurisdiction of any state pursuant to the application of enforcement measures under chapter 7. [174] Unlike a Hobbesist sovereign, however, the U.N. Security Council does not directly command a monopoly of power. The military agreements contemplated by article 43 have never been concluded. But the states comprising the membership of the Security Council and, in particular, the five permanent members (viz., China, France, the Soviet Union, the United Kingdom, and the United States) as a group possess an overwhelming preponderance of military force—without question, enough military power to impose their collective will upon the rest of the world if they so desire. The essential purpose of the Security Council is thus to provide a source of legal and institutional legitimacy, recognized by all parties to the U.N. Charter, whereby the major military powers could rule the world to the extent they can mutually agree to do so and, in addition, acquire the benefits accruing from having such rule accepted as legitimate by all members of the international civil society.

Of course the great powers, or even the United States and the Soviet Union together, could agree to impose their collective will upon the rest of the world outside the context of the United Nations Organization, either jointly by a condominium arrangement, or severally through division of the world into spheres of influence. But the crucial difference would be that U.N. members have formally consented to be ruled by the Security Council, whereas pure great power fiat not expressed by means of the U.N. apparatus possesses absolutely no claim whatsoever to international legitimacy. Power endowed with legitimacy (i.e., the rule of law) is far more powerful and effective than mere power alone. The legitimacy of the Security Council's absolute rule, when agreed upon by its members, flows from the prior consent of those states governed. This is an explicitly Hobbesist notion.

CHARTER ARTICLE 27(3) AND THE VETO POWER

The real impediment to the Security Council ever constituting a genuine Hobbesist sovereign is the veto power over substantive matters granted by Charter article 27(3) to the five permanent members.[175] According to Hobbes, the sovereign must speak with a voice that is not subject to the vicissitudes of any individual member.[176] It is obvious therefore that the U.N. Security Council was never intended to be a Hobbesist sovereign. Consequently it is inappropriate to evaluate the performance of the Security Council in maintaining international peace and security by Hobbesist criteria: Namely, whether it can effectively enforce the peace absolutely, at all times, under all circumstances, and against all potential violators. Any assertions, hopes, beliefs, or illusions to the contrary that were generated before, during, or after the San Francisco Conference were completely unsubstantiated and unrealistic.

When evaluated in accordance with the dictates of Hobbes' *Leviathan*, however, the U.N. Security Council has operated much more effectively than might have been predicted on that basis alone. At the time of the U.N.'s foundation the most that could have been reasonably expected was that the Security Council could somehow preserve and extend the uneasy wartime alliance among the great powers into the postwar world upon the basis of its fundamental underlying condition—unanimity. To the degree that the permanent members could maintain, or at least selectively reinstitute, their World War II coalition in order to handle postwar international crises, the U.N. Security Council would provide a mechanism to enforce the peace of the world in a manner accepted as legitimate by the remainder of the international civil society.

Viewed from this non-Hobbesist perspective, the founders of the United Nations were certainly not utopian or naive but, to the contrary, as hardheaded and realistic about the peacekeeping potential of the Organization as they could be under the circumstances. A Security Council without a great power veto would have been a non-starter from the beginning. And there was always the possibility that once brought into existence the United Nations as a whole could somehow generate enough momentum of its own in order to transcend some of its congenital limitations. That possibility has been partially realized in the postwar world, for example, by means of the Uniting for Peace Resolution.[177] But the failure to achieve a mere potentiality must not be allowed to detract from the non-Hobbesist significance of the Security Council and, in general, of the United Nations as a whole.

BREAKING OUT OF THE CIRCULARITY OF HOBBESISM

Most international political scientists and many international legal positivists have mistakenly adopted Hobbesist criteria for evaluating the usefulness of international law and international organizations for the preservation of world peace. When international political scientists collectively assert that international law and organizations are essentially "irrelevant" to violent conflict between states over matters of vital national interest, their conception of "relevance" is determined by Hobbesist criteria. Likewise, contemporary public international lawyers commit a similar mistake when they tacitly concede the political scientist's objections to the "relevance" of international law and organizations during international crises, and instead concentrate on examining the compliance by states with international law in all the non-conflictual aspects of international relations. Each group's conscious or unconscious application of Hobbesism to law on the international level of analysis confuses more than it clarifies.

To criticize the "relevance" of international law and international organizations when it comes to the threat or use of force from a Hobbesist perspective is simply to commit the cardinal methodological sin described by international political scientists as ignoring the "level-of-analysis" problem. Although Hobbesism might still prove to be a useful analytical tool for understanding the nature of domestic politics, law, and government, such limited utility must not result in its automatic application to international politics, law, and organizations because the operational dynamics of the international level of analysis are essentially different from those of the domestic level of analysis. Commission of such a fundamental methodological error so distorts whatever substantive conclusions are obtained as to render them severely defective if not meaningless.

This becomes especially clear when it is realized that the three Hobbesist states of nature/war (i.e., the New World, civil war, international relations) were defined so as to consist of simple negativisms of the underlying conditions of civil society. Hence a Hobbesist analysis of international law and international organizations creates an analytical circularity. For Hobbes the law among nations was, by explicit definition, the law of nature, which essentially amounted to the antinomian "law" of Machiavellian power politics—i.e., no "law" whatsoever.

The typical Hobbesist objections to the "relevance" of the Security Council, the United Nations, and international law in general simply obscure their vital functions in developing a better understanding of the nature of international crises and the means whereby the latter can be prevented, forestalled, and controlled. Hobbesism must therefore be abandoned and replaced by a non-Hobbesist approach to the study of international law and organizations. For this reason, the primary emphasis of a functionalist analysis is upon the operational process of management, not upon the Hobbesist promulgation and enforcement of rules. The cardinal task of functionalism is thus to analyze the ability of international law and organizations to contribute to the successful management of international crises and the peaceful resolution of the underlying disputes.

International Law, Peace, and the Status Quo

This line of analysis raises a set of general issues in regard to the political nature of international law and international organizations. A functionalist analysis must consider: (1) whether international law and organizations inevitably tend to work for the institution or preservation of any legal status quo no matter how inherently unjust, unfair, immoral, inequitable, or irreligious; (2) whether the prohibition on the forcible disruption of a status quo effectively precludes its timely rectification; (3) whether there subsist in international relations some elements of the geopolitical status quo which are so fundamental to the existing system that they cannot be altered in any way other than by the threat or use of force. If any of these criticisms proves to be sound, the functionalist must further inquire whether international law and international organizations should be considered to constitute legitimate sources for the promulgation of normative standards in the first place. Framing the problem more concretely: Why should states or peoples who believe they are oppressed and will be destroyed by the existing status quo accept the illegitimacy of the threat or use of force to save themselves from destruction?

Those who feel that they are being destroyed by the maintenance of the status quo (e.g., the PLO) will resort to violence in the name of self-preservation. For this reason, a status quo which is perceived to be inherently unjust or unfair by a significant group cannot expect to remain unchallenged by the threat or use of force for long. The peace derived from the maintenance of such a status quo will prove to be ephemeral. This was the lesson of the Treaty of Versailles, learned and put to good use by the Western victors of the Second World War when it came to a decision upon the postwar treatment to be accorded a vanquished Germany and Japan.[178] The defeated Axis powers were given a stake in the maintenance of a status quo in which they had someting to lose and which, therefore, they should be willing to maintain. The subsequent history of international relations has so far testified to the wisdom of what was, in effect, a policy of political co-optation into a legal status quo of those previously displaced from it. One can only hope that a similar policy will ultimately prove to be the underlying sentiment of the Camp David Accords[179] and, pursuant thereto, the dormant Israeli-Egyptian negotiations over the institution of some form of "autonomy" for the Palestinian people in the Gaza Strip and West Bank. At least until that time, the legal status quo in the Middle East will be forcefully attacked by those completely dispossessed from it such as the Palestinian people.[180]

A system of international law and international organizations which, by its very nature, operates to discourage the violent disruption of the status quo can only be recognized as legitimate if it provides an effective and timely procedure for the peaceful evolution of a new legal status quo in which a more just and fair condition may be approximated for all participants. A short-term solution to an immediate crisis does not necessarily serve as a long-range amelioration of the underlying conditions that gave rise to it. Until those conditions are resolved, similar crises can be expected to recur. And so the Entebbe crisis was followed in relatively short order by hostage crises and rescue operations at Mogadishu, Somalia and Larnaca, Cyprus.

The Lessons of Mogadishu and Larnaca

In the aftermath of the West German raid at the Mogadishu airport in Somalia, it was publicly revealed that a large number of states had created special commando groups for the express purpose of undertaking Entebbe-like rescue operations.[181] Unlike the Entebbe raid, however, the raid at the Mogadishu airport was undertaken with the consent of the Somali government.[182] Fortunately, it too was successful.[183] The Entebbe hijacking had been supervised by PFLP leaders located in Mogadishu, undoubtedly with the knowledge of the Somali government. Perhaps the precedent of the Israeli raid at Entebbe exerted a chastening influence upon President Siad Barre when it came to granting permission for the West German raid.

But like the Entebbe raid, the Egyptian raid at the Larnaca airport in Cyprus did not have the permission of the territorial government.[184] The consequences there were tragic.[185] Larnaca clearly demonstrated that Entebbe could have easily become a human disaster of the first magnitude. How would the Security Council's vote on the Entebbe raid have changed if this admittedly high-risk operation had failed and most or all of the remaining hostages were killed together with substantial loss of life on the part of Israeli and Ugandan soldiers? Would the Security Council have been more inclined to adopt a condemnatory or at least critical resolution against Israel?

At a minimum, the African states might have pressed their three-power draft resolution to a vote, and an American veto could have resulted. In any event, it would have been difficult for Israel to have claimed that the non-adoption of a Security Council resolution on a calamitous Entebbe operation was tantamount to tacit approval of the raid. Whatever the precise outcome of the debates and vote, it would have been hard to avoid the conclusion that the raid was a mistake both legally and politically.

Legality and Success or Failure

The proposition that Israel's actions would more likely have been deemed mistaken had the Entebbe raid failed is almost self-evident when it comes to an evaluation of the political consequences of an unsuccessful raid. But why should the success or failure of a military operation have any bearing whatsoever upon a determination of its ultimate legality or illegality? A public international lawyer would object to the ex post facto nature of such characterizations. An international political scientist might remark that this alleged shortcoming is merely a result of the irrelevance of international law and organizations to international political crises involving vital national interests. Once again, both would be wrong because each perceives international law in strictly legal positivist terms.

A functionalist analysis indicates that governmental policy decisions in time of international crisis consist of both legal and political dimensions in a constant state of dynamic interaction with each other. Since they are essentially inseparable, inevitably each decisional dimension— legal and political—is evaluated in light of the outcome they jointly produce. Just because public international lawyers and international political scientists may mistakenly believe that international law can be isolated from international politics, it is wrong to think that legality or illegality is essentially independent of political success or failure.

By its very nature, international law represents an attempt to legitimate preexisting or proposed power relationships, an attempt that either succeeds or fails. Consequently, determinations of legality or illegality are essentially dependent upon the political success or political failure, respectively, of the course of state conduct at issue. A pattern of successful political action creates new legal rules through legitimization of that state behavior by lack of effective political opposition to it. An accumulation of political failures also creates law by generating political pressures to establish legal rules prohibiting the unsuccessful political conduct in the future. This success phenomenon is responsible for the development of customary international law. The failure syndrome oftentimes leads to the conclusion of a treaty on the subject. Conversely, successful international legal rules create the political environment necessary and conducive to the passage of more of the same. Unsuccessful international legal rules are either formally terminated by agreement or informally abandoned by a pattern of successful contrary political practice that evolves into the formation of a new customary legal regime. Once again, international law is and becomes international politics and vice versa.

The Problem of Change

Since it is absurd to believe that states would adopt international legal rules that are dangerous, ineffective, or useless for the promotion of their respective national interests, it is more plausible to assume that extant international legal rules originally possessed none of the above characteristics but rather were safe, effective, and useful in advancing individual national interests. The major problems of both international law and international politics arise because governmental perceptions of the requirements of national interest vary with the ineluctable change in historical conditions. International law must, therefore, change in order to maintain its vital link with both.

Simultaneously, as international law evolves and alters the international political milieu, national interests must change to maintain their vital link with international law and organizations. Although not intuitively obvious, this latter proposition becomes evident when one realizes that status quo powers define their vital national interests to include adherence to international law by themselves and other states because such behavior naturally tends towards the peaceful preservation of the status quo. Those states which already possess the major benefits of international relations do not want to lose them through war or violence. Almost by definition, then, obedience to international law lies within the respective national interests of status quo powers.

The successes and failures of this dynamic interaction among international law, national interests, and historical conditions thus constitute the essence of international politics. In regard to Entebbe, Mogadishu, and Larnaca, universal fear of permitting the development of a failure syndrome for hostage rescue operations proved to be the motivating force behind the negotiation and adoption of an international convention against the taking of hostages. This rapid succession of similar crises demonstrated to the entire international community the urgent need to suppress the incidence of transnational hostage taking and thus to attenuate the conditions conducive to non-permissive hostage rescue interventions. Here the analysis enters upon the fifth and final function of international law and organizations in time of crisis. This consists of an examination of the political processes by which the legal standards of acceptable political behavior are redefined for all actors within the international system in light of the successes and failures of this dialectical interaction between existing legal rules and political practice that are produced and illustrated by an international crisis.

10

The Function of Redefinition as Performed
by the U.N. General Assembly

This last function of international law concentrates upon the process by which standards for state behavior are redefined by the international community in order to improve international legal standards existing before the outbreak of a crisis. Entebbe revealed an entire complex of unresolved problems concerning hostage taking, state responsibility in such crises, and foreign military intervention to rescue hostages. During the Security Council Entebbe debates, a general consensus emerged that the taking of hostages for any reason violates a fundamental principle of international law and international politics. The Entebbe crisis generated the momentum necessary to propel this consensus into the establishment of a U.N. committee for the drafting of a convention against the taking of hostages. A draft hostages convention codified the elements of the Entebbe debate consensus, thereby attempting to remedy those problems of international law and international politics exposed by Entebbe and provide a deterrent to the outbreak of similar crises in the future, or at least a means for their more effective management if they should recur.

The German Initiative

The first major initiative undertaken by the Federal Republic of Germany (FRG) in the United Nations after becoming a member in 1973 was its request, made during the Security Council Entebbe debates, for the preparation of an international convention on measures against the taking of hostages. The German delegate suggested that the next session of the General Assembly take up this matter. Pursuant to that suggestion, the FRG Vice-Chancellor and Minister for Foreign Affairs, Hans-Dietrich

Genscher, addressed a letter of September 28, 1976, to the U.N. secretary-general requesting the inclusion in the agenda of the 31st session of the General Assembly of a separate item entitled "Drafting of an international convention against the taking of hostages."[186] An attached explanatory memorandum stated that the taking of hostages not only threatened the lives of those directly involved "but the security of many other people as well and frequently also endanger[ed] international peace and transnational relations."[187] Undoubtedly, this was an allusion to the Israeli raid at Entebbe. Because of its legal importance, the proposed item was referred to the Sixth Committee of the General Assembly.

In the Sixth Committee, the FRG proposed a draft resolution for consideration by the General Assembly calling for the drafting of an international convention against the taking of hostages with a key requirement that contracting parties either prosecute or extradite hostage takers.[188] In response thereto, Libya introduced an amendment that would have added the word "innocent" before the word "hostages" throughout the text of the proposed draft resolution.[189] The effect of the Libyan amendment would have been to differentiate between "innocent" and "non-innocent" hostages and thus to have raised the issue of whether citizens or political leaders of a state against which a war of national liberation has been declared (e.g., Israel or South Africa) are "innocent" and therefore entitled to the protection of a hostages convention. In an apparent compromise, the sponsors of the FRG draft resolution agreed to drop the provision calling for mandatory prosecution or extradition of hostage takers, and the Libyan delegate agreed not to press his amendment.[190]

The final resolution adopted by the General Assembly, upon recommendation of the Sixth Committee, contained neither a reference to "innocent" hostages nor a requirement that a convention provide for the mandatory prosecution or extradition of alleged hostage takers. It simply decided to establish an Ad Hoc Committee on the Drafting of an International Convention against the Taking of Hostages (hereinafter referred to as the Hostages Committee) with instructions to draft "at the earliest possible date" an international convention against the taking of hostages.[191] The Hostages Committee was requested to submit a draft convention to the General Assembly for consideration at its 32d session and such an item was included in the latter's provisional agenda.[192]

Circumvention of the Terrorism Committee

On that same day, December 15, 1976, and in reference to the immediately prior agenda item, the General Assembly adopted resolution

31/102 on measures to prevent international terrorism, etc.[193] Unlike the hostages resolution which was adopted by consensus,[194] there was dissent on the terrorism resolution; the vote was one hundred in favor to nine against (Australia, Belgium, Canada, Israel, Japan, Luxembourg, Netherlands, United Kingdom, United States), with twenty-seven abstentions.[195] The terrorism resolution expressed deep concern over increasing acts of international terrorism endangering or taking innocent human lives or jeopardizing fundamental freedoms, and urged states to continue to seek just and peaceful solutions to the underlying causes giving rise to terrorism. On the other hand, resolution 31/102 reaffirmed the inalienable right to self-determination and independence of all peoples under colonial and racist regimes and other forms of alien domination and upheld the legitimacy of their struggle, in particular the struggle of national liberation movements, in accordance with the purposes and principles of the Charter and relevant U.N. resolutions. The General Assembly condemned the continuation of repressive and terrorist acts by colonial, racist, and alien regimes denying peoples their legitimate right of self-determination, independence, and other human rights and fundamental freedoms. Finally, the 31st General Assembly invited the Ad Hoc Committee on International Terrorism to continue its work.

The Ad Hoc Committee on International Terrorism (hereinafter referred to as the Terrorism Committee) had been established by General Assembly resolution 3034 (XXVII) of December 18, 1972,[196] but its work had been suspended since 1973.[197] The proceedings of the Terrorism Committee had broken down over several interrelated problems: (1) the definition of international terrorism; (2) the right of national liberation movements to commit putative terrorist acts as part of their struggle; (3) the matter of so-called "state terrorism," which allegedly gives rise to and legitimates national liberation movements; and (4) whether a thorough study of the causes of terrorism should precede any recommendation on measures to deal with it or vice versa.[198] Third World members of the Terrorism Committee feared that a campaign against international terrorism would be turned into a weapon against national liberation movements, such as the PLO in the Middle East and those operating in Southern Africa.[199] Hence the deadlock.

The Entebbe incident generated sufficient enthusiasm among U.N. members to reinvigorate the mandate of the Terrorism Committee. But the focus of the enthusiasm was over hostage taking, and so the General Assembly created the Hostages Committee to circumvent the deadlock that had developed in the Terrorism Committee.[200] Entebbe had demonstrated the severe threat to international peace and security produced by the phenomena of transnational hostage taking and responsive non-consensual military interventions. Entebbe created the international political climate conducive to the adoption of a "piecemeal" approach to international terrorism by isolation of hostage taking from its other elements. Both the time and the circumstances were ripe for a definitive settlement of this problem.

Hostage taking had to and could be removed from the agenda of the Terrorism Committee and handed over as the sole item of business to its own independent committee charged with the mandate to draft a convention on that subject alone. There, progress towards a convention would be much more likely than if, for example, the deadlocked Terrorism Committee had been directed to draft a hostages convention. Suggestions had previously been made in the Terrorism Committee for the adoption of a "piecemeal" approach to the regulation of international terrorism by drafting several conventions, each of which would prohibit a specific type of reprehensible terrorist activity.[201] A convention against the taking of hostages was among the earlier suggestions but did not materialize.[202]

National Interest and Hostage Rescue Operations

An abstract commitment to principles of international peace and security by U.N. members does not alone account for the breakthrough on a hostages convention. On the level of pure national self-interest, the Israeli raid at Entebbe illustrated quite dramatically the marked vulnerability, in future hostage-taking crises, of most Third World states to similar self-help measures by militarily advanced countries. Failure to control transnational hostage taking might simply prompt stronger countries to intervene militarily into weaker countries for the purpose of rescuing hostages or, worse yet, encourage the use of hostage rescue operations as pretexts for accomplishing additional, non-humanitarian objectives, such as a coup d'état. Self-help generally works in only one direction. As a remedy it cannot be relied upon by a weak state against a strong state, or even by the weak against the weak. Conversely, the adoption of a hostages convention could undermine a militarily advanced state's purported right to undertake self-help measures and thereby deter or at least terminate an intervention. In this regard, a hostages convention would be especially valuable to prevent non-consensual military intervention in cases where the state of landing was genuinely attempting to secure the safe release of all hostages.

Even foreign military intervention genuinely limited to the humanitarian purpose of securing the release of hostages represents a distinct threat to the internal political security of the established government of the target state. The domestic political question will inevitably arise: What good is this government if it cannot protect the country from outside attack? For example, in the aftermath of the Entebbe raid there were severe disturbances within the Ugandan army and among the students at Makerere University directed against the Amin regime.[203] Rumors of a coup d'état were followed by brutal governmental repression against both the army and students with a further destabilization of what was already a volatile situation.[204]

Militarily weak states had everything to gain from a hostages convention and little to lose—except for a few propaganda points that might possibly be gained from insisting upon the principle that national liberation movements had a right to take hostages as part of their struggle. But why should Third World governments jeopardize their own internal stability for such a tenuous principle? Weighted within the utilitarian calculus of international politics, U.N. non-regulation of hostage taking by national liberation movements came out short in comparison to the dangers that foreign military intervention presented to the domestic security of governments that were fairly unstable to begin with. Entebbe had demonstrated that the negotiation of a convention against the taking of hostages would promote the vital national interests of almost all Third World states. Hence the establishment of the Hostages Committee.

Formation and Composition of the Hostages Committee

Pursuant to paragraph 2 of resolution 31/103, the president of the U.N. General Assembly appointed thirty-four states as members of the Hostages Committee. Of the fifteen members of the Security Council at the time of the Entebbe debate, all six of those which had voted in favor of the U.S.-U.K. draft resolution (France, Italy, Japan, Sweden, U.S., U.K.) and three which had not participated in the vote on the U.S.-U.K. draft resolution (Libya, U.S.S.R., Tanzania) were appointed to the Hostages Committee.[205] In addition, five non-members of the Security Council which had participated in the Entebbe debates were also appointed to the Hostages Committee (Federal Republic of Germany, Guinea, Kenya, Somalia, Yugoslavia).[206] There was thus a carryover of fourteen states from the Security Council Entebbe debates to membership on the Hostages Committee.[207] Moreover, nineteen members of the Terrorism Committee were appointed to the Hostages Committee.[208]

The First Session of the Hostages Committee

The first session of the Hostages Committee convened at U.N. Head-quarters from August 1 to 19, 1977.[209] The main working paper before it was a draft convention against the taking of hostages submitted by the Federal Republic of Germany.[210] Its key provision was article 7, which required a contracting state to extradite or prosecute an alleged offender found within its territory. Unfortunately, the first session of the Hostages Committee was unable to make any substantive progress on the FRG draft convention. It concluded only with the adoption of a resolution recommending that the 32d session of the U.N. General Assembly invite the Hostages Committee to continue its work in 1978.[211]

ELEMENTS OF DISSENT IN ITS DEBATES

The first session of the Hostages Committee deadlocked over the same general issue that had led to the breakdown of the Terrorism Committee: How should a hostages convention deal with recognized national liberation movements? In both the Terrorism and Hostages Committees, the Arab and African states wanted a guarantee that a hostages convention would not be used as a legal-political weapon against legitimate national liberation movements.[212]

For example, a working paper submitted by Lesotho and Tanzania, later joined by Algeria, Egypt, Guinea, Libya, and Nigeria, would have defined the term "taking of hostages" for the purposes of a hostages convention as not including any act or acts carried out in the process of a national liberation struggle by movements recognized by the United Nations or regional organizations.[213] The Libyan delegate submitted a working paper that would have defined the term "taking of hostages" to include the concept of "state terrorism."[214] And in a most prophetic utterance the delegate from Democratic Yemen put the problem as follows: "Either there would be an internationally accepted convention against the taking of hostages which did not apply to acts carried out by recognized national liberation movements in the course of their struggle or there would be no convention at all."[215] Although it might have sounded strident at the time, his first alternative was in fact to come true, but without the extreme negative consequences he apparently intended.

In addition, the earlier disputes over inclusion of a requirement for prosecution or extradition of hostage takers and the protection of only "innocent" hostages were revived.[216] To this confusion was added a request for the preservation in any hostages convention of a state's right to grant political asylum.[217] Finally, underlying these problems was the seminal question raised by the Entebbe crisis itself: Could a state use force to rescue hostages held within the territory of another state under any circumstances?

The Israeli raid at Entebbe haunted the proceedings of the first session of the Hostages Committee, and numerous allusions to Entebbe were made throughout its debates.[218] The delegate from Algeria put the matter quite correctly when he surmised: "It was obvious that an effort was being made to find a way out of that impasse [i.e., in the Terrorism Committee] through the drafting of a convention against the taking of hostages."[219] In his opinion, this was unfortunate since "there had been too quick a surrender to the emotion aroused by the renewed outburst of violence [i.e., Entebbe] when the request had been made to include in the agenda of the General Assembly the question of the taking of hostages and of the adoption of prompt measures to punish certain acts which undeniably constituted a threat to international order."[220] Over his objections, in the Hostages Committee as in the General Assembly, the Entebbe crisis would work to create a consensus from which a hostages convention could eventually emerge.

ELEMENTS OF CONSENSUS IN ITS DEBATES

Despite these matters of disagreement at the first session of the Hostages Committee, strong elements of consensus were manifest within the debates as well. In effect, they patterned the elements of consensus contained within the Security Council Entebbe debates. It was argued that since the laws of war severely condemned the taking of hostages during international and civil war, this practice should not be tolerated by the laws of peace either.[221] In the opinion of the Polish delegate, a hostages convention would rectify a situation where "international law did not contain any general prohibition against taking hostages in time of peace."[222]

As for the treatment accorded to national liberation movements by a hostages convention, the U.S. delegate observed that those government members of the Hostages Committee expressing strong support for national liberation struggles had already endorsed the principle that liberation movements should not take hostages at the Diplomatic Conference on the Reaffirmation and Development of International Humanitarian Law Applicable in Armed Conflicts.[223] In June of 1977, that Conference had adopted two protocols additional to the Geneva Conventions of 1949.[224] Article 1 of the First Protocol applied the entirety of the four Geneva Conventions of 1949 to wars of national liberation.[225]

This would include the prohibitions against the taking of hostages contained in article 3, common to all four conventions, and in article 34 of the Fourth Geneva Convention. Article 75 of the First Protocol specifically affirmed the prohibition against the taking of hostages during national liberation struggles;[226] article 4 of the Second Additional Protocol reiterated this prohibition for armed conflicts not of an international character.[227]

Therefore, the German delegate argued, it was unnecessary for the FRG draft hostages convention to deal with hostage taking by national liberation movements.[228] When the Additional Protocols to the Geneva Conventions entered into force, liberation struggles would be regarded as international conflicts to which the prohibition on hostage taking applied. In the meantime, a national liberation struggle would be treated as an armed conflict not of an international character within the meaning of article 3 of the Fourth Geneva Convention. Article 147 of the Fourth Convention regards the taking of hostages as a "grave breach," and thus article 146 of the Fourth Convention would require the prosecution or extradition of hostage takers. Therefore, the taking of hostages in violation of article 3 would obligate a contracting state to prosecute or extradite the hostage taker in accordance with articles 146 and 147 of the Fourth Geneva Convention. However, the FRG delegate did not specifically address the difficult issue of whether articles 146 and 147 can in good faith be applied to violations of article 3, since the latter is generally considered to constitute a "mini-convention" for non-international armed conflict that stands apart from the rest of the Fourth Convention, which applies only to international armed conflict. Arguably this technical distinction could leave a "loophole" for hostage takers who are members of recognized national liberation movements until the Additional Protocols actually come into force.

As far as "state terrorism" was concerned, the German delegate explained that article 1 of the FRG draft hostages convention covered the case of a person who, acting on behalf of a public institution or a state, committed an offense of hostage taking within the terms of the convention.[229] The Mexican delegate subseqently observed that the granting of political asylum to a hostage taker would not prevent prosecution under the terms of the convention.[230] Finally, no member of the Hostages Committee was prepared to argue for the inclusion in a draft hostages convention of a provision explicitly granting a state the right to use force to rescue hostages within the territorial domain of another state when the latter violated the convention. Nevertheless, the delegates were similarly unwilling to adopt proposals specifically denying the right to use force to rescue hostages.[231] However, it did appear that the members of the Hostages Committee would be willing to settle for the inclusion of a general reaffirmation of the principles of the U.N. Charter in the text of the hostages convention. This outcome hinted at a general prohibition against the use of transnational force, but essentially left the seminal question of the Entebbe raid unanswered.

To be sure, such a compromise would avoid a neat positivist resolution of the issue by failing to render a definitive determination of the legality or illegality of hostage rescue operations under international law. Yet insistence upon a clear-cut solution to this abstract problem by either side in the Hostages Committee would have killed the hostages convention in so far as it would have been interpreted by both the opponents and the partisans of the Israeli raid at Entebbe as a *sub silentio* adjudication of the merits of that dispute. All members of the Hostages Committee abstained from a revival of the Security Council debates on the legality of the Entebbe raid precisely in order to avert a breakdown of the Committee proceedings. Instead, they operated on the foundation of the least common denominator among them and drafted a hostages convention on that compromise basis. Hopefully, under the regime of a hostages convention, an Entebbe-like crisis would not recur, and even if one did, it could be dealt with at that time and on its own terms. It would be foolish to defeat an apparent present gain for international law and politics because of a possible future loss or a past concluded tragedy.

The West German Raid at Mogadishu

Progress on a hostages convention was sustained by the sequence of events surrounding the October 13, 1977 hijacking of a Lufthansa airliner with eighty-seven passengers and crew on board over the French Riviera and, after several intermediate stops, its eventual diversion to the Mogadishu airport in Somalia.[232] In return for release of the hostages, the hijackers demanded freedom for eleven members of the Baader-Meinhof gang imprisoned in West Germany and for two Palestinians held in Turkish jails. On October 18, 1977, a West German commando group stormed the aircraft.[233] This special unit had been founded as an anti-terrorism force in the aftermath of the 1972 massacre of Israeli athletes at the Munich Olympic Games,[234] Unlike Entebbe, however, the Mogadishu raid was conducted with the permission of the territorial government;[235] like Entebbe, it was enormously successful. Eighty-six hostages were freed and all hijackers killed.[236] Unfortunately, the pilot of the plane had already been murdered by one of the hijackers in Aden,

Democratic Yemen, where the plane touched down before flying to Mogadishu. [237]

In response to the pilot's murder, the International Federation of Airline Pilots Associations (IFALPA) generally denounced governments for failing to act decisively against hijackers, [238] and threatened to call a two-day strike against worldwide air operations unless forceful action was taken by the United Nations against air piracy. [239] Diplomats and officials at the United Nations attempted to use the momentum generated by the Lufthansa events to stimulate the General Assembly into taking more stringent measures against hijacking and the taking of hostages. [240] In a press conference of October 19, the U.N. secretary-general announced that he had urged the chairman of the Assembly's Sixth Committee to give priority to its discussion of the drafting of an international convention against the taking of hostages. [241] The report of the Hostages Committee was currently before that body for consideration and recommendations to the General Assembly.

On October 21, the U.N. secretary-general, the president of the General Assembly, and the president of the International Civil Aviation Organization (ICAO) met with the president of IFALPA in an effort to forestall the strike. At this meeting, the secretary-general indicated that a special item would be presented to the General Assembly dealing with the safety of international civil aviation. Afterwards, the IFALPA president stated publicly that in view of this assurance, IFALPA had postponed plans for a cessation of international airline operations. On October 25, the General Assembly allocated to its Special Political Committee an additional item entitled "Safety of international civil aviation." The Assembly asked that the item be accorded due priority by the Committee. [242]

Upon recommendation of the Special Political Committee, the General Assembly, on November 3, 1977, adopted by consensus resolution 32/8 on the safety of international civil aviation. [243] In that resolution the Assembly called upon all states to take all necessary steps to prevent acts of aerial hijacking or other wrongful interference with civil air travel. It appealed to all states which had not yet become parties to the Tokyo, Hague, and Montreal Conventions to give urgent consideration to their ratification or accession. It also called upon ICAO to undertake urgently further efforts to ensure the security of air travel, and appealed to all governments to commence serious studies of the abnormal situation relating to hijacking.

The original text of resolution 32/8 was modified to meet objections from Arab and other Third World countries. One modification was specifically directed against Israel. It modified the text to include a statement that actions taken against hijacking should be "without prejudice to the sovereignty or territorial integrity of any State." This language was intended to approve the Mogadishu raid because the Somali government had consented to it, while simultaneously to disapprove the Israeli raid at Entebbe because of the absence of Ugandan consent. After the vote had been taken in the General Assembly, the Israeli delegate, Chaim Herzog, criticized the resolution as a weak compromise with the forces of international terrorism: "The International Pilots Association has been taken for a ride."[244]

Next, on December 16, 1977, the General Assembly adopted resolution 32/147,[245] by a vote of ninety-one in favor to nine against (Australia, Belgium, Canada, Israel, Japan, Luxembourg, Netherlands, United Kingdom, United States), with twenty-eight absentions.[246] The resolution invited the Terrorism Committee to continue its work, first by studying the underlying causes of terrorism, and then by recommending practical measures to combat terrorism. Thus, the General Assembly solved the old problem of priority between these two tasks in favor of those state members of the Terrorism Committee which had strongly advocated the position of national liberation movements.

Nevertheless, on that same day, the General Assembly adopted by consensus resolution 32/148, in which it decided that the Hostages Committee should continue to draft, at the earliest possible date, an international convention against the taking of hostages.[247] Before the vote on the Hostages Committee, however, the Tanzanian delegate stated that the taking of hostages could not be treated in isolation from the phenomenon of international terrorism, and that those delegations willing to compromise on a draft resolution against the taking of hostages were unwilling to do so when it came to the passage of a consensus resolution on international terrorism. If the same obstructionism was displayed in the future, the Tanzanian delegate threatened to call for a vote on the draft resolution against the taking of hostages when the item came up along with the resolution on international terrorism.[248] Fortunately, the Mogadishu crisis had served to renew and strengthen the U.N. Entebbe consensus so that a draft convention against the taking of hostages could proceed on its own accord.

Larnaca and the Second Session of the Hostages Committee

The second session of the Hostages Committee was held from February 6 to 24, 1978, in Geneva, but the Committee still could not agree upon the text of a draft convention. It did recommend that the 33d General

Assembly invite the Hostages Committee to continue its work in 1979.[249] Although progress was made on several draft articles, those issues arising from the status of national liberation movements under a future hostages convention remained unresolved. In order to break the deadlock, the Committee established two working groups. Working Group I was requested to examine the "thornier questions" connected with the drafting of a hostages convention and to try to find some common ground for compromise.[250] Working Group II was requested to deal with draft articles that were not generally controversial and with texts on which Working Group I had come to an agreement.[251]

The chairman of Working Group I identified several issues to focus upon: (1) the scope of the convention and the question of national liberation movements; (2) the definition of taking of hostages; (3) extradition and right of asylum; and (4) respect for the sovereignty and territorial integrity of states with regard to the release of hostages.[252] The report of Working Group I stated that negotiations revolved around the generally agreed principle that the taking of hostages was an act prohibited under international law: "no one should be granted an open license for taking hostages."[253] Even the proponents of safeguards for the right of national liberation movements maintained that they were not suggesting that those movements should be granted the right to take hostages as part of their struggle.[254] They insisted, however, that a clear distinction must be drawn in the convention between genuine activities of national liberation movements and acts of terrorist groups which had nothing in common with them.[255] Although they denied it, this position represented a distinct about-face by supporters of national liberation movements from their position at the first session of the Hostages Committee. There, they had argued that national liberation movements had a right to seize at least a "non-innocent" hostage such as Ian Smith, then prime minister of Rhodesia, or John Vorster, then prime minister of South Africa, as part of their struggle.[256] During the interim between the first and second sessions of the Hostages Committee, delegates from Third World countries had apparently verified the assertion made by the First World members of the Committee that national liberation movements had been prohibited from taking hostages in Additional Protocol One to the 1949 Geneva Conventions.

Within Working Group I there arose the realization that the deadlock over the treatment to be accorded national liberation movements could be broken by the establishment of a "link" between the hostages convention and "other international legal instruments."[257] The concept of a "link" between a hostages convention and the Geneva Convention protocols had been suggested by Syria during the first session of the Hostages Committee.[258] Two distinctive approaches emerged as to how this "link" should be established. A proposal submitted by Mexico at the first session of the Hostages Committee,[259] a modified version of which received the endorsement of Algeria, inter alia, at the second session, would have provided that the hostages convention did not apply to "any act or acts covered by the rules of international law applicable to armed conflicts," which would include legitimate national liberation struggles.[260] On the other hand, First World states suggested that the scope of the hostages convention should be broad enough to encompass all cases of hostage taking and therefore that the provisions of the convention would "supplement" the Geneva Conventions of 1949 and its 1977 Additional Protocols.[261] In that connection, France proposed that the preamble of the hostages convention should include the statement that "the taking of hostages is and must be proscribed always, everywhere and in all circumstances."[262]

The problem of "state terrorism" was disposed of by recognizing that under the proposed convention individual responsibility would arise if a government official of any state committed an act of hostage taking.[263] On the other hand, the questions of the right of asylum and of respect for the sovereignty and territorial integrity of states with regard to the release of hostages were deemed to constitute "minor problems."[264] Related to the problem of asylum, however, was a suggestion that the proposed convention contain a provision similar to article 13 of the Strasbourg Convention allowing refusal of extradition if there were grounds to believe that the request was made for reasons of political, ethnic, or religious persecution.[265] On these issues, too, it seemed that a compromise was possible.

The prospects were bright indeed near the end of the second session of the Hostages Committee for the conclusion of a draft hostages convention. And once again fate intervened to invigorate the mandate of the Hostages Committee and give its work a renewed sense of urgency. For on February 18 and 19, 1978, just prior to the final two meetings of the second session of the Hostages Committee on February 24,[266] the hostage taking at Larnaca airport in Cyprus and the deadly Egyptian rescue operation unfolded toward their tragic denouement.[267] The major concessions discussed above were readily accepted by the members of the Committee at these final meetings in a remarkable spirit of harmonious compromise,[268] and then artfully woven into the textual fabric of the Committee's second report to the General Assembly. Entebbe, Mogadishu, and now Larnaca had all decisively impacted upon international politics and were therefore soon to impact upon the international legal order by redefining international law to include a hostages convention which would, in turn, redefine the contours of international political relations.

The Third Session of the Hostages Committee

On November 29, 1978, the General Assembly adopted by consensus Resolution 33/19, deciding that the Hostages Committee should continue its work and should make every effort to submit a draft convention against the taking of hostages to the 34th General Assembly session.[269] The Hostages Committee held its third session in Geneva from January 29 to February 16, 1979.[270] There it decided to reestablish Working Groups I and II under the same conditions as the previous year.[271] This enabled it to finish its preparation of a draft international convention against the taking of hostages,[272] and in its final report, to recommend the draft convention to the General Assembly for further consideration and adoption.[273]

Of the two alternative concepts for the scope of the convention, the Committee decided to accept textual language that would preclude the application of the draft hostages convention wherever the Geneva Conventions of 1949 or the Additional Protocols of 1977 were applicable to a particular act of hostage taking committed in the course of armed conflicts as defined in the Conventions and Protocols.[274] In effect, the Third World countries prevailed on this point, and the prophecy by the delegate from Democratic Yemen came true. The draft hostages convention would not, as suggested by First World states, "supplement" the Geneva Conventions and Additional Protocols by rendering an act of hostage taking subject to the provisions of both regimes. Nevertheless, the draft convention would serve the purpose of closing the final loophole in international law on hostage taking. The hostages convention would apply to all instances of transnational hostage taking not covered by the Geneva accords.[275]

Language was also adopted in Working Group I to the effect that nothing in the hostages convention shall be construed to justify the violation of the territorial integrity or political independence of a state in contravention of the U.N. Charter.[276] Finally, there was general agreement that the provisions of the hostages convention should not be interpreted to impair the right of asylum.[277] Nevertheless, a grant of asylum by a state party to a hostage taker would not relieve it of the obligation to submit the case to its competent authorities for the purpose of prosecution.[278]

The Hostages Convention and Teheran

The 34th General Assembly referred the draft hostages convention to the Sixth Committee, which substantially upheld the compromises therein. Then once again fate intervened to add momentum to the hostages convention, propelling it successfully through the final stages of the adoption procedure in both the Sixth Committee and the General Assembly. On November 4, 1979, Iranian "student-militants" entered the embassy of the United States in Teheran and seized and detained the U.S. diplomatic staff on the premises.[279] The subsequent course of the Iranian hostages crisis would dramatically illustrate the pressing need for the adoption and ratification of a hostages convention by the General Assembly and its members.

Within the Sixth Committee, the main controversy focused on the text of article 9, which provided that a request for extradition of an alleged offender should not be granted if the requested state party had substantial grounds to believe that the request for extradition had been made for the purpose of prosecuting or punishing a person on account of race, religion, nationality, ethnic origin, or political opinion.[280] Article 9 was eventually adopted by the Sixth Committee by a recorded vote of 103 to 10, with 4 abstentions,[281] Israel and Laos not participating.[282] Solid opposition to article 9 came from the Soviet bloc: Bulgaria, Byelorussia, Cuba, Czechoslovakia, East Germany, Hungary, Mongolia, Poland, Ukraine, and the U.S.S.R.[283] This was pursuant to their long-standing position that the most effective way to deal with hijackers or hostage takers was mandatory return to the state in whose aircraft or territory the violation had been originally committed.[284]

The Sixth Committee then adopted, without vote, a recommendation to the General Assembly that it adopt a draft resolution and annex containing the proposed international convention against the taking of hostages.[285] On December 17, 1979, the General Assembly adopted this as resolution 34/146 without a vote.[286] There was, however, a separate vote on article 9, with 125 in favor, 10 against, and 3 abstentions.[287]

The Hostages Convention and Entebbe

No effort will be made here to analyze the provisions of the Hostages Convention paragraph by paragraph or to compare them with the FRG draft hostages convention or with the terms of the various debates in an attempt to determine their precise meaning or to delineate future problems of interpretation.[288] Once again, that task is part of a legal positivist approach to public international law, and more than one article discharging that duty has appeared in print.[289] It would seem useful, however, to examine from a functionalist perspective the central provisions of the Hostages Convention by reference to the very crisis to which it responded—Entebbe.

Notice first that the Hostages Convention would have applied to the Entebbe situation, since the PLO disavowed the Entebbe operation from the outset.[290] Therefore, even if the First Additional Protocol to the Geneva Conventions of 1949 had already come into force, and the PLO undertook to apply it pursuant to article 96 of the First Protocol,[291] according to article 12 of the Hostages Convention, the provisions of the latter would apply in full.

Article 1 of the Hostages Convention would have defined the crime of "hostage taking" to include the acts of the Entebbe hostage takers and their accomplices. Since responsibility under the convention is imputable to individuals and not to governments, article 1(2)(b) would have rendered Amin guilty as an accomplice of the offense of taking of hostages. Article 2 would have required Uganda to make the offense of hostage taking punishable by appropriate penalties which take into account its grave nature. Article 3 would have obligated Uganda to take all measures it considered appropriate to ease the situation of every hostage, "in particular, to secure his release and, after his release, to facilitate, when relevant, his departure." By article 4, Uganda would have been required to take all practicable measures to prevent preparations within its territory for the Entebbe hostage taking.

Under article 5, Uganda was under a duty to take measures necessary to establish its jurisdiction over the hostage takers and their accomplices. Article 6 would have required Uganda to take them into custody or take other measures to ensure their presence for any criminal or extradition proceedings to be instituted against them. Article 8 would have required Uganda, if it did not extradite the hostage takers, to submit their case to its competent authorities for the purpose of prosecution through proceedings in accordance with its laws "without exception whatsoever." Those authorities must make their decision to prosecute in the same manner as in the case of any ordinary offense of a grave nature under Ugandan law.

Article 9 would have provided an exception to the requirement for extradition of an alleged offender if Uganda had substantial grounds for believing that the request was made for purpose of persecution on account of race, religion, nationality, ethnic origin, or political opinion. Even assuming Uganda had grounds under article 9 to resist an extradition request for the PFLP hostage takers by Israel (which would have had jurisdiction over the offense under articles 5(c) and (d)), it would have been difficult, if not a violation of the Hostages Convention, to invoke article 9 to deny a request for extradition by, inter alia, France (which would have had jurisdiction under article 5(a)), Great Britain (jurisdiction under article 5(d)), or West Germany and Switzerland (jurisdiction under article 5(c)).[292] And even if Uganda granted the Entebbe hostage takers asylum, pursuant to article 8 it still would have been compelled to submit their case to its competent authorities for the purposes of prosecution.

Finally, article 14 states that nothing in the Hostages Convention shall be construed as justifying the violation of the territorial integrity or political independence of a state in contravention of the Charter of the United Nations. An explicit prohibition on the threat or use of force to rescue hostages was not included in the Hostages Convention despite draft provisions to this effect submitted to the Hostages Committee by Third World states.[293] Consequently, the Entebbe raid would not have been precluded by the terms of the Hostages Convention. But neither could Israel have claimed that the Hostages Convention had sanctioned the Entebbe raid. Under the terms of the Convention, that issue would have remained unresolved. The legality or illegality of the Entebbe raid would still have had to be determined in accordance with the terms of public international law described above in Chapter 7 (pp. 83–88) under the concept of *definition*, and, in addition, by reference to the provisions of the Convention itself.

Arguably, the existence of the Hostages Convention at the time of the Entebbe crisis and its gross violation by Uganda might have provided additional impetus for the launching of the Israeli raid. On the other hand, the existence of the Hostages Convention's mandatory requirement of prosecution or extradition of hostage takers might successfully have deterred the PFLP hijacking in the first place, or at least have prevented Ugandan complicity in the hostage taking. In either event, the preexistence of a Hostages Convention would probably have made a substantial difference to the outcome of the Entebbe crisis.

From the perspective of an international legal positivist or of an international political scientist, failure by the Hostages Convention to confront head-on the difficult issue of the legality of hostage rescue operations might be construed to mean that the Convention itself is fatally defective or essentially meaningless for future international crises like Entebbe. Application of a functionalist analysis of international law in time of crisis, however, indicates that this shortcoming is not unduly significant when placed within its overall context. An Entebbe-type rescue operation may be unnecessary in the future precisely because of the existence of the Hostages Convention and, more importantly, because of the profound effects that the entire sequence of events which led to its adoption over the three-and-one-half-year period after Entebbe exercised upon the state members of the international system. The significance for the future of international relations lies not in the precise terms of the Hostages Convention itself, but rather in the solidification of international opinion against the phenomenon of transnational hostage taking. It is that opinion which will serve as the ultimate force for the implementation of the provisions of the Hostages Convention in the future.

The Hostages Convention and the Iranian Hostages Crisis

Within the international community, the longstanding Entebbe consensus against the taking of hostages that had been sustained by Mogadishu and Larnaca and finally codified with the adoption of the Hostages Convention, was to serve a highly useful purpose for the United States government in the promotion of its perceived vital national interests during the course of the Iranian hostages crisis. Entebbe had redefined the contours of international law and international politics prior to Teheran in a manner highly supportive of the American position. By November of 1979, all state members of the international system had accepted the fundamental principle that hostage taking is absolutely prohibited under all circumstances, whether during international war, civil war, wars of national liberation, or times of peace. The Hostages Convention represented the concatenation of international opinion against the phenomenon of transnational hostage taking, and this consensus repeatedly manifested itself in tangible assistance provided to the United States from all quarters (e.g., even by the PLO and Libya) throughout its confrontation with Iran. Here the dialectical interaction between vital national interests and international law demonstrated once again the critical relevance of international law and international organizations to the resolution of even severe international crises and to the preservation of peace and stability throughout the entire system of international relations.

On the domestic level, before the outbreak of the Iranian hostages crisis, it was doubtful whether the United States government would eventually ratify any hostages convention because of domestic opposition to some of its alleged "loopholes" for "terrorists" since it did not "supplement" the Geneva accords as previously explained. Yet in the immediate aftermath of the Iranian hostages crisis, the United States Senate unanimously (98-0) gave its advice and consent to the ratification of the Hostages Convention on July 30, 1981.[294] The Iranian hostages crisis had propelled the end-product of the Entebbe hostages crisis through the difficult and unpredictable U.S. Senate treaty-making procedure.[295] The International Convention against the Taking of Hostages finally entered into force on June 3, 1983.[296]

Part Three of this book will examine in greater detail the interaction between the national and international legal and political dimensions of the Iranian hostages crisis from the functionalist perspective developed above. The Iranian hostages crisis provided dramatic confirmation of the proposition that it is virtually impossible to analyze the phenomenon of international crisis without a sound comprehension of the profound impact international law and organizations exert upon the structure and process of international conflict. It is difficult to understand how any scholarly analyst or governmental decision maker could have prescribed a viable course of conduct for the United States during the Iranian hostages crisis without possessing a thorough training in the rules of international law and the procedures of international organizations for the peaceful settlement of disputes. This is the reason why those American academics who publicly offered creative suggestions for the peaceful resolution of the Iranian hostages crisis were generally public international lawyers of a non-positivist persuasion. The vast majority of commentaries generated by political scientists offered no solution other than the application of brute military force in order to redeem America's illusive national honor.

Within the Carter administration, this dichotomy between international law and Machiavellianism was typified by the diametrically opposed attitudes of Secretary of State Cyrus Vance, a lawyer, and National Security Adviser Zbigniew Brzezinski, a political scientist. The latter's Machiavellian approach only produced the disastrous hostage rescue mission aborted in the Iranian desert. By contrast, the patient continuation of Vance's international law approach by his successor Edmund Muskie ultimately resulted in the safe release of all the hostages. Part Three's analysis of the Iranian hostages crisis will demonstrate the glaring need for international political scientists to overcome their longstanding, inbred, realist prejudices against the relevance of international law and organizations to "high international politics." Only then can they proceed to draw upon the rich body of insights into the nature of international conflicts and the means whereby they can be prevented or controlled already generated by those public international lawyers who have broken out of the international legal positivist paradigm.

II

The Increments of International Law and Politics

Theoretical Propositions concerning the Five Functions
of International Law and Organizations during the
Entebbe Crisis

The state members of the international community have attempted, through the principles of international law and the techniques of international organizations, to redefine the behavioral standards of international politics in order to rectify the deficiencies that Entebbe revealed. This does not mean, however, that transnational hostage-taking crises will never erupt again. They undoubtedly will. Yet their unfortunate recurrence will not prove that this entire experience with international law in time of crisis, from the Entebbe raid to the adoption of the Hostages Convention to Teheran and beyond, is a meaningless exercise demonstrating the futility and essential irrelevance of international law and organizations in crisis situations. This would be the precipitous conclusion of those public international lawyers and international political scientists who consciously or unconsciously pursue a legal positivist approach to the study of international law and politics.

From a functionalist perspective, however, another hostage crisis would not indicate that international law and international organizations had somehow "failed." Likewise, no purpose would be served by elucidating some pseudo-definitive determination of which parties in any future hostages crisis were "right" and "wrong," regardless of how those terms are defined. Instead, a functionalist analysis shifts the focus of attention to the five crucial roles of international law and organizations in time of crisis described above by utilizing the key concepts of (1) definition, (2) decision, (3) adjudication, (4) resolution, and (5) redefinition. A functionalist analysis examines the dynamic interaction between law and politics throughout the course of the crisis, its successes and failures at each stage, and, more importantly, the reasons responsible for the entire process. From that vantage point, a functionalist analysis can then work toward achieving a better knowledge of how the system of international relations can be redesigned to improve its operations in light of these demonstrated strengths and weaknesses.

From a functionalist perspective, therefore, a new crisis must not become an excuse for more professional defeatism, but rather should be treated as an opportunity for more intellectual creativity. It makes no sense to vilify international law and international organizations when they constitute some of the most effective tools available to governmental decision makers for the purpose of both solving an immediate crisis and preventing or controlling similar crises in the future. A functionalist analysis operates upon the fundamental assumption that the main task of government decision makers is to render international law and international organizations even more relevant to international crises than they are currently. That objective is no longer an article of faith. In the strategic nuclear world of the 1980s, it has become an historical imperative.

An international crisis might some day prove to be the penultimate cause for the destruction of the entire system of international relations by precipitating a nuclear exchange between the two superpowers. Therefore, international politics, international law, and international organizations are saliently defective in their mutual inability to deal with the phenomenon of international crisis on a prospective and comprehensive basis, since decision makers continue to rely instead upon ad hoc, improvisational techniques of crisis management. It is essential to prevent or forestall international crises to the maximum extent humanly possible, and to discover the means whereby they can be successfully managed once underway. How this should be done can be determined through an examination of the ways in which past international crises have started, developed, and ended. Hence, it becomes necessary to follow Thucydides' suggestion and employ "an exact knowledge of the past as an aid to the interpretation of the future, which in the course of human things must resemble if it does not reflect it."[297] For this purpose, the following theoretical propositions concerning the five functions played by international law and organizations in time of crisis from the Entebbe raid to the adoption of the Hostages Convention are offered for the reader's consideration:

DEFINITION

1. In time of international crisis, governmental decision makers will define their vital national interests to include considerations of international law and vice versa.

2. In the perceptions of crisis management decision makers, international legal rules not technically binding upon parties to a crisis, yet relevant to its subject matter, will nevertheless be treated as obligatory and acted upon accordingly.

3. An international crisis will generate momentum for the closure of a loophole in the definitional context of international law illustrated by the crisis that can be exploited for this purpose.

DECISION

1. Prior to the time of an international crisis, the institution of a procedure for the routine inclusion in the standard crisis management decision-making team of the cabinet level minister in charge of the government's legal bureaucracy will allow for an effective injection of international legal considerations throughout the course of the crisis management decision-making process.

2. Members of a crisis management team will request the justice minister's opinions on the legality of their proposed courses of conduct, will accept his opinions as correct, and will weigh his opinions together with the diplomatic, military, political, and other factors involved in order to make their decision.

3. Crisis management decision makers will rely upon international law and organizations extensively in order to revolve the crisis in a manner favorable to their interests.

4. A party to an international crisis will not resort to a competent political/legal forum (e.g., the U.N. Security Council) when it does not believe that a peaceful and satisfactory resolution of the dispute is possible there.

5. In time of international crisis, a government will initially pursue those viable options it perceives to be the "least violative" of the international legal order.

6. If a government decides to use violence in an international crisis, force will be employed to the minimum extent perceived to be necessary for the accomplishment of the operation's objectives. (This proposition is actually a corollary to the "least violative" principle since an "economic use" of violence is always required by international law.)

7. Considerations of international law will enter into the decision-

making process of even non-state actors engaged in a violent course of transnational conduct (e.g., so-called international terrorists).

ADJUDICATION

1. The prior existence of a competent political/legal forum for the hearing and adjudication of an international crisis will facilitate its settlement.
2. The types of arguments not made in a political/legal forum will be as significant as the types of arguments that are made.
3. Non-arguments will reveal the presence of a general consensus on fundamental principles among the members of a political/legal forum.
4. Arguments expressed in terms of the existence of rules or the source of reference for rules will prove to be unmanageable within such a political/legal forum during a crisis.
5. Arguments expressed in terms of the inclusivity, priority, interpretation, and application of rules as well as over the facts themselves will prove to be manageable in such a political/legal forum during a crisis.
6. In a political/legal forum, a purely factual argument will estop its proponent from denying the obligatory nature of the rule in reference to which the argument is made.
7. In a political/legal forum the non-adoption of a draft resolution will not necessarily mean the disapproval of the principles contained therein.

RESOLUTION

1. A party to an international crisis will resort to a competent political/legal forum when it believes that a peaceful and satisfactory resolution of the dispute is possible there.
2. In time of international crisis, resort to a competent political/legal forum may provide a party with a face-saving way out of the crisis.
3. In time of international crisis, submission of the dispute by a party to a competent political/legal forum will significantly impair that party's ability to pursue unilateral military action.
4. In time of international crisis, non-action by a competent political/ legal forum can be a form of action itself which legitimizes the status quo.
5. In time of international crisis, a political/legal forum will be unable to institute and maintain a status quo significantly out of line with the merits of the dispute between the parties.
6. In time of international crisis, a successful course of arguably illegal

conduct will more likely be acceptable to a political/legal forum than an unsuccessful course of arguably illegal conduct.

7. A consistent pattern of either successful or unsuccessful political behavior will generate momentum for the creation of international legal rules specifically permitting or prohibiting, respectively, such conduct in the future.

REDEFINITION

1. An international crisis will generate momentum for commencing negotiations within a political/legal forum for the closure of a loophole in the coverage of international law illustrated by the crisis.

2. An international crisis will generate momentum for breaking a preexisting deadlock within a political/legal forum in negotiations over subject matter related to the crisis that can be exploited for this purpose.

3. Negotiations over subject matter related to the crisis will more likely prove successful if they are isolated and divorced from other issues by consignment to their own separate political/legal forum.

4. The types of arguments that are not made in a political/legal forum will be as significant for the progress of such negotiations as the types of arguments that are made.

5. Non-arguments will reveal the presence of a general consensus on fundamental principles among the members of a political/legal forum which will facilitate the progress of the negotiations.

6. Negotiations precipitated by an international crisis will be interpreted by the members of a political/legal forum in reference to that crisis.

7. In negotiations precipitated by the crisis, ambiguous compromises that leave some fundamental issues unresolved will be necessary for progress to occur.

8. A similar international crisis will generate renewed momentum for the progress of the negotiations that can be exploited for this purpose.

9. Negotiations precipitated by an international crisis will make more progress if they are linked to preexisting arrangements already accepted by the members of the political/legal forum.

How to Construct the General Theoretical Model

Quite obviously, this set of theoretical propositions concerning the five functions played by international law and organizations in time of crisis raises more questions than it answers. That is precisely what it is intended to do. In a similar fashion, a series of international crises (such as those occurring in Korea, Suez, Cyprus, Cuba, Congo, Dominican Republic, and Iran) could be used to determine the general validity of each particular theoretical proposition derived from the Entebbe experience. Moreover the theoretical framework of analysis elaborated above can be applied to other crises in the series to derive additional theoretical propositions. These in turn could be tested for the purpose of verification by reference to other crises in the series.

At the conclusion of this process, there will exist a set of theoretical propositions for each crisis whose validity has been tested in reference to the other crises. Those propositions which were verified by a substantial number of crises would be retained in the collection for further analysis, while those which seemed too particularized would be qualified or discarded. The resulting set of theoretical propositions would allow the construction of a general theoretical model for the role of international law and organizations in time of crisis. This would constitute that third stage in the previously described fivefold process of generating (1) descriptive statements, (2) theoretical propositions, (3) a general model, (4) predictive hypotheses, and (5) prescriptive recommendations.

In this regard, consider the "least violative" principle and its "economic violence" corollary described in the set of theoretical propositions derived from the Entebbe crisis:

> In time of international crisis, a government will initially pursue those viable options it perceives to be the least violative of the international legal order.
>
> If a government decides to use violence in an international crisis, force will be deployed to the minimum extent perceived to be necessary for the accomplishment of the operation's objectives.

In addition to Entebbe, the operation of both the "least violative" principle and its "economic violence" corollary can be detected in the Cuban missile crisis. There, among the various alternative courses of conduct considered by the United States government (namely, invasion, surgical airstrike, blockade, and quarantine), it chose to implement a selective quarantine of Cuba with the endorsement of the Organization of American States (OAS). OAS approval testifies to the validity of another Entebbe proposition: "In time of international crisis, a successful course of arguably illegal conduct will more likely be acceptable to a political/legal forum than an unsuccessful course of arguably illegal conduct."

Either the "least violative" principle or its "economic violence" corollary, or both, can also be found at work in, among other international crises, the U.S. intervention in the Korean War and sponsorship of the Uniting for Peace Resolution in the U.N. General Asembly; in the refusal of the United States to support its allies—France and Great Britain—during the 1956 Suez crisis and the establishment of UNEF under the Uniting for Peace procedure; during the U.N. operation in the Congo; throughout the sequence of events surrounding the establishment of UNFICYP; during the U.S. intervention into the Dominican Republic and creation of the Inter-American Peace Force; and in the Iranian hostages crisis. The operation of the Entebbe "success/failure" principle, whereby successful conduct is approved and failures condemned, was prevalent throughout these crises as well.

Thus, at least three theoretical propositions derived initially from the Entebbe crisis are tentatively identified to have functioned conjointly during the course of several other international crises. This coincidence tends to indicate that perhaps each proposition represents part of some characteristic of the interaction between international law and politics in time of crisis which can be accounted for by a fundamental unifying principle. Such a relationship might be expressed in terms of the following theoretical proposition: In time of international crisis, a state's threat or use of force that is arguably but not excessively illegal could very well succeed in terminating the crisis. In other words, a useful solution to an international crisis that is not perfectly legal must nevertheless fall within the penumbra of legality in order to succeed. Conversely, according to the Entebbe "success/failure" principle, the penumbra of legality will afterwards be extended to include successful solutions or contracted to exclude failures.

The Time-lag Phenomenon

Although these hypotheses, if verified by empirical research, might seem disturbing to international legal positivists, they must not become the grounds for despair that international political scientists might disdainfully call them. A functionalist analysis of international law in time of crisis points the direction out of many of the apparent dilemmas created if the "least violative" principle, its "economic violence" corollary, the "success/failure" principle, and the principle of "arguable illegality" turn out to be the operative dynamics of international crises. Since the interaction between international law and international politics is presumed to be dialectical, the process of interaction should take a substantial period of time to work its way through the system of international relations. Consequently, there should exist a significant time lag between the promulgation of new international legal rules on the threat or use of force and state practice in this area. Thus, present state behavior can be expected to conform, not with the current rules of international law concerning the use of force, but rather with the rules that were in existence during the immediately previous, distinct era of international relations—say, before the Second World War. Likewise, the rules of international law concerning the use of force which are in existence today might very well indicate not how states act presently, but how they will behave a generation from now.

The reasons for the existence of this time-lag phenomenon can be derived from the functionalist analysis of international law and organizations in time of crisis. The promulgation of new international legal rules concerning force will *redefine* the international legal and political environment most effectively and completely for the *next* generation of foreign policy decision makers. The rules that today's decision makers negotiate, draft, sign, and ratify may be perceived by them as innovative goals for which one should strive but not necessarily obey in all circumstances. Since those rules are the products of the decision makers' own labor, they are seen to be eminently susceptible to manipulation in order to accomplish self-serving objectives. After all, creators of rules cannot really be expected to possess an overwhelming degree of respect for their own creations.

Yet this inherent degree of disrespect for newly created legal rules disappears among the succeeding generation of international decision makers. They approach these rules as facts of international life given to them by their forebears and sanctified by the passage of time. The successor generation of decision makers should, therefore, be much less inclined to violate these rules than were their creators. The rules which today's decision makers think to be innovative, conditional, and qualified will have become internalized, accepted, and followed as a matter of course by the decision makers of tomorrow. Over the course of a generation or so, international legal rules thought to be essentially *de lege ferenda* (even if codified into treaty form) will be treated as *lex lata* in the practice of international relations.

By definition, then, new international legal rules concerning the use of force will stay at least one generational step ahead of state behavior. It is thus quite inappropriate to expect that states will instantly obey new rules on the threat or use of force. It is more realistic to expect observance of these rules to develop over an extended period of time. So even if today's international legal and political order tolerates a particular form of violent state conduct because it is only arguably illegal, that same behavior will not be tolerated in the future because by then it will have become clearly or egregiously illegal.

How to Test the Predictive Hypotheses

The fourth stage of Part Two's analytical process—suggesting predictive hypotheses—can now be described, albeit somewhat hesitantly. Empirical research should be able to determine whether current state practice roughly conforms with the rules of international law concerning the use of force existing before World War II; whether state behavior during the interwar period coincided with the international legal rules concerning the use of force before World War I; whether state practice during the nineteenth century followed the rules of international law before the French Revolution and Napoleonic Wars; and so on backwards through time until the foundation of the modern system of international law and politics with the Treaty of Westphalia and Grotius. Some research along these lines has already been conducted. Its tentative results appear to support the proposition that at least a generation passes before innovative international legal rules on the use of force are fully internalized and implemented by government decision makers.[298]

The Importance of Prescriptive Recommendations

Verification of such predictive hypotheses through empirical research would lead to the fifth and final stage of the analytical process proposed in Part Two: offering prescriptive recommendations. Such results would tend to indicate that there does indeed exist a great value in the creation of new international legal rules respecting the threat or use of force which are somewhat, but not too far, ahead of current state practice. The adoption of these rules should not lead to the expectation that the states of today's world will adhere to them immediately, but to the belief that nations will basically respect these rules within a generation or so. This is not to suggest that the mere enactment into multilateral treaty form of the Clark-Sohn proposals would permit the international community to sit back and watch as a world government gradually, yet inevitably, comes into being.[299] International law must remain one step ahead of international practice—no more, but certainly no less. Therefore, the codification of current international behavior into positive treaty law is simply not enough. The promulgation of new and realistic rules further limiting the threat or use of force by state and non-state actors is essential.

Perhaps we might not live to experience their benefit, but hopefully the next generation will. For without our strenuous efforts to improve the international legal order today, there might not be a next generation for tomorrow.

Conclusion

It is often the case in foreign affairs decision making that a policy which is based upon sound considerations of international law and organizations typically represents a good and eventually successful policy. However, it is almost invariably the case that a foreign policy decision which violates fundamental principles of international law and organizations constitutes an unsound and unworkable approach that is usually counterproductive in the short-term and ultimately self-defeating over the long-haul course of international relations. This is because the rules of international law and the procedures of international organizations for the peaceful settlement of international disputes actually incarnate the essence of those rights which most members of the international community believe they are entitled to; of those rights which they perceive other states to be entitled to; and of what they think constitutes rational and reasonable international behavior. In the estimation of the vast majority of the international community, when one state flagrantly violates basic principles of international law and organizations, it rudely defeats their expectations and seriously infringes upon their perceived rights. The predictable response is diplomatic, political, and economic opposition, at a minimum, and violent military action, if possible, when deemed required by the gravity of the violation.

From this perspective, the major problem with the great bulk of contemporary literature in the field of international law and organizations becomes its inability to articulate policy prescriptions in a manner that is useful to real-world government decision makers. Instead, most of the literature adopts a legal positivist approach to the subject of international relations that simplistically consists of a sterile, mechanistic determination of the legality or illegality of a proposed or completed course of international deportment. International legal positivists make little effort to explain to government decision makers both why and how obedience to the rules of international law and reliance upon the procedures of international organizations for the peaceful settlement of international disputes clearly falls within the vital national security interests of their respective states, whether considered parochially in terms of advancing their narrow self-interests or expansively in terms of promoting world public order.

Even more seriously, international legal positivism impedes the ability of an analyst to comprehend and operationalize the undeniable fact of international political life that in real-world situations, and especially in times of international crisis, government decision makers must often choose the least bad as good. The primary reason why the legal positivist approach to analyzing international relations proves to be "irrelevant" to international political decision making is because it represents a completely dichotomous and static viewpoint of the world. Rejecting the typical legal positivist approach to international relations, this author would like to postulate the existence of a spectrum of incremental degrees in legality or illegality for the purpose of analyzing international political behavior.

A functionalist perspective would distinguish between seven degrees of state behavior by reference to international law: conduct which is (1) egregiously illegal; (2) clearly illegal; (3) arguably illegal; (4) arguably illegal or legal; (5) arguably legal; (6) clearly legal; and (7) perfectly legal. Moreover, functionalism does not premise that there exist hard and fast dividing lines between any two of these degrees, but instead that each degree imperceptibly shades off into its immediate neighbors along this continuum of international deportment. Finally, a functionalist analysis can better take account of the fact that it is also possible for a particular policy (P) to become more or less legal or illegal over time (T). These two contending approaches to conceptualizing the relationship between international law and politics can be schematically illustrated by means of the diagrams in Figure 1.

As can be seen from comparing these graphic representations of positivism and functionalism, a legal positivist approach prevents an analyst from making any discriminations between degrees of legality or illegality for the purpose of evaluating the propriety of a particular foreign policy decision and, consequently, from discerning any gradual improvement in or deterioration of the policy during the course of its development. From a legal positivist perspective, a foreign policy decision is either legal or illegal, once and for all time. International political decision making cannot realistically be conducted on the basis of such a completely dichotomous and static viewpoint of the world, especially during a severe international crisis.

By contrast, application of a functionalist analysis can delineate several points of choice at key moments in time during the historical development of a foreign policy decision-making process where a serious examination of the rules of international law and the procedures of international organizations for the peaceful settlement of disputes might very

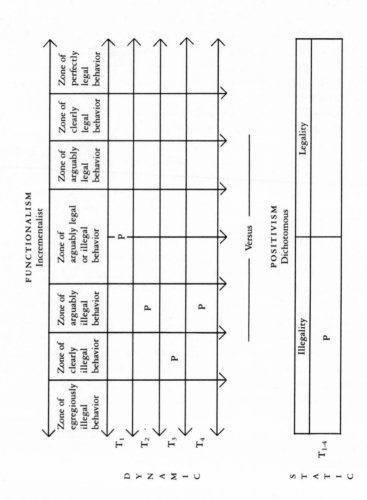

Figure 1.

well produce better and more successful policies. A functionalist analysis could indicate to government decision makers that some contemplated policies are better or worse than others; that some proposed policies should be rejected out of hand; and that other policy options should be vigorously pursued. A functionalist analysis would enable government decision makers to select that policy or combination of policies which could move their decision-making process along this incremental spectrum of legality/illegality in the direction away from egregious illegality and towards perfect legality. This policy selection would occur not in the expectation that the latter objective could in fact be achieved in the foreseeable or even distant future, but in the belief that government decision makers could and should promote policies that are more lawful, when possible, or at least less illegal, when necessary, over those which are less lawful or more illegal, respectively. In this manner a functionalist approach to foreign policy decision making could constitute a sound, coherent, and consistent government strategy for formulating a more successful foreign policy either during the course of an international crisis or over the long run of international relations.

Unlike a legal positivist approach to international relations, adoption of a functionalist analysis permits such incremental judgments to be made and therefore prepares the way for gradual improvements in foreign policy decision making to occur. A functionalist analysis can provide a mechanism for generating progressive movement out of many of the difficult predicaments that confront contemporary international political decision makers. Describing how that process can be performed will become the task of the third and final part of this book. Part Three will delineate precisely why and how international law and organizations could have been used more effectively by the U.S. government as the basis for conducting its foreign policy during a series of major international crises beginning with and precipitated by the Iranian hostages crisis. If U.S. government decision makers had paid more serious attention to considerations of international law and organizations from 1979 through 1984, an entire series of severe international crises could have been avoided in the first place, or else more effectively managed from the outset. A functionalist analysis of the relationship between international law and politics could have forestalled the perilous state of international relations as of today.

Part Three

*International Law and Organizations
as a Basis for Conducting
American Foreign Policy*

A New Philosophy for American Foreign Policy

The Death of Power Politics

Power politics as a philosophy of international relations is dead. Its demise was publicly decreed by its modern founder, Hans Morgenthau, in a stunning lecture delivered in May of 1978, some two years before his own death, as recounted above in Chapter 5. Morgenthau declared that power politics must be replaced as the intellectual basis for the conduct of American foreign policy decision making because ultimately its continued pursuit will only instigate a suicidal third world war with the Soviet Union. Nevertheless, the utility of power politics is still proclaimed by Morgenthau's numerous disciples and famous protégés, the foremost of whom is Henry Kissinger,[1] mentor to former Secretary of State Alexander Haig. When at the outset of the Reagan administration they lamented the dire need for a "geopolitical" approach to foreign affairs, one premised on a "grand theory" or "strategic design," they meant no more but certainly no less than a theory of power politics. Suffice it to say here that a succinct recapitulation of its cardinal principles can be found in Machiavelli's *The Prince*. For what such "political realists" pass off to an unwitting world as "pragmatic" solutions to the complex problems of contemporary international affairs consist essentially of a highly refined and superficially rationalized Machiavellianism updated to and qualified by the stark and brutal realities of global strategic nuclear warfare.

According to this "political realist" school, nothing essential has changed since Thucydides first articulated the cardinal principles of power politics some 2,500 years ago in the Melian Dialogue.[2] There,

Thucydides argued that in situations of unequal power distribution between states in time of incessant warfare, considerations of justice must be deemed irrelevant by foreign policy decision makers, for without life itself such an intangible and transcendent value is meaningless. Nevertheless, one implication of this passage is that in a non-belligerent situation, where the major international actors possess a rough equivalence of military power and thereby establish a "balance of power" between them, considerations of justice do and should come into play. It follows that in peacetime an effective balance of military power between major international actors could indeed support and sustain an effective system of international law and organizations for the peaceful settlement of disputes in order to forestall the development of a general systemic war. On the other hand, the collective pursuit of power politics by states during peacetime will only produce the self-fulfilling prophecy of war.

If Thucydides was the first teacher of power politics, then Machiavelli was the atypical student genius who carried his master's lessons to such logically extreme conclusions that they would have been spiritually objectionable to the teacher himself if given the opportunity for further reflection. Here Stanley Hoffmann's classic distinction between "moderate" and "revolutionary" international political systems becomes relevant,[3] for they each find their respective philosophical counterparts in the theories of power politics propounded by Thucydides and Machiavelli. Thucydides' *The Peloponnesian War* is the treatise for a relatively moderate theory of power politics in comparison to Machiavelli's *The Prince*. The latter reads like a revolutionary manifesto for the most radical version of power politics known to Western philosophical thought.

The differences in degree of intensity between the two authors are attributable to their contradictory attitudes toward the concept of the "balance of power" and the ability of man's free will to change historical conditions.[4] Thucydides believed that man must resign and accommodate himself to the inevitability of the balance of power system in order to survive. By contrast, Machiavelli argued that the prince must destroy the balance of power system completely in order to achieve historical glory even if he perishes in the process.

In *The Prince*, Machiavelli called for the complete destruction of the status quo in Renaissance Italy, which had assumed the form of a rough "balance of power" between competing political units that kept the peninsula in a condition of internecine warfare. Machiavelli wanted one Italian prince ruthlessly to consolidate his internal position, then to unite Italy by conquest of her disparate city-states, and finally to liberate her from foreign interventionists in order to establish a second Roman

Empire.[5] Machiavelli sought to replace Italy's internal balance of power system with what contemporary international political scientists call a "directive [i.e., authoritarian] hierarchical system."[6] Modern theorists of power politics correctly understand, however, that the probability of "total warfare" in an advanced industrial and nuclear age precludes taking Machiavellian power politics to the logical conclusion of universal hegemony. Restraint is the only alternative to thermonuclear suicide. So instead of preaching the Machiavellian destruction of the international balance of power, modern "political realists" assert the fundamental importance of maintaining the balance of power system for the preservation of world peace. In a nuclear world the balance of power has become an historical imperative to which the Machiavellian pursuit of power politics must accommodate itself. The implementation of Machiavellianism by a government in its conduct of foreign affairs must therefore occur only within the confines and for the express purpose of "upholding" or "restoring" the balance of power itself.[7]

The principal (and fatal) defect of modern "realist" theory is its supposition that Machiavellianism can actually be subordinated to the objective of preserving a balance of power system. This handmaiden of foreign policy decision making will ineluctably become its master. By its very nature, Machiavellian power politics requires the employment of violence against putative adversaries in order to achieve ultimate objectives. This dictate traps governments into an interminable cycle of force and counterforce from which mankind cannot escape except by thermonuclear destruction. Machiavellianism's presumed need for states to engage in the threat and use of force creates an insoluble set of problems for the conduct of foreign affairs in regard to both the short-term issues confronting governmental decision makers and to the long-haul course of international relations. For either prospect Machiavellian power politics is a suicidal proposition.

From a long-term perspective, power politics tends to undermine the balance of power system because it demands of states the constant threat and use of force in their mutual relations. Even a "moderate" theory of international power politics prescribes the purposeful institution of hostilities between major actors, perhaps a systemic war itself, in order to "uphold" or "restore" the balance of power.[8] Machiavellian power politics and war are essentially inseparable phenomena precisely because Machiavellianism amounts to nothing more sophisticated than a flimsy philosophical justification and transparent psychological rationalization for pursuing a foreign policy that basically consists of waging a permanent and universal war of aggression.[9]

Of course, modern theorists of power politics reject the inevitability of war by postulating the existence of some sort of "invisible hand" that will miraculously maintain the balance of power system by ensuring that states' recourse to violence will somehow fall short of global nuclear war because of overwhelming considerations of rational self-interest. This assumption naively relies on the alleged ability of governments to control their international political environment and nuclear weapons systems. The Machiavellian modern man possesses too much faith in his own rationality, too much trust in the strength of his intellect, and too much conviction in the power of his free will to manipulate men and machines for the good of his own survival. Today's foreign policy decision makers must adopt a more Thucydidean respect for the impersonal forces of history that severely limit the ability of man's free will to determine his own fate. Otherwise, humankind will succumb to a combination of its technological perfections and Machiavellian predilections.

In the short-term perspective, Machiavellian power politics offers no truly substantive prescriptions for the day-to-day conduct of foreign affairs. Despite its claim to be a "grand theory" of international relations, power politics simply recommends a series of ad hoc calculations of national self-interest and power aggrandizement at the direct expense of other states in order to win the supposed "zero-sum game"[10] of international relations. Power politics provides no indication of how these decisions should be integrated into a unified, coherent, and consistent policy except for its vacuous injunction that the "balance" must be "preserved" at all costs. Because of its impracticability, therefore, power politics must be rejected as a theory for the conduct of foreign policy. Yet the reality of power must never be ignored in the formulation of a constructive alternative.

The Alternative of International Law and Organizations

One viable alternative to power politics as a basis for the conduct of international relations by the United States can be found in the principles of international law and the procedures of international organizations for the peaceful settlement of international disputes. Adherence to the rules of international law is consistent with American national security interests whether considered expansively in terms of furthering world public order or parochially in terms of satisfying selfish policy goals. The classic Machiavellian dichotomy between the "is" and the "ought to be" does not hold true for American foreign policy decision making.[11] That which is expedient and that which is just coincide and reinforce each other.

This situation exists because the United States is the outstanding example of a status quo power in the post–World War II system of international relations. By virtue of its victory in that war, the preservation of the resulting political, economic, and military status quo is to American advantage. America's national security interests are best served by obedience to international law as a policy for itself as well as other states because such conformity upholds the status quo. To the degree a state enjoys the benefits of the existing configuration of international relations, the greater should be its commitment to upholding international law and to the creation of effective international organizations for the peaceful settlement of disputes.

Phenomenologically, law is the instrument par excellence for the peaceful preservation and transformation of any political or economic status quo, whether domestic or international. By its very nature, the international legal order represents an attempt by advantaged international actors to legitimate (i.e., to impart a moral value content to), preexisting and proposed power relationships. A fundamental transformation in the international balance of power produced by systemic warfare results in the creation of new international law and organizations, which in turn endow these new power relationships with a connotation of moral value. Conversely, a change of international moral values (e.g., self-determination of peoples) produces new international law and organizations (e.g., U.N. General Assembly resolutions and committees to promote decolonization), which in turn transform the existing international balance of power (e.g., the creation of a plethora of new states). Throughout this dialectical process, the rules of international law and the institutions of international organizations play the key role of intermediating agent between power and politics, on the one hand, and values and morality, on the other.

For these reasons, this author has emphatically rejected the reigning international legal positivist doctrine that there actually exists some radical phenomenological dichotomy between politics, law, and morality. In Part Two of this book, I have argued instead that there persists a process of dynamic interaction between international politics and international law, whereby the former continuously is and becomes the latter and vice versa. From such a "functionalist" perspective, moral value considerations are yet another element of this dialectical process that constitutes the essence of international political relations.

Because of their inherent propensity for successfully performing such a mediative role for the entire international system, international law and organizations can function as superlative instruments for the peaceful preservation and transformation of the international political and economic status quo even among international actors striving to realize their different and at times diametrically opposed national interests and moral values. International law enunciates those rules which the actors in the international system have found to constitute the least common denominator for that which is both essential and valuable for international life. And that which is both essential and valuable for international life becomes embodied in the rules of international law.

The principles of international law and the existence of international organizations for the peaceful settlement of disputes create a median way between the idealism of human values and aspirations and the reality of disparate power and economic conditions for all states in the international system. There is no realistic alternative for any state on the face of this planet to protect its vital national interests and to promote its cherished national values with due respect for the right of all other states to do the same. Whatever the defects of the contemporary international legal order might be, its improvement is far preferable to the pursuit of Machiavellian power politics, the threat and use of force, and nuclear war. The U.S. government must become the first to re-recognize the critical relevance of international law and organizations for the continued preservation of world peace.

The Relevance of International Law to Crisis Management Decision Making

One corollary to this thesis is that in time of international crisis, the government of a leading status quo state such as the United States should not rely upon dubious international legal principles such as retaliation, retorsion, reprisal, military intervention, counter-intervention, humanitarian intervention, self-help, etc. as a basis for its conduct of crisis management decision making. These alleged principles of customary international law are relics of nineteenth century "gunboat diplomacy" that were inflicted by the world's major imperial powers upon militarily inferior international actors and coveted colonial territories, but which have now been almost universally discredited in the post–U.N. Charter era.[12] Nevertheless, in the late twentieth century, the validity of some of these principles is still stubbornly insisted upon by the great powers and their allies. Yet because of the fundamental transformation in the nature of the international system that has occurred since the mid-nineteenth century, it is precisely these status quo states that should be working most assiduously towards the complete extinction of such retrogressive principles from the recognized corpus of public international law and the established patterns of interstate behavior. When major status quo powers threaten or use force for reasons not explicitly sanctioned by contemporary standards of international law that have been formally accepted by all states of the world community, they undermine the integrity of that very international legal order which they have constructed to protect their vital national interests in the first place. Consequently, those states that currently reap and possess the major benefits of international relations should not unwittingly endeavor to lose them through resort to or encouragement of illegitimate violence and coercion by themselves and others.

In the modern world of international relations, the only legitimate justifications and procedures for the perpetration of violence and coercion by one state against another are those set forth in the U.N. Charter. The Charter alone contains those rules which have been consented to by the virtual unanimity of the international community that has voluntarily joined the United Nations Organization. Therefore, in times of international crisis, a major status quo power such as the United States must in good faith exercise its own threats or use of transnational force in strict accordance with the exact conditions prescribed by the United Nations Charter. These include and are limited to the right of individual and collective self-defense in the event of an "armed attack" as prescribed by article 51; "enforcement action" by the U.N. Security Council as specified in chapter 7; "enforcement action" by the appropriate regional organizations acting with the authorization of the Security Council as required by article 53 and specified in chapter 8; and the so-called peacekeeping operations organized under the jurisdiction of the Security Council pursuant to chapter 6, or under the auspices of the U.N. General Assembly in accordance with the Uniting for Peace Resolution,[13] or by the relevant regional organizations acting in conformity with their proper constitutional procedures and subject to the overall supervision of the U.N. Security Council as specified in chapter 8 and articles 24 and 25.

For a leading status quo power such as the United States to threaten or use force on the basis of alleged justifications derived from antiquated and oppressive principles of customary international law ruthlessly practiced in a relatively primitive and essentially colonialist era of international relations risks generating a tremendous degree of political, economic, and military opposition from both the intended victim and all those states that share in common with it a history of repeated victimization by means of the same set of transparent pretexts for imperialistic intervention, occupation, and exploitation. Such a neo-imperialist policy also risks either nonexistent or minimal support from, or else outright opposition by, America's allied major status quo states acting in sympathy with such victims because the former have finally realized the need to eliminate the last vestiges of their own imperial behavior from the contemporary system of international relations after having experienced its pernicious consequences for themselves. It therefore lies within the vital national interest of a leading status quo power such as the United States for its crisis management decision makers to adopt and firmly adhere to an almost irrefutable presumption against any threat or use of force that does not squarely fit within the extremely few and severely restricted justifications and procedures for transnational violence and coercion set forth in the United Nations Charter. Thus, rather than relying upon doctrinal relics of the colonial past, or inventing novel international legal artifices (e.g., Kennedy's "quarantine" of Cuba), American foreign policy decision makers must restore the Charter as the fundamental operative premise for both the management of international crises and the overall conduct of its international affairs.

The Asymmetries of International Law and Politics

The continued invocation of these outmoded and dangerous principles of customary international law purporting to justify transnational violence and coercion by the government of a leading status quo power such as the United States demonstrates its subliminal attachment to an interconnected set of formal legal propositions. These principles are: (1) that the rules of international law should operate in a perfectly symmetrical manner upon equal and independent sovereign states in their mutual relations; and (2) that the normal condition of strict reciprocity in legal obligations between equal and independent sovereign states generally counsels derogation from a fundamental norm of international law by the government of one state in the event of a prior violation directly affecting it by another sovereign. These basic assumptions of equality, symmetry, and reciprocity in state behavior usually serve their intended purpose of facilitating the routine of day-to-day international relations. But in times of severe international crises, they can quickly prove to be totally dysfunctional for the purpose of crisis management decision making.

Admittedly, it is an elementary principle of international law that all states must be treated as equal and independent since each is sovereign within its own territorial domain. Even though this precept drastically departs from the glaring political, military, and economic inequalities of international life, the doctrine propounding the sovereign equality of states is essential to the preservation of world peace. It impedes the strong from inflicting unbridled depredation on the weak and thus forestalls a cataclysmic struggle among the strong over the division and conquest of the weak.

Nevertheless, although all states are, by definition, equal under international law, they do not all benefit equally from the rules of international law. The major status quo powers in today's world obtain comparatively greater benefits from the current international legal order because, in the aftermath of the Second World War, they possessed the overwhelming degree of political, military, and economic power requisite to promulgate and impose rules designed to operate to their distinct advantage. Thus, the international legal order is an inherently asymmetrical system. It functions to the proportionate advantage of states to the degree they benefit from the existing political, military, and economic status quo. And leading status quo powers such as the United States have the greatest stake in upholding the integrity of the extant international legal order.

It follows, then, that a violation of an international legal rule by a minor state against a leading status quo power must not be treated by the latter as a sufficient condition for the responsive use of transnational violence and coercion (e.g., retaliation, retorsion, reprisal, intervention, self-help, etc.) in order to protect, assert, or enforce its alleged rights. If the victim of the violation enjoys a greater relative advantage than the violator in the maintenance of the status quo and thus the preservation of the international legal order, the government of the victim state must consider the long-term detrimental effects its arguably unjustifiable counterviolation will inflict on the stability of the entire international system. As a general proposition I should like to suggest that the damage to both its own national security interests and to the international legal, political, and economic status quo resulting from a counterviolation of international law by a leading status quo power almost invariably far outweighs any harm to either that might arise from both the original violation of international law by a minor state together with the supposed harm that might occur from the great power victim not unilaterally prosecuting its rights through illegitimate transnational violence and coercion. In this sense, then, a leading status quo power would be wise to follow Socrates' advice that it is better to suffer injustice than it is to inflict injustice,[14] in the event of an offense perpetrated upon it by a minor state. This conclusion recommends that major status quo states such as the United States rely exclusively on the panoply of rules, techniques, and institutions afforded by the contemporary international legal order for the peaceful settlement of their disputes with minor states.

This recommendation is further strengthened by the observation that the international legal order simultaneously consists of elements and processes of both distributive justice and rectificatory justice as classically defined by Aristotle in book 5 of *The Nicomachean Ethics*.[15] It is fundamentally unfair, transparently hypocritical, and ultimately self-defeating for a major status quo state in conflict with a minor adversary to insist upon its alleged right to rectificatory justice by means of retaliation, retorsion, reprisal, intervention, or self-help when the distributive elements and processes of the international system—whether pertaining to political power, economic wealth, or military might—are already overwhelmingly apportioned and inexorably operating to the former's distinct advantage. In a system of unequally distributed power, it becomes foolish for decision makers in a major status quo state stubbornly to insist upon fulfillment of the punctilio of rectificatory justice in regard to their claims, while at the same time they blithely ignore the claims of a distributive (and rectificatory) nature advanced by a minor adversary. As will be demonstrated herein, exclusive reliance upon a rectificatory and positivistic approach to international law and organizations by the United States government throughout the Iranian hostages crisis produced a series of unmitigated disasters for American foreign policy, undermined the integrity of the international legal order, and set back the cause of world peace.

International Law and Machiavellianism

Of course this line of analysis should not lead a major status quo power such as the United States to tolerate behavior violative of elementary norms of international law directed against it or any other state by another great power such as the Soviet Union, or by another major power against a minor state. Such fundamentally disruptive conduct by a powerful actor must be resisted by all states acting in accordance with the rules, institutions, and techniques of the international legal order. If utilized intelligently this integrated collection of remedies should prove sufficiently flexible and effective to accomplish successfully the task of ultimately defeating grievous threats to or breaches of international peace and security. It would be a serious mistake, however, for a leading status quo state such as the United States to respond to an alleged Machiavellian assault on the status quo by a great power adversary such as the Soviet Union through the counterpractice of Machiavellian power politics either against the latter or against some minor third state supposedly aligned with the Soviet Union, like Cuba. Yet just such a Machiavellian response was exactly what the Reagan administration officially advocated under its euphemistic doctrine known as "horizontal escalation."

The United States has a far greater stake than either the Soviet Union or any of its allies in maintaining the integrity of the international legal system in order to preserve the existing political, military, and economic status quo still substantially weighted in America's favor. So long as there persists a rough equivalence of military power between the two nuclear superpowers and their respective alliance systems, the counterpractice of Machiavellian power politics by the United States and allied major status quo states weakens and eventually destroys the effectiveness of the entire system of international law and organizations that they established after the Second World War for the express purpose of preserving a favorable status quo in the first place. The use by leading status quo powers of Machiavellian power politics will either completely eliminate or else magnitudinally decrease the tremendous advantages afforded to them by reliance instead on the strength of the contemporary international legal order.

Even Machiavelli himself quite perceptibly observed that the two principal foundations of all states must consist of good laws and good armed forces.[16] A government committed to the preservation of the status quo must learn how to "fight" by means of the law.[17] For the status quo state in today's international political system, the wisdom of the fox is just as important as the strength of the lion.[18]

It is beyond the scope of Part Three to elaborate a comprehensive manner in which American foreign policy decision makers can utilize international law and organizations to conduct international relations on a day-to-day basis. One fruitful step in this direction, however, would be to apply the foregoing considerations to develop a "functionalist" analysis of the crises over Iran, Afghanistan, Cuba, and the SALT II Treaty which marked the latter half of President Jimmy Carter's administration. This examination will illustrate several "points of choice"[19] in which a greater degree of sensitivity to the requirements of international law and a more heightened awareness of the potential of international organizations for the peaceful settlement of disputes by the Carter administration either could have avoided these crises or have substantially contributed to their more effective management and successful termination.

Too many legal and political analysts deduced the wrong "lessons" from these crises for application to the future conduct of American foreign policy by the Reagan administration. When it came to foreign affairs, President Carter certainly did not manifest the wisdom of the fox, and undoubtedly Machiavelli would have classified him into that third category of princes who are "useless" because they neither understand things on their own nor perceive what their advisers understand.[20] Yet the Reagan administration improperly concluded that the correct antidote to Carter's shortcomings was exclusive reliance on prodigious display of the lion's strength in international relations. If this viewpoint is permitted to pass unchallenged, a different but no less dangerous set of international crises (e.g., Lebanon, Central America, Cuba, Persian Gulf) seems destined to afflict U.S. foreign policy. Like the Iranian hostages crisis, they will, to a great extent, be the products of American, not foreign, manufacture. Conversely, if the correct "lessons" of these previous crises are articulated now they can provide a workable guide for sorting out the monumental disarray in American foreign policy that chronically plagued the Reagan administration from the outset. This book will develop an analytical framework for these crises on the basis of international law and organizations that eschews the intellectual defects of both the Carter approach and the Reagan anti-Carter approach to international relations.

The Definitional Context of the Iranian
Hostages Crisis

International Terrorism

The Iranian hostages crisis did not begin with the seizure of the U.S. diplomats in Teheran in November 4, 1979. Instead, it was precipitated by President Carter's decision to admit the deposed Shah of Iran into the United States for medical treatment readily available elsewhere,[21] contrary to advice by his advisers and intelligence services,[22] and in full awareness that seizure of the embassy and the detention of its personnel would be a likely reaction.[23] The president's exculpatory explanation that he had relied on Iranian Prime Minister Mehdi Bazargan's prior assurance of protection for the embassy is unconvincing. It was obvious at the time that Bazargan exerted little control over the government itself, then under the domination of the Revolutionary Council led by Ayatollah Ruhollah Khomeini, let alone over the various revolutionary factions that roamed the streets of Teheran. Bazargan was a figurehead and his government a mere chimera in light of Khomeini's then unofficial authority.

For example, on February 14, 1979, the U.S. embassy in Teheran had been seized by members of the Communist Tudeh Party and of the People's Fedayeen. After a three-hour mêlée, the seizure terminated with the arrival of forces loyal to Khomeini as requested by U.S. Ambassador William Sullivan.[24] President Carter should never have counted on the recurrence of a similar fortunate outcome when, some eight months later, he decided to admit the Shah into the United States.

From this perspective, the public debate during the 1980 presidential election campaign concerning the means whereby the U.S. government should deter future instances of "international terrorism" launched against it akin to Teheran was completely misdirected. No amount of legal, political, economic, or military deterrence can prevent a severe crisis in relations with another country when the president of the United States willfully provokes the crisis in the first place. The most effective deterrent to presidential instigation of another hostage-taking crisis like Iran will hopefully prove to be the overwhelming rejection of President Carter by the American people on November 4, 1980.

The incoming Reagan administration's subsequently proclaimed intention to replace President Carter's emphasis on "human rights" with a "war" against "international terrorism" (e.g., renewed military and economic assistance for the then repressive regimes in Argentina, Guatemala, and Chile, or "destabilization" of Colonel Qaddafi in Libya) as the keystone of its foreign policy should have been seriously reexamined and ultimately repudiated. "Terrorism" is a vacuous and amorphous concept entirely devoid of an accepted international legal meaning, let alone an objective political referent. The standard cliché that one man's "terrorist" is another man's "freedom fighter" is not just a clever obfuscation of values. It indicates that the international community has yet to agree upon a legal or political definition for the term "terrorism."[25] This pejorative and highly inflammatory term has been used by the governments of the United States, Great Britain, the Soviet Union, and Israel, inter alia, to characterize acts of violence ranging from common crimes to legitimate wars of national liberation recognized by the appropriate international organizations. Invoking a holy war against "international terrorism" may constitute effective governmental propaganda to manipulate public opinion in support of a foreign policy premised on considerations such as Machiavellian power politics,[26] but it cannot serve as the basis for conducting a coherent and consistent global foreign policy in a manner that protects and advances a state's legitimate national security interests in accordance with the requirements of international law.

The Myth of Intelligence Failure

Blaming events in Southwest Asia on alleged U.S. intelligence failures was likewise misconceived. Despite President Carter's public wrist-slapping charade played out with C.I.A. Director Stansfield Turner,[27] there never really was a failure by U.S. intelligence agencies to predict the ouster of the Shah.[28] The Carter administration apparently invented the fiction of "intelligence failure" in order to avoid assuming direct political responsibility for failing to act more vigorously to prevent the Shah's downfall. That decision could and should have been publicly

defended on its merits alone without resort to such a potentially dangerous subterfuge. Consequently, there was no need for the Reagan administration to "unleash"[29] the C.I.A. from those restrictions on its operations drawn up following the revelation of its commission of a gross
pattern of foreign and domestic abuses by the Rockefeller Commission
Report[30] and the Senate committee investigations under the chairmanship of Frank Church.[31]

This concocted myth of "intelligence failure" should never have been
allowed to serve as a pretext for the imposition of additional obstacles in
the way of private citizens or the press to investigate and expose C.I.A.
malfeasance (e.g., the proposal for the C.I.A.'s complete exemption from
the Freedom of Information Act,[32] the Intelligence Identities Protection
Act[33]) or to free the C.I.A. and the F.B.I. to engage in practices of
dubious constitutionality within the United States on the alleged grounds
that they concern foreign intelligence activities or the war against "international terrorism." Nor must the claim of intelligence failure be allowed
to justify the renaissance of covert interventions abroad (e.g., abrogation
of the Clark Amendment[34] prohibiting covert intervention in Angola, or
violations of the Boland Amendment that prohibited U.S. support for
paramilitary operations to overthrow the Sandinista government in Nicaragua[35]), undertaken in express violation of international law.[36] Such
activities not only work to the detriment of the international legal rights
and human dignity of alien peoples, but undermine the civil liberties of
American citizens both at home and abroad.[37] They thus subvert the very
foundations of the American constitutional system of government based
upon the rule of law. From this perspective, the Executive Order on
United States Intelligence Activities signed by President Reagan on
December 4, 1981,[38] which revoked President Carter's Executive Order
12036 on the same subject,[39] represented an unfortunate retrograde
step. Because of its demonstrative susceptibility to abuse, the president's
discretionary control over the Central Intelligence Agency should finally
be codified by congressional enactment of a formal legislative charter
applicable to all U.S. intelligence agencies and activities.

The Deportation of Innocent Iranian Students

Similar criticism applies to President Carter's decision to expel from the
country those Iranian students found to be violating their visa requirements.[40] Unfortunately, the president seemed to possess the appropriate
combination of statutory and constitutional authorization necessary to
effectuate this unjust, unfair, and discriminatory policy on his own

accord.[41] This decision aimed to satisfy the American public's insistence that the government do something to express outrage at the injustices perpetrated in Teheran by the students' cohorts.[42] Any attempts to justify Carter's decision by arguing that deportation created a safety valve for the relief of public pressure to use military force against Iran must fail. The Carter administration allowed, if it did not encourage, American public opinion to work itself up into a collective furor over the incident in the first place.

As a matter of sound constitutional policy, the U.S. government should never carry out a large-scale deprivation of someone's civil liberties in the mistaken belief that this will permit it to achieve any foreign policy objectives. In the case of these Iranian students, vicarious retribution inflicted upon a selected group of innocent aliens undermined the basic exercise of civil liberties by all Americans. Especially in times of severe international crises, rather than the simplistic rally-round-the-president phenomenon that this country has so tragically yet repeatedly witnessed, the exercise of civil liberties by citizens and aliens alike is essential to restrain governmental folly and illegality. Legislation should be enacted prohibiting the president from ever again selecting out a group of aliens peacefully residing in this country for purposes of political persecution or manipulation. Just as the United States has come to regret the internment of Japanese-Americans during the Second World War, someday America may hope for eventual repentance of its deportation of these innocent Iranian students.

U.S. Intervention Abroad

Because the promise for a full-scale congressional investigation of the Iranian hostages crisis remains unfulfilled, all the facts surrounding President Carter's decision to admit the Shah into the United States have yet to be exposed. The publicly stated reason was that somehow "we owed it to him" for humanitarian reasons because he had proved himself to be a valued and faithful ally.[43] Carter allegedly undertook that "humanitarian" decision on the basis of a medical report concerning the Shah's condition submitted to the White House by a doctor in the employ of David Rockefeller, then chairman of the Chase Manhattan Bank, which had a vested economic interest in the cultivation of the Shah's well-being.

Carter's rationale also ignored a consistent pattern of gross violations of those fundamental human rights recognized by the Universal Declaration of Human Rights[44] (affirmed, ironically enough, by the 1968 Proclamation of Teheran[45]), committed by the Shah's secret police organization (SAVAK)[46] against the Iranian people, with the assistance of the American C.I.A.[47] On a level of pure American national self-interest, Carter's rationale overlooked the Shah's role as a leading price-hawk within the Organization of Petroleum Exporting Countries (OPEC), whereby enormous oil revenues enabled the Shah to construct a military establishment far beyond Iran's legitimate security needs. This was accomplished in part for the express purpose of intimidating Persian Gulf countries through threats of force, covert intervention, and outright aggression,[48] all in violation of article 2(4) of the U.N. Charter.[49] In this endeavor the Shah was encouraged by the so-called Nixon Doctrine,[50] whereby regional surrogates were intended to help the United States "police" its spheres of influence throughout the world and thus shoulder their proper share in its so-called "burdens" of peace. The Shah was to be America's "policeman" in the Persian Gulf.

This "indebtedness" argument sounded particularly strange coming from the Carter administration. Carter had decided not to intervene overtly to buttress the Shah against the domestic revolution that led to his downfall in January 1979. That decision was essentially correct, despite its domestic unpopularity, because it comported with the general principle of international law prohibiting foreign intervention into the domestic affairs of another state.[51] The Iranian people possessed the exclusive right to determine how their government should be constituted without overt or covert interference by the United States. This elementary principle of equal rights and self-determination of peoples took precedence over any putative U.S. national security interest in the free flow of oil from the Persian Gulf.[52] It was the long history of American overt and covert intervention in support of the Shah that paved the way for the Iranian hostages crisis in the first place. By contrast, the decision not to intervene overtly in Iran during the events of 1978–79 may have averted even greater catastrophes. The United States must learn from this tragic experience that it is both just and expedient not to assist a repressive regime to conduct an all-out war against its own people. Here the basic rule of international law dictating nonintervention in the domestic affairs of another country perspicaciously tells the United States what is in its best interest anyway.

The appropriate lesson to be derived from the downfall of the Shah for application to U.S. "friends" around the world (e.g., in El Salvador, Guatemala, Saudi Arabia, the Philippines, South Korea, and South Africa) is that the American government should refrain from intervention in the domestic affairs of another state in order to prop up a regime that, according to a good faith judgment by the United States, has forfeited the support of its own people. On the other hand, the United States must make clear that it is prepared to assist another state, at its request, in case of outright aggression by a third state, in accordance with the terms of the right of collective self-defense as defined by article 51 of the United Nations Charter.[53] Most tragically, because it was tied down by the self-generated Iranian hostages crisis, the Carter administration was unable to forestall the Soviet invasion of Afghanistan at the end of 1979, a blatant case of aggression. This same rule would counsel provision of military assistance by the U.S. government to the people of Afghanistan in their struggle against the Soviet invasion.[54] Such help would uphold article 51 and could facilitate a negotiated settlement of the dispute under the auspices of the United Nations by convincing the Soviets that they cannot win the war in Afghanistan at any cost acceptable to them.[55]

The Case for Iran

In light of this unsavory historical background, the hypothetical legal arguments in defense of the Iranian seizure and detention of the American diplomatic personnel in Teheran certainly deserved serious consideration. The decision to admit the Shah demonstrated a shocking degree of insensitivity by the Carter administration to the legitimate concerns and real fears of the Iranian people. Once before they had ousted the Shah, only to see him restored to the throne by the C.I.A.[56] With the Shah actually in the United States, it reasonably appeared to them that a repetition of this scenario was more than a distinct possibility.

On the eve of the Shah's departure from Iran, Zbigniew Brzezinski, President Carter's National Security Adviser, had asked the U.S. Ambassador in Teheran, William Sullivan, about the feasibility of instigating a countercoup by the Iranian military to prevent Ayatollah Khomeini's imminent ascent to power.[57] Presumably his request was made with the full knowledge and approval of President Carter. The mission of General Huyser to Teheran has been reported to have been part of the same unsuccessful plan.[58] It is undeniable that the U.S. embassy in Teheran was engaged in extensive intelligence activities, that U.S. intelligence agents were stationed there under cover as diplomatic personnel,[59] that the embassy was serving as a primary source for channelling intelligence information back to the United States, and that American intelligence services were maintaining close contact with the Paris entourage of Shahpur Bakhtiar, the Shah's self-designated successor, as a possible replacement for Khomeini.[60] The Iranian apprehension of an American sponsored coup d'état was undoubtedly reasonable and serious as far as they were concerned.

On the basis of these facts, a fairly compelling argument could be made that the seizure and detention of the American diplomats was a legitimate exercise of Iran's right of individual self-defense under article 51 of the U.N. Charter, which, under these imminent circumstances, took precedence over Iran's obligations under Charter articles 2(3),[61] 2(4), and 33[62] as well as over the 1961 Vienna Convention on Diplomatic Relations,[63] the 1963 Vienna Convention on Consular Relations,[64] and the 1973 Convention on the Prevention and Punishment of Crimes Against Internationally Protected Persons, Including Diplomatic Agents,[65] inter alia. The seizure arguably fits within the doctrine of anticipatory self-defense enunciated by U.S. Secretary of State Daniel Webster in the famous case of *The Caroline*. This test requires "the necessity of that self-defence [to be] instant, overwhelming, and leaving no choice of means and no moment for deliberation."[66] To be sure, this author does not approve of recognizing the validity of the doctrine of anticipatory self-defense in the post–U.N. Charter world. Yet viewed from the Iranian perspective, the American diplomats were justifiably seized and detained in order to forestall another decisive and perhaps fatal coup d'état sponsored by the United States government operating in explicit violation of international law.[67] The hostage takers acted to preserve the fruits of the second anti-Shah revolution purchased at the cost of so much bloodshed, in furtherance of the Iranian people's legitimate right of self-determination.

Accordingly, the demand by the Iranians for the extradition of the Shah in return for the release of the hostages was likewise justifiable. From Teheran's perspective, there was no other effective recourse to defend Iran from a second pro-Shah coup launched with the assistance of the American government. Of course, under U.S. domestic law, the Carter administration could not have extradited the Shah to Iran because there was no extradition treaty in force between the two countries.[68] Nevertheless, an argument can be made that by analogy to article 146 of the Fourth Geneva Convention of 1949, the U.S. government had an affirmative obligation either to bring the Shah before its own courts, or else to hand him over for trial to another High Contracting Party (e.g., Iran) for the commission of "grave breaches" (e.g., willful killing, torture or inhuman treatment, or willfully causing great suffering or serious injury to bodily health) as defined by article 147 during the course of an article 3 non-international armed conflict.[69] Yet Congress has failed to enact the necessary implementing legislation in order to fulfill its obligations under article 146 of the Fourth Geneva Convention, so that those like the Shah who are alleged to have committed "grave breaches" can be extradited or tried within U.S. municipal courts.[70] The Iranian government could have plausibly argued that the United States was derelict in its legal duties under article 146 by not having previously enacted such implementing legislation. Consequently, the United States could not plead the infirmity of its domestic law to excuse the violation of international law arising from its refusal either to extradite or to try the Shah.[71] Moreover, because it was obvious at the time of the admission of the Shah that neither alternative was possible under U.S. domestic law, the Carter administration's favorable response to the Shah's request willfully placed the U.S. government in violation of international law.

The United States has no conceivable national security interest in granting political asylum to or becoming a "safe haven" for deposed dictators who have allegedly committed "grave breaches" of the Fourth Geneva Convention or have engaged in a consistent pattern of gross violations of the fundamental human rights of their own citizens. A rudimentary knowledge of international human rights law and the body of international humanitarian law governing armed conflict would have clearly indicated that the Carter administration not admit the Shah into this country for any reason except to prosecute him or return him to Iran. In other words, a serious examination of the rules of international law would have quite perspicaciously told the Carter administration not to admit the Shah into the United States, and thus the entire crisis could have been easily avoided.

The outbreak of the Iranian hostages crisis in response to the admission of the Shah indicates quite clearly that Congress must pass the necessary implementing legislation required under the appropriate provisions of the Geneva Conventions and, in addition, that the United States should ratify the Genocide Convention and enact its necessary implementing legislation as soon as possible.[72] This elementary statutory framework would officially put on notice current and deposed dictators who have allegedly committed "grave breaches" or acts of genocide against their own citizens that they risk criminal prosecution or extradition to their homelands if they travel to the United States. Such a publicly stated American policy should deter their requests for admission in the first place, and thus forestall international complications arising from them like the Iranian hostages crisis. Such a preventive approach to this problem would also enable the United States to maintain normal diplomatic relations with successor governments.

Carter's Positivistic Delusions of Self-Righteousness

The above arguments are not intended to excuse or condone the Iranian seizure and detention of U.S. diplomats, but only to point out that there was a plausible legal argument on the Iranian side that should have been taken into account by the Carter administration. This is a basic fact that every American lawyer learns in the first year of law school and constantly confronts throughout professional life; yet, it is all too readily forgotten in the heat of severe international crises involving the United States. At a minimum the Iranian people *felt* they possessed legitimate fears of, and substantial grievances against, the United States that motivated the embassy seizure and personnel detention. No amount of gainsaying by the American government could have altered their perceptions. From this functionalist perspective, therefore, it was immaterial to the resolution of the crisis whether the Iranians had a grievance that could be proved to the satisfaction of the International Court of Justice.

Irrespective of the positivistic legal technicalities characterizing their feelings, the Carter administration should have dealt with these Iranian perceptions as part of the definitional context of the crisis. Instead, the Carter administration never recognized the validity of the Iranian position to any extent. It crudely manipulated the symbolic meaning of the crisis as part of an overall strategy to convince domestic and international public opinion that the United States was completely in the right and Iran completely in the wrong. In the real world of international affairs, no state is ever perfectly right and no state is ever perfectly wrong. The realities of political life and historical fact are not properly subject to such dogmatic assertions from which positivistic foreign policy recommendations can be derived. For crisis management decision makers to believe otherwise is simply an exercise in self-delusion; and for crisis management decision makers in a popular democracy to convince their domestic constituency of the veracity of this absurd proposition is not an achievement, but an entrapment in the world of their own delusions.

The Carter administration, for example, insisted that the hostage takers be called "terrorists"[73] instead of university "students" (which they were)[74] or even "militants,"[75] a more neutral term used by the American news media. This terminology obfuscated the fact that President Carter's precipitation of the crisis was the immediate cause of the students' "terroristic" behavioral response. Carter's characterization was calculated to produce the maximum degree of revulsion among the American people and thus to build public support for his administration's indefensible handling of the crisis. The intended message was that the hostage takers

were just like PLO/Baader-Meinhoff/Red Brigade "terrorists" who indis-
criminately kill innocent men, women, and children for no ostensible
reason. The Iranian "terrorists" were merely part of the monolithic bloc
known as "international terrorism" that is a conspiracy directed against
the vital national interests of the United States and the entire "Free
World" and which, therefore, must be destroyed at all costs.

This manipulative tactic produced a self-fulfilling prophecy: The
United States thereafter could not accede to Iranian requests no matter
how legitimate some may have been because it could not be seen catering
to the demands of "international terrorism." You do not make concessions to "terrorists" because one concession simply encourages more
"terrorism" elsewhere in the world. Indeed, you do not even negotiate in
good faith with "terrorists"—you kill them!

This positivistic characterization of the crisis locked the Carter administration into a position from which it was more difficult to negotiate its
way out, and rendered the ultimate costs of negotiation for the United
States much higher than otherwise would have been the case. Since it was
obvious from the outset of the crisis that negotiation and compromise
would prove to be necessary, there was no point in making the process
any more difficult than it apparently was going to be. To the contrary, by
attempting to manipulate the crisis to its own advantage in this fashion,
the Carter administration lost a substantial amount of control over its
development.

Even after the release of the hostages, the Reagan administration's
persistent characterization of the Iranian hostage taking as an act of
"international terrorism" impeded the formulation of a rational policy
towards Iran that could protect America's legitimate national security
interests in a manner consistent with the requirements of international
law. Apparently, this positivistic perception blindly led the Reagan
administration to foment a comprehensive campaign to destabilize the
Khomeini government by means of U.S. sponsorship for paramilitary
raids launched from Turkey and Iraq into Iran by various Iranian opposition groups,[76] and for an internal military countercoup,[77] among other
illegal projects. These developments represented a serious retrograde step
for both American national security interests in the Persian Gulf and the
international legal order.

14

A Functionalist Approach to U.S.
Crisis Management Decision Making

Alternatives of International Law and Organizations

In its description of the events surrounding the Iranian hostages crisis, the Carter administration purposefully truncated the beginning of the sequence in a conscientious effort to present the dispute with Iran in a manner most favorable to the position of the United States. The Carter administration unfairly portrayed Iran as the instigator of the crisis when in fact the United States was its true author. In an effort to defuse the crisis, the Carter administration should have publicly admitted its legal and political responsibility for starting it in the first place.

At the very outset of the crisis, President Carter should have publicly acknowledged that the Iranian people had presented a series of grave complaints against the United States under international law and that the American government was prepared to submit the entire dispute immediately to the U.N. Security Council or the International Court of Justice or any other mutually acceptable international tribunal or forum. Such acknowledgement and offer would have interjected an element of fluidity into the crisis that could have facilitated a negotiated solution. Conversely, persistent and stubborn refusal by the Carter administration to even intimate that Iran might have possessed arguably legitimate claims against the United States doomed any prospects for a negotiated settlement of the crisis from the start.

This self-induced delusion of absolute righteousness was behind the Carter administration's opposition to an early suggestion by then Acting Foreign Minister Abolhassan Bani-Sadr to bring the crisis before the U.N. Security Council.[78] Its positivistic rationale was that the Iranians had committed an act of terrorism beyond the bounds of international law and diplomatic practice and therefore were not entitled to air any complaints against the United States in an international forum until the hostages were freed.[79] The Carter administration should have accepted the Bani-Sadr proposal with alacrity.[80] Even if it did not terminate the crisis immediately, acceptance would have strengthened the authority of Bani-Sadr (who, at the time, was genuinely committed to a negotiated settlement of the crisis)[81] within the struggle for power in Iran. Failure of the Bani-Sadr initiative contributed to his ouster as acting foreign minister[82] and his departure from the center of the political stage until his election as president in January 1980.[83] The absence of Bani-Sadr's moderating influence during this crucial phase of the crisis probably contributed substantially to a hardening of the Iranian position.

The Carter administration was correct *finally* to bring the matter to the attention of the Security Council,[84] and right again to go to the International Court of Justice to secure an indication of provisional measures[85] and a final judgment against Iran.[86] Decisions by the Council and the Court calling for the immediate release of the hostages contributed significantly to the resolution of the crisis by authoritatively defining this affirmative legal obligation of Iran to the satisfaction of the entire international community. Unfortunately, however, at the same time these decisions induced the Carter administration to adopt an essentially rectificatory and positivistic approach to the Iranian hostages crisis whereby it acted as if it were a plaintiff vindicated on all counts of its petition.

Although an American crisis management team must always take international law and organizations into account, in a thermonuclear age its immediate objective must be to resolve the crisis, even, if necessary, by sacrificing technically flawless legal arguments and positions in its favor. This is the fundamental distinction between a positivistic and rectificatory attitude towards crisis management decision making and an approach that draws creatively upon the functional potential of international law and organizations as tools for the peaceful settlement of international disputes. Blinded by self-righteousness and paralyzed by a deep-seated fear of adverse electoral consequences, the Carter administration failed to follow the elementary rule of crisis management: Place yourself in the shoes of your adversary as part of a sincere effort to locate some grounds for compromise, then proceed to take the first steps in that direction.[87]

There was no point in the Carter administration's stubborn insistence upon the certification of its legal purity by the International Court of

Justice or the Security Council during the course of its dealings with Iran. The Carter administration's primary concern should not have been how to compel the Iranian government to obey the decisions of the World Court and the Security Council, but how to convince the Iranian students that release of the hostages could be accomplished in a manner consistent with the principles the students were advocating. Throughout the Iranian hostages crisis, the Carter administration should have been seeking to satisfy the concerns of the student hostage takers, who operated beyond the control of their government. They were essentially demanding that the United States make some relatively cost-free concessions on matters of principle in return for the release of the hostages. They were not pressing for U.S. concessions of a political, military, economic, or strategic nature. Under these circumstances, the most prudent course for the Carter administration would have been to institute a conscientious effort to de-escalate the crisis gradually by announcing a series of unilateral concessions on principle to the Iranian students without asking for or even expecting immediate reciprocal gestures.[88]

To support this effort, the Carter administration should have taken the public position that the crisis was not a life-or-death confrontation between two nations, but only an unfortunate incident, essentially beyond the control of the Iranian government, that could be settled peacefully by a good faith effort on the part of it and the United States. Accordingly, the Carter administration should have stated its formal legal position that, due to the revolutionary conditions in Iran, the United States would not hold the Iranian government legally responsible for the hostage taking by the students or for the continued well-being of the hostages because the incident was most appropriately characterized as an act of mob violence that under generally recognized principles of international law did not traditionally engage state responsibility.[89]

Even if the Iranian government felt compelled to repudiate this benign interpretation of the event and to formally associate itself with the student hostage taking, as it subsequently did, the Carter administration should have persisted in maintaining the "mob violence" characterization of the crisis. The Iranian government's voluntary assumption of international legal responsibility for the student hostage taking became a valuable political asset to those revolutionary factions seeking a confrontation with the United States in order to bolster their internal power position. The Carter administration carelessly played into their hands. With some patience and fortitude, American treatment of the hostage taking as an act of mob violence (which it legally and factually was) might have facilitated a gradual de-escalation of the crisis by providing those Iranian leaders who favored release of the hostages some room to maneuver against their adversaries. This functionalist approach to the management of the Iranian hostages crisis stood just as good a chance of gradually developing into the same type of self-fulfilling prophecy that the alternative life-or-death scenario actually degenerated into. An international crisis can sometimes be successfully transformed into a non-crisis if the party possessing overwhelming political, military, and economic power resolutely sets out to do so. Unfortunately, the Carter administration's instigation and mismanagement of the Iranian hostages crisis must testify to the validity of the converse of this proposition.

As another element of this concerted effort to defuse the crisis, President Carter should have announced his sponsorship of the formation of a congressional committee à la Allende to investigate the history of C.I.A. activities in Iran, especially the agency's role in the 1953 restoration of the Shah. Carter should have promised that all executive branch documentation relevant to the investigation and the committee's final report would be published serially as soon as they were produced.[90] Carter also should have proposed the immediate creation of an impartial international commission, whose composition was mutually acceptable to Iran and the United States, possessing the necessary competence to investigate and adjudicate the respective claims of each government. Such a commission would have circumvented the Iranian objection to the jurisdiction of the International Court of Justice. American consent to the creation of an international commission should have been given without the incapacitating condition, obstinately imposed by the Carter administration, that the hostages be freed before the commission issue its final report.

Carter should have publicly stated his intention to apologize for any violations of international law committed by the U.S. government that were proved to the satisfaction of the international commission, and his readiness to recommend that Congress pay reparations to Iran for such violations in an amount to be determined by the commission. If necessary to the success of this plan, the Carter administration should have indicated its willingness to disclaim any right to a setoff from Iran for damages arising as a result of any violations of international law connected with the seizure and detention of the hostages. In this manner the Carter administration could have tacitly conceded that if the students' seizure of the hostages was actually motivated by genuine fears of an American-sponsored coup d'état against Khomeini, their action could reasonably be construed to constitute a measure of anticipatory self-defense which, under the attendant circumstances, was excusable.

The Carter Administration's Honor

Even if the cumulative effect of all these actions still did not immediately obtain the release of the hostages, the Carter administration could have represented that it had scrupulously fulfilled even the most exacting requirements of international law concerning the peaceful settlement of international disputes with a minor state. Instead, the primary obstacle to a speedy negotiated solution to the crisis proved to be the Carter administration's insistence that the "honor" of the United States precluded any American apology to Iran as demanded by the latter.[91] It was never the "honor" of the United States that was at stake during the Iranian hostages crisis, but only the "honor" of the Carter administration and its ability to get reelected at all costs. The "honor" of a superpower such as the United States is never at stake until a president purposely decides to put it at stake, and thus to risk its loss.

The classic argument against foreign policy decision makers taking "honor" into consideration during a crisis can be found in the aforementioned Melian Dialogue by Thucydides.[92] Honor was at the very root of Homeric Greek society founded upon the ethos of shame. Yet it too was discarded by the brutal logic of Thucydides' theory of power politics. Epic heroes such as Hector and Achilles had become an anachronism; collective heroism, a fatal liability. A pure theory of power politics must deem "honor" to be inconsequential for calculations of power and national interest in foreign policy decision making. Yet on this point modern political realists depart from Thucydides when they attribute some independent significance to considerations of "honor" or, its variant, the "prestige" of a state in international relations. In an era when honor and shame counted for far more in the estimation of man than they have at any other time in the history of Western civilization, Thucydides rejected this notion as a dire threat to human survival.

By contrast, the Carter administration shamelessly manipulated America's "honor" to its distinct electoral advantage throughout the 1980 presidential campaign that effectively began in September 1979. Exploiting the rally-round-the-president mentality of the American people during an international crisis, Carter overcame Senator Edward Kennedy's substantial lead in the polls, defeated Kennedy decisively in a series of key primaries, and clinched the Democratic party nomination by May 1980.[93] Once that task was accomplished, Carter's campaign quite cynically abandoned its "Rose Garden strategy," and downplayed the significance of the crisis throughout the summer of 1980 so that Ronald Reagan would not be tempted to use its instigation and prolongation as prima facie evidence of Carter's rank incompetence in foreign affairs.[94] The crisis did not revive as a major campaign issue until just before the November 4 election when the Iranian parliament finally announced its conditions for the release of the hostages.[95] Once Carter had lost the election, the crisis worked its way rapidly toward a successful outcome, subject only to delays caused by American banks haggling with Iran over the price of the hostages' freedom.[96]

The Carter administration's inexcusable concentration of such an extraordinary degree of attention upon the domestic electoral consequences of its handling of the Iranian hostages crisis provided one compelling argument in favor of the passage of a constitutional amendment that limits an American president to a single, six-year, non-renewable term of office. For reasons already discussed above, one major component of America's vital national security interests must consist of upholding the integrity of the international legal order, especially in regard to its own foreign affairs behavior. The achievement of this objective requires U.S. foreign policy decision makers to understand that the long-range interest America has in strengthening the international legal order almost invariably must take precedence over any short-term benefit that might conceivably be gained from acting illegally to resolve an immediate crisis. Yet the four-year presidential reelection cycle almost automatically guarantees that short-term interests prevail over such long-range considerations, usually to the severe detriment of the international legal order. The U.S. presidential election system must be restructured so that the president and his top advisers are freed to consider the long-term interest America has in promoting its vital national security concerns in a manner consistent with the requirements of international law and in full cooperation with the relevant international institutions.

The Counterproductivity of the Carter Administration's Coercive Measures

To its great credit the Carter administration did not resort to a military blockade or invasion of Iran and did attempt to pursue a relatively peaceful resolution of the crisis—at least near the outset. Yet the Carter administration insinuated that the use of military force remained open as a viable option under unspecified circumstances,[97] and this specter totally undercut the significance of its peaceful overtures to Iran. If Carter seriously intended to pursue a peaceful negotiated settlement, it was counterproductive to engage in any hint, threat, or use of force, or to take any coercive, punitive, or retaliatory measures against Iran. Nevertheless, Carter undertook several such actions, including an embargo on the importation of Iranian oil; massing two U.S. naval task forces with assault troops in the Indian Ocean and Arabian Sea;[98] freezing Iranian governmental assets in order to protect the vested interests of U.S. banks while the Shah remained at liberty to secrete his assets abroad;[99] deporting innocent Iranian students;[100] seeking economic sanctions against Iran at the U.N. Security Council[101] and, failing because of a Soviet veto in the aftermath of its Afghan invasion,[102] imposing economic sanctions unilaterally[103] and in conjunction with U.S. allies.[104] Predictably foolish was the Carter administration's severance of diplomatic relations with Iran.[105] This step incredibly complicated and extended the final stages of the hostage release negotiations.[106]

Without these measures the Carter administration could have preserved the effectiveness of an essentially peaceful approach to the settlement of the crisis. But, as was often the case during his administration, Carter's foreign policy represented a predictably unworkable compromise between the diametrically opposed approaches of Brzezinski (i.e., Machiavellian power politics) and Secretary of State Cyrus Vance (i.e., international law and organizations). The Carter adminstration's simultaneous pursuit of these two mutually inconsistent "tracks" cancelled each other out and produced a stalemate in negotiations with Iran.

To overcome this predicament, President Carter should have given explicit pledges before the U.N. Security Council repudiating the threat or use of force to resolve the hostages crisis under any circumstances, and promising that the United States would never again intervene in Iran's domestic affairs. Such pledges would have been consistent with the moral values upon which the United States is supposed to be founded. Indeed, such pledges would have simply amounted to a formal reiteration of American obligations under the U.N. Charter and general principles of international law anyway.

Moreover, there has been considerable concern that one important reason why the Soviet Union decided to invade Afghanistan in late December 1979, was its prediction that the United States intended to take military action against the Khomeini government soon after the hostage release negotiations had stalemated and, incidental thereto, the Soviets' fear that Carter planned to replace Khomeini with another stridently pro-American, anti-Russian regime located right on Soviet borders as the U.S. had done in 1953.[107] A firm Soviet military foothold in Afghanistan would offset this anticipated geopolitical reversal of the advantageous consequences flowing from the anti-Shah revolution. By contrast, prompt, forthright, and creditable U.S. pledges not to use force or covert intervention during the Iranian crisis, supported by abstention from a buildup of American military forces in Southwest Asia, could have undercut the position of those in the Kremlin who might have been making this argument, inter alia, to justify an Afghan invasion.

The Rescue Mission Fiasco

The outstanding example of an ill-advised use of force was the American hostage rescue operation in April of 1980. The mission was a blunder in conception, planning, and execution that fortunately aborted before resulting in even greater catastrophes:[108] the deaths of over half the hostages, substantial casualties among the rescuers and Iranian citizens, hostilities between the United States and Iran, permanent embitterment of their mutual relations, and further opportunities for Soviet penetration and destabilization of Iran. The counterargument that a "successful" rescue operation had the merit that it would at least decisively terminate the crisis one way or another and thus restore some semblance of normality to the situation overlooks that fact that it was the United States which provoked the crisis in the first place and mismanaged it from the outset. In one fell stroke, Carter destroyed all the initiatives for peaceful settlement of the dispute then being pursued by Secretary of State Vance and sidetracked the negotiations for the hostages' release until the fall of 1980.

It was understandable, therefore, that Vance decided to resign in advance of the operation,[109] that American allies retreated from imposing economic sanctions despite a prior agreement,[110] and that the U.S. earned the enmity of the Islamic world.[111] The rescue operation demolished the principled nature and appeal of the American position that had been carefully constructed by Vance and the legal adviser's office on the solid foundation of international law and organizations. From this point on, the Carter administration could no longer convincingly argue in its bid for active support from foreign governments that the U.S. was completely in the right and Iran was completely in the wrong.

Based on the sketchy details so far made available in the public record, it seems that the Carter administration planned a military operation that was far more than just a simple rescue mission (e.g., an anti-Khomeini coup). Until all the facts surrounding the raid are disclosed, tentative conclusions as to its legality under international law are completely unwarranted. And since the U.S. government has so far refused to discharge its weighty burden of proof on this matter, the rescue mission must remain presumptively illegal.

Vance was the only one of Carter's top advisers who opposed the rescue operation. Yet he was not even present when the decision to intervene was made.[112] His deputy, Warren Christopher, attended the decisive meeting while Vance was away on a brief vacation.[113] Christopher was previously unaware of the rescue mission plan, and naturally assumed that Vance had already given his consent to a matter of such fundamental importance. On his return to Washington, Vance was confronted with the bureaucratically impossible task of reversing a decision that had already been unanimously agreed to by the president and the department chiefs without his participation.[114] The psychological phenomenon known as "dissipating" cognitive dissonance undoubtedly and predictably had already come into operation in order to defeat Vance's arguments against the wisdom of the raid before the reconvened crisis management decision-making team.[115]

The absence of Vance, the lone dissenter, was probably more than just a coincidence. Presumably Vance was specifically excluded from the first determinative meeting precisely in order to avoid a direct and heated confrontation between him, on one side, and Carter and the administration's other top crisis management decision makers on the other, who apparently had already made up their minds in favor of a raid. Arguably, the fateful decision to launch the raid might not have been made, despite the latters' personal preferences, if Vance had been afforded the opportunity to be present at the crucial first meeting, had offered his arguments against the raid, and, if necessary, had bolstered his opposition with a threat to resign if the raid was ultimately sanctioned. A threat by Vance to resign that was made before the decision to launch the raid could have exerted a far more profound impact upon the decision-making process than his implicit threat to resign if an affirmative decision already taken in favor of the raid was not subsequently reversed.

In the aftermath of Vance's resignation, Carter skillfully selected Senator Edmund Muskie to succeed him in order to head off a proposed full-scale investigation into the bungled rescue mission, if not the entirety of the crisis, by the Senate during the course of its confirmation hearings on any successor. The senators could be expected to and did in fact treat one of their own number with the soft kid gloves normally required by senatorial courtesy. Nevertheless, Muskie's patient continuation of Vance's international law approach successfully culminated in the safe release of all the hostages on January 20, 1981. This peaceful resolution of the crisis fully vindicated Vance and his reliance upon international law and organizations. By contrast, the dead bodies of eight American servicemen killed in the Iranian desert will stand for all time as a testament to the moral and intellectual bankruptcy of Brzezinski and his penchant for Machiavellian power politics.

The Need for a Reorganization of U.S. Crisis Management Procedures

The exclusion of the secretary of state from the crucial decision to launch the Iranian raid indicates that the standard crisis management procedures of the U.S. government had completely broken down. Such a breakdown illustrates a basic structural deficiency in the bureaucratic channels by which considerations of international law and involvement with international organizations are presented to the top level of American foreign policy decision makers. The task of rendering legal opinions to them is within the organizational prerogative of the secretary of state with the assistance of the legal adviser and his office.[116] The attorney general is not routinely included in international crisis management teams. Therefore, the secretary of state must consider and balance both the political and the legal aspects of the situation before he makes his final recommendation to the crisis team. This practice risks subordination, or at least diminution, of legal considerations to the political dimension of the crisis. Worse yet, legal arguments are likely to be manufactured as ad hoc or ex post facto justifications for decisions taken on the grounds of Machiavellian power politics in express violation of international law. The legal adviser (who has a rank equivalent to assistant secretary of state) is not bureaucratically situated to protect America's long-term but vital national security interest in preserving the integrity of the international legal order during an immediate crisis.

One promising initiative to correct this defect would be to mandate by statute that the U.S. attorney general sit as a permanent member of the National Security Council and any subsidiary bodies established for the purpose of crisis management decision making.[117] This reform would permit the attorney general, drawing on the expertise of international lawyers in both the Justice and the State Departments, to interject considerations of international law and organizations directly into the highest echelon of crisis management. Justice would have a voice and a vote equal to and independent from those for Defense, Foreign Affairs, and Intelligence. The legal aspects of the crisis would not risk dilution by the foreign policy dimension in a stage penultimate to their presentation before the determinative body.

Of course, once the legal aspects are presented they will have to compete in the marketplace of ideas drawn from other perspectives. But it is significant that those legal ideas would be presented, and on a direct, equal, and independent basis, in the first place. With the presence of the attorney general, international law and organizations would gain their own personal advocate to compete for influence over the formulation of American foreign policy with those leaders advocating reliance instead on Machiavellian power politics. Chapter 7 in Part Two of this book, describing the *Decision* stage in the analytical framework applied to the Entebbe crisis, provides ample support for the validity of this proposition on the basis of the Israeli experience in crisis management decision-making procedures during the tenure of the former Labor government.

15

The Carter Administration's Responsibility for the Death of Détente

The Positions of Henry Kissinger

One factor that played an important role in the admission of the Shah into the United States was the reported threat by Henry Kissinger to oppose ratification of the SALT II Treaty if President Carter did not acquiesce.[118] Starting in the late 1950s, the Shah had funnelled much of Iran's oil money through the Chase Manhattan Bank,[119] whose chairman was David Rockefeller, and Kissinger had been a Rockefeller family protégé throughout his public career.[120] During the Nixon and Ford administrations, Kissinger was the master architect of the policy known as détente,[121] the centerpiece of which was the Strategic Arms Limitation Talks (SALT). A substantial portion of SALT II (approximately 75 percent) had been negotiated under his personal direction.[122]

By the late summer of 1979, however, Kissinger seemed primarily concerned with pre-positioning himself for reappointment as secretary of state in a new Republican administration. Except for John Anderson, all the major Republican presidential aspirants opposed ratification of SALT II, and it was clear that whoever the candidate was going to be, a frontal assault upon the treaty would constitute a major component of the Republican party's strategy to defeat President Carter in the 1980 election. Kissinger could not have hoped to win another coveted term at State if he publicly and unequivocally supported SALT II. Consequently, Kissinger's testimony on the treaty before the Senate Committee on Foreign Relations on July 31, 1979, became a remarkable exercise in dissimulation and obfuscation over a matter concerning the vital national security interests of the United States and the fate of the entire world. At the hearings, Kissinger conditioned his tepid support of SALT II on, among other measures, a significant arms buildup and the Senate's imposition of debilitating restrictions[123] on the ability of the president to engage in future strategic arms negotiations. Undoubtedly Kissinger would have castigated the latter as a dangerous and unconstitutional infringement upon the president's power to conduct the foreign affairs of the United States had he been in office.

Kissinger's lukewarm and highly qualified support for SALT II was so evanescent as to be meaningless, and his testimony proved so innocuous that it alone could not have seriously jeopardized whatever his reappointment prospects were without it. Yet Kissinger's self-interested refusal to speak out clearly, unequivocally, and forcefully in order to save his own progeny during the Senate hearings and throughout the course of the public debate over the ratification of SALT II substantially contributed to the "death" of the treaty. Kissinger might have deserved some credit for resisting the enormous temptation to repudiate SALT II entirely at that time if he had not attempted to bargain his continued non-opposition in return for admission of the Shah. That decision set into motion a chain of events which ultimately produced the Soviet invasion of Afghanistan and Carter's decision to withdraw SALT II from consideration by the Senate.

About fifteen months after his Senate testimony on the treaty, and immediately before the 1980 presidential election on November 4, Kissinger publicly supported candidate Ronald Reagan's proposal to withdraw SALT II from consideration by the Senate and to move directly into negotiations for SALT III.[124] By the summer of 1982, however, Kissinger veered into the exact opposite direction of publicly advocating the ratification of SALT II![125] Kissinger's venal posturing on both the Iranian hostages crisis and the ratification of SALT II was so highly opportunistic and unprincipled that the American people should deem him to be permanently estopped from ever again offering his pseudo-Machiavellian advice on the proper conduct of U.S. foreign policy.

Carter's Cuban Crisis

Kissinger's active support for (or at least continued non-opposition to) SALT II became critical at that particular time because the treaty would hang by a thread in the Senate due to President Carter's self-induced fiasco concerning the Soviet "combat brigade" stationed in Cuba. As pressure rose on Carter to redress the nonexistent Soviet military threat to Latin America and the Caribbean, the president finally declared that the status quo in Cuba was "unacceptable."[126] Presumably, the Soviets must either remove their combat troops from Cuba, or else eliminate their allegedly offensive military capabilities. When the Soviets refused to budge, however, the president was forced to accept the previously unacceptable. Yet these events proved calamitous for SALT II's chances in the Senate. There Senator Frank Church, then chairman of the Senate Foreign Relations Committee, which was still conducting hearings on the treaty, had formally "linked" its ratification to Carter achieving a change in the Cuban status quo.

President Carter bears significant responsibility for Church's joining of this "linkage" even though Carter halfheartedly opposed it. When intelligence sources confirmed that Soviet combat troops were stationed in Cuba, Carter was about to begin a vacation aboard the *Delta Queen*, slowly paddle-wheeling down the Mississippi River to provide some excellent "photo-opportunities" for his soon-to-be-launched Democratic presidential primary campaign. With Carter's knowledge, Secretary Vance directed the State Department to reveal the information to Church, apparently with the intention that Church would have the privilege of being the first to make the intelligence public. This would give Church an opportunity to appear to be a hard-liner on defense matters at the start of a difficult reelection campaign against vigorous conservative opposition inspired in part by his liberal image on foreign affairs. Presumably a tough stand on the Soviet troops in Cuba would permit Church to take the "soft" stand of supporting SALT II, which he favored. But the plot boomeranged on Carter, much to his inexcusable surprise. Church called for vigorous counteractive measures by the Carter administration, and backed up his demands with the "linkage" to SALT II. At the request of Church, the Senate Foreign Relations Committee adopted a declaration that Carter could not ratify SALT II until he had assured the Senate that the Soviet troops in Cuba "are not engaged in a combat role." Out of deference to Church, the White House acquiesced in this publicly acknowledged instance of "linkage."[127] All this posturing was to no avail, however, for Church, like Carter, was defeated in his bid for reelection in November 1980.

Of course, "linkage" was a concept pioneered by Henry Kissinger during the Nixon and Ford administrations.[128] The theory stemmed in part from his congenital inability to perceive that strategic arms limitation agreements between the two nuclear superpowers transcend any Machiavellian maneuvers on the geopolitical chessboard of power politics. "Linkage" is a tool of power politics, not of international law and organizations. Predictably, therefore, linking SALT II with the Soviet "combat brigade" in Cuba proved disastrous for the future of nuclear arms control and reduction agreements between the two superpowers.

Carter's gross mismanagement of what should have been a Cuban non-crisis provided critics with additional evidence of his basic incompetence in foreign affairs and defense policy. Before uttering any hasty pronouncements on Soviet troops in Cuba while SALT II teetered in the balance, Carter should have waited for the production of further intelligence information. This eventually confirmed that such troops had been stationed in Cuba with the full knowledge of previous American administrations[129] as part of the Kennedy-Khrushchev agreement which terminated the Cuban missile crisis of October 1962. As publicly proclaimed, the heart of this deal was that the Soviets would remove their medium and intermediate range ballistic missile installations and jet bombers from Cuba in return for a U.S. pledge not to invade that country overtly or covertly à la the Bay of Pigs.[130] Soviet conventional troops remained in Cuba in order to secure the pledge. They served as a "trip-wire" against American invasion, making it likely that any outright assault on Cuba would immediately escalate into a direct superpower confrontation.[131]

From the Soviet perspective, it was Carter, not they, who strove to reverse the status quo in Cuba by reneging on the Kennedy-Khrushchev agreement. It reasonably appeared to the Soviet Union that the U.S. government was using the threat of SALT II's non-ratification as a geopolitical club to force it into granting unjustified and humiliating concessions over Cuba which would undermine its positions of influence throughout the world. Hence, the Soviet Union understandably refused to capitulate to Carter's demands, and he had to content himself with face-saving countermeasures tantamount to an acceptance of the previously "unacceptable" status quo in Cuba.[132]

The "Soviet troops" fiasco could have perhaps been written off to routine presidential electoral posturing if not for the fact that this experience inflicted irreparable damage upon SALT II. This exercise in "linkage" must have induced any optimists in the Soviet leadership seriously to doubt the sincerity of Carter's commitment to SALT II and détente. Kremlin pessimists must have concluded that Carter was somehow trying to trick them out of the mutual benefits promised by the SALT II Treaty just signed at Vienna in June. Because of his inept creation and monumental mishandling of this Cuban non-crisis, President Carter must assume full responsibility for fatally jeopardizing the safe passage of SALT II through the U.S. Senate treaty ratification process, together with all of its incalculably adverse consequences for international peace and security.

Carter's ICBM Cuts

Even before the "Soviet troops" in Cuba fiasco, President Carter had already substantially retarded the progress of the strategic arms limitation talks with the Soviet Union on at least two prior occasions. Shortly after his inauguration, President Carter unilaterally called for substantial qualitative limitations on and quantitative reductions in land-based intercontinental ballistic missile (ICBM) systems, inter alia, much to the astonishment of the Soviet Union.[133] Such cuts would have redounded to the strategic disadvantage of the Soviet Union because of its preponderant reliance on ICBMs. In contrast to America's more evenly balanced "triad" of strategic nuclear warheads dispersed between heavy bombers (27 percent), submarines (50 percent), and ICBMs (23 percent), the Soviets have about 72 percent of their strategic nuclear warheads on ICBMs, 23 percent in submarine launched ballistic missiles (SLBMs), and 5 percent on strategic nuclear bombers.[134] This Carter initiative in effect renounced the 1974 Vladivostock agreement[135] concluded between President Ford and General Secretary Brezhnev on the basic principles for future SALT negotiations: namely, an equal overall aggregate ceiling of 2400 strategic nuclear delivery vehicles (ICBMs, SLBMs, and heavy bombers) and a sublimit of 1320 multiple independently targetable reentry vehicle (MIRV) systems for each side. As a result, Secretary of State Vance's mission to Moscow with Carter's suggestions at the end of March 1977 failed.[136] The Soviet Union insisted upon a return to Vladivostock in order to continue the negotiations. Carter eventually had to give in, withdraw his proposals, and return to the Vladivostock consensus. But this blunder had sidetracked negotiations on the SALT II Treaty for several months.[137] No serious progress was made on SALT II until the fall of 1977.

Carter's "China Card"

About one year later SALT II negotiations were again set back by six months because of the badly timed decision by the Carter administration to grant diplomatic recognition to the People's Republic of China (PRC). The decision was announced in December of 1978, to be effective January 1, 1979.[138] This act represented the culmination of former Secretary of State Henry Kissinger's "grand strategy" of establishing a three-way "balance of power" between the United States, the Soviet Union, and mainland China. By instituting an American relationship with the PRC, Kissinger sought to generate a new source of leverage over the Soviet

Union that could be exploited on numerous other issues, e.g., the Viet Nam War, détente, and SALT. It was a textbook example of the practical application of the Machiavellian theory of power politics on a global scale in the nuclear age.

Yet because of Carter's decision to "play the China card" at this time, the Soviet Union balked at making the final set of SALT II compromises. It was not until late June of 1979, therefore, that the treaty was finally signed in Vienna,[139] a moment too perilously close to the beginning of the 1980 presidential campaign. This six month hiatus meant that SALT II would inevitably become hostage to the vicissitudes of American electoral rites and could not conceivably be evaluated by an objective and dispassionate analysis of its merits alone. Or to phrase this proposition more precisely, the ratification of SALT II was ultimately and quite properly recommended on its merits alone by the Senate Committee on Foreign Relations in a nine to six vote, subject to certain reservations, understandings, and declarations,[140] but never came to fruition because of domestic political reasons that were totally extraneous to the treaty's intrinsic value as an arms control measure.

Another disastrous consequence of Carter's mistimed diplomatic recognition of the PRC was the subsequent visit of Deputy Prime Minister Deng Xiaoping to the United States in late January of 1979. Deng used this opportunity to utter bellicose pronouncements against Viet Nam,[141] which had invaded and conquered Cambodia. Deng successfully manipulated his visit so that America appeared to grant tacit consent to China's punitive and thus illegal invasion of Viet Nam some two weeks later, almost immediately after Deng's return home,[142] in reaction to the Vietnamese invasion of Kampuchea, formerly known as Cambodia. Ironically, therefore, Deng shrewdly counterplayed his "American card" against the Soviet Union in order to forestall Soviet military retaliation against China for the invasion of their Vietnamese ally. From the Soviet perspective, the Carter administration had become a witting accomplice to Chinese aggression. It must have been hotly debated among the Kremlin leadership whether to further advance a long-term Soviet strategy for "containment" of the newly belligerent China by the invasion and occupation of Afghanistan. Perhaps as a precautionary measure, therefore, the Soviet Union substantially escalated its provision of military equipment to the Marxist Afghan government in March of 1979.[143] China seemed to be moving toward a formal military alignment with the United States. Indeed, on April 20, 1979, Deng Xiaoping offered to cooperate with the United States in the establishment of electronic intelligence-gathering stations on Chinese territory. These stations would monitor Soviet missile test sites previously observed from stations in Iran that were shut down after the Shah's ouster.[144]

The MX Missile Decisions

As it turned out, SALT II actually accelerated the pace of the nuclear arms race considerably. Part of the price Carter chose to pay for approval of SALT II by his joint chiefs of staff was the decision to deploy a land-based MX missile system,[145] first in a "racetrack" basing mode,[146] later changed to a "dragstrip" proposal—both of which were equally absurd.[147] The racetrack/dragstrip basing modes were founded upon the dubious assumption that the Soviet Union would reciprocate by building a similar semi-fixed mobile ICBM system of its own in order to permit "adequate verification" for the purpose of future arms control agreements. But this further assumed that the Soviet Union had a genuine commitment to "adequate verification" in the first place and, more importantly, that it was willing to undertake such a vast expenditure of funds to replicate such a cost-inefficient system. Although the U.S. economy might be strong enough to sustain such massive waste, the Soviet economy definitely is not. The Soviet Union will, in all probability, develop a cost-efficient, land-based, fully mobile ICBM system that might not be "adequately verifiable"—for example, on railroad cars. If so, then the racetrack/dragstrip MX would have proven to be an economic, strategic, and environmental folly.

Moreover, despite the Pentagon's contrary arguments, the Soviet Union could MIRV its missiles more cheaply than the U.S. could have built additional racetracks/dragstrips. And a racetrack/dragstrip MX shelter would not have been hardened, so it could be taken out by only one Soviet reentry vehicle (RV), not the standard two.[148] Thus, any alleged U.S. ICBM "vulnerability" problem would still not have been solved by a racetrack/dragstrip MX. Consequently, President Reagan was quite correct to have abandoned the Carter administration's harebrained basing mode for the MX. And fortunately, the Reagan administration's own plan to substitute for it the implementation of another equally ridiculous basing mode—the "closely spaced basing" system, more popularly known as the "dense-pack"[149]—was soundly rejected by both Congress and the Scowcroft Commission Report, which then was quickly endorsed by President Reagan.[150]

The twin decisions to deploy the MX and to do so in a racetrack basing mode immediately preceded and quickly followed, respectively, the Carter-Brezhnev summit in Vienna for the signature of SALT II. The MX decisions destroyed whatever good will, trust, and momentum for the future that would be and had been generated there, and poisoned the atmosphere for the proposed SALT III negotiations concerning theater nuclear forces in Europe. Instead of the projected date of January 1980, this new round of nuclear arms limitation talks was not to meet until October of that year and then under circumstances so inauspicious that they were doomed to failure from the outset. The SALT III negotiations would ultimately be resumed by the Reagan administration, but only after an extended hiatus.

With its ten to fourteen MIRVs, each possessing near pinpoint accuracy, the land-based MX threatened to exercise a profoundly destabilizing impact on the strategic nuclear balance of terror between the two superpowers. It purported to provide the United States with an offensive first-strike capability against Soviet ICBM silos, which constitute about 72 percent of their strategic nuclear forces. Because of this imbalance in comparison to the American triad, the land-based MX will create a "vulnerability" problem for the Soviet Union that is far more serious and threatening than the so-called "window of vulnerability" alleged to be facing U.S. ICBMs for the rest of this decade by groups such as the Committee on the Present Danger.[151] The Soviet Union will be forced to respond by deploying a fully mobile "light" ICBM system of its own in order to counter the U.S. MX threat. Mutual deployment of one "light" ICBM system by each superpower, as permitted by SALT II,[152] will complete the first stage in the post SALT II nuclear arms race. An even more disturbing prospect is that the U.S. first-strike MX missile might, in the alternative, force the Soviet Union to adopt a "launch-on-warning" policy[153] that places the future of the world community at the mercy of inherently defective computers and predictably faulty standard military operating procedures.

NATO's TNF Decision

The final assault on SALT II and détente came on December 12, 1979, when NATO announced its decision to deploy 108 Pershing 2 rockets and 464 ground-launched cruise missiles in Europe starting in 1983, allegedly for the purpose of offsetting the deployment of 300 Soviet SS-20s.[154] Yet, alternatively, the deployment of fast and highly accurate American Pershing 2s in West Germany could also provide the United States with a seemingly effective "surprise" offensive first-strike capability against hardened command centers and strategic ICBM silos targeted against the American heartland that are located within the Soviet Union.[155] From the Politburo's perspective, this decision purportedly concerning only the "modernization" of theater nuclear forces (TNF) substantially undermined the value of the SALT II limitations on the American strategic nuclear weapons force. On its face, NATO's TNF decision specifically violated article XII of the SALT II treaty, providing that "each Party undertakes not to circumvent the provisions of this Treaty, through any other state or states, *or in any other manner.*"[156] In a statement to the North Atlantic Council on June 29, 1979, the U.S. government stated its unilateral opinion that "the non-circumvention provisions will not affect existing patterns of collaboration and cooperation with its Allies, *nor will it preclude cooperation in modernization.*"[157] With good cause, the Soviet government emphatically rejected this self-serving interpretation of the non-circumvention clause of the just signed, yet unratified SALT II Treaty.[158] By its sponsorship of and participation in NATO's 1979 TNF decision the United States government willfully violated the basic rule of customary international law enunciated in article 18 of the Vienna Convention on the Law of Treaties: "A State is obligated to refrain from acts which would defeat the object and purpose of a treaty when: (a) it has signed the treaty . . . until it shall have made its intention clear not to become a party to the treaty. . . . "[159]

Finally, NATO's 1979 TNF decision also reneged upon an unpublicized yet crucial element of the bargain struck between Kennedy and Khrushchev to terminate the 1962 Cuban missiles crisis: Soviet offensive nuclear weapons systems were withdrawn from Cuba in implicit exchange for the removal of U.S. Jupiter and Thor missiles from Italy and Turkey, both NATO members.[160] Irrespective of how anyone positivistically characterizes the binding nature of this understanding, thereafter, the Soviet Union had a perfectly legitimate and reasonable expectation that American Intermediate Range Ballistic Missiles (IRBMs) such as the Pershing 2 would not be reintroduced into Europe. President Brezhnev's subsequent reactive threat to take retaliatory measures that would place the United States "in an analogous position"[161] if NATO's new IRBMs were deployed raised the specter of another Cuban missile crisis under circumstances far less auspicious for the United States in an era of nuclear equality as opposed to the halcyon days of American nuclear superiority when it could successfully intimidate the Soviet Union as it did in 1962. The planned deployment of Pershing 2s in West Germany definitely did not constitute a "modernization" of NATO's theater nuclear forces, but rather the creation of a new and destabilizing U.S. IRBM first-strike counterforce system in Europe. Just as the stationing of Soviet IRBMs in Cuba precipitated a crisis-threatening nuclear war with the United States, so too the emplacement of American IRBMs in Germany could have readily precipitated a crisis-threatening nuclear war with the Soviet Union.

The Soviet Invasion of Afghanistan

Whatever the merits of this Euromissile trade-off, the timing and accumulation of such major nuclear weapons decisions, coupled with the Soviet "combat brigade" fiasco and the then proposed trip of Secretary of Defense Harold Brown to China, undercut the creditability of the U.S. government with the Soviet Union in regard to arms control and détente. With SALT II effectively "dead" in the Senate, the MX missile very much alive, new IRBMs on the way for NATO, a flowering American military rapprochement with the PRC, a massive U.S. military buildup in the Persian Gulf, Arabian Sea, and Indian Ocean in response to the Iranian hostages crisis, and indications that the U.S. might invade Iran and replace Ayatollah Khomeini with another American surrogate right across Russian borders under the pretext of the crisis, the Soviet Union was given every incentive and confronted with no deterrent to violate the so-called code of détente[162] by invading Afghanistan. There was neither "carrot" nor "stick" for the United States to offer or wield in an effort to forestall this aggression. The Soviet invasion of Afghanistan led President Carter to withdraw SALT II from consideration by the Senate, and the centerpiece of the Carter administration's foreign policy towards the Soviet Union collapsed. In Afghanistan the Soviet Union turned America's specter of "linkage" upon its perverted head.

This author does not subscribe to the benign thesis that the Soviet invasion of Afghanistan was an essentially defensive maneuver designed primarily to prevent the spread of Islamic fundamentalism from Khomeini's Iran into Soviet Central Asia by shoring up a tottering client regime in Afghanistan.[163] Nor do I believe that the Soviet march into Afghanistan was just another step along the road of some masterplan for world conquest. As is characteristic of behavior by both superpowers, the Soviet Union exploited a target of opportunity gratuitously handed to it by the gross ineptitude of American decision makers who lost substantial control over the development of international political conditions. If there had been no "racetrack" MX decisions, no Cuban brigade fiasco, no new theater nuclear weapons announced for Europe, no threatening U.S. military rapprochement with China, no Iranian hostages crisis and buildup of U.S. military forces in the Arabian Gulf and Indian Ocean; if SALT II had been ratified and preparations were under way for the SALT III negotiations; if détente was still alive and flourishing, or even if all these disturbing events had not been occurring at approximately the same time, there was a good chance the Soviet Union would have refrained from an outright invasion of Afghanistan and instead have contented itself with maintaining the level of military assistance provided to Nur Mohammed Taraki throughout the summer of 1979, and despite the mid-September coup by Hafizullah Amin.

The key analytical question, therefore, is not *why* the Soviet Union invaded Afghanistan. From its perspective, there were several sound strategic reasons for going in with its own troops. Rather, the focal point should be why the Soviet Union invaded Afghanistan *when* it did at the end of December 1979. I submit that the correct answer to this question lies in the Carter administration's instigation and mismanagement of this series of severe international crises. As described above, these predicaments resulted in significant part because of the Carter administration's gross insensitivity to the requirements of international law and to the full potential usefulness of international organizations for the peaceful settlement of its disputes.[164]

This argument is not intended to excuse or condone the Soviet invasion of Afghanistan, but simply to illuminate some of the motivations that might have induced such drastic Soviet action at that particular time. There is no point in debating the "real" motivations behind the Afghan invasion because most probably they will never be accurately known. Whatever they might have been originally, this aggression created a new geopolitical status quo in Southwest Asia that had to be dealt with on its own terms by the U.S. government. The Soviet threat to Iran and Pakistan was incontestably real, and beyond them lay the Persian Gulf mini-states, Saudi Arabia, and the Indian subcontinent. Yet throughout the Iranian crisis, the Carter administration lost sight of the true U.S. national security interest at stake in this region: to keep the Soviet Union at a safe distance from the Persian Gulf oil lifeline to Western Europe and Japan. Instead, for domestic political purposes, it chose to concentrate an inordinate and counterproductive degree of attention on the hostages situation.

Several elements of the Carter administration's frenzied reaction to the Afghan invasion were best explained by its irresistible impulse to be reelected at all costs: the predictably porous grain embargo,[165] curtailment of Soviet fishing rights,[166] suspension of Soviet contracts and a freeze on sophisticated technology transfers,[167] boycott of the Moscow Olympic Games,[168] an ineffective draft registration,[169] the $400 million in "peanuts" for Pakistan,[170] Brzezinski's near fatal jaunt to the Khyber Pass,[171] Mohammed Ali's embarrassing pep talks in African capitals,[172] and Clark Clifford's war scare.[173] This motley collection of uncoordinated half-measures amounted to tough talking, but not a foreign policy. They accomplished little more than grandstanding to the American people for votes. Each action was a one-shot affair incapable of exerting a compelling military, political, or economic impact upon the Soviet Union. Together they were predicated on the monumental misreading of Russian history to the effect that the Soviet government would disgorge a significant geopolitical gain because of relatively inconsequential economic and moral pressures brought to bear by a group of rank diplomatic amateurs fighting for their electoral lives. None was effectively designed to redress the geopolitical situation produced by the Afghan invasion. The Carter administration was too preoccupied chasing the tail of its "honor" in Iran and a ghost "combat brigade" in Cuba to focus the necessary attention and resources on the really serious crisis developing in Afghanistan during the fall of 1979.

The Carter Doctrine and His Rapid Deployment Force

The Carter administration claimed to deal directly with the Afghanistan invasion when it announced Carter's "Doctrine" for the Persian Gulf, whereby the president committed the U.S. government to use military means to prevent "any outside force [i.e., the Soviet Union] to gain control of the Persian Gulf region."[174] Even if supported by a creditable Rapid Deployment Force (RDF),[175] the Carter Doctrine was a dangerous bluff whose potential for nuclear confrontation and escalation was immeasurable. A Pentagon report has concluded that the United States cannot by itself successfully defend Iranian oil fields from a Soviet invasion unless, perhaps, America resorts to the first-use of tactical nuclear weapons.[176] Their deployment in a conventional conflict with the Soviet Union could easily degenerate into strategic nuclear warfare between the two superpowers. Similarly, later intimations by the Reagan administration that it was prepared to counteract a Soviet thrust into Iran with an invasion of Cuba (euphemistically called "horizontal escalation") risked the same suicidal result.[177] Neither course of conduct could be justified under fundamental principles of international law. In the former case the principle of "proportionality" would be violated; in the latter, U.N. Charter article 2(4).

Neither the RDF in the Gulf nor the Soviet "combat brigade" in Cuba are really designed to be effective against the overwhelming superiority of conventional forces fielded by the other superpower near its heartland. But in the Machiavellian calculus of power politics, American RDF troops are deemed expendable because only the prospect of their certain death can supposedly deter by serving as a nuclear trip-wire.[178] Yet just because the Soviet Union adopted this ridiculous approach to protect the strategically insignificant island of Cuba provides no sound reason for the United States to construct a similar nuclear trip-wire for the crucial Persian Gulf. Cuba and the Persian Gulf are not analogous situations. The requirements for apparently successful deterrence in these respective regions are so fundamentally dissimilar that they require the pursuit of different foreign and military policies by the two superpowers.

Likewise, the RDF cannot succeed at its two other appointed tasks of seizing and operating Persian Gulf oil fields against the wishes of the local governments in the event of another cutoff as occurred in 1973, or of protecting petroleum facilities from destruction by opposition movements indigenous to the region or by externally supported saboteurs. Such disruptions are beyond the substantial capacity of the RDF (now called the U.S. Central Command) to counteract. Consequently, since the Carter Doctrine can neither deter a Soviet invasion, nor stem the tide of revolutionary change in the Gulf, the Reagan administration should have consigned it to Trotsky's "dustbin" of history.

Nevertheless, somewhat paradoxically, the Reagan administration eagerly embraced this ill-conceived, rhetorical flourish by a former opponent, hastily uttered during the heat of an unsuccessful election campaign,[179] as the cornerstone of its policy toward the Persian Gulf. Worse yet, the Reagan Corollary improvidently extended the Carter Doctrine to ordain U.S. opposition to internally-based interference with the free flow of Saudi Arabian oil.[180] The U.S. government must not be tempted to enter into de facto alliances with feudal or reactionary regimes in order to guarantee their continued survival against internal adversaries in return for stable supplies of expensive oil, especially at the calculated risk of precipitating a theoretically "limited" tactical nuclear war with the Soviet Union. As demonstrated by the Iranian revolution, even a perceptibly radical successor regime will recognize the need to sell oil to Western Europe, Japan, and the United States for the hard currency necessary to finance imports essential to fulfilling the basic human needs of its citizenry (e.g., U.S. food supplies), let alone to pay for an economic development program.

Similarly, providing military assistance to African and Middle Eastern countries (e.g., Morocco, Somalia, Kenya, Oman) in return for RDF access rights or facilities was a policy of doubtful utility that could only undermine the domestic legitimacy of host governments and enmesh the United States on the wrong side of regional disputes. It was foolish and counterproductive for the Carter administration and, later, the Reagan adminstration, to offer economic and military assistance to the governments of President Siad Barre in Somalia and of King Hassan II in Morocco for the purpose of securing U.S. access rights to these countries incident to some prospective intervention by the RDF in the Persian Gulf region. The former leader used American support to continue his covert war against Ethiopia in the Ogaden, thus perpetuating the presence of Cuban troops and Soviet advisers in the horn of Africa, while the latter employed American weapons to consolidate his unjustified hold over the western Sahara, thus further destabilizing relations in northern Africa between Morocco, Mauritania, Algeria, Tunisia, and Libya. Since both of their policies expressly violated some of the most fundamental norms of the contemporary international legal order concerning the prohibition on transnational violence, the inviolability of international borders, the right to self-determination of peoples, and the peaceful settlement of international disputes, the United States should have completely dissociated itself from either regime for any purpose other than using its influence to facilitate negotiated solutions to the Saharan and Ogaden conflicts under the auspices of the Organization of African Unity, or the United Nations, or both.

Finally, because of the RDF's demonstrated susceptibility to abuse and illegal use under international law, Congress must amend the War Powers Act of 1973 to provide that the president of the United States cannot order the introduction of RDF troops into hostilities or into situations where imminent involvement in hostilities is clearly indicated by the circumstances without prior authorization by a joint resolution of Congress.[181] A narrowly drawn exception to this amendment could permit the president to use RDF troops solely for the purpose of rescuing a substantial number of American citizens from situations where they face imminent danger of death without the need for prior congressional authorization, though subject to the other requirements of the Act. Without such an amendment any American president will be constantly tempted to order the RDF into combat for all sorts of reasons and under a variety of pretexts simply because of the existence of a seemingly effective U.S. interventionary force subject to his unfettered discretionary command.

16

Restoring Persian Gulf Security

The Iran-Iraq War

The consummation of some scenario for U.S. military intervention in the Persian Gulf was perhaps far closer to actuality than generally believed. The report by columnist Jack Anderson that the Carter administration was contemplating an invasion of Iran to seize the oil fields in the fall of 1980 as a last minute fillip to bolster his prospects for reelection coincided with a substantial increase in U.S. forces stationed in the Indian Ocean and Arabian Gulf.[182] Anderson's allegations warranted a full-scale congressional investigation. This did not occur, however, in a Congress which later accepted the Reagan administration's tendentious assertions that the War Powers Act did not restrict the continued presence of U.S. military advisers in El Salvador.[183]

Likewise, there were several indications from the public record[184] that the Carter administration tacitly condoned, if not actively encouraged, the Iraqi invasion of Iran in September of 1980 because of its shortsighted belief that the pressures of belligerency might expedite release of the hostages. Presumably, the Iraqi army could render Iranian oil fields inoperable, and, unlike American marines, do so without provoking the Soviet Union to exercise its alleged right of counter-intervention under articles 5 and 6 of the 1921 Russo-Persian Treaty of Friendship.[185] These articles were unilaterally abrogated by Iran on November 5, 1979, the day after the American diplomats were seized in Teheran.[186] At the time, the Soviet government protested the Iranian abrogation and, in the aftermath of the Anderson exposé ten months later, raised the specter of counter-intervention, apparently successfully, in order to ward off an American invasion.

In any event, American efforts to punish, isolate, and weaken the Khomeini regime because of the hostages crisis simply paved the way for Iraq to invade Iran.[187] The American policy of "neutrality" towards the Iran-Iraq War, first announced by the Carter administration and supposedly continued by its successor, misrepresented fact if not the law.[188] A substantial body of diplomatic opinion believed that the American government consistently "tilted" in favor of Iraq despite its public proclamation of "neutrality."[189] Even if the United States had been factually as well as legally "neutral" in the Iran-Iraq War, that position was itself shocking and indefensible under the most rudimentary principles of international law. When, before, in the post–U.N. Charter world has the United States ever been "neutral" in the face of outright aggression? As the U.S. government should have learned from the tragic history of American "neutrality" toward widespread acts of fascist aggression committed during the 1930s, peace is indeed indivisible. In a thermonuclear age, aggression per se is the most dangerous threat to world peace. The United States could not have possibly been consistent, believable, or effective in condemning the Soviet invasion of Afghanistan without likewise condemning the Iraqi invasion of Iran. America's rank hypocrisy fooled no one but itself.

The Carter Administration's Dilatory Settlement of the Hostages Crisis

THE EFFORTS TO PROTECT AMERICAN BANKS

Once the "honor" of the Carter administration was no longer at stake in the Iranian hostages crisis because of his resounding defeat by Ronald Reagan on November 4, 1980, the path was opened to a negotiated settlement on the basis of the four conditions laid down by the Iranian parliament on November 2: (1) a U.S. pledge of non-interference in the domestic affairs of Iran, (2) termination of the U.S. freeze on approximately $8 billion of Iranian government assets, (3) cancellation of all legal and financial claims by the U.S. government and U.S. companies against Iran, and (4) transfer of the late Shah's assets from the United States to Iran.[190] The earlier demand for the issuance of a formal U.S. apology to Iran was dropped.

Despite repeated protestations by the top lawyers in the Carter administration, it was obvious from the moment of their promulgation that the president possessed all the constitutional and statutory authority he needed to comply almost immediately with these four terms for the release of the hostages. Upon close examination of their text, it appears fairly certain that the four conditions set down by the Iranian parliament on November 2 were drafted with the advice of someone possessing a fairly sophisticated knowledge of U.S. domestic law relating to international claims settlements so that they could have been expeditiously complied with by the Carter administration.[191] Instead of doing this, however, top lawyers in the Carter administration argued in public that the president lacked the necessary legal authority to fulfill unconditionally the terms relating to the return to Iran of the Iranian governmental assets and those of the late Shah. But Congress had clearly given such powers to the president for exercise under such extraordinary circumstances by means of the 1977 International Emergency Economic Powers Act[192] and the 1868 "Hostages Act."[193] In this matter, the president's statutory authority was further bolstered by his independent power under article II of the Constitution to enter into international agreements for the purpose of settling claims with foreign governments.[194]

This self-denigrating argument by the Carter administration was probably intended to serve as a smokescreen for its decision to vigorously protect the vested economic interests of U.S. banks with loans outstanding to Iran.[195] Some of those loans had been illegally procured by the Shah, his family, and their entourage with the banks' willing connivance. These loans were thus in severe jeopardy of being quite properly repudiated by the Khomeini government. Yet as part of the overall settlement resulting in the release of the hostages, Iranian loans owed to U.S. banks were eventually paid off at full face value directly out of the Iranian government assets when unfrozen by the Carter administration before the residue was repatriated to Iran.[196] In other words, even the supposedly fraudulent loans were liquidated, and the Iranian government was left with the daunting task of pursuing its remedies against the banks in U.S. courts.

The Carter administration's conscious decision to put the venal interests of the banks ahead of both the vital national security interests of the United States and the well-being of the hostages during this final stage of the crisis delayed the latters' release until mid-January of 1981. There was absolutely no valid reason or excuse for the hostages to have rotted in captivity for this additional amount of time while the banks and the Carter administration bargained over the cost of their freedom with Iran. Congress should have conducted a thorough investigation into precisely whose interests were being furthered during this final stage of the Iranian hostages/assets negotiations. In particular, if Carter's top lawyers were actually telling the president that he did not have the authority to do what the Constitution, relevant statutes, and cases clearly gave him the authority to do, then serious questions arise as to whether they were either grossly incompetent or else completely corrupted by the expectation of significant economic gain to prospective clients and themselves. To be sure, in the alternative, the Carter administration's top lawyers could have calculated that such public posturing would obtain a better economic deal from Iran on behalf of the banks. But this argument simply raises the question of why they put the financial interests of the banks before the vital national security interests of our country and before the personal welfare of the hostages and their families in having the crisis terminated immediately. In any event, American international lawyers have nothing to be proud about for the role they played in the Iranian hostages/assets negotiations.

UPHOLDING THE DECLARATIONS OF ALGIERS

Despite these sordid aspects of the settlement, the Reagan administration was quite correct to take an affirmative decision to "honor"[197] the terms of the Declarations of Algiers[198] concluded by President Carter that produced the termination of the Iranian hostages crisis in January of 1981. Admittedly, under general principles of international law the United States government could have properly denounced the entire settlement. According to article 52 of the 1969 Vienna Convention on the Law of Treaties, a treaty is void *ab initio* if its conclusion was procured by the threat or use of force in violation of the principles of international law embodied in the United Nations Charter.[199] Such a violation had already been definitively established to have occurred by the International Court of Justice in its May 24, 1980 Final Judgment in the *Case Concerning United States Diplomatic and Consular Staff in Teheran*.[200] Therein the World Court held, thirteen votes to two, that by its actions Iran had violated obligations owed to the United States under various international conventions in force between the two countries and under long-established principles of customary international law. In addition, the World Court unanimously decided that Iran must immediately terminate its unlawful detention of the U.S. hostages, release them from its custody, and ensure their safe departure from Iran. Pursuant to articles 36, 53, 59, and 60 of the Statute of the International Court of Justice, this decision was binding, final, and without appeal irrespective of the fact that Iran contested the jurisdiction of the World Court to decide the case and consequently failed to participate in its proceedings.[201]

The United States and Iran had signed but not yet ratified the Vienna Convention on the Law of Treaties. Nevertheless, the United States government, the foreign ministries of other countries, and even the World Court itself had all indicated that the rules enunciated in the Vienna Convention were declaratory of principles of customary international law in respect to treaties.[202] Therefore, the grounds for denunciation set forth in article 52 can be relied upon by parties, signatories, and non-signatories alike in their treaty relations with each other. Furthermore, to deny a state the right to denounce an agreement concluded under duress would contravene the fundamental principle enunciated in article 2(4) of the U.N. Charter that all states must refrain from the threat or use of force in their international relations. Since this settlement was not binding under international law, President Reagan was under no obligation derived from either international law or the U.S. Constitution to adhere to its terms simply because it was signed by his predecessor.

Despite this legal positivist conclusion, however, there were several compelling reasons of world order — strategic-military, geopolitical, and international economic in nature — which argued in favor of the Reagan administration deciding to carry out the terms of the settlement that remained to be discharged in the future. These executory provisions included, essentially, voiding the suits of creditors brought in U.S. courts, submitting their claims to international arbitration, repatriating the residue of Iranian governmental assets still in this country or in foreign branches of U.S. banks, and assisting Iran in its attempts to recover sums allegedly misappropriated by the Shah, his family, and their associates by means of permitting proceedings to be brought in U.S. courts. It was obvious from the text of the Declarations of Algiers that President Reagan possessed all the legal authority he required under the U.S. Constitution and relevant statutes and cases to carry out these terms and that his power to do so would ultimately be upheld by the U.S. Supreme Court, as subsequently happened in the unanimous decision of *Dames & Moore v. Regan*.[203] Yet, as a matter of sound constitutional policy, such an extraordinary intrusion by the Executive into the normal operations of the Judiciary — an independent and coordinate branch of government under America's constitutionally mandated separation-of-powers system — can only be justified by a situation which concerns the most vital national security interests of the United States in its conduct of foreign affairs. The Reagan administration's adherence to the Iranian hostages settlement fulfilled this weighty criterion.

The foremost consideration supporting adherence to the settlement was that the U.S. government had a critical long-term interest in demonstrating to all states of the world, and especially those of the Middle East and Southwest Asia, that it possessed a serious, sincere, and meaningful commitment to the peaceful settlement of its disputes with other countries, especially with minor powers, and even if its adversary was clearly in the wrong. To have denounced the hostages settlement at that time would have destroyed those benefits the United States had already undeniably received from its relatively restrained behavior throughout the hostages crisis, and consequently undercut its ability to capitalize upon them in the future. Even more seriously, to have denounced the Iranian hostages settlement would have shaken the very foundations of American negotiating credibility with respect to even its valid international legal obligations.

For reasons previously explained, the Reagan administration's adherence to the terms of the settlement did not, as generally supposed, represent a compromise with the forces of "international terrorism" that ultimately would encourage similar incidents of hostage taking or other violent actions perpetrated against American embassies and diplomats around the world. The immediate cause for the seizure of the hostages was President Carter's grossly provocative decision to admit the Shah into the United States. Hopefully, future American presidents will be sufficiently chastened by the example of Carter's stunning electoral defeat in 1980 should they seriously contemplate the willful precipitation of a crisis with another country. But in the most unfortunate event that the U.S. government is ever again in a situation where it becomes essential to negotiate its way out of a severe international crisis, it was crucial to firmly establish the precedent that America will adhere to such agreements even if they are void under international law.

Given the enormous consequences of these issues related to the Iranian hostages settlement, the claims by U.S. companies that the agreement should have been repudiated because their economic interests were not, somehow, adequately protected, especially compared to the favorable treatment received by the banks, evaporate into relative insignificance when scrutinized under the bright light of the text. Admittedly, although the protections afforded to U.S. companies by the settlement were extensive, they were certainly not airtight. Yet there have never been absolute, guaranteed protections for U.S. companies which voluntarily choose to do business abroad in countries where revolution is more than a distinct possibility. Because of this settlement, American companies facing losses in Iran were placed in a far better position than those which have invested in other countries where revolutionary regimes adopted a policy of expropriating critical sectors of the national economy and, ancillary thereto, engaged in an extensive pattern of contractual breaches. For example, in the claims settlement agreement concluded between the United States and the People's Republic of China in 1979, U.S. claimants received only forty-two cents on the dollar which, when discounted for almost thirty years of unpaid interest and adjustments for inflation, came out to the grand sum of roughly twelve cents.[204] The net percentage of recovery has not been all that much dissimilar throughout the history of U.S. claims settlement agreements negotiated with other revolutionary regimes after the Second World War.[205] At least the U.S. non-bank creditors of Iran were afforded the protections of binding international arbitration, by an impartial tribunal, in accordance with fair and expeditious procedures, and, most importantly, with an opportunity to obtain payment at full face value for their legitimate claims.

As for those companies which entered into contracts calling for submission of disputes arising thereunder to Iranian courts—which were excluded from international arbitration by the settlement—there was no persuasive reason why the U.S. government should have effectively rewritten their contracts in order to give them more benefits than they originally bargained for with Iran and therefore rescue them from their own improvidently concluded business deals. Even those companies excluded from international arbitration could have still claimed the benefits of U.S. income tax deductions for their legitimate business losses in Iran. Hence, a substantial percentage of their losses were paid for indirectly by the U.S. Treasury and thus ultimately subsidized by U.S. taxpayers. Since U.S. companies were not denied due process of law by the Iranian hostages settlement, their self-interested objections were quite properly not allowed to stand in the way of its implementation by the Reagan administration.

America's Future Relations with Iran

Furthermore, the Reagan administration was quite correct to have publicly taken the position that there would be no formal punitive retribution exacted by the United States against Iran for the latter's violation of several of the most sacrosanct principles of international law and politics by the seizure and detention of the American embassy and its diplomats in Teheran. The United States, its NATO allies, and Japan possess vital national security interests in preventing the disintegration of Iran due to factional strife, regionally based autonomous breakaway movements, or external aggression or subversion originating from Iraq or the Soviet Union. Continued destabilization of Iran only generates further opportunities for Soviet penetration and exploitation. Although Western economies have so far successfully coped with the partial interruption of oil supplies from Iran and Iraq because of their war, the United States must not permit the development of a permanent threat to Saudi Arabia and to the free flow of Gulf oil through the Straits of Hormuz by encouraging conditions that might lead to the installation of an Iranian regime acting at the behest of the Soviet Union, or worse yet, the occupation of one shore thereof by Soviet troops. Nevertheless, it is crucial to reiterate that the Iranian people possess the exclusive right to determine their own form of government without overt or covert U.S. intervention, even if this means the continuation of an Islamic fundamentalist regime in Teheran.

In order to achieve the compelling objectives of American national security interests and the maintenance of the international legal order in the Persian Gulf, the Reagan administration should have moved to restore normal diplomatic relations with Iran as expeditiously as possible and without any prior conditions. With the hostages crisis behind it, the Reagan administration should have immediately reversed the Carter administration's position of alleged "neutrality" towards the Iran-Iraq War. The American government should have officially labeled Iraq as the aggressor in the Gulf war, and publicly called for an immediate ceasefire and Iraqi withdrawal from occupied Iranian territory. The Reagan administration should have attempted to convince its NATO allies to terminate their provision of military equipment, weapons, and supplies to Iraq.[206] Operating in conjunction with them and Iran, the United States should have worked at the U.N. Security Council for the formal adoption of this program and its implementation by a U.N. peacekeeping force designated to replace departing Iraqi and Iranian troops on a transitional basis.[207] The Security Council should have demanded that the dispute between Iraq and Iran over the Shatt al-Arab estuary be submitted to the procedures for compulsory arbitration set forth in article 6 of the 1975 Iran-Iraq Treaty on International Borders and Good Neighborly Relations.[208] Although insufficient to justify a counter-invasion of Iraq, Iranian demands for the payment of war reparations and for the deposition of President Saddam Hussein because of Iraq's war of aggression were quite reasonable and fully supportable under fundamental principles of international law. These Iranian concerns should have been recognized as valid by the U.S. government and should have been accommodated to some extent within whatever framework was ultimately adopted for the peaceful settlement of this dispute by the U.N. Security Council.

Of course, the improvement of American relations with Iraq was a desirable objective as well. But it should not have been purchased by derogation from the fundamental principle of international law requiring the condemnation of aggression and by writing off Iran to its own fate, or to the account of the Soviet Union. Indeed, if the Reagan administration truly believed that the major U.S. strategic objective in the Persian Gulf was to counteract a threatened Soviet thrust through Iran towards Saudi Arabia, the best American defense could be mounted, not from the borders of Iraq, but from the eastern and northern frontiers of Iran, at the request of the Iranian government and with the assistance of the Iranian army. Within this context, a credible Rapid Deployment Force could play an effective role consistent with the requirements of international law. Such action would be in furtherance of the right of collective self-defense recognized by article 51 of the U.N. Charter. In the meantime, to the extent Persian Gulf oil can be transported via pipelines terminating on the Red Sea, the strategic importance of controlling the Straits of Hormuz diminishes.

The criticism that such a dramatic reversal of American policy in the Persian Gulf would have alienated friendly regimes in Egypt, Saudi Arabia, Kuwait, and Jordan, inter alia, overlooks the fact that American "neutrality" in the Gulf war simply encouraged these Arab countries temporarily to put aside their deep-seated animosities for the purpose of aligning themselves with Iraq against non-Arab Iran. Restoring peace to the Persian Gulf demanded vigorous American leadership acting in strict accordance with the rules of international law and in full cooperation with the relevant international institutions. Unfortunately, despite its continued protestations of "neutrality" towards the war, the Reagan administration seems to have "tilted" even more strenuously in favor of Iraq than did Carter.

Apparently Reagan succumbed to the temptation of exploiting the American public's paranoid fear over the "spread of Islamic fundamentalism" from Khomeini's Iran throughout Persian Gulf oil fields in order to justify a covert alignment by the United States, its European allies, and Middle Eastern friends with the Iraqi aggressor and its allied anti-Khomeini military and paramilitary forces both within and outside Iran. This misguided policy should have been reversed immediately before it completely destroyed America's ability someday to reestablish normal diplomatic, political, and military relations with Iran in order to forestall any potential for Soviet invasion under the pretext of the 1921 Russo-Persian Treaty. Under these apocalyptic circumstances, the most prudent course for the Reagan administration would have been to work towards the establishment of a strong, stable, and secure government in Teheran, able to undertake the military measures necessary to offset

Soviet divisions massed on Iran's borders. As for the Iranian threat to close the Straits of Hormuz in the event Iraq escalated its attack against Iranian oil installations and foreign oil tankers, world public opinion should hold the U.S. government's illegal pro-Iraqi policies fully accountable for whatever political, military, and economic catastrophes might result therefrom.

U.S. Arms Sales in Southwest Asia

Despite the foregoing criticisms of the Carter administration's handling of the Iranian hostages crisis, overall the United States demonstrated a remarkable degree of restraint for a superpower by abstaining from the use of potentially overwhelming military force to terminate the incident one way or another. This example stands in stark contrast to the Soviet invasion of Afghanistan and its longstanding threat of military intervention into Poland. If there had ever been any doubt as to where the two nuclear superpowers really stood on the basic issues of peace, freedom, and justice, it was decisively clarified for all countries of the world by these parallel events of the years 1979–80. In the wake of the Afghan invasion there has been a fundamental realignment of political relations among the nations of Southwest Asia, acting in fearful response to the Soviet thrust through their midpoint.[209] By its comparative forebearance in Iran, however, the United States created a magnificent opportunity to work with the states of this area to create those individual and collective self-defense arrangements necessary to ameliorate or prevent the development of conditions inviting additional Soviet or intra-regional aggression.

In regard to measures promoting individual self-defense by the states of this region, the purveyance of sophisticated American weapons systems and technology to Israel, Saudi Arabia, Jordan, Pakistan, and China is a most disturbing factor. As events in Iran demonstrated, arms sales can easily become counterproductive. Any U.S. arms transfer policy must be required by the legitimate defensive needs of these countries as defined by international law and interpreted in good faith by the American government. Unilateral policy determinations by these foreign governments do not provide adequate criteria. Thus the Reagan administration should not have planned to provide weapons to Saudi Arabia simply to curry favor and thus secure a stable flow of expensive oil to the West; to China as a geopolitical "card" to be played in some Machiavellian balancing game of power politics with the Soviet Union; or to Jordan for the purpose of creating a surrogate force for illegal military intervention throughout the Persian Gulf.

Nor must such weapons be given to any state in this or other regions of the world that manifests a tendency to employ them in a manner either the U.S. government or the U.N. Security Council deems violative of international law. Hence the Israeli air strikes with American-made planes against the Iraqi nuclear reactor and the PLO headquarters in Beirut, and Israel's threat to bomb Syrian anti-aircraft missiles in Lebanon during the summer of 1981, followed by its patently illegal invasion of that country one year later, should have been grounds for additional concern and reevaluation by the Reagan administration. The same can be said for Pakistan's three wars with India and its frantic pursuit of a nuclear weapons capability. All of these states bore heavy burdens of proof in regard to pending American arms transfers that were not discharged in a manner satisfactory to the requirements of international and U.S. domestic law. [210] Unfortunately, the Reagan administration apparently chose to rely upon the wholesale provision of American military equipment to various governments around the globe as an ineffectual and ultimately self-defeating substitute for the hard task of formulating a set of coherent princples for the conduct of American foreign policy on some basis other than the Machiavellian predilections of former Secretary of State Haig, which his successor, George Shultz, quite unthinkingly came to embrace.

The Gulf Cooperation Council

From a long-term perspective on Persian Gulf Security, the Reagan administration should have abandoned Haig's Machiavellian objective of creating a formal anti-Soviet "strategic consensus" under American tutelage, and substituted for it a policy that promoted the foundation of an effective, regional, collective self-defense and policing arrangement. Consequently, the Reagan administration should have vigorously encouraged the efforts of six local states to form a viable Gulf Cooperation Council. [211] Such an organization could someday metamorphose into an effective Gulf Security Organization, affiliated with the United Nations under chapter 8 of the Charter, and possessing a standing peacekeeping force, or the ability to field one on short notice. Though the Council aims to keep both superpowers out of the region, a Gulf Security Organization could only advance the interests of the United States, its NATO allies, and Japan by the establishment of some modicum of peace, order, and stability in this volatile area.

Geography gives the Soviet Union advantages the West cannot match without supporting the creation of an effective regional collective self-defense and policing system. A Gulf Security Organization would be far more successful at the pacific settlement of local disputes, opposition to intra-regional aggression, and the suppression of externally fomented disturbances than the American Rapid Deployment Force ever could. The United States must not become a member of, or play any formal role within, such a Gulf Security Organization so as not to undermine its claim to regional legitimacy and its independence from superpower politics. Nevertheless, America should make clear its intention to provide military assistance to such an organization in the event of an armed attack upon one of its members by an extra-regional power like the Soviet Union. Such assistance would be in furtherance of the right of collective self-defense recognized by article 51 of the U.N. Charter.

Finally, as current events in the Middle East indicate, the success of any American foreign policy in the Persian Gulf cannot be divorced from the issue of peace between Israel and its Arab neighbors. The security of the Persian Gulf oil lifeline to Europe and Japan cannot be preserved without the attainment of an overall peace settlement between Israel and the adjacent Arab states. Consequently, an absolute precondition to Persian Gulf security becomes active American support for progress towards implementing the international legal right of the Palestinian people to self-determination in accordance with the rules of international law and in full cooperation with the relevant international institutions.[212] Otherwise, the primary political objective of Gulf states will continue to be to organize their efforts and substantial resources in opposition to both Israel and the United States. In the meantime, the Reagan administration's decision to assign troops from the 82d Airborne Division, already selected as part of the Rapid Deployment Force, to serve as a component unit within the multinational peacekeeping force designated to police the easternmost section of the Sinai desert in the aftermath of Israel's withdrawal pursuant to the terms of its 1979 peace treaty with Egypt, was egregiously shortsighted. The monumental peace between Egypt and Israel should not have been linked in any way to the prospect of illegal American military intervention in the Persian Gulf.[213]

17

The Israeli Invasion of Lebanon

Haig's "Strategic Consensus"

Despite the conclusion of the preceding chapter, there are several indications from the public record that the Reagan administration willingly consented in advance to the Begin government's flagrantly illegal invasion of Lebanon shortly after Israel had completed its withdrawal from the Sinai on April 25, 1982.[214] At the outset of the Reagan administration, Secretary of State Alexander Haig quite myopically viewed the myriad of problems in the Middle East and Persian Gulf primarily within the context of a supposed struggle for control over the entire world between the United States and the Soviet Union. Haig erroneously concluded that this global confrontation required the United States to forge a "strategic consensus" between itself and Israel, Egypt, Jordan, and Saudi Arabia in order to resist anticipated Soviet aggression in the region.

Haig's vision of founding a U.S. centered "strategic consensus" in the Middle East was simply a reincarnated version of Kissinger's "Nixon Doctrine," whereby regional surrogates were intended to assist the United States "police" its spheres of influence throughout the world by virtue of massive American military assistance. Israel would become America's new "policeman" for stability in the Middle East, filling the position recently vacated by the deposed Shah of Iran, whom the Nixon/Kissinger administration had unsuccessfully deputized to serve as America's "policeman" for Southwest Asia. Hence, according to Haig's "strategic consensus" rationale, the United States had to more fully support the Israeli government of Prime Minister Menachem Begin even during the pursuit of its blatantly illegal policies in Lebanon and in the territories occupied as a result of the 1967 and 1973 wars, because of Israel's overwhelming military superiority (courtesy of the United States) over any Arab state or combination thereof except Egypt, which had been effectively neutralized by its 1979 peace treaty with Israel.

Whereas the Shah fell over internal domestic conditions that were only exacerbated by the large-scale U.S. military presence in Iran, Haig's scheme was tragically flawed from the very moment of its conception. Haig totally disregarded the fundamental realities of Middle Eastern international politics, where traditionally all regional actors have been far more exclusively concerned about relationships with their surrounding neighbors than about some evanescent threat of Soviet aggression. The more immediate danger to stability in the Middle East and Persian Gulf is not the distant prospect of Soviet intervention, but rather a continuation of the ongoing Arab-Israeli dispute. Nevertheless, the Begin government shrewdly manipulated Haig's delusions in order to generate American support for Israel's plan to invade Lebanon in the summer of 1982 for the express purpose of destroying the PLO and, as a result of the process, further consolidating its military occupation of the West Bank. The Israeli invasion of Lebanon was probably intended to serve as a prelude to its progressive de facto annexation of the West Bank in explicit violation of international law.

The Illegality of the Invasion

This most recent invasion of Lebanon by the Israeli government constituted a clear-cut violation of U.N. Charter articles 2(3) and 33, mandating the peaceful settlement of international disputes, as well as the article 2(4) prohibition on the threat or use of force in international relations against the territorial integrity or political independence of any state. Despite arguments by the Begin government to the contrary,[215] the invasion could not be excused as a legitimate exercise of the right of self-defense, recognized by article 51 of the Charter and by accepted principles of customary international law concerning the use of force. To be sure, the PLO was likewise bound by the obligations enunciated in articles 2(3), 2(4), and 33 and the Lebanese government must not have allowed its territory to be used in a manner violative of international law. Nevertheless, according to the rationale of the International Court of Justice in the *Corfu Channel Case*, the Lebanese government's failure to discharge that obligation was not sufficient to justify the Israeli invasion.[216]

Moreover, the PLO could not be held legally responsible for every act of violence perpetrated against Israel that occurred anywhere in the world. In such matters involving allegations based on circumstantial evidence, the burden of proof was upon Begin to produce sufficient facts from which inferences that the PLO sanctioned specific military operations could permissibly be drawn, "provided that they leave *no room* for reasonable doubt."[217] Begin completely failed to discharge this weighty burden of proof, let alone the far less rigorous standard of "clear and convincing" evidence.

Indeed, the record of evidence clearly established that during the year preceding the invasion, the PLO had in good faith adhered to the terms of the cease-fire applicable to the Lebanese-Israeli border that had been successfully negotiated in the summer of 1981 by President Reagan's special envoy for the crisis, Philip Habib.[218] Consequently, the PLO did not launch any "armed attack" from Lebanon upon Israel as required by article 51 before the latter could resort to the use of force to defend itself. To the contrary, it was Israel that perpetrated an "armed attack" upon Lebanon and the PLO in explicit violation of its U.N. Charter obligations, and thus triggered their respective rights of individual self-defense under international law to resist this unlawful invasion.

Nor could the Begin government appropriately invoke the stockpiling of weapons by the PLO in Lebanon as a legitimate justification for the invasion of that country. Even assuming for the purpose of argument that the contemporary international legal order still recognizes an alleged right of anticipatory self-defense under the U.N. Charter, the Israeli invasion of Lebanon failed to meet the test of *The Caroline* case. According to this classic formulation, the "necessity of that self-defence [must be] instant, overwhelming, and leaving no choice of means, and no moment for deliberation."[219] In a front-page interview published by the *Wall Street Journal* in July of 1982, Prime Minister Begin candidly admitted that this most recent invasion of Lebanon was not necessary to ensure the existence of the state of Israel.[220] Begin emphatically repeated this assertion in an August 8, 1982 speech at the National Defense College, and specifically stated that the invasion of Lebanon "does not really belong to the category of wars of no alternative."[221] By his own words Begin voluntarily conceded those very facts which definitively repudiated the claim that this invasion was a legitimate act of self-defense in accordance with any generally recognized test of public international law, all of which depend upon fulfilling the basic requirement of "necessity."

Finally, the Israeli invasion of Lebanon violated the basic principle of customary international law dictating proportionality in the use of force.

This requirement of "proportionality" applies to even a legitimate exercise of the right to self-defense under international law. The enormous scale of death, destruction, dislocations, and suffering inflicted by the Israeli army in Lebanon was egregiously disproportionate to any harm that had been perpetrated upon Israel or to any serious threat to its legitimate national security interests posed by the presence of the PLO in Lebanon. For example, during the course of the invasion Eliahu Ben-Elissar, chairman of the Knesset's key Foreign Affairs and Defense Committee, brazenly stated in a *New York Times* interview that Israeli counterstrikes in Lebanon "won't be proportionate."[222] The tragic history of repeated violence between the PLO and Israel does not alter the admitted facts that this invasion did not fulfill the two fundamental conditions of "necessity" and "proportionality" required by international law before any government can justify the use of transnational force.

The Applicability of the Geneva Conventions

The four Geneva Conventions of 1949 applied in their entirety to the conduct of hostilities by Israel in Lebanon. Since the start of the invasion in June of 1982, the Israeli government imprisoned a sum total of approximately nine thousand people at the Ansar prison camp in southern Lebanon. Soldiers of the PLO who had been captured by the Israeli army in Lebanon were entitled to full-scope protections as "prisoners of war" within the meaning of the Third Geneva Convention of 1949[223] pursuant to article 4(a)(2) thereof extending such treatment to members of organized resistance movements, or to article 4(a)(3) protecting regular armed forces professing allegiance to an authority not recognized by a detaining power, or to article 4(a)(6) protecting inhabitants of non-occupied territory who form themselves into a *levée en masse* upon the approach of an invading army. Furthermore, article 5 specifies that in the event any doubt arises as to whether persons, having committed a belligerent act and having fallen into the hands of the enemy, belong to any of the categories enumerated in article 4, such persons shall enjoy the protection of the Third Convention until such time as their status has been determined by a competent tribunal. Finally, article 130 of the Third Convention states that the willful deprivation of a prisoner of war's right of fair and regular trial prescribed in the Convention is a "grave breach" requiring the imposition of "effective penal sanctions" upon the perpetrator in accordance with article 129.

In any event, even if PLO soldiers were appropriately deprived of their prisoner-of-war status, together with captured officials of the PLO and other individuals affiliated with them, as well as all Lebanese and Palestinian civilians, they were entitled to the full panoply of protections set forth in the Fourth Geneva Convention[224] and the customary international law of belligerent occupation.[225] Statements by the Israeli government that captured PLO soldiers and officials were to be treated as "terrorists" and thus presumably deprived of their protected status under the Geneva Conventions would have, to the extent acted upon, constituted a grave violation of the humanitarian laws of armed conflict that have been universally accepted by all civilized states.[226]

As a party to the four Geneva Conventions of 1949 the United States government had an absolute obligation under common article 1 to respect and to ensure respect for their observance in all circumstances by other contracting powers such as Israel.[227] This obligation became irresistibly compelling in a situation where Israel was enabled to invade Lebanon by means of weapons, munitions, and supplies provided primarily by the U.S. government at concessionary rates. Under these circumstances of complicity, the Reagan administration had an absolute duty to employ the tremendous leverage over Israel afforded by its arms supply relationship and economic subsistence in order to secure strict obedience to the humanitarian laws of armed conflict by Israel and its allied Phalange and Haddad militias, and to obtain Israel's immediate and unconditional withdrawal from Lebanon as required by U.N. Security Council resolution 508 (1982)[228] and resolution 509 (1982),[229] both of which were legally binding on Israel and the United States under Charter article 25.[230]

Application of the Nuremberg Principles
to the Kahan Commission Report

Article 6(a) of the 1945 Charter of the International Military Tribunal established at Nuremberg[231] to prosecute and punish Nazi war criminals defined the term "crime against peace" to mean "planning, preparation, initiation or waging of a war of aggression, or a war in violation of international treaties, agreements or assurances, or participation in a common plan or conspiracy for the accomplishment of any of the foregoing." Nuremberg Charter article 6(b) defined the term "war crime" to include "murder, ill-treatment or deportation to slave labour or for any other purpose of civilian population of or in occupied territory, murder or ill-treatment of prisoners of war or persons on the seas, killing of hostages, plunder of public or private property, wanton destruction of cities, towns or villages, or devastation not justified by military necessity." Article 6(c) of the Nuremberg Charter defined the term "crime against humanity" to include "murder, extermination, enslavement, deportation, and other inhumane acts commited against any civilian population." Article 6 also provided that leaders, organizers, instigators, and accomplices participating in the formulation or execution of a common plan or conspiracy to commit crimes against peace, crimes against humanity, and war crimes are responsible for all acts performed by any persons in execution of such plan. Article 7 of the Nuremberg Charter denied the applicability of the "act of state" defense by making it clear that the official position of those who have committed such heinous crimes "shall not be considered as freeing them from responsibility or mitigating punishment." Finally, article 8 provided that the fact an individual acted pursuant to an order of his government or of a superior shall not free him from responsibility, but may be considered in mitigation of punishment if justice so requires.

The principles of international law recognized by the Charter of the Nuremberg Tribunal and the Judgement of the Tribunal itself were affirmed by a unanimous vote of the U.N. General Assembly in resolution 95(1) on December 11, 1946.[232] Since that time, the Nuremberg Principles have universally been considered to constitute an authoritative statement of the rules of customary international law dictating individual criminal responsibility for crimes against peace, crimes against humanity, and war crimes. Indeed, in the seminal case of *Eichmann v. Attorney-General of the Government of Israel*, the Supreme Court of Israel specifically held that the Nuremberg Principles "have formed part of the customary law of nations 'since time immemorial.'"[233]

Under the Nuremberg Principles, to the extent the U.S. government permitted Israel to use American weapons in explicit violation of international law and of U.S. domestic statutes applicable to arms transfer agreements,[234] it must assume full legal responsibility before the entire international community for all crimes against peace, crimes against humanity, and war crimes committed or condoned by Israel and its allied Phalange and Haddad militia forces operating in Lebanon. Such American responsibility would include the savage massacre of several hundred innocent Palestinian and Lebanese civilians by organized units of the Phalangist militia at the Sabra and Shatila refugee camps in West Beirut, at that time under the control of the occupying Israeli army. As the Occupying Power in West Beirut at the time, Israel was fully responsible for the barbarous treatment inflicted upon these innocent Palestinian and Lebanese refugees by the Phalange militia. Article 29 of the Fourth Geneva Convention clearly provides that a Party to the conflict (i.e.,

Israel), in whose hands protected persons may be, is responsible for the treatment accorded to them by its "agents," irrespective of any individual responsibility which may be incurred. Utilizing language reminiscent of Nazism, the Begin government specifically ordered the Phalangists into these refugee camps for the express purpose of "purging," "cleansing," and "purifying" them of Palestinian "terrorists."

In regard to this matter of personal culpability, despite the terminology employed by the Kahan Commission Report,[235] international law does not recognize the existence of the phenomenon therein denominated as "indirect responsibility" for war crimes and crimes against humanity. The test of individual responsibility for such heinous crimes recognized by customary international law is succinctly stated in section 501 of the U.S. Army Field Manual on *The Law of Land Warfare* (1956), which in turn is based upon the famous case of General Yamashita.[236] According to this test, any Israeli government official or military commander who "has actual knowledge, *or should have knowledge*, through reports received by him or through other means, that troops *or other persons subject to his control* are about to commit or have committed a war crime and he fails to take the necessary and reasonable steps to insure compliance with the law of war or to punish violators thereof" shall be responsible for such crimes.[237] Applying this test to the factual findings of the Kahan Commission Report, and taking the latter at face value, it was evident that Prime Minister Begin, Defense Minister Sharon, Foreign Minister (later Prime Minister) Shamir, Chief of Staff Rafael Eitan, Director of Military Intelligence Saguy, and Generals Drori and Yaron, inter alia, must assume full personal responsibility under international law for all war crimes and crimes against humanity perpetrated by the Phalange militia units at Sabra and Shatila. Furthermore, article 147 of the Fourth Geneva Convention defines such atrocities to constitute "grave breaches" that require the government of Israel to impose "effective penal sanctions" upon such perpetrators in accordance with article 146, which was never done. Finally, that same article 146 also requires the U.S. government to bring such suspected war criminals, regardless of their nationality, before American courts for the purpose of prosecution and the imposition of effective penal sanctions should they decide to enter U.S. territory. That was never done either.

The Phalange Militia

There were several indications of additional elements of legal responsibility on the part of the U.S. government for the September massacre. The

Reagan administration played the leading role in securing the withdrawal of PLO troops from Beirut in return for American and Israeli
guarantees of protection for Palestinian civilians left behind, and then
prematurely evacuated U.S. marines from Lebanon.[238] A report in the
Sunday Times of London stated that U.S. officials in Beirut learned of an
ongoing massacre in these undefended refugee camps on the evening of
Thursday, September 16, only a few hours after the Israeli Defense Forces
(IDF) had ordered the Phalangists to enter them.[239] Yet U.S. officials
refused to act upon this information so as not to compromise the source
of their intelligence. Under these horrendous circumstances the burden
of proof should be upon the U.S. government to refute any allegations of
complicity in the massacre.

The need for a thorough investigation of U.S. responsibility for violations of the laws of humanitarian armed conflict by the Phalangists
throughout Lebanon is rendered even more imperative by the reported
fact that the C.I.A. had been providing military and financial assistance
to the Phalange since at least March of 1981.[240] At the very minimum,
the Phalange militia was bound to observe common article 3 of the four
Geneva Conventions of 1949, which applies in the case of an armed
conflict not of an international character occurring in the territory of one
of the High Contracting Parties (i.e., Lebanon).[241] Other reported violations of common article 3 and the laws of humanitarian armed conflict
committed by the Phalange in southern Lebanon and the Bekaa Valley
included extortion, abductions, killings, rapes, and the intimidation
and harassment of the civilian population, especially Palestinians. As the
Occupying Power in southern Lebanon and the Bekaa Valley, the Israeli
government must assume full responsibility for failing to suppress such
atrocities and to punish their Phalange perpetrators.

The Arab Deterrent Force

The Begin government was not entitled to invoke the lawful presence of
the Arab Deterrent Force in Lebanon as a reason to justify the continuation of its undeniably lawless military occupation of that country. The
Arab Deterrent Force (ADF), composed primarily of Syrian troops, had
been stationed in Lebanon and conducted its peacekeeping operation
with the consent of the Lebanese government and with the approval of
the League of Arab States. The League was the appropriate regional
organization under chapter 8 of the U.N. Charter for the purpose of
sanctioning such international peacekeeping activities in a member state
such as Lebanon.

Admittedly, Syrian troops originally intervened into the Lebanese civil war in 1976 to protect the Maronite Christian forces from destruction by the PLO without obtaining prior approval from the Lebanese government. [242] But in this matter Syria simply followed the international legal precedent already set by the U.S. government during 1965 in order to legitimize, on an ex post facto basis, its arguably illegal military intervention into and occupation of the Dominican Republic. Thereafter, the Johnson administration resorted to the Organization of American States for its approval to transform American soldiers into an Inter-American Peace Force. [243] In a May 5, 1965 *Memorandum on the Legal Basis for United States Actions in the Dominican Republic* distributed by the U.S. State Department, its legal adviser argued as follows: "The propriety of a regional agency 'dealing with such matters relating to the maintenance of international peace and security as are appropriate for regional action' is expressly recognized by Article 52 of the Charter of the United Nations." [244]

This author does not intend to defend the propriety of the U.S. intervention into the Dominican Republic under international law, but rather to argue that because of the legal position it formally adopted to justify its Dominican occupation, the U.S. government was effectively estopped from denying that the League of Arab States could lawfully authorize the occupation of Lebanon by Syrian troops integrated into the Arab Deterrent Force, provided (1) the ADF had the consent of the Lebanese government, (2) it was subject to the overall supervisory jurisdiction of the League, and (3) it operated for the limited purpose of ameliorating the civil war that then mercilessly raged throughout the country. Especially after having encouraged the Syrian intervention in 1976, the United States government should never have treated the egregiously illegal presence of the Israeli army in southern Lebanon on the same footing as the technically lawful presence of the Arab Deterrent Force in eastern and northern Lebanon.

This conclusion, however, is not intended to obscure the fact that in the Syrian occupied zone of the Bekaa Valley and Tripoli, credible reports emerged of numerous instances where Syrian troops engaged in acts of intimidation, harassment, physical mistreatment, arbitrary detention, kidnappings, and extortion of protection money directed against the civilian population. These actions violated Syrian obligations as an Occupying Power under the Fourth Geneva Convention and the customary international law of belligerent occupation. In addition, Syrian troops failed to keep the peace in the territory they occupied in the Bekaa and in northern Lebanon so that a variety of paramilitary groups and militias, such as the Front for Liberating Lebanon from Foreigners, remained free to take advantage of the civilian population and to perpetrate similar outrages upon them. Finally, Syria permitted Iranian and Libyan "volunteer" troops to enter the territory it occupied in the Bekaa and therefore must assume full responsibility for their behavior and compliance with the laws of war.

The Role of UNIFIL

The Begin government had no right under international law to intervene in the domestic affairs of Lebanon by dictating the terms of its government or of some "peace treaty" as conditions for the withdrawal of the IDF. Because it was procured by means of the blatant threat and use of force in egregious violation of the most basic principles of international law, the May 17, 1983 Agreement on Troop Withdrawal[245] concluded between the regime of Amin Gemayel and the Begin government under the auspices of the United States was void *ab initio* under article 52 of the Vienna Convention on the Law of Treaties.[246] The agreement was entitled to absolutely no international legal significance whatsoever. Indeed, the mere attribution of any semblance of legal validity to this document would have simply constituted a reward to the Begin government for the aggression it perpetrated against Lebanon.

The foreign and domestic future of the Lebanese government must be determined by the Lebanese people themselves without interference or compulsion from any external source. The most effective means to ensure the success of this endeavor would have been for Israel immediately to withdraw its troops from Lebanon and to turn over evacuated territory to the United Nations Interim Force in Lebanon (UNIFIL) without any prior conditions. Israeli charges that UNIFIL could not be trusted because the United Nations as a whole is biased against Israel obfuscated the fact that UNIFIL operated under the auspices of the Security Council (not the General Assembly), where the United States could, if appropriate, exercise a veto power. The record of evidence clearly established that UNIFIL proved to be quite effective at preventing the large-scale infiltration of PLO fighters across the Israeli-Lebanese border from 1978 through 1982.[247] A renewed and strengthened mandate for UNIFIL would have enabled it to continue to perform this task until the Lebanese army was reconstituted as an effective and independent military force under the control of a functioning and truly representative central government.

The precedent of the U.N. military force sent by the Security Council to the Congo from 1960 to 1964, known by its French acronym ONUC,[248] indicated that UNIFIL could have been fortified with sufficient manpower, weapons, and authorization to use force offensively, if necessary, in order to accomplish its mission of guaranteeing the territorial integrity and political independence of Lebanon. Such a strengthened mandate for UNIFIL could have permitted the withdrawal of the Arab Deterrent Force by the League of Arab States at the request of a truly representative Lebanese government, and the deployment of UNIFIL troops along the Lebanese-Syrian border in its place. UNIFIL could have remained in Lebanon for as long as a truly representative government felt it was needed to ensure the restoration of internal peace and stability to that country and in its foreign relations with immediate neighbors.

By contrast, as part of a conscientious and coordinated effort with Israel to eviscerate UNIFIL, the Reagan administration sought first to supplant it with U.S. marines, and then to induce its NATO allies to contribute troops toward the formation of a "multinational force" that had no authorization from either the United Nations or any regional organization to perform peacekeeping activities in Lebanon. The War Powers Act of 1973[249] mandated that the president remove the American marine contingent he introduced into Lebanon on September 29, 1982, within sixty days, unless Congress specifically authorized their continued use. Yet the marines remained in Lebanon and needlessly endured enormous casualties until February 1984.

The U.S. Congress should have adamantly insisted upon the president respecting its constitutional and statutory prerogatives in this matter, and thus have demanded that all American military forces be immediately withdrawn from Lebanon and their positions occupied by UNIFIL troops. UNIFIL would have proven far more effective at keeping the peace among the various factions in Lebanon and at protecting the lives of innocent Palestinian and Lebanese civilians from additional gross violations of their fundamental human rights by the Phalangists, the Haddad militia, and other irregular paramilitary groups organized by the IDF than American marines and some "multinational force" ever could. The presence of the "multinational force" operating in Beirut that consisted of troops drawn from NATO countries only raised the specter of rapid escalation into a general European war in the event of an Israeli-inspired clash with Soviet troops stationed in Syria or operating in the Bekaa Valley.

The "multinational force" should likewise have been withdrawn immediately, and UNIFIL troops should have been designated to take their positions throughout the environs of Beirut. Yet even after the collapse of the "multinational force" in February 1984, the primary obstacle to the interposition of a U.N. force in Beirut proved to be the Reagan administration's obstinate refusal to withdraw the U.S. Sixth Fleet beyond the firing range of Lebanese territory, thus precipitating the Soviet Union to veto the adoption of such a plan by the U.N. Security Council. The Reagan administration was more interested in retaining the military option to engage in the further illegal threat and use of American force in support of the Gemayel regime, than in securing a genuine peace settlement in that tormented country under the auspices of the U.N. Security Council.

As this book went to press in the fall of 1984, the new Israeli coalition government organized under the joint leadership of Shimon Peres and Yitzhak Shamir indicated that Israel would finally be prepared to accept an expanded role for UNIFIL as a major element of some force withdrawal agreement with Lebanon. The height of tragic irony is that the Begin government, acting in cooperation with the Reagan administration, could have easily obtained a renewed and invigorated mandate for UNIFIL from the U.N. Security Council in the summer of 1982. But for their own demented reasons, Begin and Sharon, aided and abetted by Haig and Reagan, preferred an IDF invasion to a UNIFIL expansion. As a direct result, over twenty thousand people were wantonly killed in Lebanon, including six hundred Israeli soldiers and almost three hundred American soldiers and civilians, all of whom needlessly lost their lives. The Israeli invasion of Lebanon shall stand as one of the great international crimes of the post–World War II era. And yet so far neither Israeli nor American domestic public opinion has held their respective popularly elected leaders accountable for the commission of these grave crimes against peace, crimes against humanity, and war crimes. Have both the Israeli and the American people so readily forgotten the Principles of Nuremberg?

The Gemayel Regime

The regime of Amin Gemayel exerted effective control over only certain limited sectors in the city of Beirut. Therein it was bound to observe, at a minimum, common article 3 of the four Geneva Conventions of 1949, which applies to the case of an armed conflict not of an international character. Nevertheless, there were repeated and credible reports that authorities in the Gemayel regime and members of the Lebanese army subject to its authority engaged in a widespread pattern of violations of fundamental human rights directed against the civilian popoulation of Beirut. Of special concern was a fairly extensive policy of harassment, intimidation, and discrimination practiced against Palestinian residents and refugees that seemed purposefully calculated to drive the entire Palestinian population out of Lebanon.

Similarly, in the aftermath of the Israeli occupation of West Beirut, the Gemayel regime proceeded to disarm Moslem militia forces operating in the city. Yet it completely failed to disarm the Phalange and other Christian militias in Beirut, which exploited this opportunity to perpetrate additional outrages on the civilian population of the city, particularly Palestinians. Given the circumstances surrounding the creation of the Gemayel regime amidst a cordon of Israeli troops, it could accurately be characterized under international law as a "puppet government" established by the United States and Israel for the express purpose of accomplishing their illegitimate political and military objectives in Lebanon. Consequently, according to article 29 of the Fourth Geneva Convention, both Israel and the United States were fully responsible for all violations of the laws of humanitarian armed conflict inflicted upon the civilian population of Beirut, especially Palestinians, by their "agent," the Gemayel regime.

Furthermore, since it was always a creation of and surrogate for the Israeli and American governments that never represented anything more than a minority faction among several groups fighting for control of Lebanon, the Gemayel regime possessed absolutely no authority under international law to request U.S. military intervention for the purpose of defeating its internal adversaries. The Reagan administration's accession to its puppet government's request constituted an impermissible intervention into the Lebanese civil war that violated the international legal right of the Lebanese people to self-determination as recognized by article 1(2) of the U.N. Charter. The basic principle of international law and politics dictating non-intervention in the domestic affairs of another state indicated quite clearly that the Reagan administration should have refrained from taking sides in the Lebanese civil war and instead worked in conjunction with the U.N. Security Council to create political, military, and economic conditions in Lebanon that could eventually permit the installation of a truly free and representative government. By contrast, for thoroughly Machiavellian reasons, the Reagan administration pursued the exact opposite course of conduct, which produced predictably disastrous consequences for the Lebanese people as well as for U.S. marines and diplomats.

The Haddad Militia

The Reagan administration should have actively opposed any proposals by the Israeli government to establish some type of semi-permanent international police force in Lebanon that was not under the jurisdiction of the U.N. Security Council, or worse yet, to create some form of "security zone" policed by Israeli or American or NATO troops in southern Lebanon or the Chouf mountains. Indeed, since its first invasion of Lebanon in 1978, Israel had already been obliged to dismantle the Lebanese Christian enclave it illegally constructed along the border under the command of the late Major Saad Haddad, whose followers steadfastly resisted the interposition of UNIFIL troops with the active collusion of the Israeli government. As a direct result of the 1982 Israeli invasion, the Haddad militia forces were able to extend their control over a zone in southern Lebanon that soon reached from the Israeli border to the Awali bridge north of Sidon, and with the support of the IDF refused to permit the introduction of even Lebanese army troops into this expanded zone. Within the territory it controlled, however, the Haddad militia forces were bound to observe, at a minimum, common article 3 of the four Geneva Conventions of 1949, which applies in the case of an armed conflict not of an international character. Nevertheless, there were credible reports that the Haddad militia forces launched a campaign of violence, terror, and intimidation directed against the local Palestinian population as part of a calculated effort to drive them out of Lebanon.

Article 29 of the Fourth Geneva Convention makes it clear that a party to the conflict such as Israel, in whose hands protected persons may be, is responsible for the treatment accorded to them by its "agent." Given the historical role the Israeli government played in the creation of the Haddad militia and its continued provision of political, military, and economic support, it was clear that the term "agent" included the Haddad militia. Article 49 of the Fourth Geneva Convention absolutely prohibits individual or mass forcible transfer or deportations of protected persons from occupied territory to any other country for any reason whatsoever, and article 147 defines such offenses to be a "grave breach" of the Convention requiring the imposition of "effective penal sanctions" upon perpetrators in accordance with article 146. As the Occupying Power in southern Lebanon, the Israeli government must assume full legal responsibility for all violations of the humanitarian laws of armed conflict committed by its "agent," the Haddad militia, which the IDF either encouraged, permitted, or failed to suppress and punish. And because of their criminal nature, the U.S. government must actively oppose any attempt by Israel to establish an allegedly independent "police" role in southern Lebanon for its surrogate Haddad militia forces (now under the command of General Antoine Lahad and renamed the Southern Lebanese Army) as part of some future troop withdrawal agreement that Israel might attempt to illegally impose upon Lebanon with or without the connivance of Syria.

A Role for the United Nations

If the United Nations proved to be largely ineffective during this latest stage in the Lebanese civil war, it was only because the United States actively opposed the Security Council's adoption of any effective measures against Israel in order to ensure the latter's compliance with the most elementary rules of international law. At the initiative of its other members, the Security Council should have invoked its enforcement powers under chapter 7 of the U.N. Charter by determining that the Israeli invasion and occupation of Lebanon was a "breach of the peace" and an "act of aggression" under article 39[250] warranting the imposition of a universal embargo upon the sale or provision of arms, munitions, and military supplies to Israel along the lines of the U.N. mandated arms embargo against South Africa.[251] If an arms embargo proved insufficient to obtain Israeli withdrawal, Charter article 41 authorized the Security Council to require all other members of the United Nations to impose the sanctions of "complete or partial interruption of economic relations and of rail, sea, air, postal, telegraphic, radio and other means of communications, and the severance of diplomatic relations" upon Israel. If the U.S. government continued to veto Security Council resolutions designed to secure Israel's immediate and unconditional withdrawal from Lebanon as required by Resolutions 508 and 509, the United Nations General Assembly should have acted under the terms of its Uniting for Peace Resolution[252] to recommend that all U.N. members impose such sanctions against Israel on their own accord. Since the United States government originally proposed and sponsored the passage of the Uniting for Peace Resolution in the General Assembly for the express purpose of circumventing the abusive exercise of the veto power by the Soviet Union in the Security Council during the Korean War,[253] the Reagan administration would have been estopped to deny that such collective measures against Israel by the membership of the General Assembly were lawful. In this way the Israeli government's grievous transgressions against the Lebanese and Palestinian peoples could have been effectively opposed by all members of the world community in a manner consistent with the requirements of international law despite the complicitous obstructionism of the Reagan administration.

The Right of the Palestinian People to Self-Determination

Because of the presence of almost 350,000 Palestinian refugees in Lebanon, a long-term solution to the problems of that country can only be found when Israel is willing to recognize the international legal right of the Palestinian people to self-determination. Despite the Camp David Accords,[254] neither Egypt, Israel, the United States, Jordan, nor for that matter any other state, has a right under international law to negotiate on behalf of the Palestinian people. Both the U.N. General Assembly and the League of Arab States have determined that the PLO is the legitimate representative of the Palestinian people.[255] That determination must be respected by Israel and the United States for the purpose of negotiating an overall settlement on the ultimate disposition of the West Bank, the Gaza Strip, and Jerusalem. Mutual and simultaneous recognition of their respective rights under international law by Israel and the PLO must be the next stage in the development of the Middle East peace process.

The Israeli government has repeatedly stated that under no circumstances will it ever recognize the PLO as the legitimate representative of the Palestinian people because the group is said to be a "terrorist" organization. To be sure, the Palestinian National Charter of 1968[256] calls explicitly for the destruction of the state of Israel and its replacement by a secular Palestinian state on the territory of what was once the League of Nations Mandate for Palestine awarded to Great Britain after World War I. And article 10 of the National Charter proclaims that commando action constitutes the nucleus of the Palestinian popular liberation war.[257] On the other hand, one of those passages from the Bible that the Begin government apparently relied upon to support its farfetched claim to sovereignty over the West Bank because "Judea and Samaria" are said to be part of the "Promised Land" granted by God to the Hebrew people contains the following injunction for dealing with the native inhabitants by means of genocide: "But of the cities of these people, which the Lord thy God doth give thee for an inheritance, thou shalt save alive nothing that breatheth. Thou shalt utterly destroy them; namely, the Hittites, and the Amorites, the Canaanites, and the Perizzites, the Hivites, and the Jebusites; as the Lord thy God hath commanded thee."[258]

The Begin government's illegal invasion of Lebanon in order to destroy the PLO, its gross violations in Lebanon of the Geneva Conventions of 1949 and the humanitarian laws of armed conflict, directed against Palestinians as such, its illegal annexation of the Golan Heights, and its repeated violations of the Fourth Geneva Convention and the customary international law of belligerent occupation in all of the occupied territories (e.g., construction of Jewish settlements, deportation of inhabitants, collective punishments, and the "Milson Reforms"[259]) tend to indicate that Prime Minister Begin, a devoutly religious man, took God's genocidal command at face value. Under his lawless and misguided leadership, Israel gradually became a pariah state within the international community, a disgraceful position it shamelessly shared with the apartheid regime of South Africa, one of its few remaining allies besides the United States. The time was long past for the United States government to pull America out of this "unholy alliance" with Israel against the Palestinian people. Yet near the very outset of his administration President Reagan callously declared that Israeli settlements in the Occupied Territories were "not illegal," thus violating the U.S. obligation under article 1 of the Fourth Geneva Convention of 1949 to ensure respect for the terms of the convention (here article 49) by another party such as Israel.

Revision of Resolution 242 (1967)

The only way out of this conundrum of "terrorism" in the Middle East is for Israel and the PLO to accord each other mutual and simultaneous recognition of their respective rights under international law, thus decisively breaking the cycle of violence, retaliation, and counter-retaliation that has developed between them. The U.S. government can facilitate this objective by sponsoring an amendment to U.N. Security Council resolution 242 (1967)[260] that would explicitly affirm the international legal right of the Palestinian people to self-determination, including an independent state of their own if they so desire. On the other hand, in regard to ensuring Israel's existence, a revised resolution 242 would continue to affirm the necessity for "[t]ermination of all claims or states of belligerency and respect for and acknowledgement of the sovereignty, territorial integrity and political independence of every state in the area and their right to live in peace within secure and recognized boundaries free from threats or acts of force," and should be amended to specifically protect the state of Israel by name. Such a revised resolution 242 could then be accepted by Israel and the PLO as a prelude to negotiations over the ultimate disposition of the West Bank, the Gaza Strip, and Jerusalem. With these negotiations underway, there would be no need for the PLO to launch any military operations against Israel from Lebanon, Jordan, the occupied territories, or elsewhere, and no reason for Israel to continue its war against the PLO and the Palestinian people.

The PLO is neither a "state" nor a "government" within the contemplation of international law, but only the legitimate representative of the Palestinian people for the purpose of negotiating procedures leading to implementation of their recognized international legal right of self-determination. Thereafter, the future status of the PLO must be determined by the Palestinian people themselves. In the meantime, however, the United Nations Charter, the international laws of humanitarian armed conflict, and general principles of customary international law absolutely prohibit Israel from using force in an effort to exterminate the PLO and, in the process, oppress the people of Lebanon as well as Palestinian refugees located there. Unfortunately, under the influence of Alexander Haig, the Reagan administration acquiesced in Israel's illegal attempt to destroy the PLO by means of American weapons, munitions, supplies, and money. The great tragedy of the current stage in the Middle East crisis was that the Reagan administration either explicitly or implicitly approved Israel's flagrant and repeated violations of international law and of U.S. domestic statutes applicable to arms transfer agreements in Lebanon.

The Reagan Peace Plan

In his Senate confirmation hearings, George Shultz indicated that he was thinking along these lines. He should have seized the opportunity presented by a transition in power to completely repudiate the misconceived policies of his Machiavellian predecessor. The so-called Reagan Peace Plan, announced September 1, 1982,[261] and drafted under Shultz's auspices, represented a welcome departure from Haig's tragically flawed "strategic consensus" approach to America's Middle East foreign policy decision making. At least the Reagan Peace Plan recognized that the dispute between Israel, on the one hand, and its neighbor states and the Palestinian people, on the other, must be resolved on its own merits. Yet from the perspective of international law, the Reagan Peace Plan was severely deficient for a number of basic reasons.

First, and foremost, was that the U.S. government had no legal right or standing to exclude unilaterally and in advance of any negotiations the creation of an independent sovereign state on the West Bank and Gaza Strip from among the various options open to the Palestinian people when they finally have the opportunity to exercise their international legal right of self-determination. The self-determination of peoples has been a fundamental principle of American foreign policy and of international law and politics since President Woodrow Wilson's famous Fourteen Points address of January 8, 1918, to a joint session of Congress. It set forth the war aims and peace terms acceptable to the U.S. government, the last one of which laid the cornerstone for the foundation of the League of Nations.[262] The fundamental interdependence of universal peace among nations and the principle of equal rights and self-determination of peoples was explicitly recognized and reaffirmed in article 1(2) of the U.N. Charter, the successor to the Covenant of the League. That principle was the motivating force behind the General Assembly's adoption of resolution 181 (II) of November 29, 1947,[263] that called for the creation of independent Arab and Jewish states (joined in an Economic Union) and an international trusteeship for the city of Jerusalem after the termination of the League of Nations Mandate for Palestine. That promise for the creation of a Jewish state in the mandated territory has been fulfilled, whereas that promise for the creation of an independent Arab state remains to be carried out. The international legal right of the Jewish people to found the sovereign state of Israel stands on the same legal footing as the international legal right of the Palestinian people to found a state of their own on the West Bank and Gaza Strip.

The Begin government's pursuit of a policy tantamount to genocide[264] against the Palestinian people in Lebanon demonstrated precisely why they require an independent state of their own in order to better protect their physical existence and to preserve their cultural heritage. In the aftermath of the Second World War, identical sentiments motivated the international community to support the creation of the state of Israel for the protection of the Jewish people against a repetition of the Nazi holocaust. Despite dramatic improvements in the utility of international human rights law in direct reaction to the genocidal horrors of World War II, as Woodrow Wilson correctly foresaw, an independent state still remains the only effective means that the international community has so far devised to defend one national group from physical and cultural annihilation by another national group.

There will be no peace in the Middle East until the Palestinian people are likewise given the opportunity to exercise their international legal right of self-determination in whatever manner they choose, not in accordance with a limited set of alternatives preselected for them by the United States in collusion with Israel, Egypt, or Jordan. When the Reagan administration unilaterally foreclosed the option of an independent sovereign state to the Palestinian people, it betrayed the fact that the keystone of its foreign policy toward the Middle East remained considerations of Machiavellian power politics. By definition, these motivations were not entitled to the respect of other nations or the support of the American people.

This conclusion was corroborated by the fact that the progenitor of the Reagan Peace Plan was none other than Henry Kissinger himself, today's leading proponent of practicing Machiavellian power politics in international relations.[265] Unfortunately Shultz, like Haig before him, was willing to give Kissinger's outmoded and dangerous ideas another chance. Yet the world might not survive another Kissingerian "nuclear alert" of U.S. forces during some future Middle East War, as occurred in 1973.[266] It is high time for the U.S. government to discard both Kissinger and his Machiavellianism into the dustbin of history.

18

The Future of Nuclear Arms Control
between the Superpowers

Presidential Campaign Rhetoric

After the Soviet invasion of Afghanistan, the vituperative rhetoric of the 1980 presidential campaign intervened into the SALT II debate and obscured several points about the treaty that are crucial for ensuring the future progress of nuclear arms control and reduction agreements between the two superpowers. The Carter administration's constant refrain that all the SALT II restrictions applied to the Soviet Union, and none to the United States,[267] constituted pure electoral propaganda. The SALT II Treaty per se never was a truly effective and meaningful arms control measure. It placed no real restrictions on either side, but left both superpowers essentially free to build all their currently planned weapons systems.[268] For example, General David Jones, the chairman of the U.S. Joint Chiefs of Staff, forthrightly admitted during his testimony on SALT II that the treaty would not impede the U.S. nuclear weapons program to any significant extent.[269] And Secretary of Defense Harold Brown, among others, testified to the same effect.[270]

Both countries agreed to limit the number of MIRVs per missile that, in any case, they would not be technologically able to exceed until after the expiration of SALT II in 1985. The Soviet Union agreed to dismantle obsolete weapons systems scheduled to be replaced anyway. The freeze on the number of Soviet "heavy" SS-18s at 308 did not matter much since that figure seems to have represented their planned deployment run of "heavy" ICBMs in the first place, and was simply carried forward from the SALT I Interim Agreement of 1972[271] and the Vladivostok Accord. Rather than constructing extra "vulnerable" SS-18 silos, the Soviet Union seemed to be more interested in deploying a mobile "light" ICBM system as permitted by SALT II. In this regard, there were reports that the Soviet Union engaged in testing the deployment of a mobile "light" ICBM system on railroad cars.

SALT II possessed little more than symbolic significance without a SALT III and SALT IV. Yet the great value of SALT II was that it could have paved the way for successful SALT III negotiations concerning theater nuclear forces in Europe and for genuine nuclear arms reduction agreements between the two superpowers and their allies in the future. Moreover, there was always the probability that SALT II could have been informally extended by the two superpowers after its expiration in 1985, much as they did with the SALT I Interim Agreement.[272] At that point, the SALT II numerical restrictions could begin to serve as an effective limitation on the development of both U.S. and Soviet strategic nuclear weapons systems.

The value of SALT lay less in the limitations formally set out in each treaty than in the process of negotiation itself. The technology of mass destruction develops too rapidly to be controlled, given the cumbersome, time-consuming, and highly politicized procedures for treaty negotiation and ratification. The SALT process could not stop and reverse the arms race until it first controlled the technology race. In the meantime, however, continuation of the SALT process served the useful function of purporting to regulate technological evolution in the nuclear arms race. SALT made the arms race appear more understandable, predictable, less irrational, and thus susceptible to governmental control. Undoubtedly these appearances were illusions that could someday become suicidal for mankind. But since nuclear deterrence is essentially a psychological phenomenon anyway, in the absence of genuine arms reductions such illusions rendered the strategic balance of terror between the two superpowers to appear more stable and therefore less dangerous than would be the case without them.

The Window of Vulnerability

On the other hand, charges by groups such as the Committee on the Present Danger (COPD)[273] and later, under its influence, the Reagan campaign, that SALT II somehow undermined the very foundations of Western strategic nuclear deterrence were without any merit whatsoever.[274] However, since the COPD's strategic nuclear assumptions (e.g., the "window of vulnerability") came to dominate the defense and foreign policies of the Reagan administration, they should have been seriously reexamined and ultimately repudiated. The COPD's outlandish assumptions did not justify the enormous nuclear and conventional weapons buildup undertaken by the Reagan administration, which, it quite callously admitted, was to be financed directly by huge cuts from scarce resources previously allocated to social welfare programs and human services. Nothing could have constituted a greater present danger to the peace, stability, security, and prosperity of the United States both at home and abroad than this wasteful and unnecessary arms buildup America experienced under the misguided stewardship of those COPD members who assumed high governmental positions in the Reagan administration.

The COPD concept of a "window of vulnerability" was a lot of strategic nonsense. It was based upon the dubious assumption that the Soviets can and will arm each of their 308 SS-18s with 40 reentry vehicles (RVs), each possessing enough pinpoint accuracy to take out hardened U.S. ICBM silos.[275] So far in the technical literature it does not appear that the Soviet Union has or will have the capability to arm an SS-18 with more than 10 RVs, each with enough accuracy to destroy silos, or that it aspires to have this technology, even assuming it is possible.[276] As the number of RVs and their accompanying decoys and penetration aids per missile increases, beyond a certain point the accuracy of each RV necessarily decreases. Indeed, if SALT II had been duly ratified in 1979, Soviet SS-18s would have been limited to 10 RVs each, the SS-17 to 4 RVs, the SS-19 to 6 RVs, the new "light" ICBM permitted by SALT II (e.g., the Soviet equivalent of the U.S. MX) to 10 RVs, SLBMs to 14 RVs, and air-to-surface ballistic missiles (ASBMs) to 10 RVs.[277] The Soviet Union's long-range mobile SS-16 was banned altogether by SALT II because its first two stages were indistinguishable from the intermediate range SS-20.[278] So those Reagan administration officials who decried intelligence indications that the Soviet Union was deploying SS-16s had only themselves to blame for opposing the ratification of SALT II.[279]

Article III of SALT II would have carried forward Vladivostok's equal overall aggregate ceiling of 2,400 strategic nuclear delivery vehicle launchers for both sides and would have required the Soviet Union to reduce that number to 2,250 by January 1, 1981.[280] Article V of SALT II contained the Vladivostok sublimit of 1,320 for all MIRVed systems and within that number it established a sublimit of 1,200 on launchers of MIRVed ICBMs, MIRVed SLBMs, and MIRVed ASBMs; within the latter number it established a sublimit of 820 on MIRVed ICBMs.[281] Likewise, if SALT II had been duly ratified in 1979, Soviet production of the Backfire bomber would have been limited to thirty per year under the terms of a separate but related statement by Brezhnev.[282] These SALT II limitations would have decisively impeded the ability of the Soviet Union to exploit the throw-weight advantage of its heavier ICBMs by the process of additional MIRVing, which was the primary concern of the COPD. Furthermore, an indefinite extension of the life of a ratified SALT II treaty beyond its contemplated 1985 expiration date could permanently forestall the development of any hypothetical "window of vulnerability" problem for both the U.S. and the Soviet land-based ICBM systems.

Even assuming the "worst-case scenario" envisioned by the COPD that by the end of this decade the Soviet Union will have acquired the necessary technological sophistication to quadruple the number of RVs per SS-18 and to design each one of these 12,230 reentry vehicles with the degree of computer-simulated "accuracy" necessary to destroy hardened U.S. ICBM silos, the COPD's assertion that there would then exist a "window of vulnerability" for the U.S. Minuteman ICBM force was still a lot of strategic nonsense. The COPD maintained that under these circumstances the Soviet Union would be able to launch a "disarming" surprise first strike upon the great bulk of U.S. ICBM silos, using only a portion of their own ICBM force while holding the remainder of their ICBMs in reserve for a threatened second strike upon U.S. population centers.[283] Presumably, the Politburo would then issue an ultimatum to the American president (or, more likely, his successor) that he either surrender or face the total annihilation of the U.S. population by the rest of the Soviet ICBM force. Consequently, according to COPD, the president would then be presented with only two unpalatable options: (1) ordering an all-out nuclear attack upon Soviet population centers by America's unscathed SLBM force in full knowledge that this action would precipitate Soviet destruction of American cities by their left-over ICBMs, or (2) capitulation. Shorn of his own ICBMs, the president would be incapable of pursuing a third and more rational alternative of ordering a limited nuclear strike on the remaining Soviet ICBM force[284] because American SLBMs do not possess the pinpoint accuracy necessary to be used in a countersilo as opposed to a countercity mode.

The COPD argued that without this third option available, any sane, intelligent, and "moral" American president might choose to surrender rather than proceed any farther down the path toward nuclear Armageddon. Hence, the COPD postulated the need to "close" this "window of vulnerability" by generating such a third option, enabling the president to launch a limited nuclear strike on reserve Soviet ICBM silos by means of proceeding immediately with the deployment of a force of "survivable" U.S. ICBMs.[285] Originally, the Reagan administration had interpreted this requirement to mean the deployment of the new MX missile into a land-based mode that could "absorb" a Soviet first strike with enough missiles left intact in order to destroy any remaining Soviet ICBMs.

No point would be served by spending much time examining in great detail the absurd nature of this interconnected set of improbable assumptions underlying the COPD's worst-case scenario because there exists at least one definitive line of refutation that can be quickly explained and readily comprehended. As Carter's Secretary of Defense Harold Brown indicated during his testimony on SALT II before the Senate Committee on Foreign Relations in the summer of 1979, even under the worst-case scenario envisioned by the COPD, the president of the United States would still be able to implement the third alternative—a limited nuclear strike on any reserve Soviet ICBM forces by means of American B-52 bombers armed with air-launched cruise missiles (ALCMs), which do possess enough accuracy to be used in a countersilo capacity and can penetrate Soviet air defenses. Admittedly the bomber/ALCM attack would take eight to ten hours to complete, whereas a U.S. MX counterstrike could theoretically occur in only thirty minutes to an hour, assuming the best of circumstances.[286] But this brief time differential does not validate the limited nuclear war assumptions of the COPD's worst-case scenario.

During those eight to ten hours, the U.S. president could simply sit tight while the bombers/ALCMs fly to the outskirts of Soviet airspace in order to perform their mission of destroying any residual ICBM force. With the bombers/ALCMs on their way, the next move in the COPD's hypothetical scenario for limited nuclear war would be up to the Soviet Union. During those eight to ten hours the Soviet leadership would be confronted with three basic options, presented here in an estimated increasing order of probability: (1) absorb the U.S. bomber/ALCM attack and then do nothing; (2) absorb the U.S. bomber/ALCM attack and then launch the rest of their strategic nuclear forces upon American population centers; or (3) launch any remaining ICBMs together with the rest of their strategic nuclear forces upon American population centers before the U.S. bombers/ALCMs arrive. In the event the Soviet leadership should decide upon alternatives 2 or 3, the U.S. president could still effectively retaliate by ordering the destruction of Soviet cities by means of the intact U.S. SLBM force. Yet, given the enormous uncertainties underlying all these outlandish scenarios for waging a limited nuclear war, in the most improbable event that the Soviet Politburo someday decides to launch a surprise nuclear attack upon the continental United States, it would most probably order a simultaneous and coordinated all-out assault by the entirety of its strategic nuclear weapons systems upon American population centers, industrial complexes, ICBM silos, in-port SLBM forces (40 percent), and strategic bomber bases. In that event, an American president (or his successor) could still totally devastate the Soviet Union by means of America's invulnerable at-sea SLBM force (60 percent) alone, or in conjunction with U.S. quick-alert bombers.

The Superfluousness of the MX Missile

The need to guarantee this outcome of "mutual assured destruction" (MAD) for both superpowers under a variety of such worst-case scenarios had already been foreseen and exploited by previous American administrations to justify construction of the redundant "triad" dispersion of U.S. strategic nuclear weapons systems among bombers, SLBMs, and ICBMs in the first place. Indeed, after the passage of over two years into the Reagan administration, the Scowcroft Commission Report, enthusiastically endorsed by President Reagan, definitively "closed" this mythical "window of vulnerability" by arguing quite persuasively that the COPD's worst-case scenario for a "successful" Soviet limited nuclear attack upon the Minuteman ICBM force was never a realistic possibility to begin with precisely because of the existence of the U.S. "triad." Despite the outrageous claims by the Committee on the Present Danger and, under its influence, by the Reagan administration, there was thus absolutely no need to make the "triad" any more redundant than it already was by deploying a first-strike MX missile system in a vulnerable basing mode to "close" a nonexistent "window of vulnerability" allegedly threatening the current U.S. Minuteman ICBM force.

If the Reagan administration was in fact seriously concerned about the existence of some such theoretical "window of vulnerability," it would not have stridently advocated the admittedly vulnerable basing mode for the MX missile known as the "dense-pack." From the COPD's strategic nuclear perspective, the dense-pack was far less "survivable" than the Carter administration's racetrack/dragstrip proposal. Moreover, Pentagon devotees of the dense-pack and, before it, of the racetrack/dragstrip, tacitly conceded that ultimately any fixed or semifixed land-basing modes for the MX missile would require the deployment of an anti-ballistic missile (ABM) defense in order to "finally" solve the hypothetical "vulnerability" problem.[287] This of course assumes that the United States can indeed develop and deploy an effective ABM system in the first place. If that is the case, however, it would have made more sense for the Reagan administration to have abrogated the ABM Treaty[288] when it came up for review in 1982 (or again in 1987) so as to deploy an ABM defense around the entire U.S. Minuteman ICBM system as soon as feasible, and thus abandon the multibillion dollar first-strike and destabilizing MX missile. Apparently, the Pentagon was more concerned with the acquisition of a potentially disarming first-strike missile against Soviet ICBMs than it was with "closing" some nonexistent "window of vulnerability" for U.S. ICBMs.

Furthermore, from the COPD's strategic nuclear perspective, both the dense-pack and the racetrack/dragstrip basing modes were far inferior for closing the "window of vulnerability" to the deployment of the MX missile on railroad cars—a system the Soviet Union seemed to be experimenting with for its new mobile "light" ICBM. Although a U.S. "railway" or "roadway" MX has the advantage that it would not require an ABM defense, the problem with a fully mobile land-basing mode (e.g., the Scowcroft Commission's suggested "Midgetman") is that if it is adopted by either one or both superpowers it might not be "adequately verifiable" for the purpose of negotiating future nuclear arms control and reduction agreements.[289] Assuming the Reagan administration really possessed a serious commitment to that objective, then these considerations led inevitably to the Garwin-Drell proposal of basing the MX in offshore diesel-powered submarines cruising somewhere above the U.S. continental shelf.[290] The Garwin-Drell proposal would have been cheaper, more capable of surviving a Soviet first strike, would not have required any ABM defense, could have been "adequately verified," and would not have created any domestic political or environmental problems. If the MX missile was ultimately deployed, as the Reagan administration seemed determined to do, it should have been placed under the ocean, not on the land. The primary reason why this solution to the nonexistent "vulnerability" problem was not adopted by either the Carter or Reagan administration is better explained in terms of bureaucratic politics within the Pentagon than by strategic, economic, environmental, or arms control considerations: The Air Force did not want to lose the MX mission to the Navy.[291]

Indeed, the Navy was currently engaged in the process of deploying an offensive first-strike strategic nuclear weapons system by means of its Trident 2 program. Each Trident 2 missile is to be armed with fourteen Delta-5 warheads, each possessing enough pinpoint accuracy to destroy hardened Soviet ICBM silos and thus to be used in a counterforce mode as opposed to the traditional SLBM countercity mode.[292] In other words, the Navy's Trident 2 program rendered the Air Force's MX program superfluous.

*The Dangers of Developing an American First-Strike
Capability*

With the explicit approval and active support of both the Carter and
Reagan administrations, the Pentagon has proceeded apace with the
design, testing, and deployment of three separate, independent, and
potentially offensive first-strike counterforce nuclear weapons systems:
the Air Force's MX, the Navy's Trident 2, and the Army's Pershing 2. To
this formidable arsenal should also be added the new MK12A warhead
for the MIRVed (3 RVs) Minuteman III ICBM system that can also exercise
a substantial countersilo capability.[293] This is an astounding and truly
disturbing situation!

This author is confident the Soviet leadership could not even begin to
comprehend why the United States government, professing a genuine
commitment to nuclear arms control, would want to field four offensive
first-strike nuclear weapons systems at the same time. Based upon all the
evidence then available, the most likely and logical conclusion for the
Politburo to have drawn was that the Reagan administration was actively
exploiting the American public's paranoid fear over the COPD's worst-case
scenario for a defensive limited nuclear war (i.e., the "window of vulnerability") in order to obtain the necessary high degree of popular support
for the expenditure of funds exorbitant enough to construct new weapons
systems that would provide the U.S. president with the theoretical capability to wage a "successful" offensive limited nuclear war against Soviet
ICBM silos.

The American government's completion of its planned deployment of
the MK12A, MX, Trident 2, and Pershing 2 systems near the end of this
decade would effectively reverse the respective positions of the two superpowers in the COPD's hypothetical worst-case scenario for a limited nuclear
war. But the "window of vulnerability" then facing the Soviet Union
would be far more tangible and dangerous because of its preponderant
reliance on ICBMs. Then the Politburo's adoption of a "launch on warning" policy would become a real possibility, if not an inevitability. It is
likely, then, that the U.S. government would feel compelled to respond
in kind. The mutual adoption of "launch on warning" policies by both
nuclear superpowers would then create an enormous, almost inexorable
incentive for either one to launch a preemptive first strike with part or all
of its nuclear weapons systems in the event a serious geopolitical crisis
should break out between them.

This author sincerely hopes that the U.S. government would never
give serious consideration to launching a surprise nuclear attack upon the

Soviet Union for any reason. But the fate of the entire world depends upon the American people not becoming overly complacent with the supposed certainty of this result.[294] For example, at the beginning of the Cuban missile crisis in October of 1962, a substantial majority of the U.S. governmental decision-making team created to deal with the crisis (the Executive Committee) believed that a "surprise surgical air strike" against Soviet missile sites and bombers in Cuba was the most appropriate and effective measure to take.[295] Yet Robert Kennedy stridently opposed this "sneak attack" option because it was completely inconsistent with the moral values upon which the United States was founded. For this reason, he joined ranks with Secretary of Defense Robert McNamara in advocating the imposition of a naval blockade around Cuba, coupled with U.S. resort to the Organization of American States (OAS) for its endorsement.[296] Eventually the blockade alternative prevailed over the surprise attack scenario, and the United States received the unanimous support of the OAS for its "quarantine" of Cuba.[297] Solid Western hemispheric support for the arguably legal U.S. position before the OAS proved to be a key factor in convincing Khrushchev to withdraw Soviet missiles and bombers from Cuba. On the other hand, the egregiously illegal response of a "sneak attack" could have readily produced World War III.

The world can only hope that some future American president under similarly excruciating crisis conditions would likewise have the patience, courage, and foresight to override the advice given by a majority of his top advisers and refuse to order an illegal "surprise surgical airstrike" upon Soviet ICBM silos by first-strike counterforce strategic nuclear weapons systems such as the MK12A, MX, Trident 2, and Pershing 2. Yet to provide an American president with the military option of ordering such an illegal offensive "surprise limited nuclear attack" upon Soviet ICBM silos by means of the prior deployment of the MK12A, MX, Trident 2, and Pershing 2 only makes it that much more likely that these systems will in fact someday be so used. As Robert Kennedy is reported to have said in regard to the members of the Executive Committee during the Cuban missile crisis: "The fourteen people involved were very significant. . . . If six of them had been President of the U.S., I think that the world might have been blown up."[298] Because there does not exist such a phenomenon deceptively called the "window of vulnerability," these inherently offensive systems cannot serve any conceivable defensive or deterrent purpose, and they are certainly not necessary for a retaliatory attack upon Soviet population centers.

There is thus no legitimate reason under international law for the U.S.

government to develop and deploy any one of these first-strike strategic nuclear weapons systems, let alone all four simultaneously. Rather, considerations of international law forthrightly tell the American people and their representatives in Congress not to provide the president with that combination of weapons systems which would, for the first time, give him the theoretical capability of launching a "successful" preemptive nuclear strike upon the Soviet Union. If the American people deny him that capability now, he will not even be able to consider this option tomorrow. If the American people give him this capability today, he undoubtedly will consider this option in a future crisis. Consequently, Congress should have taken an affirmative decision against deploying any land-based MX, the sea-based Trident 2, and the European-based Pershing 2 systems.

The Reagan Administration's Expansion of Carter's Presidential Directive 59

Despite the nonexistence of any "window of vulnerability" for American ICBM silos, the Carter administration, under relentless attack from the Reagan campaign for being "soft" on defense, officially proclaimed Presidential Directive 59 (P.D. 59) in August 1980, just as his unsuccessful presidential campaign was entering into the home stretch. P.D. 59 naively contemplated the possibility of America fighting a "limited nuclear war," whereas its more dangerous successor, promulgated by Reagan's Secretary of Defense Caspar Weinberger in his 1982 Five-Year Defense Guidance Statement, expanded upon P.D. 59 by proclaiming as its objective the capability for America to "prevail" in a "protracted nuclear war." Under the pernicious influence of the Committee on the Present Danger, the U.S. government's basic strategic nuclear doctrine shifted from one of deterring nuclear war, to fighting and winning a nuclear war.[299] This was utter folly because any strategic nuclear doctrine possesses some degree of inherent propensity for becoming a self-fulfilling prophecy.

Related to the Reagan administration's pursuit of a first-strike nuclear capability against the Soviet Union became the necessity for the United States to develop a seemingly effective anti-ballistic missile defense in order to defeat any anticipated retaliatory attack by the residue of Soviet nuclear forces. Hence President Reagan's proposals to defend a multi-billion dollar land-based MX with multibillion dollar land-based and space-based anti-ballistic missile systems compounded one folly with another to create strategic and economic insanity.[300] It should have been made emphatically clear to the Soviet Union that the United States would not terminate the life of the 1972 U.S.-U.S.S.R. Anti-Ballistic Missile Systems Treaty when it came up for review in 1982, 1987, or beyond. Instead Reagan's so-called Strategic Defense Initiative of March 23, 1983, constituted nothing less than a formal announcement by the U.S. government of its intention to pursue a policy that will essentially amount to an anticipatory breach of the ABM Treaty. Undoubtedly the Soviet Union will respond in kind, and the monumental ABM Treaty will gradually fall into desuetude even if not specifically denounced or abrogated by either party.

In a similar vein, the Reagan administration refused to support the ratification of the Threshold Test Ban Treaty of 1974, the Peaceful Nuclear Explosions Treaty of 1976, and the SALT II Treaty of 1979, in addition to renouncing the long-standing objective of the U.S. government to negotiate a Comprehensive Test Ban Treaty (CTBT) with the Soviet Union, among others. The Carter administration had made substantial progress with the Soviet Union in the CTBT talks, but meaningful negotiations were effectively suspended in the aftermath of its Afghan invasion.[301] The theory behind the CTBT was that if governments could not test nuclear weapons, measuring their capabilities becomes difficult; this uncertainty in calculations deters their offensive use. By contrast, in adhering to the COPD's dangerous credo, the Reagan administration became primarily concerned with achieving the opposite result.

Even if the Soviet leadership might someday set out to develop an offensive first-strike capability against U.S. ICBM silos, its pursuit of such a patently illegal policy would still not provide any sound reason for the U.S. government to do the same. America must analyze the strategic nuclear equation in light of both its own vital national interests and its own cherished national values. Despite the Machiavellian assumptions held by the Reagan administration, America must not abandon or pervert its deep-seated values simply because its primary adversary might not share them. If America automatically and routinely proceeds to mimic Soviet behavior, then America gradually becomes like the U.S.S.R., and eventually becomes indistinguishable from the Soviet Union in the eyes of U.S. allies, friends, neutrals, adversaries and, most tragically of all, its own people. In other words, the U.S. government will become just as Machiavellian in its conduct of both foreign affairs and domestic policy as the Soviet government allegedly is, though this author does not subscribe to such a demonical interpretation of Soviet behavior.

The American people must not allow the Soviet Union to dictate our nuclear weapons policy to us simply because of our own government's obtuseness. If the SALT II Treaty had been duly ratified by the United States in 1979, as it was by the Soviet Union, there would never have existed any hypothetical rationale, justification, or excuse for either super-power to pursue the development of a first-strike nuclear weapons strat-egy and capability. The main obstacle to the prevention of a first-strike nuclear arms race between the two superpowers proved to be the Carter administration's failure and the Reagan administration's refusal to obtain the advice and consent of the U.S. Senate to the ratification of the SALT II Treaty. Contrary to the popular myth, therefore, when the chips were down, it was America, not the Soviet Union, that lacked the will for real arms control.

Reagan's "Zero-Option"

If on November 5, 1980, President-elect Ronald Reagan really had possessed a sincere commitment to the negotiation of nuclear arms control and reduction agreements with the Soviet Union, he would have an-nounced that immediately upon assumption of office his administration intended to renew the suspended SALT III negotiations concerning the "modernization" of theater nuclear forces (TNF) in Europe: SS-20s, the Pershing 2, ground-launched cruise missiles, the neutron bomb, the Backfire bomber, and other U.S. Forward Based Systems (FBS). The Reagan administration finally did this in November of 1981, but only after having wasted almost ten precious months before starting negotia-tions.[302] An examination of the various proposals put forth by the Reagan administration on TNF (later euphemistically called INF for "intermediate range nuclear forces") reveals that the U.S. government was not really conducting these negotiations in good faith. The so-called zero option proclaimed by President Reagan was simply a sop thrown to the people of Western Europe in order to get them to agree to the deployment of the Pershing 2s and ground-launch cruise missiles toward the end of 1983.

NATO's TNF decision in December of 1979 was two-tracked: the new TNF would be developed, but negotiations would occur so that hopefully they would not have to be deployed.[303] From all the indications in the public record, it was obvious from the outset that the Reagan adminis-tration intended to arm to the teeth first, and maybe negotiate seriously later. In this regard, President Reagan's persistent refusal to include consideration of the French and British nuclear forces within the TNF negotiations was singularly unreasonable.[304] The December 21, 1982 proposal by General Secretary Yuri Andropov to reduce Soviet intermedi-ate range ballistic missiles in Europe to the number of missiles fielded by Great Britain and France (i.e., 162) in return for NATO's abandonment of its plan to deploy the 572 medium range missiles toward the end of 1983 seemed to stake out an eminently reasonable position for the start of serious negotiations between the two superpowers.[305] Moreover, on May 4, 1983 Andropov modified and extended his proposal to call for equality in the number of warheads, not just missiles, on both sides of the Euromissile equation.

The Soviet demand that British and French nuclear weapons systems somehow be taken into account during the TNF/INF negotiations with the United States was fully supportable by basic considerations of international law. According to article 5 of the North Atlantic Treaty of 1949, an armed attack against any one or more of the members of NATO in Europe or North America "shall be considered an attack against them all" that requires each of them to assist the member or members so attacked "by taking forthwith, individually and in concert with the other Parties, such action as it deems necessary, including the use of armed force, to restore and maintain the security of the North Atlantic area."[306] The Reagan administration could never have realistically expected the Soviet Union to ignore this solemn international legal obligation incumbent upon the United States, Great Britain, and France, both individually and collectively, to come to the assistance of any other NATO member in the event of an armed attack perpetrated by the Soviet Union. The Reagan administration's stubborn adherence to this unreasonable position, together with its heedless decision to move forward with the deployment of the first-strike Pershing 2 missiles in West Germany as of December 1983, in explicit defiance of both the non-circumvention provision of the SALT II Treaty and the 1962 Kennedy-Khrushchev understanding on the removal of U.S. IRBMs from Europe, predictably resulted in the Soviet decision to discontinue the INF negotiations on November 23, 1983 and, shortly thereafter, the Strategic Arms Reduction Talks (START). Conversely, if any progress is to be made in renewed nuclear negotiations with the Soviet Union, the U.S. government must realize that Soviet demands for the removal of Pershing 2s from Europe and for equality in the number of INF systems deployed by the members of NATO and the Warsaw Pact, respectively, are reasonable and therefore should be accommodated.

The START Negotiations

In regard to the START discussions, President-elect Ronald Reagan should have called for an immediate opening of formal negotiations concerning those strategic systems not prohibited by SALT II: the "light" ICBM, long-range cruise missiles, high energy, anti-satellite, space-based weapons, and so on. By early 1981 the United States and the Soviet Union were already caught up in this post–SALT II stage of the nuclear arms race. The two superpowers, in conjunction with their allies, should have negotiated immediately and comprehensively to prevent the loss of all control over the development of these new and destabilizing weapons systems. Regrettably, the Reagan administration wasted one year of precious time debating whether even to participate in its subsequently proposed Strategic Arms Reduction Talks with the Soviet Union.[307]

To undergird movement in this direction, the Reagan administration was correct to announce its informal adherence to the terms of the unratified SALT II treaty on the condition of reciprocal behavior by the Soviet Union. But ultimately, the formal ratification of SALT II or of some cosmetic substitute by the U.S. government will prove to be the necessary precondition for any further progress in negotiating nuclear arms control and reduction agreements with the Soviet Union. President Carter's unfortunate experience in unexpectedly calling for massive nuclear weapons cuts on the part of both superpowers, especially in the area of ICBMs, clearly indicated that the best course of action for the Reagan administration would have been to announce its support for the immediate ratification of SALT II before America proceeded to negotiate any strategic arms reduction proposals with the Soviet Union, and then to have worked diligently to secure the advice and consent of the Republican-controlled Senate to the treaty. Future progress could only have been made upon the basis of consolidating past gains.

START could only have succeeded within the context of a ratified SALT II. This former objective could then have been accomplished by both superpowers agreeing to modify a ratified SALT II by significantly lowering its numerical limitations on strategic nuclear delivery vehicle launchers and upon an indefinite extension of the life of such a ratified treaty as so amended. The Soviet Union indicated that it was prepared to proceed in this manner within the context of the START negotiations.[308] The Russians proposed an equal ceiling for both superpowers of 1,800 long-range missiles and bombers, which would have required the Soviet Union to reduce from its current level of 2,500 and the United States from 2,000. In addition, the Soviet Union expressed a willingness to establish an overall ceiling on the number of nuclear warheads carried by long-range missiles and bombs carried by bombers. Furthermore, the Soviet Union stated a desire to retain "the best elements of" SALT II and a readiness to consider modifications. Nevertheless, the Reagan administration rejected that forthcoming overture because it still stubbornly insisted that the SALT II Treaty was in some mysterious way "fatally flawed." The time was long past for the Reagan administration to have abandoned the rhetoric of the Reagan campaign against Carter.

Nuclear Non-Proliferation

In an equally reactionary manner, the nebulous non-proliferation policies of the Reagan administration seemed to consist primarily of dismantling President Carter's strict anti-proliferation regime and replacing it by the promiscuous philosophy of America becoming a "reliable supplier" of nuclear knowledge, training, technology, materials, and expertise to selected countries—in other words, a reliable proliferator.[309] Certainly the greatest preventive to further nuclear weapons proliferation would be a massive reduction in both the U.S. and Soviet nuclear weapons inventories. No anti-proliferation regime can eventually succeed unless and until the two superpowers take seriously their obligations under article 6 of the Nuclear Non-Proliferation Treaty (NPT) "to pursue negotiations in good faith on effective measures relating to the cessation of the nuclear arms race at an early date and to nuclear disarmament, and on a general and complete disarmament under strict and effective international control."[310] The totality of the Reagan administration's nuclear weapons policies constituted a clear-cut violation of NPT article 6, which threatened to produce the further proliferation of nuclear weapons around the world. Conversely, in regard to nuclear non-proliferation as well, only the political will was needed for the U.S. government to take the first step away from nuclear catastrophe for the entire world by ratifying SALT II. Otherwise the specter of nuclear Armageddon, envisioned most recently by such pragmatic and experienced leaders as Hans Morgenthau, George Kistiakowski, George Kennan, and Hyman Rickover, will envelop the earth for all eternity.

The Repudiation of Linkage

Both the Carter and Reagan administrations should have repudiated their adoption of Henry Kissinger's Machiavellian theory of "linkage" between considerations of geopolitical power politics (e.g., Afghanistan, Poland, and El Salvador) and those of nuclear weapons control.[311] Human survival depends on the success of these endeavors to control the nuclear arms race by the principles and techniques of international law and organizations. Handicapped, defective, and imperfect they may be, but they represent the only short-term and long-range substitutes for the increasing risk of global nuclear war.

As for the so-called "linkage in fact," if the politicized treaty ratification procedure in the U.S. Senate still proves to be a major obstacle to the realization of the foregoing agenda, future presidential administrations must submit their nuclear arms control and reduction agreements with the Soviet Union for approval by a joint resolution of Congress.[312] Such apocalyptic agreements must not be held hostage to the self-interested votes of a few senators. Failure by the Senate to support the Treaty of Versailles and the Covenant of the League of Nations was in part responsible for World War II. Senate obstinacy over a revised SALT II or SALT III or START I must not be permitted to pave the way for World War III.

19

International Lawlessness in the
Caribbean Basin

The Inter-American System of International
Law and Politics

On April 12, 1984, U.S. Ambassador to the United Nations Jeane
Kirkpatrick delivered a speech before the 78th annual convention of the
American Society of International Law in which she attempted to justify
the Reagan administration's twin decisions to mine the harbors in Nicaragua and to withdraw from the compulsory jurisdiction of the International Court of Justice in regard to disputes concerning Central America
for a period of two years in order to avoid Nicaragua's suit against the
United States over this and numerous other instances of violent and
illegal conduct perpetrated upon it.[313] The gist of Kirkpatrick's argument was that since the adversaries of the United States often engage in
behavior that is completely lawless, thoroughly reprehensible, and occasionally barbaric, the U.S. government had both the right and the duty
to do exactly the same thing. Needless to say, her audience found her
"argument" appalling. Yet such a rectificatory attitude toward international law was simply characteristic of the Reagan administration's misguided approach to world politics from the moment it came to office in
1981.

For reasons explained more fully in Chapter 12, it is a serious mistake
for U.S. government decision makers to operate on the hard-nosed "realist"
premise that the international legal order is a perfectly symmetrical
system in which a violation of international law by a supposed U.S.
adversary should necessarily result in the reciprocal counterviolation of
international law by the United States government, especially when the

dispute involves minor powers such as Nicaragua and Cuba. This rectificatory approach to international law and politics is essentially based upon the misleading assumption that there exists a perfect symmetry of international legal rights and duties between equal, independent, and sovereign states. Whatever the merits of recognizing this legal fiction for the purpose of maintaining international peace and security, it obscures the fact that all states do not benefit equally from the rules of international law. The U.S. government has the most to lose in the event its active participation in a reciprocal cycle of violations and counterviolations of international law severely undermines the post–World War II international legal order embodied in the U.N. Charter.

Nevertheless, whatever position one might take concerning the wisdom of adopting this insight for application to the conduct of U.S. foreign policy around the world, the rectificatory approach to international law and politics exemplified in Kirkpatrick's speech possesses absolutely no validity for application to the states of the Western hemisphere, most of which are members of the Organization of American States (OAS). In this region of the world, for the past century the U.S. government has taken the pioneer role in the development of a distinctively inter-American system of international political, legal, and economic relations that was purposely designed to be superior to the principles of interaction governing relations among non-American states or between American states and non-American states.[314] This longstanding objective of U.S. foreign policy commenced with Secretary of State James Blaine's 1881 call for the convocation of the First International American Conference at Washington, D.C., that eventually met in 1889,[315] and culminated almost six decades later with the Ninth International American Conference held at Bogota in 1948, which adopted the OAS Charter.[316]

To be sure, the creation of a viable and discrete inter-American system was intended to advance the United States government's perceived vital national security interest in getting and keeping the European mother countries out of the affairs of the Western hemisphere for good. But at the same time this inter-American system of international relations was originally conceived to be different from, if not antithetical to, the pre–U.N. Charter European system of public international law and politics, which was grounded in monarchism, the balance of power, spheres of influence, war, conquest, imperialism, and the threat and use of force. By contrast, the inter-American system was to operate upon the principles of sovereign equality, state independence, non-interventionism, the peaceful settlement of international disputes, international law and organizations, international arbitration and adjudication, mutual cooperation, and a fundamental commitment to democracy as the ideal form of government.

These philosophical bonds between sister American republics found their common origin in the intellectual ferment of the European Enlightenment and were tempered by the shared experience of revolutions for independence against the Old World mother countries. This similar heritage created a profound awareness among all states in the inter-American region that they possessed a joint and several interest in the advancement of superior rules for international behavior applicable to their mutual relations that at some time in the not-too-distant future could hopefully be expanded to include relations between all states in the international community. For these reasons it was thought possible to create a system of international law and politics in the Western hemisphere that was governed by a set of international legal rules that were more exacting, humane, enlightened, liberal, and moral than those currently in operation between the states of the Old World, especially when it came to threat and use of transnational force, and notwithstanding the fact that American states might have to continue to adhere to such regressive and bankrupt rules in their relations with non-American states.

The Reagan Administration's Embrace of the Roosevelt Corollary to the Monroe Doctrine

It was against the democratic principles upon which the American republics had affirmed their unity that the Reagan administration argued that supposed Nicaraguan and Cuban violations of international law in the Western hemisphere or in Africa either could or should justify U.S. counterviolations of international law in Central America or elsewhere. Despite the lessons of history, the Reagan administration, in its pervasive arrogance of power and its elemental disrespect for both domestic and international law, soundly repudiated the progressive development in the conduct of U.S. foreign policy toward the states of the Western hemisphere, which had fostered the growth of the distinctively inter-American system of international law and politics during the past century. In place of this system the Reagan government publicly claimed to be adhering to the so-called Roosevelt Corollary to the Monroe Doctrine as the nucleus of its violent and destabilizing foreign policy towards Central America and the Caribbean basin.

As initially stated by President James Monroe in his message to Congress of December 1, 1823, the Monroe Doctrine proclaimed that the American continents were no longer considered by the U.S. government to be appropriate subjects for future colonization by any European powers; that the countries of Europe must not seek to extend their political systems to the Western hemisphere; that the United States would not interfere in the affairs of any current European colony or dependency in the Western hemisphere; that the United States would remain neutral in the war between Spain and the newly independent governments of South America, but not to the point of permitting a reimposition of Spanish rule; and, finally, that the United States would continue to obey the dogma of Washington's farewell address by preserving its neutrality in the affairs of Europe except when its rights were seriously jeopardized.[317] The Polk Corollary to the Monroe Doctrine subsequently created an additional prohibition that a European power could not acquire territory in the Western hemisphere by means of cession from another European power.[318]

From a Latin American perspective, the Monroe Doctrine as originally defined was not theoretically objectionable since it was well understood that this U.S. policy position was in part responsible for the ability of Latin American states to achieve and maintain independence from their European mother countries.[319] The real problem arose from the so-called Roosevelt Corollary to the Monroe Doctrine, announced by President Theodore Roosevelt in his annual message to Congress on December 6, 1904.[320] Although phrased in general terms to apply to any international delict committed by a Western hemispheric state, the essence of this precept meant that the U.S. government would exercise an alleged right of preemptive intervention into the domestic affairs of Central American and Caribbean countries delinquent in the payment of their public debts to private creditors in European states. The alleged justification for the Roosevelt Corollary was that in order to prevent military intervention by European creditor states to collect on their nationals' debts in the Western hemisphere, and thus to forestall potential breaches of the Monroe Doctrine, the U.S. government must arrogate to itself a supposed right to impose upon Latin American debtor countries a formal regime for the proper administration of their public finances and the retirement of their public debts under direct U.S. supervision. If deemed necessary, this objective would be accomplished by the forceful seizure and occupation of foreign territory and customs houses by armed U.S. troops.

From a Latin American perspective, the Roosevelt Corollary announced a unilateral policy of hegemonial imperialism by the U.S. government toward the states of the Western hemisphere that was akin to the balance of power politics and spheres of influence system then being pursued around the world by the great powers of Europe. For example, Argentine Minister of Foreign Affairs Luis M. Drago argued quite vigorously that the United States should not assume the functions of a public debt collector for Latin American countries on behalf of Europe as it was then doing in the Dominican Republic.[321] Latin America was not a U.S. sphere of influence and the U.S. had no right to exercise such "international police functions" throughout the region. The Roosevelt Corollary explicitly contradicted the underlying principles of non-interventionism, state equality, and sovereign independence so fundamental to preserving the integrity of the Monroe Doctrine that they must be applied to international relations among all Western hemispheric states, and especially by the United States in its dealings with Latin American countries. Even former U.S. Secretaries of State Richard Olney and Elihu Root—the first to President Cleveland, the latter to Theodore Roosevelt—eventually joined the Latin American protests, insisting that the true essence of the Monroe Doctrine did not require the United States to become the "international policeman" of the Western hemisphere or a debt collection agent for the benefit of European creditor states and their nationals.[322]

The formal promulgation of the Roosevelt Corollary to the Monroe Doctrine had been precipitated by the dire economic situation in the Dominican Republic, where the government had literally fallen into a state of international bankruptcy and was faced with the imminent prospect of military intervention by European powers in order to enforce collection on debts owed to their nationals.[323] Pursuant to a Convention effectively imposed by the Roosevelt administration upon the Dominican Republic government in 1907, the president of the United States was authorized to appoint a General Receiver for the collection and proper administration of all Dominican customs duties revenues.[324] This 1907 Convention did not explicitly grant the United States a right to intervene in the Dominican Republic for the purpose of securing the discharge of any of its underlying obligations, though according to article II the United States could provide the General Receiver and his assistants with "such protection as it may find to be requisite for the performance of their duties."[325] Under the specter of the Great War in Europe, on November 29, 1916, President Woodrow Wilson decided to intervene and placed the Dominican Republic under military occupation over an alleged failure to fulfill the terms of the Convention.[326] The marines were withdrawn in 1924, but the customs receivership was not terminated until 1940.[327]

The 1907 Dominican Republic Loan Convention proved to be a rough-and-ready model for the negotiation of economic receivership agreements between the United States and Honduras in 1911, which was not ratified;[328] between the United States and Nicaragua in 1911, not ratified,[329] and again in 1914, which was ratified;[330] and between the United States and Haiti in 1915.[331] The United States marines intervened in Nicaragua in 1912, occupied the country until 1925, returned the next year, and finally withdrew in 1933.[332] U.S. marines occupied Haiti from 1915 through 1934, though the receivership was maintained until 1947.[333] The marines landed in Hondruas in 1924 and were not withdrawn until the following year.[334] In this manner "dollar diplomacy" and "gunboat diplomacy" were to merge and proceed hand-in-hand in the formulation of U.S. foreign policy towards Central America and the Caribbean basin.[335]

Military interventionism became the keystone of U.S. foreign policy towards the Western hemisphere from the time of the 1898 Spanish-American War until at least a decade after the conclusion of the First World War. Politically the policy was justified by the Roosevelt Corollary to the Monroe Doctrine. In addition, legally the policy was supposedly justified either by the terms of some treaty or by the asserted right under customary international law for the U.S. government to intervene militarily in order to protect the lives and property of its nationals abroad from dangerous civil conditions allegedly degenerating beyond the control of the host government—invariably a pretext at best. Strategically, the fulcrum of U.S. interventionist foreign policy toward Central America and the Caribbean essentially turned upon the need to protect the Panama Canal Zone, which linked the two American coasts and served as the highway for political, military, and economic communications between the U.S. mainland and its recently acquired possessions in the Far East.

For the first three decades of the twentieth century the United States government would fruitlessly try to cope with the problem of curing endemic political, military, and economic instability in Central America, the Caribbean basin, and Mexico by the crude techniques of actual or threatened military intervention and occupation. This interventionist policy expressly contravened the emotional sentiments, philosophical principles, and numerous international legal conventions the U.S. government was simultaneously promoting for general application within the inter-American system of international relations that it was actively seeking to create in the Western hemisphere. The ramifications of the Roosevelt Corollary's elemental characteristics of military interventionism and economic imperialism have chronically plagued and hopelessly perplexed U.S. foreign policy decision making toward Central American and Caribbean countries up to and including the present era.

Yet contemporaneously with the implementation of the Roosevelt Corollary it was also recognized by many members of the U.S. foreign policy establishment that unilateral military intervention by the United States into the domestic affairs of Central American and Caribbean countries under whatever legal and political justifications or pretexts was in itself undesirable and ultimately self-defeating over the long run, and certainly far less preferable than founding some system sanctioned by all Western hemispheric states that would provide for their collective intervention when necessary in order to ensure that each lives up to its international responsibilities.[336] Such notions, prevalent among several generations of U.S. foreign policy decision makers, eventually proved to be the motivating force behind the foundation of the OAS and the inclusion of chapter 8 in the U.N. Charter for the express purpose of guaranteeing the effectiveness of this organizational structure to maintain international peace and security in the Western hemisphere. But by failing to learn the tragic lessons derived from the unsuccessful history of unilateral U.S. military interventionism in the Western hemisphere throughout the past eighty years, the Reagan administration has condemned the peoples of all American states to repeat the mistakes of the Roosevelt Corollary.

The Illegality of the U.S. Invasion of Grenada

Arguments like those by the Reagan administration, purporting to justify the U.S. invasion of Grenada under international law, must not be allowed to manipulate the U.S. populace into supporting yet another violent intervention into the domestic affairs of some other independent American state such as Nicaragua. Throughout the twentieth century, the U.S. government has routinely concocted evanescent threats to the lives and property of U.S. nationals abroad as pretexts to justify armed interventions into and military occupations of sister American states. The transparency of these pretexts was just as obvious then as it is today.

The Reagan administration had the burden of proof to establish by means of clear and convincing evidence that there did in fact exist an immediate threat to the lives of U.S. citizens in Grenada, which it never discharged.[337] Even if it had, such a threat could have justified, at the very most, only a limited military operation along the lines of the Israeli raid at Entebbe for the sole purpose of evacuating the major concentration of U.S. nationals studying at the St. George's School of Medicine.[338] The alleged threat to U.S. nationals was totally insufficient to justify a full-scale military invasion and occupation of the country, together with the forceful deposition of the Austin-Coard regime.

Nor could the Reagan administration's alternative rationale of terminating the "chaotic conditions" allegedly then present in Grenada be properly invoked to justify the military invasion, occupation, and regime ouster.[339] Even when it actually exists, chronic disorder in a country does not permit neighboring states to intervene for the purpose of re-establishing minimum public security, let alone imposing a democratic form of government.[340] Under article 51 of the U.N. Charter, neighboring states do possess a right of individual or collective self-defense to protect their own borders from external attack originating from some unstable neighbor.[341] But there was absolutely no evidence that any faction in Grenada was engaged in or about to inflict any overt or covert attack upon some neighboring Caribbean state by means of armed troops, guerillas, or "terrorists."[342] If such clear and convincing evidence had existed, the U.S. government could have responded immediately with measures necessary and proportionate to protect the victim, at its request, in accordance with the right of collective self-defense recognized by U.N. Charter article 51.

As for the so-called request for assistance by the then deposed governor-general of Grenada, Sir Paul Scoon, there is no point in fruitlessly debating whether or not he might have possessed some residuum of constitutional powers to request foreign military intervention under the circumstances prevalent in Grenada after the Austin-Coard coup. The fact of the matter was that President Reagan gave the "green light" for the Grenadian invasion to the Pentagon on Saturday, October 22, 1983.[343] According to Sir Paul's own account of his role, it was not until late Sunday evening that he even considered external assistance to be necessary, and then what he asked for was not an invasion but help from outside.[344] Since Sir Paul's request for assistance came well after Reagan's order to invade, the former becomes completely immaterial to analyzing the legality or illegality of the U.S. invasion. As the distinguished, conservative, and generally pro-American *Economist* concluded in a special report of March 10, 1984: "The Scoon request was almost certainly a fabrication concocted between the OECS and Washington to calm the post-invasion diplomatic storm. As concoctions go, it was flimsy."[345] Those international lawyers and Reagan administration apologists who purport to attribute any semblance of legal validity to this bogus request must gut the truth in order to do so.[346]

Any such violent intervention into the domestic affairs of Grenada by the U.S. government operating in conjunction with a motley collection of Caribbean states required the explicit authorization by the U.N. Security Council acting under chapter 7 of the U.N. Charter, or at the very least by the appropriate regional organization acting in accordance with U.N. Charter chapter 8 and subject to the overall approval of the U.N. Security Council. In this case, the Organization of American States was the only collective agency mandated by the regional community of states to maintain international peace and security in the Western hemisphere, and all the participants in the Grenadian invasion (i.e., United States, Jamaica, Barbados, Dominica, St. Lucia, St. Vincent, and Antigua) as well as Grenada itself were members of the OAS.[347] Article 18 of the OAS Charter specifically provides that no state or group of states has the right to intervene, directly or indirectly, for any reason whatever, in the internal or external affairs of any other state.[348] Article 20 declares that the territory of a member state is inviolable and therefore may not be the object, even temporarily, of military occupation or of other measures of force taken by another state, directly or indirectly, on any grounds whatever. Finally, article 21 reiterates the solemn obligation of article 2(4) of the U.N. Charter that American states will not have recourse to force except in cases of self-defense pursuant to existing treaties. In direct violation of these rudimentary international legal obligations, the Reagan administration quite forthrightly admitted that it invaded Grenada for the illegitimate purpose of deposing the leftist military junta that had seized power after the coup against Prime Minister Maurice Bishop,[349] and then installing a government more favorably disposed to the United States. As such, the invasion constituted a Crime against Peace as defined by the Nuremberg Principles.

The members of the Organization of Eastern Caribbean States (OECS) could not have lawfully authorized the U.S. invasion of Grenada. To be sure, article 22 of the OAS Charter provides that measures adopted for the maintenance of international peace and security in accordance with existing treaties do not constitute a violation of the principles set forth in the aforementioned OAS Charter articles 18 and 20. So, let us assume for the sake of argument that OAS article 22 actually applies to the subsequently concluded OECS Charter (1981).[350] Apparently Secretary of State George Shultz believed some such interconnection to exist when he argued that the OECS was the functional equivalent to the Rio Pact for the English-speaking countries of the Caribbean basin.[351] Schultz's argument, however, was merely an effort to muddy the waters of the debate.

The United States and the Spanish-speaking countries of the Western hemisphere are parties to the 1947 Inter-American Treaty of Reciprocal Assistance (called the Rio Pact),[352] which is a collective self-defense agreement concluded under U.N. Charter article 51. The Rio Pact is the Western hemisphere's functional equivalent to the North Atlantic Treaty,[353] the essence of which can be found in the requirement of Rio article 3 (NATO article 5) that an armed attack by any state against a member state shall be considered as an attack upon all member states and, consequently, that each member state undertakes to assist in meeting the attack in accordance with the inherent right of individual or collective self-defense recognized by U.N. Charter article 51. But collective self-defense agreements concluded under U.N. Charter article 51 such as the Rio Pact or NATO do not and cannot provide member states with any legal authority to intervene into matters which are essentially within the domestic affairs of another member state.[354]

Since the English-speaking countries of the Caribbean basin were not parties to the Rio Pact, by means of OECS Charter article 8 several of them decided to establish a Defense and Security Committee that would merely coordinate measures for their collective self-defense. But article 8 restricted OECS competence in such security matters to situations amounting to an "external aggression" and then only in accordance with the right of individual or collective self-defense recognized by U.N. Charter article 51.[355] Hence article 8 provided no authority for OECS intervention into the turbulent domestic affairs of Grenada produced by the anti-Bishop coup. Furthermore, OECS article 8 required unanimous agreement by member states on the Defense and Security Committee before any action could be taken, and that condition was never fulfilled.[356]

In the alternative event that the invasion was supposedly approved by the OECS Authority of Heads of Government of the Member States of the Organization, OECS article 6(5) specifically required that all decisions taken by the Authority must receive the affirmative vote of all member states present and voting at the meeting of the Authority at which such decisions were taken, "provided that such decisions shall have no force and effect until ratified by those Member States, if any, which were not present at that meeting." Grenada was not present at the OECS meetings which purported to authorize its invasion.[357] And for reasons previously explained, the bogus Scoon "request" could not constitute a valid ex post facto ratification of the illegal and ultra vires OECS decision to invade. So the invocation of article 8 by OECS members was completely ineffectual to justify their invasion of Grenada and, *a fortiori*, unable to serve as the legal basis for its invasion by non-members such as the United States, Jamaica and Barbados.[358]

The Precedential Significance of the Cuban Missile Crisis and the Dominican Republic Civil War

If the Reagan administration and the members of the OECS had honestly believed the very existence of the Austin-Coard regime in Grenada could have created a serious threat to the *future* peace and stability of the Caribbean, the appropriate remedy would have been to bring the situation to the attention of the OAS. In the relatively recent past the U.S. government and other Western hemispheric states have successfully resorted to the OAS on more than one occasion in order to deal with matters they considered to jeopardize the peace and security of the region.[359] For example, during the 1962 Cuban missile crisis the U.S. government decided to turn to the OAS when the Kennedy administration realized it was not able to justify its "quarantine" of Cuba under U.N. Charter article 51 because there existed no immediate threat of armed attack or armed aggression by Cuba against the United States.[360] At the request of the United States, the Council of the OAS decided to act provisionally as the Rio Pact's Organ of Consultation and unanimously approved the "quarantine" of Cuba on the jurisdictional basis of Rio Pact article 6, covering threats to the peace of the region other than armed attack, instead of Rio Pact article 3, covering cases of armed attack.[361] The OAS's overwhelming support for the U.S. position exercised a profound impact upon Khrushchev's decision to remove the missiles and terminate the crisis, thus avoiding World War III. (Nevertheless, the Kennedy administration argued somewhat incredulously that the OAS "quarantine" of Cuba was not an "enforcement action" that required explicit "authorization" by the U.N. Security Council as required by U.N. Charter article 53 because the "quarantine" was only recommendatory, not mandatory by nature.)[362]

Similarly, during the course of the U.S. military intervention into the Dominican Republic in 1965, the Johnson administration realized its obvious lack of legal authority to remain in the country for the purpose of terminating the civil war raging in Santo Domigo and then reestablishing a democratically elected government.[363] Consequently, it resorted to the OAS in order to obtain approval for a continuation of the U.S. military occupation (though not for the invasion itself) under the jurisdiction of the OAS. Upon the submission of the crisis by the United States to the OAS Council, the latter convoked a meeting of the Organ of Consultation, not under Rio Pact article 6 as during the Cuban missile crisis, but under then article 39 of the OAS Charter dealing with "problems of an urgent nature and of a common interest to the American states."[364] The reason why Rio Pact article 6 was not invoked as the jurisdictional basis for the convocation of the Organ of Consultation was that it was not believed the Dominican Republic civil war constituted a fact or situation that might endanger the peace of America. Eventually the Tenth Meeting of Consultation of Ministers of Foreign Affairs created an Inter-American Peace Force (IAPF) operating under its authority in the Dominican Republic that incorporated the U.S. troops already on the island, inter alia.[365] Nevertheless, the U.S. government again argued somewhat disingenuously before the U.N. Security Council that the Inter-American Peace Force was not an "enforcement action" that required the explicit "authorization" of the Security Council under article 53 of the U.N. Charter.[366]

This author does not intend to confer any endorsement upon the legal propriety or political wisdom of either the "quarantine" of Cuba or any aspect of the U.S. intervention into the Dominican Republic. Instead, my intention is to contrast U.S.-requested OAS involvement in these two incidents with the fact that the Reagan administration never even bothered to bring the post-Bishop situation in Grenada to the attention of the OAS as it easily could have done under the new article 59 of the revised OAS Charter,[367] which is the successor to the former article 39 relied upon by the Johnson administration during the Dominican Republic civil war. Clearly the situation in Grenada produced by the anti-Bishop coup was not nearly as serious internally or as potentially dangerous externally as the civil war in Santo Domingo that confronted the Johnson administration. Yet unlike Johnson, President Reagan did not even bother to request the OAS to intervene in Grenada for the limited purpose of organizing and supervising popular elections leading to the installation of a democratic government and the termination of the U.S. military occupation of the island. The total lack of such an OAS imprimatur will raise serious doubts concerning the international legitimacy of any successor government in Grenada that is elected under the auspices of U.S. military occupation.

The Mirror-Imagery of the Johnson and Brezhnev Doctrines

In the immediate aftermath of the Grenadian invasion, 11 members of the U.N. Security Council[368] and 108 members of the U.N. General Assembly,[369] among both groups several staunch U.S. allies, deplored this invasion as a gross violation of the most fundamental principles of international law enshrined in the U.N. Charter. The U.S. government suffered the most serious setback to its traditional role in upholding the integrity of the international legal order in the Western hemisphere since President Johnson's strikingly similar invasion of the Dominican Republic in 1965.

Historically, any U.S. foreign policy founded upon such blatant violations of international law has proven to be counterproductive and ultimately self-defeating over the long haul. For example, even though Johnson subsequently obtained OAS approval for U.S. military occupation of the Dominican Republic under the guise of the IAPF, this maneuver was followed in relatively short order by Leonid Brezhnev's promulgation of a reincarnated version of the so-called Johnson Doctrine as the primary justification for the Soviet invasion of Czechoslovakia in 1968. In an effort to justify the U.S. invasion of the Dominican Republic, the Johnson Doctrine proclaimed that although revolution in any country is normally a matter for that country to deal with, it becomes a matter calling for hemispheric action when the objective is the establishment of a communist dictatorship.[370] In a similar vein the Brezhnev Doctrine stated that "when the internal and external forces hostile to socialism seek to revert the development of any socialist country toward the restoration of the capitalist order, when a threat to the cause of socialism in that country, a threat to the security of the socialist community as a whole, emerges, this is no longer only a problem of the people of that country but also a common problem . . . for all socialist states."[371] There is a remarkable degree of similarity between the arguments put forth by the U.S. government before the U.N. Security Council in 1965 to justify its invasion of the Dominican Republic and the arguments employed at the Security Council by the Soviet Union to justify its 1968 invasion of Czechoslovakia.[372] It is almost as if the later Soviet diplomats obtained a verbatim record of the earlier Security Council debates over the Dominican Republic invasion, and adopted wholesale the gist of the legal arguments set forth by the U.S. government in order to justify their Czechoslovak invasion. However, the Warsaw Pact was obviously a collective self-defense agreement concluded under article 51 of the U.N. Charter and therefore could provide absolutely no legal justification for military intervention into the domestic affairs of one member state by any or all other member states. Brezhnev's transmuted version of the Johnson Doctrine would return to vex U.S. foreign policy decision making as one of the justifications for the Soviet's patently illegal invasion of Afghanistan in 1979.[373]

U.S. military action in egregious violation of international law sends a strong message to the entire international community that in the opinion of the U.S. government the conventional rules restricting the transnational threat and use of force found in the U.N. and OAS Charters no longer apply in settling the myriad of contemporary international disputes. When even the United States flouts international law, the only consequence can be an increasing degree of international violence, chaos, and anarchy around the globe. U.S. military forces are certainly not up to the task of "policing" all of Central America and the Caribbean basin, let alone the entire world. And as the War Powers Act proves,[374] the American people would not permit them to do so anyway despite the bellicose inclinations of the Reagan administration. It was not just an unfortunate coincidence that relatively soon after the C.I.A. had mined harbors in Nicaragua, submarine mines mysteriously appeared to destroy international shipping in the vital Suez Canal and Red Sea.

The Reagan Administration's Undeclared War
Against Nicaragua

Reagan's lawlessness in Grenada haunts the future of U.S. foreign policy around the world and especially in the Western hemisphere. Yet shortly after the Grenada invasion the Reagan administration seemed to be planning an identical fate for the Sandinista government in Nicaragua under the subterfuge of reviving the moribund Central American Defense Council Pact (CONDECA).[375] As a matter of international law, CONDECA is functionally analogous to the Rio Pact in that it constitutes a collective self-defense agreement concluded under U.N. Charter article 51, and thus can only be triggered in the event of an armed attack or external aggression upon member states. Consequently, the Reagan administration attempted to provoke the Sandinista government into attacking the opposition *contra* groups at their bases of supply in Honduras, which could then serve as a pretext for the intervention of U.S. and Central American military forces under the guise of "the right of collective self-defense." Such policies undertaken by any administration of any government present the immediate danger of a region-wide war in Central America. Thus, Congress, to safeguard against any further employment of these policies, must enact a Central American equivalent to the Clark Amendment for Angola,[376] which would expressly prohibit the expenditure of any U.S. governmental funds in support of overt or covert military or paramilitary operations in the Western hemisphere without explicit congressional authorization.

Actions like those pursued by the Reagan administration to organize and support military operations launched by opposition *contra* groups from bases of supply in Honduras and Costa Rica against the Sandinista government are illegal, irresponsible, and counterproductive for maintaining international peace and security for all states in Central America. Such actions seem more concerned with obtaining an outright military victory against the Sandinista government in Nicaragua and against the insurgents in El Salvador at any cost, than they are to restore some semblance of peace and stability to Central America. They are merely a continuation of Theodore Roosevelt's antiquated "big stick" policy of unilateral U.S. military intervention, undertaken as a chimerical panacea for curing the widespread instability indigenous to Central America and the Caribbean basin.

Despite protestations to the contrary by "realist" politicians, there does indeed exist a realistic alternative to intervention by U.S. troops or doing nothing in Central America. In order to head off a U.S.-instigated border war between Honduras and Nicaragua, as well as to prevent the militarization and consequent destabilization of Costa Rica, an independent peacekeeping force and/or observer group organized by the OAS or (if Nicaragua continues to object to the OAS's involvement, by the U.N. Security Council) should be stationed both on the border between Honduras and Nicaragua and on the border between Costa Rica and Nicaragua. Its mission would be to interdict any alleged flow of arms from Nicaragua into El Salvador as well as to prevent the infiltration of all paramilitary forces into Nicaragua from its immediate neighbors.

For good cause, Nicaragua objected to the implementation of such an independent peacekeeping role by the OAS because the Sandinistas correctly perceived the organization to have been historically under the predominant influence of the U.S. government. For example, in 1979 the Carter administration attempted to convince the OAS to send an international peacekeeping force to Nicaragua in order to prevent the Sandinistas from assuming power in light of the then impending departure of Anastasio Somoza. Even though ultimately unsuccessful, this U.S. strategem created legitimate suspicions about the creditability of the OAS in the eyes of the Sandinistas.[377] The U.S. government must strive to convince the Sandinistas that submission of the matter to the OAS will be pursued in good faith and that the U.S. government will abide by whatever resolution is eventually worked out by the rest of the OAS members. In addition, for reasons that will be discussed below, Cuba should be reintegrated into the OAS in order to provide the Sandinistas with a favorable interlocutor and as a demonstration of good faith and impartiality by both the United States and the OAS as a whole.

If Nicaragua nevertheless proves to be reluctant to have the matter submitted to the OAS, the U.N. Security Council still possesses concurrent jurisdiction to deal with the situation in Central America under U.N. Charter articles 34, 35, and 52. For quite some time the U.N. Security Council has proven to be extremely effective at the deployment of observer groups and peacekeeping forces along border regions engulfed in serious transnational conflict.[378] Just because the OAS might ultimately prove to be institutionally incapable of serving as an effective intermediator in the dispute between the United States and Nicaragua, its incapacity neither can nor should prevent the U.N. Security Council from exercising its "primary responsibility" for the maintenance of international peace and security in the Western hemisphere under U.N. Charter article 24.

As for the Reagan administration's mere rhetorical support for the so-called Contadora Group, such gestures generated only the smokescreen of a multilateral approach, while the adherents of "big stick" diplomacy pursued a unilateral and illegal alternative based upon violence, threats, and coercion. With all due respect for the good intentions of the members of the Contadora Group (Mexico, Panama, Venezuela, and Colombia) they cannot serve as an effective substitute for the formal involvement by either the OAS or the U.N. Security Council. Their sincere efforts to obtain a peaceful resolution of the conflicts in Central America have in the past only been deceptively manipulated by the Reagan administration to provide the veneer of a plausible legal argument why neither the OAS nor the U.N. Security Council should exercise its recognized jurisdiction to deal with the matter.

The Alleged Connection Between Reagan's Policies Toward Nicaragua and El Salvador

In the pursuit if its patently illegal policy to overthrow the Sandinista government in Nicaragua, the Reagan administration contemptuously violated the essential provisions of both the U.N. and OAS Charters and numerous principles of customary international law concerning the use of transnational force, including the terms of the 1907 Hague Convention Relative to the Laying of Submarine Mines,[379] to which Nicaragua and the United States are parties. The C.I.A.'s mining of the Nicaraguan harbors constituted a War Crime within the meaning of the Nuremberg Principles that created personal criminal responsibility under international law for all U.S. government officials who participated in the formulation and execution of this reprehensible policy. In a category just as heinous were the repeated violations of U.S. domestic law perpetrated by the Reagan administration to pursue its internationally lawless policies in Central America: the War Powers Act,[380] the Neutrality Act,[381] the Ethics in Government Act,[382] the Boland Amendment,[383] and the Intelligence Oversight Act,[384] among others.

Capping this list was the Reagan administration's sordid attempt to withdraw from the compulsory jurisdiction of the International Court of Justice in regard to disputes concerning Central America for a period of two years in order to avoid Nicaragua's suit against the United States. This action represented an unconstitutional usurpation by President Reagan of the power to amend a treaty that received the advice and consent of two-thirds of the Senate without receiving the additional advice and consent of two-thirds of the Senate to the amendment. The Reagan administration's concerted effort to undermine the compulsory jurisdiction of the World Court constituted a pernicious assault upon the integrity of the entire post–World War II international legal order. Similarly, the Reagan administration flouted its obligation to terminate immediately all support for the opposition *contra* groups in accordance with the Interim Order of Protection issued by the International Court of Justice on May 10, 1984.[385]

The amalgamation of Reagan's foreign policies toward Central America constituted nothing less than a gross pattern of violations of the most fundamental requirements of U.S. domestic law, international law, and the U.S. Constitution. Reagan officials have attempted to justify this gross pattern of domestic and international lawlessness by the specious argument that the various measures they have inflicted upon the Sandinista government are part of a legitimate collective self-defense effort undertaken to protect the government of El Salvador against alleged Nicaraguan aggression.[386] Concerning this latter allegation, however, there exists a serious question of proof because the Reagan administration never adduced clear and convincing evidence that the Sandinista government was currently providing weapons, equipment, and supplies to the insurgents in El Salvador, pleading that such revelations might possibly compromise sensitive intelligence sources and methods.[387] Irrespective of the self-serving nature of these assertions, international law placed the burden of proof on this matter squarely upon the shoulders of the Reagan administration.[388]

The Reagan administration's refusal to produce clear and convincing evidence that after the spring of 1981 Nicaragua was sending weapons, equipment, and supplies to the insurgents in El Salvador, forfeited any claim to the support of the American people, the OAS, and the members of the international community for measures involving the threat or use of force against the Sandinista government on the grounds of collective self-defense for El Salvador. The evidence in the public record clearly indicated that the Sandinista government terminated the large-scale provision of military assistance to the insurgents in El Salvador by the spring of 1981,[389] shortly after Reagan came to power uttering dire threats of economic, political, and military reprisals if Nicaragua's undoubtedly impermissible conduct did not cease. Since the success of those threats, however, the primary focus of the Reagan administration's policies towards Central America became achieving the quite illegal goals of deposing the Sandinista government in Nicaragua and defeating the insurgents in El Salvador's civil war.

Even assuming that Nicaragua provided limited amounts of weapons, equipment, and supplies to the insurgents in El Salvador after the spring of 1981, that fact, if established by means of clear and convincing evidence, would still not have justified the violent policies that the Reagan administration subsequently pursued toward Nicaragua. For example, U.S. instigation of and support for the *contra* groups operating out of Honduras and Costa Rica cannot be justified as a legitimate act of collective self-defense under the terms of U.N. Charter article 51 because the Reagan administration willfully violated the basic terms of both the U.N. and OAS Charters mandating the peaceful settlement of international disputes, and prohibiting the threat or use of transnational force directed against the political independence of a state.

Procedurally, the Reagan administration was first obliged by U.N. Charter articles 33 and 52 to attempt in good faith to obtain a peaceful resolution of the conflict under the auspices of the OAS. Reagan's purposeful failure to do so, or in the alternative to bring the matter to the attention of the U.N. Security Council under Charter article 35, vitiated his claim of a right to use force in collective self-defense of El Salvador. Substantively, even if the Reagan administration had in good faith exhausted all measures for the peaceful settlement of this dispute without success, its instigation of the *contra* groups for the express purpose of overthrowing the Sandinista government in Nicaragua could still not be justified as a legitimate measure of collective self-defense under U.N. Charter article 51.

The Boland Amendment to the Continuing Appropriations Act for Fiscal Year 1983 provided the proper distinction under international law that should have been drawn and applied to this situation:[390]

> None of the funds provided in this Act may be used by the Central Intelligence Agency or the Department of Defense to furnish military equipment, military training or advice, or other support for

military activities, to any group or individual, not part of a country's armed forces, for the purpose of overthrowing the Government of Nicaragua or provoking a military exchange between Nicaragua and Honduras.

In other words, under the doctrine of collective self-defense the U.S. government could only have provided military and economic assistance, at the request of legitimate governments in El Salvador and Honduras, for the limited purpose of interdicting any alleged flow of arms from Nicaragua through Honduras into El Salvador, but not to any extent for the unlawful purpose of overthrowing the Sandinista government in Nicaragua. Yet the Reagan administration never paid any attention to this flat prohibition of the Boland Amendment, and a pusillanimous Congress proved quite willing to permit a popular president to flout this and several other of its basic laws in Central America.

Although the military operations of the *contras* might have had as an incidental consequence the interdiction of arms supplies from Nicaragua through Honduras into El Salvador, that has probably never been their primary objective. Hence, U.S. support for the *contras* was prohibited by both the terms of the U.N. Charter and the OAS Charter. Moreover, whatever putative "right" the U.S. government might have in theory to interdict such arms in cooperation with legitimate governments in Honduras and El Salvador, due to the prior history of the Reagan administration's abusive manipulation of the *contras*, it would be far preferable for some combination of observer groups and/or independent peacekeeping forces operating under the auspices of the OAS or the U.N. Security Council to take the place of both the *contras* and U.S. troops along the concerned Central American borders in order to patrol for the purpose of interdicting any transnational flow of arms and guerillas.

Illegal U.S. Intervention into El Salvador's Civil War

The Reagan administration illegally intervened into the civil war in El Salvador by providing enormous amounts of military and economic assistance to a brutal dictatorship that used it to perpetrate a gross and consistent pattern of violations of the most basic human rights of the people of that country. Fundamental principles of international law and politics dictate non-intervention into a civil war by outsiders because the determination of one state's form of government is universally considered to fall essentially within its domestic jurisdiction. The Reagan administration's illicit intervention into El Salvador's civil war contravened the international legal right of self-determination for the people of El Salvador as recognized by article 1(2) of the U.N. Charter.[391]

Nevertheless, the OAS can still be given a leading role to play in the resolution of the civil war in El Salvador. An OAS peacekeeping force could be introduced into El Salvador. It should consist of troops drawn from American states acceptable to all the internal parties to the conflict. Its mission would be to restore conditions of domestic security to a degree sufficient to permit the convocation of full-scale negotiations among representatives of all the internal factions over the terms necessary to ensure free, fair, and safe democratic elections for all Salvadorans. These elections could then be conducted under the supervision of the OAS, and would necessarily require a cessation of hostilities and some degree of reduction in military forces on both sides of the conflict. Eventually the OAS peacekeeping force could be gradually phased out of the country sometime after the installation of a broadly based, democratically elected government that is free from the tutelage of the United States. This is not the case with the current government of José Napoleón Duarte.

The historical record clearly establishes that with the active support of the Johnson administration, such OAS facilitation of the transition from civil war to a democratic government in an American state succeeded once before in the Dominican Republic, which has remained a democracy until today. As of this writing, however, the primary obstacle to implementing a similar OAS-sponsored peacekeeping approach in El Salvador has proven to be politics of the "big stick" variety, namely, obstinate refusal by the Reagan administration to abandon the pursuit of some phantasmagorical unilateral military victory against the insurgents. The alleged fact that Nicaragua might have impermissibly intervened into the Salvadoran civil war by providing weapons, equipment, and supplies to the insurgents cannot justify any alleged right of counter-intervention by the U.S. government so long as the OAS or the U.N. Security Council can be successfully utilized to deescalate the conflict. By contrast, the Reagan administration implemented a foreign policy towards Central America that seemed purposefully designed to produce an escalation of military hostilities to the point of precipitating armed intervention by U.S. troops into combat against both the insurgents in El Salvador and the Sandinista government in Nicaragua.

The Need for a New U.S. Foreign Policy Toward Cuba

Any serious effort by the United States government to restore and then maintain international peace and security throughout Central America

and the Caribbean basin must be supported by a thorough reevaluation of
U.S. foreign policy toward Cuba in accordance with the requirements of
international law. The best way to "neutralize" Castro as a supposed
anti-U.S. actor in the Western hemisphere excludes the means hitherto
used: viz., military invasion, naval blockade, covert operations, economic
sanctions, and political destabilization measures—all of which clearly
violate international law.[392] Rather, the United States should seek to
reestablish normal diplomatic relations with the Castro government as
soon as feasible; to remove all U.S. economic sanctions imposed against
Cuba;[393] to prosecute Cuban refugee groups located in the United States
that prepare armed expeditions against the Castro government in violation of U.S. neutrality laws[394] and to employ U.S. military forces to
thwart such expeditions whenever detected as required by U.S. law;[395] to
reverse the 1962 Punta del Este Resolution by the Eighth Meeting of
Consultation of the Ministers of Foreign Affairs of the American Republics that illegally excluded the Castro government from participation in
the OAS;[396] and, finally, to include Cuba within President Reagan's program for the economic development of the Caribbean basin. Such a
comprehensive U.S. policy could free Castro from Cuba's burdensome
and, at times, counterproductive and unwanted reliance on the Soviet
Union for military defense and financial subsistence. The pursuit of such
a new Cuban policy by the U.S. government could also promptly facilitate the search for a peaceful settlement to the conflicts now raging in
Central America and southern Africa.

Historically the U.S. government has adopted the absurd position that
because the Punta del Este Resolution did not formally expel the state of
Cuba from the OAS, but only excluded the Castro government from
participation in the organization's activities, Cuba is still bound by the
terms of the OAS Charter in its relations with other American states.[397]
In response to the sophistry of this argument, the Castro government has
taken the fully warranted legal position that Cuba was effectively expelled
from the OAS in 1962, and consequently is no longer bound by the
obligations of the OAS Charter in its relations with any Western hemispheric state.[398] To be sure, Cuba continues to be bound by the terms of
the U.N. Charter in its relations with fellow U.N. members in the
Western hemisphere. But as a result of the Punta del Este Resolution,
Cuba is neither protected by nor subjected to the higher set of international legal rules established in the OAS Charter for general application
by most states of the Western hemisphere in their mutual relations.

According to the Reagan administration, the Castro government's
provision of political, military, and economic assistance to the insurgents

in El Salvador provided the justification for the policy of continuing to treat Cuba as the pariah state of the Western hemisphere. Fortunately, so far, the U.S. government has refused to accept the fervid advice of former Secretary of State Alexander Haig that it "go to the source" of the problems in Central America by taking some sort of unspecified illegal military action against Cuba.[399] The "source" of the problems in Central America lies not in Cuba but in poverty, disease, illiteracy, exploitation of the peasantry, extermination of indigenous peoples, astronomic degrees of economic inequality, and massive violations of fundamental human rights perpetrated by military dictatorships operating at the behest of economic oligarchies. At the very most, the Cuban government can only provide support to indigenous revolutionary forces already prevalent throughout Central America. Cuba can neither create nor assist a revolution that has not previously been produced by the life-threatening conditions confronting the peoples of the region.

Admittedly, for Cuba to supply political, military, and economic support to the insurgents in El Salvador violates the terms of the U.N. Charter. The Cuban response seems to be that its support for the insurgents in El Salvador can be justified by massive U.S. violations of international law with respect to Cuba for the past twenty-five years.[400] The position of the Castro government has been that it will abide by international law with states that abide by international law in their relations with Cuba. Since the U.S. government has essentially waged overt and covert military, political, and economic warfare against Cuba for the past quarter century, Cuba will provide support to those indigenous forces seeking to overthrow U.S.-backed military dictatorships throughout the Western hemisphere.[401]

Of course the great irony of the Cuban position is that it represents a mirror image of the Reagan administration's justification for its illegal policies toward Central America: violations of international law by one's adversary supposedly justify counterviolations by oneself. Except that due to its preponderant power, the quantity and quality of violations of international law committed by the United States far outweigh Cuban counterviolations in their respective degrees of deleterious significance for undermining the stability of the international legal and political order in the Western hemisphere. Once again, it is not a symmetrical situation. As a matter of sound foreign policy a superpower committed to the preservation of the international status quo neither can nor should attempt to justify an extensive pattern of international legal violations on the specious grounds that some minor adversary might be doing the same thing.

Since Cuba is not a member of the OAS, it is not bound by the obligations of the OAS Charter in its relations with any of the countries in Central America and the Caribbean, including El Salvador. However, since the United States is a party to the OAS Charter, it is bound by the terms of OAS Charter articles 18 and 20, among others, in its relations with Nicaragua. Hence, the Reagan administration cannot justify its violations of the OAS Charter with respect to Nicaragua by citing allegations of Cuban support for the insurgents in El Salvador. The United States is held to a higher standard of international legal behavior in regard to Nicaragua (i.e., both the OAS and U.N. charters) than Cuba is in regard to El Salvador (i.e., the U.N. Charter alone). The appropriate remedy for this inequality of legal rights and duties between Cuba, on the one hand, and OAS members, on the other, would be to commence the process of reincorporating Cuba into the OAS by first rescinding the Punta del Este Resolution. With its express consent, Cuba could then rejoin the OAS and thus become bound to observe the higher standards of international law enunciated by the OAS Charter in its relations with El Salvador and all other governments in Central America and the Caribbean basin. The same would hold true for U.S. foreign policy toward Cuba.

The "Linkage" Between the Reagan Administration's Caribbean and African Policies

The Reagan administration's illegal and paranoid approach to the Castro government also impelled it to abandon the Carter administration's constructive program for securing the independence of Namibia on the basis of U.N. Security Council resolution 435 (1978),[402] by instead conditioning Namibian independence upon the withdrawal of Cuban troops from Angola. Cuban troops are in Angola at the lawful request of the legitimate government of Angola to protect it from overt and covert aggression mounted by the South African apartheid regime from Namibia. There is absolutely no international legal justification for South African aggression against Angola in order to maintain and consolidate its reprehensibly illegal occupation of Namibia.

The Reagan administration's myopic concentration on the Cuban presence in Angola has led the United States further into the deadly embrace of the apartheid regime in South Africa. The Reagan administration's failure to actively support the independence of Namibia has undercut the good political and economic relations with Black African states that were successfully promoted by the Carter administration. The Reagan administration's evisceral hatred for Castro has led it to adopt policies toward southern Africa that contravene the principles of international law and the pertinent resolutions of international organizations fostering both the independence of Namibia and the destruction of apartheid in South Africa. The right of the Namibian people to self-determination had been firmly established under international law long before the South African, American, and Cuban governments decided to intervene into the Angolan civil war. Consequently, the Reagan administration had no right to obstruct the achievement of Namibian independence by conditioning it upon or "linking" it to the withdrawal of Cuban troops from Angola in any way.

The U.S. government must lead the way in developing a renewed and strengthened international commitment to achieving the independence of Namibia along the lines of the plan approved by the U.N. Security Council in resolution 435 (1978). With South Africa finally dislodged from Namibia, there would be no need for the presence of Cuban troops in Angola. The Angolan government has repeatedly stated that when South Africa leaves Namibia it will request the withdrawal of Cuban troops,[403] and Cuba has agreed to withdraw its troops whenever so requested by Angola.[404] Despite the position of the Reagan administration to the contrary, according to the relevant rules of international law, that is the proper sequence of events to be followed. In the meantime, the United States should obey the terms of the Clark Amendment prohibiting assistance of any kind for military or paramilitary operations in Angola without explicit Congressional authorization,[405] participate in the resolute condemnation by the U.N. Security Council of all South African military raids launched from Namibia into Angola, and establish normal diplomatic relations with the legitimate government in Luanda.

Integrally related to its tacit support for continued South African occupation of Namibia was the Reagan administration's policy of so-called "constructive engagement" toward the apartheid regime in South Africa. This specious policy contravened the international legal right of the people of South Africa to self-determination as affirmed by U.N. Charter article 1(2), and only encouraged discrimination and oppression against the non-white majority of that country. In the perception of many Black African states, the policy of "constructive engagement" simply rendered the Reagan administration an accomplice to the commission of the international crime of apartheid, as recognized by the 1973 International Convention on the Suppression and Punishment of the Crime of Apartheid.[406] It also facilitated aggressive conduct by the South African apartheid regime against neighboring governments in

Angola, Mozambique, Lesotho, and Zimbabwe in violation of the U.N. Charter.

The primary emphasis of the Reagan administration's foreign policy toward southern Africa was to secure the withdrawal of Cuban troops from Angola in the expectation of claiming a victory against Castro and "world communism." It had little to do with obtaining independence for Namibia, promoting self-determination and human rights for the non-white majority in South Africa, or terminating aggression by the South African apartheid regime against its neighbors. Unlike its much maligned predecessor, after a full term in office the Reagan administration had not even one major foreign policy success to its credit except for, in its demented opinion, the rape of Grenada.

The Reagan Administration's Assault
on the International Legal Order

Since January of 1981, the world witnessed a government in the United States that demonstrated little if any respect for fundamental considerations of international law or appreciation for the requirements of maintaining international peace and security. What it watched instead was a comprehensive and malicious assault upon the integrity of the international legal order by a group of men and women who were elementally lawless and thoroughly Machiavellian in their perception of international relations and in their conduct of foreign affairs. This was not simply a question of Americans giving or withholding the benefit of the doubt when it came to complicated matters of foreign affairs and defense policies to a U.S. government charged with the security of both its own citizens and those of its allies in Europe, the Western Hemisphere, and the Pacific. Rather, the Reagan administration's foreign policy represented a gross deviation from those basic rules of international deportment and civilized behavior for which the U.S. government traditionally played the pioneer role in promoting to the entire world community. By November 6, 1984, the time had long passed for the American people to put an end to the international lawlessness of the Reagan administration before it spelled disaster for the rest of the globe. For if the American people permit their government to pursue a foreign policy that is fundamentally lawless, only more setbacks for the position of the U.S. government will occur in Central America, southern Africa, the Middle East, the Persian Gulf, and in our relations with the Soviet Union.

Conclusion

The Existential Need to Struggle for International Law and Organizations

20

Machiavellianism Destroys Constitutionalism

For at least the past quarter of a century, American governmental decision makers have repeatedly tried to base their foreign policies on Machiavellian power politics. The net result has been the counterproductive
creation of a series of unmitigated disasters for the United States, both at
home and abroad, and the subversion of the entire post–World War II
international legal order that the United States, inter alia, constructed at
the 1945 San Francisco Conference in order to protect its own interests
and advance its own values. This is because Machiavellian power politics
violently contradict several of the most fundamental normative principles
upon which the United States is supposed to be founded: the inalienable
rights of the individual, the self-determination of peoples, the sovereign
equality and independence of states, non-interventionism, respect for
international law and organizations, and the peaceful settlement of international disputes. Throughout the twentieth century the promotion of
international law and international organizations has usually provided
the United States with the means for reconciling the idealism of American values and aspirations with the realism of world politics and historical conditions.

In contrast, geopolitical practitioners of Machiavellian power politics
such as Kissinger, Brzezinski, and Haig demonstrate little appreciation,
knowledge, or sensitivity to the requirements of the U.S. constitutional
system of government with its basic commitment to the rule of law. The
American people have never been willing to provide sustained popular
support for a foreign policy that has flagrantly violated elementary norms
of international law precisely because they have habitually perceived
themselves to constitute a democratic political society governed by an

indispensable commitment to the rule of law in all sectors of their national endeavors. The U.S. government's resolute dedication to the pursuit of international law and international organizations in foreign affairs has proven to be critical both for the preservation of America's internal psychic equilibrium and for the consequent protection and advancement of its global position.

But according to *The Prince*, the practice of Machiavellianism abroad requires the practice of Machiavellianism at home. The Machiavellian prince has no friends, only present and potential enemies, both foreign and domestic. So there must be no mitigation in the ferocity of the prince's application of power politics to his own subjects. These techniques become just as ruthless as those applied against the foreign enemy, though perhaps a bit more subtle and complicated. The prince must not only wage physical warfare unremittingly against foreign rivals and periodically when necessary against his own people, but he must also continuously engage in psychological warfare against his subjects in all possible ways and upon all appropriate occasions.

Thus Machiavelli counselled that the prince should appear to be "all compassion, all faithfulness, all integrity, all kindness, all religion"[1] in order to cultivate personal esteem amongst his own people, not for their benefit but solely in order to enhance his own position through the construction of a benevolent facade designed to extract the maximum degree of support from the supposedly simple and ignorant masses. Simultaneously, however, the prince must always be ready, willing, and able to inflict upon his subjects any punishment, cruelty, and atrocity required to preserve or advance his power position. In effect it was not necessary that the prince have these good qualities, but only that he appear to have them: For "men are so simple-minded and so dominated by their present needs that one who deceives will always find one who will allow himself to be deceived."[2] The ideal Machiavellian prince must be a good actor.

American foreign policy decision makers cannot realistically expect to construct a watertight compartment around their exercise of Machiavellian power politics in international relations without experiencing a serious spillover effect into domestic affairs. The Nixon-Kissinger administration was the paradigmatic example of the veracity of this proposition. Painfully aware of this interconnection, the American people cannot tolerate, but instead must and will stridently resist the practice of Machiavellian power politics by their governmental leaders both at home and abroad.

Despite the Machiavellian predilections held by international political scientists of the "realist" school, it is the inalterable nature of this "legalist" reality so intrinsic to the United States that must be understood, internalized, and effectuated by its foreign policy decision makers. The pernicious thesis incessantly propounded by international political "realists" that for some mysterious reason a democracy is inherently incapable of developing a coherent and consistent foreign policy without Machiavellianism simply reflects their obstinate refusal to accept the well-established primacy of law over power in the American constitutional system of government. International lawyers, therefore, must organize themselves into the vanguard of a struggle against the current domination of the American foreign policy establishment by the Machiavellians. They must restore the U.N. Charter and fundamental principles of international law and organizations to their rightful position as the paramount basis for conducting American foreign policy. Otherwise, the future of mankind will be left in the brutal hands of geopolitical practitioners of Machiavellian power politics such as Kissinger, Brzezinski, Haig and Kirkpatrick, and their students, associates, and protégés.

The present danger is Machiavellian power politics. The only antidote is international law and organizations. In a thermonuclear age, humankind's existential choice is stark, ominous, and compelling. America must not hesitate to apply this imperative regimen immediately before it becomes too late.

Notes

In this book, all notes will conform to The Harvard Law Review Association, *A Uniform System of Citation* (13th ed. 1981), which sets forth the standard format for legal citations. Notes are also numbered consecutively throughout each part.

Notes to Part One

1 THE RELEVANCE OF INTERNATIONAL LAW (K. Deutsch & S. Hoffmann eds. 1971).

2 Hoffmann, *International Law and the Control of Force*, in *id.* at 34.

3 *See also* S. HOFFMANN, GULLIVER'S TROUBLES, OR THE SETTING OF AMERICAN FOREIGN POLICY 17–51 (1968) [hereinafter cited as GULLIVER]; Hoffmann, *International Systems and International Law*, in THE STATE OF WAR 88 (1965) [hereinafter cited as Hoffmann 1965].

4 Even Hoffmann's brilliant analysis of American foreign policy in PRIMACY OR WORLD ORDER (1978) does not discuss the relevance of international law to the pursuit of the system of world order the author advocates. The same can be said for Hoffmann's DUTIES BEYOND BORDERS (1981). Subject to a similar criticism is Morgenthau, *Emergent Problems of United States Foreign Policy*, in THE RELEVANCE OF INTERNATIONAL LAW, *supra* note 1, at 67, an expanded version of which can be found in A NEW FOREIGN POLICY FOR THE UNITED STATES (1969).

5 *See generally* G. KENNAN, AMERICAN DIPLOMACY 1900–1950 (1951).

6 H. Kissinger, *The Nature of Leadership*, in AMERICAN FOREIGN POLICY 27 (1969).

7 *See* HARVARD LAW SCHOOL, ALUMNI DIRECTORY 395 (1978).

8 *See, e.g.*, H. KISSINGER, WHITE HOUSE YEARS 942–45 (1979).

9 Discussion with Professor Harold J. Berman, Harvard Law School, Cambridge, Mass. (Sept. 1975). *See also* KISSINGER, *supra* note 8, at 22, 31, 58–62; Berman, *Law as an Instrument of Peace in U.S.-Soviet Relations*, 22 STAN. L. REV. 943 (1970).

10 *See* E. HAAS, BEYOND THE NATION-STATE (1964).

11 *See also* I. CLAUDE, JR., SWORDS INTO PLOWSHARES (3d rev. ed. 1964); H.

STEINER & D. VAGTS, TRANSNATIONAL LEGAL PROBLEMS (2d ed. 1976); TRANS-
NATIONAL RELATIONS AND WORLD POLITICS (R. Keohane & J. Nye eds. 1971).

12 See, e.g., M. KAPLAN, SYSTEM AND PROCESS IN INTERNATIONAL POLITICS 151–65
(1957); A. Wolfers, *National Security as an Ambiguous Symbol*, in DISCORD AND
COLLABORATION 147–65 (1962).

13 See, e.g., E. H. CARR, THE TWENTY YEARS' CRISIS, 1919–1939 (1939).

14 See generally H. MORGENTHAU, IN DEFENSE OF THE NATIONAL INTEREST (1951);
H. MORGENTHAU, POLITICS AMONG NATIONS (1948); H. MORGENTHAU, SCIEN-
TIFIC MAN VS. POWER POLITICS (1946). See also H. MORGENTHAU, TRUTH AND
POWER (1970); PRINCIPLES AND PROBLEMS OF INTERNATIONAL POLITICS (H.
Morgenthau & K. Thompson eds. 1950) [hereinafter cited as Morgenthau &
Thompson]; TRUTH AND TRAGEDY (K. Thompson & R. Myers eds. 1977).

15 See D. ACHESON, POWER AND DIPLOMACY (1958); D. ACHESON, PRESENT AT
THE CREATION (1969).

16 See KENNAN, supra note 5; G. KENNAN, MEMOIRS 1925–1950 (1967); G.
KENNAN, RUSSIA AND THE WEST UNDER LENIN AND STALIN (1961); X [Ken-
nan], *The Sources of Soviet Conduct*, 25 FOREIGN AFF. 566 (1947).

17 See, e.g., KISSINGER, supra note 8; H. KISSINGER, YEARS OF UPHEAVAL (1982).

18 For an analysis of the relationship between international political realism and the
American legal realist movement of the 1920s and 1930s see STEINER & VAGTS,
supra note 11, at 346–52.

19 See generally H. MORGENTHAU, POLITICS AMONG NATIONS 4–15 (5th ed. 1973).
But cf. [Scott], *Lawyer-Secretaries of Foreign Relations of the United States*, 3 AM. J.
INT'L L. 942 (1909) (the great U.S. secretaries of state were all lawyers). Herein-
after the AMERICAN JOURNAL OF INTERNATIONAL LAW will be cited as A.J.I.L.

20 T. HOBBES, LEVIATHAN 100 (M. Oakeshott ed. 1962).

21 Hobbes asserted that international politics was one of three states of nature. The
other two were the mythical state of nature and civil war. All three, however, were
tantamount to a state of war. *Id.* at 101.

22 Compare with id. at 103–04.

23 See H. MORGENTHAU, IN DEFENSE OF THE NATIONAL INTEREST 144 (1951):
"From that iron law of international politics, that legal obligations must yield to
the national interest, no nation has ever been completely immune."

24 Political realists generally date twentieth-century legalism-moralism or utopian-
ism from Wilson. See, e.g., E. H. CARR, THE TWENTY YEARS' CRISIS, 1919–1939,
at 26–27 (2d ed. 1946); H. MORGENTHAU, POLITICS AMONG NATIONS 526–28
(5th ed. 1973). But cf. I. CLAUDE, JR., POWER AND INTERNATIONAL RELATIONS
94–204 (1962) (Wilson was in fact a realist). For the text of the speech itself see
PRESIDENT WILSON'S STATE PAPERS AND ADDRESSES 464–72 (A. Shaw ed. 1918).

25 See J-J. ROUSSEAU, *Discourse on the Origin and Foundations of Inequality Among Men*,
in the FIRST AND SECOND DISCOURSES 77 (R. Masters ed. 1964).

26 See, e.g., E. H. CARR, supra note 24, at 22–40.

27 Treaty of Versailles, June 28, 1919, 2 Bevans 42, 225 Parry's T.S. 188, *reprinted in*
13 A.J.I.L. 151 (Supp. 1919).

28 Treaty Providing for the Renunciation of War, Aug. 27, 1928, 46 Stat. 2343, T.S.
No. 796, 94 L.N.T.S. 57.

29 *Reprinted in* Dep't of State, Press Releases 41 (Jan. 7, 1932).

30 See generally W. SHIRER, THE RISE AND FALL OF THE THIRD REICH (1960); PEACE
OR APPEASEMENT? 2–5 (F. Loewenheim ed. 1965) (notorious Hossbach memo-

randum). *But see* B. RUSSETT, NO CLEAR AND PRESENT DANGER (1972); A.J.P.
TAYLOR, THE ORIGINS OF THE SECOND WORLD WAR (2d ed. 1961).

31 G. SANTAYANA, 1 THE LIFE OF REASON 284 (1905). *But cf.* E. MAY, "LESSONS"
OF THE PAST (1973).

32 *Cf.* H. HOLBORN, THE POLITICAL COLLAPSE OF EUROPE 182–93 (1951).

33 Morgenthau admitted that the Second World War played a decisive role in his
transition from international lawyer to political realist. Discussion with Professor
Hans J. Morgenthau, New York City (Apr. 1972). For a philosophical explanation
of political realism as a result of disillusioned liberalism, see J. SHKLAR, LEGALISM
123–43 (1964).

34 *See* 2 WHO'S WHO IN AMERICA 2307 (40th ed. 1978–1979); N.Y. Times, July
21, 1980, at A14, col. 1.

35 Morgenthau, *Positivism, Functionalism and International Law*, 34 A.J.I.L. 260
(1940).

36 Discussion with Professor Stanley Hoffmann, Harvard University, Cambridge,
Mass. (Sept. 1973).

37 Discussion with Professor Hans J. Morgenthau, New York City (Apr. 1973).

38 H. MORGENTHAU, *Preface* to POLITICS AMONG NATIONS at vii (2d rev. ed. 1954).

39 For histories of international political science, see generally CONTEMPORARY THEORY
IN INTERNATIONAL RELATIONS (S. Hoffmann ed. 1960); DIPLOMATIC INVESTIGA-
TIONS (H. Butterfield & M. Wight eds. 1966); MORGENTHAU & THOMPSON, *supra*
note 14; Deutsch, *Major Changes in Political Science 1952–1977*, 1978 PARTICIPA-
TION 11 (Supp.) (International Political Science Association newsletter). General
surveys of the diverse schools of international political science can be found in
CONTENDING APPROACHES TO INTERNATIONAL POLITICS (K. Knorr & J. Rosenau
eds. 1969); INTERNATIONAL POLITICS AND FOREIGN POLICY (J. Rosenau rev. ed.
1969); THE INTERNATIONAL SYSTEM (K. Knorr & S. Verba eds. 1961).

40 *See generally* FOREIGN POLICY DECISION MAKING (R. Snyder, H. Bruck & B. Sapin
eds. 1962); S. HUNTINGTON, THE COMMON DEFENSE 123–96 (1961); R.
SNYDER, H. BRUCK & B. SAPIN, DECISION MAKING AS AN APPROACH TO THE
STUDY OF INTERNATIONAL POLITICS (Princeton U. Foreign Pol'y Anal. No. 3,
1954); H. WILENSKY, ORGANIZATIONAL INTELLIGENCE 75–93 (1967); Hilsman,
The Foreign-Policy Consensus: An Interim Research Report, 3 J. CONFLICT RES. 361
(1959); Lindbloom, *The Science of "Muddling Through,"* 19 PUB. AD. REV. 79
(1959); Robinson & Snyder, *Decision Making in International Politics*, in INTERNA-
TIONAL BEHAVIOR 435 (H. Kelman ed. 1965). *See also* M. BROWN, FASHODA
RECONSIDERED (1970) (application of Snyder-Bruck-Sapin analytical framework to
French involvement in the Fashoda incident and Dreyfus affair); G. PAIGE, THE
KOREAN DECISION (1968) (application of Snyder-Bruck-Sapin framework to U.S.
intervention in Korea).

41 *See generally* R. ARON, PEACE AND WAR 19–157 (R. Howard & A. Fox trans.
1973); HAAS, *supra* note 10, at 51–85; GULLIVER, *supra* note 3, at 17–51; K.
HOLSTI, INTERNATIONAL POLITICS: A FRAMEWORK FOR ANALYSIS 29–101 (3d ed.
1977); KAPLAN, *supra* note 12; R. OSGOOD & R. TUCKER, FORCE, ORDER, AND
JUSTICE 169–79 (1967); R. ROSECRANCE, ACTION AND REACTION IN WORLD
POLITICS (1963), *reviewed in* Liska, *Continuity and Change in International Systems*, 16
WORLD POL. 118 (1963); K. WALTZ, MAN, THE STATE AND WAR (1959); Alger,
Comparison of Intranational and International Politics, 57 AM. POL. SCI. REV. 406
(1963); Brecher, *International Relations and Asian Studies: The Subordinate State System*

of Southern Asia, 15 WORLD POL. 213 (1963); Chi, *The Chinese Warlord System as an International System*, in NEW APPROACHES TO INTERNATIONAL RELATIONS 405 (M. Kaplan ed. 1968) (practical application of Kaplan framework); Franke, *The Italian City-State System as an International System*, in NEW APPROACHES TO INTERNATIONAL RELATIONS 426 (M. Kaplan ed. 1968) (another practical application of the Kaplan framework); HOFFMANN 1965, *supra* note 3, at 88; Masters, *A Multi-Bloc Model of the International System*, 55 AM. POL. SCI. REV. 780 (1961); Masters, *World Politics as a Primitive Political System*, 16 WORLD POL. 595 (1964); Russett, *Delineating International Regions*, in QUANTITATIVE INTERNATIONAL POLITICS: INSIGHTS AND EVIDENCE 317 (J. Singer ed. 1968); Waltz, *The Stability of a Bipolar World*, 93 DAEDALUS 881 (1964); Zartman, *Africa as a Subordinate State System in International Relations*, 21 INT'L ORG. 545 (1967). *See generally* L. VON BERTALANFFY, GENERAL SYSTEM THEORY (1968); MODERN SYSTEMS RESEARCH FOR THE BEHAVIORAL SCIENTIST (W. Buckley ed. 1968).

42 *See generally* J. DE RIVERA, THE PSYCHOLOGICAL DIMENSION OF FOREIGN POLICY (1968); A. GEORGE & J. GEORGE, WOODROW WILSON AND COLONEL HOUSE (1956); R. JERVIS, THE LOGIC OF IMAGES IN INTERNATIONAL RELATIONS (1970); R. JERVIS, PERCEPTION AND MISPERCEPTION IN INTERNATIONAL POLITICS (1976); Allport, *The Role of Expectancy*, in WAR 177 (L. Bramson & G. Goethals rev. ed. 1968); Greenstein, *The Impact of Personality on Politics: An Attempt to Clear Away Underbrush*, 61 AM. POL. SCI. REV. 629 (1967); Jaros, Hirsch & Fleron, *The Malevolent Leader: Political Socialization in an American Sub-Culture*, 62 AM. POL. SCI. REV. 564 (1968); Jervis, *Hypotheses on Misperception*, 20 WORLD POL. 454 (1968); Kelman, *Social-Psychological Approaches to the Study of International Relations*, in INTERNATIONAL BEHAVIOR 565 (H. Kelman ed. 1965); May, *War, Peace, and Social Learning*, in WAR 151 (L. Bramson & G. Goethals rev. ed. 1968); Tolman, *Drives Toward War*, in *id* at 159. *See also* R. BENEDICT, THE CHRYSANTHEMUM AND THE SWORD (1967); W. LANGER, THE MIND OF ADOLF HITLER (1972); Aronson, *The Theory of Cognitive Dissonance: A Current Perspective*, 4 ADVANCES IN EXPERIMENTAL SOC. PSYCH. 1 (L. Berkowitz ed. 1969); Blumer, *Society as Symbolic Interaction*, in HUMAN BEHAVIOR AND SOCIAL PROCESSES 179 (A. Rose ed. 1962).

43 *See generally* MATHEMATICAL APPROACHES TO POLITICS (H. Alker, K. Deutsch & A. Stoetzel eds. 1973); H. ALKER, MATHEMATICS & POLITICS 130–52 (1965); K. DEUTSCH, THE ANALYSIS OF INTERNATIONAL RELATIONS 132–64 (2d ed. 1978); R. FISHER, INTERNATIONAL CONFLICT FOR BEGINNERS (1969); KAPLAN, *supra* note 12, at 167–241; W. RIKER, THE THEORY OF POLITICAL COALITIONS (1962); T. SCHELLING, THE STRATEGY OF CONFLICT (1960); J. VON NEUMANN & O. MORGENSTERN, THEORY OF GAMES AND ECONOMIC BEHAVIOR (1972).

44 *See generally* H. KAHN, ON ESCALATION (rev. ed. 1968); H. KAHN, ON THERMONUCLEAR WAR (2d ed. 1961); H. KISSINGER, THE NECESSITY FOR CHOICE (1960); H. KISSINGER, NUCLEAR WEAPONS AND FOREIGN POLICY (1957); PROBLEMS OF NATIONAL STRATEGY (H. Kissinger ed. 1965); T. SCHELLING, ARMS AND INFLUENCE (1966); Wohlstetter, *The Delicate Balance of Terror*, 37 FOREIGN AFF. 211 (1959).

45 *See generally* G. ALLISON, ESSENCE OF DECISION (1971); R. WOHLSTETTER, PEARL HARBOR: WARNING AND DECISION (1962); Allison & Halperin, *Bureaucratic Politics: A Paradigm and Some Policy Implications*, 24 WORLD POL. 40 (R. Tanter & R. Ullman eds. Supp. 1972); George, *The Case for Multiple Advocacy in Making Foreign Policy*, 66 AM. POL. SCI. REV. 751 (1972); Halperin, *Why Bureaucrats Play*

Games, FOREIGN POL'Y, Spring 1971, at 70. *See generally* J. MARCH & H. SIMON, ORGANIZATIONS (1958); R. NEUSTADT, PRESIDENTIAL POWER: THE POLITICS OF LEADERSHIP (1960).

46   *See, e.g.*, R. KEOHANE & J. NYE, POWER AND INTERDEPENDENCE (1977); INTERNATIONAL REGIMES (S. Krasner ed. 1982); Haas, *Why Collaborate?*, 32 WORLD POL. 357 (1980); Haas, *Regime Decay: Conflict Management and International Organizations, 1945–1981*, 37 INT'L ORG. 189 (1983); Young, *International Regimes: Problems of Concept Formation*, 32 WORLD POL. 331 (1980).

47   *See infra* Chapter 5, Hans Morgenthau's Volte-Face.

48   *See* Boyle, *The Law of Power Politics*, 1980 U. ILL. L.F. 901, 928–29 [hereinafter cited as *Power Politics*].

49   J. AUSTIN, THE PROVINCE OF JURISPRUDENCE DETERMINED 121–26, 137–44 (1954).

50   *See* T. KUHN, THE STRUCTURE OF SCIENTIFIC REVOLUTIONS (2d ed. 1970).

51   *See* Oppenheim, *The Science of International Law: Its Task and Method*, 2 A.J.I.L. 313 (1908). *See also* Oppenheim, *Introduction* to THE COLLECTED PAPERS of JOHN WESTLAKE at x (1914); [Scott], *The Whewell Professorship of International Law*, 2 A.J.I.L. 862 (1908). *But see* Pollock, *The Sources of International Law*, 2 COLUM. L. REV. 511 (1902).

52   *Cf.* [Scott], *The Papacy in International Law*, 8 A.J.I.L. 864, 865 (1914); [Scott], *Peace Through the Development of International Law*, 8 A.J.I.L. 114 (1914).

53   *Cf.* [Scott], *Louis Renault*, 2 A.J.I.L. 152, 153 (1908).

54   *See* K. WALTZ, MAN, THE STATE AND WAR (1959); Singer, *The Level-of-Analysis Problem in International Relations*, in THE INTERNATIONAL SYSTEM 77 (K. Knorr & S. Verba eds. 1961); A. Wolfers, *The Actors in International Politics*, in DISCORD AND COLLABORATION 3 (1965).

55   Thus international legal positivists have traditionally favored the "dualist" over the "monist" argument in favor of a non-hierarchical relationship between international law and municipal law. International law is not superior to municipal law or vice versa. The two phenomena coexist with each other as interdependent and interpenetrated systems. *Cf. The Paquete Habana*, 175 U.S. 677, 700 (1900); Wright, *Conflicts of International Law with National Laws and Ordinances*, 11 A.J.I.L. 1 (1917). *But see* Starke, *Monism and Dualism in the Theory of International Law*, 17 BRIT. Y.B. INT'L L. 66 (1936).

56   *See* Root, *The Sanction of International Law*, 2 A.J.I.L. 451 (1908); Scott, *The Legal Nature of International Law*, 1 A.J.I.L. 831 (1907). *See also* Nys, *The Development and Formation of International Law*, 6 A.J.I.L. 1, 4, 20 (1912); Reeves, *The Influence of the Law of Nature upon International Law in the United States*, 3 A.J.I.L. 547 (1909) (no great influence). *But see* Lansing, *Notes on Sovereignty in a State*, 1 A.J.I.L. 105 (1907) (Austinian position); Willoughby, *The Legal Nature of International Law*, 2 A.J.I.L. 357 (1908) (critique of Scott).

57   *See, e.g.*, Stowell, *Plans for World Organization*, 18 COLUM. U.Q. 226 (1916).

58   *See* Reinsch, *International Administrative Law and National Sovereignty*, 3 A.J.I.L. 1 (1909). *See also* Baldwin, *The International Congresses and Conferences of the Last Century as Forces Working Toward the Solidarity of the World*, 1 A.J.I.L. 565 (1907).

59   *Cf.* W. HULL, THE TWO HAGUE CONFERENCES AND THEIR CONTRIBUTIONS TO INTERNATIONAL LAW 496–500 (1908) [hereinafter cited as HULL].

60   *See, e.g.*, Lansing, *Notes on World Sovereignty*, 15 A.J.I.L. 13 (1921) (written for publication in 1906); Moore, *International Law: Its Present and Future*, 1 A.J.I.L.

11 (1907); Peaslee, *The Sanction of International Law*, 10 A.J.I.L. 328 (1916); Snow, *International Law and Political Science*, 7 A.J.I.L. 315 (1913); Snow, *The Law of Nations*, 6 A.J.I.L. 890 (1912). *See also* W. KUEHL, SEEKING WORLD ORDER 88 (1969) [hereinafter cited as KUEHL].

61   N. MACHIAVELLI, THE PRINCE 127 (M. Musa trans. & ed. 1964).

62   *Id.* at 99 (need for good laws); *id.* at 145 (fighting by means of law).

63   *See* Hart, *American Ideals of International Relations*, 1 A.J.I.L. 624, 635 (1907).

64   *See* DEPARTMENT OF STATE, THE SECRETARIES OF STATE 71–85 (1978). *See also* [Scott], *supra* note 19.

65   *See* [Scott], *Editorial Comment*, 1 A.J.I.L. 129 (1907); Editorial Comment, *Societies of International Law*, 1 A.J.I.L. 135 (1907). The nucleus for the Society came from those members of the Lake Mohonk Conference on International Arbitration who wished to found an organization devoted exclusively to international law. *See also* Finch, *The American Society of International Law 1906–1956*, 50 A.J.I.L. 293, 295–98 (1956); Raymond & Frischholz, *Lawyers Who Established International Law in the United States, 1776–1914*, 76 A.J.I.L. 802, 823 (1982).

66   *Cf.* Scott, *The Revista De Derecho Internacional*, 16 A.J.I.L. 437, 438 (1922). The first issue of the AMERICAN POLITICAL SCIENCE REVIEW had been published in November of 1906.

67   *See* A. SUTHERLAND, THE LAW AT HARVARD: A HISTORY OF IDEAS AND MEN, 1817–1967, at 209 (1967); [Scott], *Editorial Comment*, 1 A.J.I.L. 129, 130, 134 (1907).

68   *See* J. RICHARDSON, 1 MESSAGES AND PAPERS OF THE PRESIDENT 205 (1911) (Farewell Address) [hereinafter cited as RICHARDSON]; *id.* at 776 (Monroe Doctrine).

69   *Cf.* [Scott], *Tripoli*, 6 A.J.I.L. 149, 155 (1912) (Mexican-American War was unjust and unjustifiable).

70   *See, e.g.*, Potter, *The Nature of American Territorial Expansion*, 15 A.J.I.L. 189 (1921). *See also* Potter, *The Nature of American Foreign Policy*, 21 A.J.I.L. 53 (1927).

71   Treaty of Peace, Dec. 10, 1898, United States–Spain, 30 Stat. 1754, T.S. No. 343, 187 Parry's T.S. 100. *See* Fenwick, *The Scope of Domestic Questions in International Law*, 19 A.J.I.L. 143 (1925) (U.S. was entitled to abate the international nuisance in Cuba in 1898). *See generally* C. FISH, THE PATH OF EMPIRE (1919); F. FREIDEL, THE SPLENDID LITTLE WAR (1st ed. 1958); P. MOON, IMPERIALISM AND WORLD POLITICS 407–56 (1928); J. PRATT, EXPANSIONISTS OF 1898 (1936).

72   *See* A. CHAYES, T. EHRLICH & A. LOWENFELD, 2 INTERNATIONAL LEGAL PROCESS 920–26 (1969).

73   *See* 9 RICHARDSON, *supra* note 68, at 7353, 7375–79.

74   Army Appropriation Act, ch. 803, § 3, 31 Stat. 895, 897 (1901).

75   *See* W. LANGER, THE DIPLOMACY OF IMPERIALISM 1890–1902, at 167–94, 385–414B, 445–83, 677–786 (2d ed. 1950).

76   *See* Wicker, *Some Effects of Neutralization*, 5 A.J.I.L. 639, 652 (1911); Winslow, *Neutralization*, 2 A.J.I.L. 366 (1908).

77   *See, e.g.*, Snow, *Neutralization Versus Imperialism*, 2 A.J.I.L. 562 (1908).

78   *See* Hart, *supra* note 63, at 624; Snow, *The American Philosophy of Government and Its Effect on International Relations*, 8 A.J.I.L. 191 (1914).

79   *See, e.g.*, [Scott], *The Baltic and the North Seas*, 2 A.J.I.L. 646 (1908); [Scott], *The Dissolution of the Union of Norway and Sweden*, 1 A.J.I.L. 440 (1907); [Scott], *The Integrity of Norway Guaranteed*, 2 A.J.I.L. 176 (1908) (purpose is to keep Russia

out of Western Europe). *See also* Editorial Comment, *The Fortification of the Aland Islands,* 2 A.J.I.L. 397 (1908).

80 *See* [Fenwick], *Mediation in the Turko Italian War,* 6 A.J.I.L. 463 (1912) (favors mediation by great powers); [Fenwick], *The Basis of Mediation in the War Between Italy and Turkey,* 6 A.J.I.L. 719 (1912) (mediation undertaken by great powers); [Scott], *Peace Between Italy and Turkey,* 7 A.J.I.L. 155 (1913) (Italy unjustified and lawless); [Scott], *The Closing and Reopening of the Dardanelles,* 6 A.J.I.L. 706 (1912); [Scott], *Tripoli,* 6 A.J.I.L. 149 (1912) (Italy violated international law by declaration of war on Turkey). *See also* Editorial Comment, *The Use of Balloons in the War Between Italy and Turkey,* 6 A.J.I.L. 485 (1912).

81 *See, e.g.,* [Scott], *Anglo-French-Italian Agreement Regarding Abyssinia,* 1 A.J.I.L. 484 (1907).

82 *See, e.g.,* Editorial Comment, *England and Russia in Central Asia,* 3 A.J.I.L. 170 (1909); Editorial Comment, *Russia and Persia,* 6 A.J.I.L. 155 (1912) (joint protectorate over Persia); Editorial Comment, *The Persian Revolution and the Anglo-Russian Entente,* 3 A.J.I.L. 969 (1909) (downfall of the Shah and intervention by British and Russian troops); Editorial Comment, *The Recent Anglo-Russian Convention,* 1 A.J.I.L. 979 (1907) (establishing spheres of influence in Persia; assigning Afghanistan to Britain and Tibet to China).

83 For the history of the establishment of the French protectorate in Morocco, see Editorial Comment, *An Antecedent Algeciras,* 8 A.J.I.L. 867 (1914); Editorial Comment, *Recent Disturbances in Morocco,* 1 A.J.I.L. 975 (1907); Harris, *The New Moroccan Protectorate,* 7 A.J.I.L. 245 (1913); [Scott], *A New Sultan in Morocco,* 3 A.J.I.L. 446 (1909); [Scott], *French Protectorate Established in Morocco,* 6 A.J.I.L. 699 (1912); [Scott], *Morocco,* 6 A.J.I.L. 159 (1912); [Scott], *The Algeciras Conference,* 1 A.J.I.L. 138 (1907); [Scott], *The Treaty of November 27, 1912, Between France and Spain Concerning Morocco,* 7 A.J.I.L. 357 (1913). *See also* [Scott], *Anglo-French Convention Respecting the New Hebrides,* 1 A.J.I.L. 482 (1907); [Scott], *Egypt a British Protectorate,* 9 A.J.I.L. 202 (1915).

84 *See* Editorial Comment, *Macedonian Railways and the Concert of Europe,* 2 A.J.I.L. 644 (1908) (end of Austro-Hungarian/Russian entente); Ion, *The Cretan Question,* 4 A.J.I.L. 276 (1910); Schelle, *Studies on the Eastern Question* (pt. 1), 5 A.J.I.L. 144, 174 (1911) (violation of Treaty of Berlin by Austria and Bulgaria was flagrant breach of international law); *id.* (pts. 2 & 3) at 394, 680; [Scott], *The Balkan Situation,* 2 A.J.I.L. 864 (1908) (violation of Treaty of Berlin); [Scott], *The Balkan Situation,* 3 A.J.I.L. 448 (1909) (satisfactory settlement of violation); [Scott], *The Balkan Situation,* 3 A.J.I.L. 688 (1909) (Austrian annexation of Bosnia-Herzegovina will be countered by renewed Russian support to Southern Slavs). *See also* [Scott], *Edward VII,* 4 A.J.I.L. 662, 664 (1910) (fear of Anglo-German war).

85 *See, e.g.,* Scott, *America and the New Diplomacy,* INT'L CONCILIATION, Mar. 1909, at 4–5.

86 *See, e.g.,* [Dennis], *The Fourteenth Lake Mohonk Conference,* 2 A.J.I.L. 615 (1908); De Sillac, *Periodical Peace Conferences,* 5 A.J.I.L. 968 (1911); Hershey, *Convention for the Peaceful Adjustment of International Differences,* 2 A.J.I.L. 29 (1908); [Scott], *Joint Resolution to Authorize the Appointment of a Commission in Relation to Universal Peace,* 5 A.J.I.L. 433 (1911); [Scott], *Lake Mohonk Conference on International Arbitration,* 1 A.J.I.L. 140 (1907); [Scott], *Mr. Roosevelt's Nobel Address on International Peace,* 4 A.J.I.L. 700 (1910); [Scott], *President Taft on International Peace,* 5 A.J.I.L. 718 (1911); [Scott], *The Fifteenth Lake Mohonk Conference on International*

Arbitration, 3 A.J.I.L. 683 (1909); Editorial Comment, *The Eighteenth Lake Mohonk Conference on International Arbitration*, 6 A.J.I.L. 725 (1912); Editorial Comment, *The Pennsylvania Arbitration and Peace Conference*, 2 A.J.I.L. 611 (1908).

87   *See, e.g.*, J. SCOTT, 1 THE HAGUE PEACE CONFERENCES OF 1899 AND 1907, at 465–66 (1909) [hereinafter cited as SCOTT]; Editorial Note, *The Congress of Nations*, ADVOCATE OF PEACE, July 1906, at 144.

88   *See, e.g.*, Baldwin, *The Membership of a World Tribunal for Promoting Permanent Peace*, 12 A.J.I.L. 453 (1918); Brown, *The Theory of the Independence and Equality of States*, 9 A.J.I.L. 305 (1915); Spencer, *The Organization of International Force*, 9 A.J.I.L. 45 (1915).

89   *See, e.g.*, KUEHL, *supra* note 60, at 91–95 (W. J. Bartnett, Justice David J. Brewer, John Bassett Moore, Joseph C. Clayton).

90   *See, e.g.*, *id.* at 134–37, 144–45, 161.

91   *Cf.* S. Hoffmann, *International Systems and International Law*, in THE STATE OF WAR 88 (1965).

92   *See, e.g.*, Editorial Comment, *Secretary Knox and International Unity*, 4 A.J.I.L. 180 (1910); Snow, *The Law of Nations*, 6 A.J.I.L. 890 (1912).

93   The great powers of Europe formally admitted Turkey to the European public international law system by the Treaty of Paris of 1856. *See* Evans, *The Primary Sources of International Obligations*, 5 AM. SOC. INT'L L. PROC. 257, 265–67 (1911).

94   Although not formally admitted like Turkey, Japan was generally considered "one of the Great Powers that lead the Family of Nations" by virtue of its military victory over China in 1895. *See* L. OPPENHEIM, 1 INTERNATIONAL LAW: PEACE 34 (R. Roxburgh 3d ed. 1920).

95   Address by John Hay to Hague Delegation (Apr. 18, 1899), in 1899 PAPERS RELATING TO THE FOREIGN RELATIONS OF THE UNITED STATES 511, 513. Hereinafter this series of documents will be cited as F.R.U.S.

96   *See* 2 SCOTT, *supra* note 87, at 15.

97   *See* General Report of the Commission of the United States of America to the International Conference at The Hague (July 31, 1899), in 2 SCOTT, *supra* note 87, at 17, 24.

98   *See* THE PROCEEDINGS OF THE HAGUE PEACE CONFERENCES: THE CONFERENCE OF 1899, at 767–72 (J. Scott ed. 1920) [hereinafter cited as HAGUE I PROCEEDINGS]; C. DAVIS, THE UNITED STATES AND THE FIRST HAGUE PEACE CONFERENCE 158–64 (1962) [hereinafter cited as DAVIS, HAGUE I]; HULL, *supra* note 59, at 297–311; 1 SCOTT, *supra* note 87, at 319–30.

99   Convention for the Pacific Settlement of International Disputes, July 29, 1899, Title IV, 32 Stat. 1779, 1788, T.S. No. 392, 187 Parry's T.S. 410, *reprinted in* 1 A.J.I.L. 107, 113 (Supp. 1907). *See* Myers, *The Origin of the Hague Arbitral Courts*, 8 A.J.I.L. 769 (1914).

100   *See* [Scott], *Treaties of Arbitration Since the First Hague Conference*, 2 A.J.I.L. 823 (1908).

101   *See* Wehberg, *Restrictive Clauses in International Arbitration Treaties*, 7 A.J.I.L. 301 (1913). *But see* Cavalcanti, *Restrictive Clauses in Arbitration Treaties*, 8 A.J.I.L. 723 (1914).

102   *See* 2 THE PROCEEDINGS OF THE HAGUE PEACE CONFERENCES: CONFERENCE OF 1907, at 47–54 (J. Scott ed. 1921) [hereinafter cited as HAGUE II PROCEEDINGS]; C. DAVIS, THE UNITED STATES AND THE SECOND HAGUE PEACE CONFERENCE 256, 258, 277–84 (1975) [hereinafter cited as DAVIS, HAGUE II]; HULL, *supra*

note 59, at 311–26; 1 SCOTT, *supra* note 87, at 330–79; Hull, *Obligatory Arbitration and the Hague Conferences*, 2 A.J.I.L. 731 (1908).

103 Final Act of The Second Hague Peace Conference, Oct. 18, 1907, *reprinted in* 2 A.J.I.L. 1, 25–26 (Supp. 1908).

104 *See* Lammasch, *Compulsory Arbitration at the Second Hague Conference*, 4 A.J.I.L. 83, 94 & n.3 (1910).

105 *See* List of Arbitration Treaties and Conventions Submitted to and Acted upon by the Senate, S. Doc. No. 373, 42d Cong., 2d Sess. 2605, 2606 (1912). *See also* Dennis, *The Arbitration Treaties and the Senate Amendments*, 6 A.J.I.L. 614 (1912); [Scott], *Arbitration Treaty with Austria-Hungary*, 3 A.J.I.L. 696 (1909); [Scott], *Recent Arbitration Treaties Concluded by the United States*, 2 A.J.I.L. 624 (1908); [Scott], *Senator Root and the Nobel Peace Prize*, 8 A.J.I.L. 133 (1914); [Scott], *The Pending Treaty of Arbitration Between the United States and Great Britain*, 6 A.J.I.L. 167 (1912); [Scott], *The Treaties of Arbitration with Great Britain and France*, 6 A.J.I.L. 460 (1912).

106 *See* 3 UNPERFECTED TREATIES OF THE UNITED STATES OF AMERICA 487 (C. Wiktor ed. 1976) [hereinafter cited as UNPERFECTED TREATIES].

107 Venezuela Preferential Case (Ger., Gr. Brit., and Italy v. Venez.), Hague Ct. Rep. (Scott) 55 (Perm. Ct. Arb. 1904).

108 Casablanca Case (Fr. v. Ger.), Hague Ct. Rep. (Scott) 110 (Perm. Ct. Arb. 1909). *See* [Scott], *The Casablanca Arbitration*, 3 A.J.I.L. 946 (1909); [Scott], *The Casablanca Arbitration Award*, 3 A.J.I.L. 698 (1909); [Scott], *The Casablanca Incident and Its Reference to Arbitration at The Hague*, 3 A.J.I.L. 176 (1909).

109 *See* DAVIS, HAGUE II, *supra* note 102, at 73–90.

110 *See* W. SCHÜCKING, THE INTERNATIONAL UNION OF THE HAGUE CONFERENCES 28 (C. Fenwick trans. 1918) (comment by Wehberg); [Scott], *The Casablanca Arbitration Award*, 3 A.J.I.L. 698, 701 (1909).

111 *See* 2 HAGUE II PROCEEDINGS, *supra* note 102, at 1016, Annex 76, art. VI.

112 Final Act of the Second Hague Peace Conference, Oct. 18, 1907, Annex to the First Recommendation Uttered by the Second Peace Conference, Draft of a Convention Relative to the Institution of a Court of Arbitral Justice, *reprinted in* 2 A.J.I.L. 1, 29 (Supp. 1908). *See* Myers, *The Origin of the Hague Arbitral Courts*, 10 A.J.I.L. 270 (1916).

113 *See* Hicks, *The Equality of States and the Hague Conferences*, 2 A.J.I.L. 530, 538–39 (1908).

114 Final Act of the Second Hague Peace Conference, Oct. 18, 1907, *reprinted in* 2 A.J.I.L. 1, 27 (1908 Supp.).

115 Scott, *The Election of Judges for the Permanent Court of International Justice*, 15 A.J.I.L. 556 (1921).

116 *See* Nys, *The Codification of International Law*, 5 A.J.I.L. 871 (1911); Root, *The Function of Private Codification in International Law*, 5 A.J.I.L. 577 (1911); [Scott], *The Third Annual Meeting of the American Society of International Law*, 3 A.J.I.L. 674 (1909).

117 *See* J. CHOATE, THE TWO HAGUE CONFERENCES 65–74 (1913) [hereinafter cited as CHOATE]; DAVIS, HAGUE II, *supra* note 102, at 190, 220–27.

118 Convention Relative to the Creation of an International Prize Court, Oct. 18, 1907, in 4 UNPERFECTED TREATIES, *supra* note 106, at 57, *reprinted in* 2 A.J.I.L. 174 (Supp. 1908). *See* Scott, *The Work of the Second Hague Peace Conference*, 2 A.J.I.L. 1, 21–22 (1908).

119   *See* J. COOGAN, THE END OF NEUTRALITY 94–100 (1981) [hereinafter cited as COOGAN]; Gregory, *The Proposed International Prize Court and Some of Its Difficulties*, 2 A.J.I.L. 458 (1908).

120   *See* Scott, *Proposed Conference for the Settlement of Certain Questions of Maritime Law*, 2 A.J.I.L. 830 (1908).

121   Declaration of London, Feb. 26, 1909, in 4 UNPERFECTED TREATIES, *supra* note 106, at 129. *See* Stockton, *The International Naval Conference of London, 1908–1909*, 3 A.J.I.L. 596 (1909).

122   *See* Coogan, *supra* note 119, at 114–17; 1 Scott, *supra* note 87, at 698–730.

123   *See* [Scott], *Approval of the Declaration of London by the United States Senate on April 24, 1912*, 6 A.J.I.L. 723 (1912).

124   *See* [Fenwick], *Naval Prize Bill and the Declaration of London*, 6 A.J.I.L. 180 (1912).

125   Naval Prize Bill, 1911, 1 & 2 Geo. 5, 7 Sessional Papers, H.L. 643. *See* Scott, *The Declaration of London of February 26, 1909*, 8 A.J.I.L. 274 (1914).

126   Declaration of London, Feb. 26, 1909, in 4 UNPERFECTED TREATIES, *supra* note 106, at 129. *See also* Myers, *The Legal Basis of the Rules of Blockade in the Declaration of London*, 4 A.J.I.L. 571 (1910).

127   *See* COOGAN, *supra* note 119, at 126 & n.7.

128   *Id.* at 145.

129   *See* Scott, *Prefatory Note* to THE DECLARATION OF LONDON, 1909, OFFICIAL DOCUMENTS, at v (J. Scott ed. 1919). *See also* Scott, *The Declaration of London of February 26, 1909*, 8 A.J.I.L. 274 (1914). *See generally* L. OPPENHEIM, 2 INTERNATIONAL LAW 546–52 (2d ed. 1912).

130   *See* DAVIS, HAGUE I, *supra* note 98, at 110–24.

131   Final Act of the International Peace Conference, July 29, 1899, *reprinted in* 1 A.J.I.L. 103, 105 (Supp. 1907).

132   *Id.* at 106.

133   *Id.*

134   *See, e.g.*, 1 SCOTT, *supra* note 87, at 61:
The means of warfare and the preparation for war will exist until a substitute for war be proposed which is not only reasonable in itself, but which is so reasonable that its non-acceptance would be unreasonable. It may be that the inter-relation and interdependence of States must be accepted in theory and practice, and that the judicial organization of the world be realized before armies and navies will cease to be used in foreign affairs, and will be confined to protecting commerce and policing the seas.
See also General Report of the Commission of the United States of America to the International Conference at The Hague (July 31, 1899), in 2 *id.* at 17, 21; Hobson, *Disarmament*, 2 A.J.I.L. 743 (1908). *But see* Trueblood, *The Case for Limitation of Armaments*, 2 A.J.I.L. 758 (1908).

135   *See* HULL, *supra* note 59, at 69–75; 1 SCOTT, *supra* note 87, at 101–06.

136   *See* DAVIS, HAGUE II, *supra* note 102, at 140–61, 215–19.

137   Final Act of the Second Hague Peace Conference, Oct. 18, 1907, *reprinted in* 2 A.J.I.L. 1, 26–27 (Supp. 1908). *See* HULL, *supra* note 59, at 69–75.

138   *See* Report of the American Delegation to the Conference on the Limitation of Armament, S. Doc. No. 125, 67th Cong., 2d Sess. (1922), *reprinted in* 16 A.J.I.L. 159 (1922).

139   Convention for the Pacific Settlement of International Disputes, July 29, 1899,

arts. 2–7, 32 Stat. 1779, 1785, T.S. No. 392, 187 Parry's T.S. 410.

140   *See* Hill, *The Second Peace Conference at the Hague*, 1 A.J.I.L. 671, 681 (1907).

141   Peace of Portsmouth, Sept. 5, 1905, Japan-Russia, I Jap. Tr. 585, 199 Parry's T.S. 144.

142   *See* Editorial Comment, *Mr. Roosevelt's Nobel Address on International Peace*, 4 A.J.I.L. 700 (1910). *See generally* Scott, *The Nobel Peace Prize*, 12 A.J.I.L. 383 (1918).

143   Convention for the Pacific Settlement of International Disputes, July 29, 1899, Title III, 32 Stat. 1779, 1787, T.S. No. 392, 187 Parry's T.S. 410. *See* HULL, *supra* note 59, at 277–88.

144   Dogger Bank Case (Gr. Brit. v. Rus.), Hague Ct. Rep. (Scott) 403 (1905). *See* Davis, Hague II, *supra* note 102, at 114; Scott, *The Work of the Second Hague Peace Conference*, 2 A.J.I.L. 1, 9 (1908).

145   *See* M. HUDSON, THE PERMANENT COURT OF INTERNATIONAL JUSTICE 40 (1943) [hereinafter cited as HUDSON].

146   *See* HULL, *supra* note 59, at 474.

147   Convention Relative to the Opening of Hostilities, Oct. 18, 1907, 36 Stat. 2259, T.S. No. 538, 205 Parry's T.S. 263, *reprinted in* 2 A.J.I.L. 85 (Supp. 1908).

148   *See* Stowell, *Convention Relative to the Opening of Hostilities*, 1 A.J.I.L. 50, 53 (1908).

149   *See* HULL, *supra* note 59, at 263.

150   *See* Editorial Comment, *Historical Extracts Showing When Hostilities Began Without Declarations of War*, 2 A.J.I.L. 57 (1908).

151   *See* DAVIS, HAGUE II, *supra* note 102, at 341–42.

152   Convention Respecting the Limitation of the Employment of Force for the Recovery of Contract Debts, Oct. 18, 1907, 36 Stat. 2241, T.S. No. 537, 205 Parry's T.S. 250, *reprinted in* 2 A.J.I.L. 81 (Supp. 1908).

153   *See* DAVIS, HAGUE II, *supra* note 102, at 255–58, 284–85; HULL, *supra* note 59, at 349–70.

154   This term was purposefully left undefined. *See* 1 SCOTT, *supra* note 87, at 416–18. Yet it was considered to include public debts. *See* HULL, *supra* note 59, at 360–63.

155   *See* 1 SCOTT, *supra* note 87, at 420–21. *See also* Scott, *The Work of the Second Hague Peace Conference*, 2 A.J.I.L. 1, 15 (1908).

156   Proposal for a Second Hague Conference (Oct. 21, 1904), 1904 F.R.U.S. 10, *reprinted in* 1 A.J.I.L. 432 (1907).

157   *See* [Scott], *The Second Peace Conference of the Hague*, 1 A.J.I.L. 431 (1907).

158   Final Act of the Second Hague Peace Conference, Oct. 18, 1907, *reprinted in* 2 A.J.I.L. 1, 28 (Supp. 1908).

159   *Id.* at 28–29.

160   *See* [Hill], *The Fifteenth Conference of the Interparliamentary Union*, 3 A.J.I.L. 180 (1909).

161   *See* DAVIS, HAGUE II, *supra* note 102, at 286–88; KUEHL, *supra* note 60, at 104.

162   *See* [Scott], *Mr. Bryan and the Third Hague Peace Conference*, 8 A.J.I.L. 330, 335 (1914).

163   Circular Note from William Jennings Bryan to U.S. Diplomatic Officers (Jan. 31, 1914), 1914 F.R.U.S. 4. *See* [Scott], *Mr. Bryan and the Third Hague Peace Conference*, 8 A.J.I.L. 330 (1914).

164   Circular Note from William Jennings Bryan to U.S. Diplomatic Officers (June 22, 1914), 1914 F.R.U.S. 10.

165   *See Chronicle of International Events*, 8 A.J.I.L. 890, 891 (1914). *See also* Editorial Comment, *Germany and International Peace*, 8 A.J.I.L. 881 (1914)

(Germany favors Third Hague Conference too).

166   *See Chronicle of International Events*, 8 A.J.I.L. 890, 892 (1914).

167   *See generally* B. TUCHMAN, THE GUNS OF AUGUST (1962).

168   *See* H. NICHOLSON, PEACEMAKING 1919 (1965).

169   *See* Schvan, *A Practical Peace Policy*, 8 A.J.I.L. 51, 59 (1914).

170   *See, e.g.*, H. HOLBORN, THE POLITICAL COLLAPSE OF EUROPE (1951).

171   Final Act of the International Peace Conference, July 29, 1899, *reprinted in* 1
       A.J.I.L. 103, 106 (Supp. 1907). *See* HULL, *supra* note 59, at 146–47.

172   Convention Respecting the Rights and Duties of Neutral Powers and Persons in
       Case of War on Land, Oct. 18, 1907, 36 Stat. 2310, T.S. No. 540, 205 Parry's
       T.S. 299, *reprinted in* 2 A.J.I.L. 117 (Supp. 1908). *See* HULL, *supra* note 59, at
       199–213; De Bustamante, *The Hague Convention Concerning the Rights and Duties of
       Neutral Powers and Persons in Land Warfare*, 2 A.J.I.L. 95 (1908).

173   Convention Respecting the Rights and Duties of Neutral Powers in Maritime War,
       Oct. 18, 1907, 36 Stat. 2415, T.S. No. 545, 205 Parry's T.S. 395, *reprinted in* 2
       A.J.I.L. 202 (Supp. 1908). *See* HULL, *supra* note 59, at 148–66; Hyde, *The Hague
       Convention Respecting the Rights and Duties of Neutral Powers in Naval War*, 2 A.J.I.L.
       507 (1908). *See also* [Finch], *The Purchase of Vessels of War in Neutral Countries by
       Belligerents*, 9 A.J.I.L. 177 (1915) (violates neutrality).

174   Convention Relative to the Laying of Submarine Mines, Oct. 18, 1907, 36 Stat.
       2332, T.S. No. 541, 205 Parry's T.S. 331, *reprinted in* 2 A.J.I.L. 138 (Supp.
       1908). *See* Stockton, *The Use of Submarine Mines and Torpedoes in Time of War*, 2
       A.J.I.L. 276 (1908).

175   Convention Relative to Certain Restrictions on the Exercise of the Right of Cap-
       ture in Maritime War, Oct. 18, 1907, 36 Stat. 2396, T.S. No. 544, 205 Parry's
       T.S. 367, *reprinted in* 2 A.J.I.L. 167 (Supp. 1908). *See* Baldwin, *The Eleventh
       Convention Proposed by the Hague Conference of 1907*, 2 A.J.I.L. 307 (1908).

176   Act of June 5, 1794, ch. 50, 1 Stat. 381.

177   Act of March 2, 1797, ch. 5, 1 Stat. 497.

178   Act of April 20, 1818, ch. 88, 3 Stat. 447 (currently reissued as 18 U.S.C.A. §
       967 (1969)).

179   Treaty of Washington, May 8, 1871, United States-Great Britain, 17 Stat. 863,
       T.S. No. 133. The three rules of article 6 provided that:
       A neutral Government is bound—
       First, to use due diligence to prevent the fitting out, arming, or equipping within
       its jurisdiction, of any vessel which it has reasonable ground to believe is intended
       to cruise or to carry on war against a Power with which it is at peace; and also to
       use like diligence to prevent the departure from its jurisdiction of any vessel
       intended to cruise or carry on war as above, such vessel having been specially
       adapted, in whole or in part, within such jurisdiction to war-like use.
       Secondly, not to permit or suffer either belligerent to make use of its ports or
       waters as the base of naval operations against the other, or for the purpose of the
       renewal or augmentation of military supplies or arms, or the recruitment of men.
       Thirdly, to exercise due diligence in its own ports and waters, and, as to all
       persons within its jurisdiction, to prevent any violation of the foregoing obliga-
       tions and duties.
       See also Report of the Delegates of the United States to the Second International
       Peace Conference at The Hague, in 2 SCOTT, *supra* note 87, at 198, 238–39, 241.

180   Pub. Res. 72, 63d Cong., 3d Sess., 38 Stat. 1226 (1915).

181   *See* [Scott], *The Joint Resolution of Congress to Empower the President to Better Enforce and Maintain the Neutrality of the United States*, 9 A.J.I.L. 490 (1915).

182   *See* Hyneman, *Neutrality During the European Wars of 1792–1815*, 24 A.J.I.L. 279 (1930); Raymond & Frischholz, *supra* note 65, at 805–07, 812–13, & 819–20.

183   Scott, *Proposed Amendments to the Neutrality Laws of the United States*, 10 A.J.I.L. 602 (1916).

184   Espionage Act, ch. 30, 40 Stat. 217 (1917). *See* Hyde, *The Espionage Act*, 12 A.J.I.L. 142 (1918).

185   "Neutrals have the right to continue during war to trade with the belligerents, subject to the law relating to contraband and blockade. The existence of this right is universally admitted, although on certain occasions it has been in practice denied." J. Moore, 7 INTERNATIONAL LAW DIGEST 382 (1906) [hereinafter cited as Moore].

186   *See generally Power Politics, supra* note 48, at 936–37.

187   *See* Stockton, *The International Naval Conference of London, 1908–1909*, 3 A.J.I.L. 596, 614 (1909). *See also* Lammasch, *Unjustifiable War and the Means to Avoid It*, 10 A.J.I.L. 689, 692, 702 (1916); Robinson, *Autonomous Neutralization*, 11 A.J.I.L. 607 (1917).

188   *See, e.g.*, Phillips, *American Participation in Belligerent Commercial Controls 1914–1917*, 27 A.J.I.L. 215 (1933).

189   *See, e.g.*, Scott, *The United States at War with the Imperial German Government*, 11 A.J.I.L. 617 (1917); Scott, *War Between Austria-Hungary and the United States*, 12 A.J.I.L. 165 (1918).

190   *Cf.* [Scott], *The Attitude of Journals of International Law in Time of War*, 9 A.J.I.L. 924 (1915).

191   *See* Dennis, *The Diplomatic Correspondence Leading up to the War*, 9 A.J.I.L. 402 (1915).

192   *See* [Scott], *Germany and the Neutrality of Belgium*, 8 A.J.I.L. 877 (1914). *But see* [Scott], *The Neutrality of Belgium*, 9 A.J.I.L. 707 (1915) (defense of invasion by Prof. Karl Neumeyer).

193   *See* [Scott], *The Binding Effect upon the German Empire of the Treaty of London of 1867 Neutralizing Luxemburg*, 9 A.J.I.L. 948 (1915).

194   [Scott], *The Hague Conventions and the Neutrality of Belgium and Luxemburg*, 9 A.J.I.L. 959 (1915).

195   *See* [Scott], *Germany and the Neutrality of Belgium*, 8 A.J.I.L. 877, 880 (1914).

196   *See* B. TUCHMAN, THE GUNS OF AUGUST 153 (1976).

197   *See, e.g.*, [Finch], *The War in Europe*, 8 A.J.I.L. 853, 857 (1914); [Scott], *The Right of Neutrals to Protest Against Violations of International Law*, 10 A.J.I.L. 341 (1916). *Cf.* COOGAN, *supra* note 119, at 193.

198   *See* Smith, *Robert Lansing and the Formulation of American Neutrality Policies, 1914–1915*, 43 MISS. VALLEY HIST. REV. 59 (1956).

199   [Scott], *The Resignation of Mr. Bryan as Secretary of State*, 9 A.J.I.L. 659 (1915).

200   [Scott], *The Appointment of Mr. Robert Lansing as Secretary of State*, 9 A.J.I.L. 694 (1915).

201   *See* Telegram from William Jennings Bryan to Ambassador Gerard (May 13, 1915), 1915 F.R.U.S. 393 (Supp.); Telegram from Secretary Lansing to Ambassador Gerard (June 9, 1915), *id.* at 436.

202   *See* Scott, *The Black List of Great Britain and Her Allies*, 10 A.J.I.L. 832 (1916); Scott, *Economic Conference of the Allied Powers*, 10 A.J.I.L. 845 (1916). *See also*

Brown, *Economic Warfare*, 11 A.J.I.L. 847 (1917); Clark, *Shall There Be War After the War?*, 11 A.J.I.L. 790 (1917).

203   See Gregory, *Neutrality and the Sale of Arms*, 10 A.J.I.L. 543 (1916); Morey, *The Sale of Munitions of War*, 10 A.J.I.L. 467 (1916); [Scott], *The Sale of Arms and Ammunition by American Merchants to Belligerents*, 9 A.J.I.L. 687 (1915); [Scott], *The Sale of Munitions of War*, 9 A.J.I.L. 927 (1915). *See also* [Scott], *American Neutrality*, 9 A.J.I.L. 443 (1915).

204   Morey, *The Sale of Munitions of War*, 10 A.J.I.L. 467 (1916).

205   See E. MAY, THE WORLD WAR AND AMERICAN ISOLATION 1914–1917, at 335–36 (1966) [hereinafter cited as MAY]; Hershey, *Some Popular Misconceptions of Neutrality*, 10 A.J.I.L. 118 (1916). *See also* Hershey, *The So-Called Inviolability of the Mails*, 10 A.J.I.L. 580 (1916).

206   See MAY, *supra* note 205, at 113–301, 387–437.

207   See Telegram from Ambassador Gerard to Secretary of State Bryan (Feb. 6, 1915), 1915 F.R.U.S. 94 (Supp.), *reprinted in* 9 A.J.I.L. 83 (Special Supp. 1915). *See also* [Finch], *Mines, Submarines and War Zones—The Absence of Blockade*, 9 A.J.I.L. 461 (1915).

208   See Telegram from Ambassador Bernstorff to Secretary of State Lansing (Jan. 31, 1917), 1917 F.R.U.S. 97, 100, 101 (1 Supp. 1917).

209   See, e.g., Declaration of London, *supra* note 121, arts. 48, 49, 50:
      Chapter IV.—Destruction of neutral prizes.
      Article 48. A neutral vessel which has been captured may not be destroyed by the captor; she must be taken into such port as is proper for the determination there of all questions concerning the validity of the capture.
      Article 49. As an exception, a neutral vessel which has been captured by a belligerent warship, and which would be liable to condemnation, may be destroyed if the observance of article 48 would involve danger to the safety of the warship or to the success of the operations in which she is engaged at the time.
      Article 50. Before the vessel is destroyed all persons on board must be placed in safety, and all the ship's papers and other documents which the parties interested consider relevant for the purpose of deciding on the validity of the capture must be taken on board the warship.

210   See Garner, *Some Questions of International Law in the European War* (pts. 3, 8 & 9), 9 A.J.I.L. 594, 612 (1915), 9 A.J.I.L. 818, 825 (1915), 10 A.J.I.L. 12 (1916).

211   See generally Scott, *Armed Merchant Ships*, 10 A.J.I.L. 113 (1916); Editorial Comment, *The Status of Armed Merchant Vessels*, 9 A.J.I.L. 188 (1915).

212   See [Finch], *The Use of Neutral Flags on Merchant Vessels of Belligerents*, 9 A.J.I.L. 471 (1915).

213   See Telegram from Ambassador Bernstorff to Secretary of State Bryan (Feb. 7, 1915), 1915 F.R.U.S. 95 (Supp.).

214   Id. at 96.

215   See Baty, *Naval Warfare: Law and License*, 10 A.J.I.L. 42 (1916); [Scott], *The Controversy Between the United States and Germany over the Use of Submarines Against Merchant Vessels*, 9 A.J.I.L. 666 (1915); Scott, *The Secretary of State on the Violations of International Law in the European War as They Affect Neutrals*, 10 A.J.I.L. 572 (1916).

216   See Scott, *The United States at War with the Imperial German Government*, 11 A.J.I.L. 617 (1917).

217   See Scott, *War Between Austria-Hungary and the United States*, 12 A.J.I.L. 165 (1918).

218 S. J. Res. 1, ch. 1, 65th Cong., 1st Sess., 40 Stat. 1 (1917).

219 Address of the President of the United States Delivered at a Joint Session of the Two Houses of Congress (Apr. 2, 1917), *reprinted in* 11 A.J.I.L. 143, 144 (Supp. 1917).

220 *See, e.g.*, Brown, *War and Law*, 12 A.J.I.L. 162, 164 (1918): "This is truly a war in defense of law." *See also* Brown, *Economic Warfare*, 11 A.J.I.L. 847 (1917) (the war demonstrates the futility of a system of international law based upon the balance of power, suppression of nationality, and denial of self-government).

221 *See* Scott, *The Dawn in Germany? The Lichnowsky and Other Disclosures*, 12 A.J.I.L. 386 (1918); Willoughby, *The Prussian Theory of Government*, 12 A.J.I.L. 266 (1918); Willoughby, *The Prussian Theory of the State*, 12 A.J.I.L. 251 (1918); American Bar Association, Resolution of Sept. 4, 1917, in 3 A.B.A.J. 576–77 (1917) (submitted by Elihu Root; adopted unanimously), *reprinted and approved in* Gregory, *The Annual Meeting of the American Bar Association*, 11 A.J.I.L. 851 (1917). *See also* Baldwin, *The Share of the President of the United States in a Declaration of War*, 12 A.J.I.L. 1 (1918) (there might exist Constitutional authority to wage war in order to secure the liberty of foreign peoples).

222 Address of the President Delivered at a Joint Session of the Two Houses of Congress (Apr. 2, 1917), *reprinted in* 11 A.J.I.L. 350, 356 (Special Supp. 1917).

223 *See also* Fenwick, *Germany and the Crime of the World War*, 23 A.J.I.L. 812 (1929) (article 231 of the Treaty of Versailles should not be interpreted as imputing moral guilt and criminal responsibility for the war to Germany, for in 1914 there was no clear basis upon which moral responsibility for a particular war could be judged); Myers, *The Control of Foreign Relations*, 11 AM. POL. SCI. REV. 24 (1917) (strong legal realist position); T. Woolsey, *Reconstruction and International Law*, 13 A.J.I.L. 187 (1919) (irrespective of idealistic motives, the war was fundamentally one of self-defense); T. Woolsey, *The Relations Between the United States and the Central Powers*, 11 A.J.I.L. 628 (1917) (after declaration of war upon Germany the United States should await the development of events before ipso facto declaring war upon Austria and Turkey).

224 *See, e.g.*, Brown, *The Theory of the Independence and Equality of States*, 9 A.J.I.L. 305 (1915); [Finch], *The Effect of the War on International Law*, 9 A.J.I.L. 475 (1915); Graham, *Neutrality and the World War*, 17 A.J.I.L. 704 (1923); Graham, *Neutralization as a Movement in International Law*, 21 A.J.I.L. 79 (1927); Hershey, *Projects Submitted to the American Institute of International Law*, 11 A.J.I.L. 390 (1917); Root, *The Outlook for International Law*, 10 A.J.I.L. 1 (1916); Spencer, *The Organization of International Force*, 9 A.J.I.L. 45 (1915); Wilson, *Sanction for International Agreements*, 11 A.J.I.L. 387 (1917).

225 *See, e.g.*, R. BARTLETT, THE LEAGUE TO ENFORCE PEACE 215–18 (1944).

226 *See* Dubin, *Elihu Root and the Advocacy of a League of Nations, 1914–1917*, 19 W. POL. Q. 439, 453–54 (1966); Root, *Amending the Covenant*, ADVOC. OF PEACE, July, 1919, at 211.

227 *See* Hyde, *The United States Accepts the Optional Clause*, 40 A.J.I.L. 778 (1946); Jessup, *Acceptance by the United States of the Optional Clause of the International Court of Justice*, 39 A.J.I.L. 745 (1945); Potter, *"As Determined by the United States,"* 40 A.J.I.L. 792 (1946); Preuss, *The International Court of Justice, the Senate, and Matters of Domestic Jurisdiction*, 40 A.J.I.L. 720 (1946); Wilcox, *The United States Accepts Compulsory Jurisdiction*, 40 A.J.I.L. 699 (1946); Wright, *The International Court of Justice and the Interpretation of Multilateral Treaties*, 41 A.J.I.L. 445 (1947).

228   *See* L. SOHN, CASES ON UNITED NATIONS LAW (2d ed. 1967).

229   *See* McDougal & Lasswell, *The Identification and Appraisal of Diverse Systems of Public Order*, 53 A.J.I.L. 1 (1959).

230   *Id.* at 6.

231   *See, e.g.*, Lasswell, *Introduction* to M. MCDOUGAL & F. FELICIANO, LAW AND MINIMUM WORLD PUBLIC ORDER at xix, xix n. 1 (1961).

232   *See, e.g.*, McDougal, Lasswell & Chen, *The Protection of Respect and Human Rights: Freedom of Choice and World Public Order*, 24 AM. U.L. REV. 919, 938–43 (1975).

233   J. Locke, *The Second Treatise of Government*, in TWO TREATISES OF GOVERNMENT 305 (P. Laslett rev. ed. 1960).

234   *See* J. BENTHAM, THE PRINCIPLES OF MORALS AND LEGISLATION (2d ed. 1823); J-J. Rousseau, *The Social Contract*, in THE SOCIAL CONTRACT AND DISCOURSE ON THE ORIGIN OF INEQUALITY 1 (L. Crocker ed. 1967).

235   *See* KARL MARX: EARLY WRITINGS (T. Bottomore trans. & ed. 1964); K. MARX, THE EIGHTEENTH BRUMAIRE OF LOUIS BONAPARTE (2d ed. 1869); BASIC WRITINGS ON POLITICS & PHILOSOPHY: MARX & ENGELS (L. Feuer ed. 1959).

236   *See* MCDOUGAL & FELICIANO, *supra* note 231, at 377–79 (Marxism is specifically rejected); M. MCDOUGAL, H. LASSWELL, & L. CHEN, HUMAN RIGHTS AND WORLD ORDER 76–79 (1980). *See generally* Berman, *American and Soviet Perspectives on Human Rights*, 22 WORLD VIEW 15 (1979).

237   *See* McDougal, *Human Rights and World Public Order: Principles of Content and Procedure for Clarifying General Community Policies*, 14 VA. J. INT'L L. 387, 412 (1974); McDougal, Lasswell & Chen, *Human Rights and World Public Order: A Framework for Policy-Oriented Inquiry*, 63 A.J.I.L. 237, 252–53 (1969).

238   K. MARX, CRITIQUE OF THE GOTHA PROGRAMME 10 (C. Dutt ed. 1938).

239   *See, e.g.*, McDougal, *The Soviet-Cuban Quarantine and Self-Defense*, 57 A.J.I.L. 597 (1963). In MCDOUGAL & FELICIANO, *supra* note 231, at 536, the doctrine of humanitarian intervention was branded "amorphous." Yet fifteen years later, the Israeli raid at Entebbe was deemed by McDougal to be "justified as a humanitarian intervention, a doctrine whose roots go back, at least, to Hugo Grotius." Letter from Myres S. McDougal and Michael Reisman to the New York Times Editor (July 9, 1976), in N.Y. Times, July 16, 1976, § A, at 20, col. 3.

240   *See* Moore, *Prolegomenon to the Jurisprudence of Myres McDougal and Harold Lasswell*, 54 VA. L. REV. 662, 676 (1968).

241   *See* G. ABI-SAAB, THE UNITED NATIONS OPERATION IN THE CONGO 1960–1964 (1978); R. BOWIE, SUEZ 1956 (1974); A. CHAYES, THE CUBAN MISSILE CRISIS (1974); T. EHRLICH, CYPRUS 1958–1967 (1974); R. FISHER, POINTS OF CHOICE (1978), *reviewed in* Rubin, *Order and Chaos: The Role of International Law in Foreign Policy*, 77 MICH. L. REV. 336 (1979).

242   T. KUHN, THE STRUCTURE OF SCIENTIFIC REVOLUTIONS 153–55 (2d ed. 1970).

243   Statement by Hans J. Morgenthau (July 1961) (copy on file with author).

244   *See* G. CLARK & L. SOHN, WORLD PEACE THROUGH WORLD LAW (3d ed. 1966). *See also* L. SOHN, CASES ON UNITED NATIONS LAW (2d ed. 1967); L. SOHN, THE UNITED NATIONS IN ACTION (1968).

245   *Quoted in* Leonard, *Danger: Nuclear War*, HARV. MAGAZINE, Nov.–Dec. 1980, at 21, 22 (brackets in original).

246   *See* Kennan, *On Nuclear War*, N.Y. REVIEW OF BOOKS, Jan. 21, 1982, at 8.

247   *See Excerpts from Farewell Testimony by Rickover to Congress*, N.Y. Times, Jan. 30, 1982, at 8, col. 1.

248   *See* C. BRENNER, AN ELEMENTARY TEXTBOOK OF PSYCHOANALYSIS 100–01 (1957).

Notes to Part Two

1   Smith & Shuster, *Drama in Hijacking of Jet to Uganda: A Long Week of Terror and Tensions*, N.Y. Times, July 11, 1976, § 1, at 1, col. 4.
2   *Id.* at 16, col. 1; *The Rescue: "We do the Impossible,"* TIME, July 12, 1976, at 21, 22 [hereinafter cited as *The Rescue*].
3   Smith & Shuster, *supra* note 1, at 16, col. 2.
4   *Id.*; *The Rescue, supra* note 2, at 22.
5   *The Rescue, supra* note 2, at 22. Actually, the French had previously released the only prisoner the hijackers demanded, and Kenya denied having any of the named prisoners in its jails. *Id.*
6   *Id.* at 23.
7   Smith & Shuster, *supra* note 1, at 16, col. 4.
8   *The Rescue, supra* note 2, at 23.
9   *Id.*
10   *Id.*
11   Smith & Shuster, *supra* note 1, at 16, cols. 5–8.
12   *Id.*
13   H. KYEMBA, A STATE OF BLOOD 166–78 (1977).
14   *See* G. ABI-SAAB, THE UNITED NATIONS OPERATION IN THE CONGO 1960–64 (1978); R. BOWIE, SUEZ 1956 (1974); A. CHAYES, THE CUBAN MISSILE CRISIS (1974); T. EHRLICH, CYPRUS 1958–1967 (1974); R. FISHER, POINTS OF CHOICE (1978). *See also* R. FISHER, INTERNATIONAL CONFLICT FOR BEGINNERS (1969); C. MITCHELL, THE STRUCTURE OF INTERNATIONAL CONFLICT (1981); INTERNATIONAL LAW AND POLITICAL CRISIS (L. Scheinman & D. Wilkinson eds. 1968); *Enhancing Order (and Law) in Future International Crises*, 70 AM. SOC. INT'L L. PROC. 123 (1976) (panel discussion by R. Bowie, T. Farer, R. Fisher, and C. Parry); Rubin, *Order and Chaos: The Role of International Law in Foreign Policy*, 77 MICH. L. REV. 336 (1979).
15   The paradigm for international legal positivism was established by Lassa Oppenheim in his article, *The Science of International Law: Its Task and Method*, 2 A.J.I.L. 313 (1908).
16   *See* THE NICOMACHEAN ETHICS OF ARISTOTLE, BOOK V, at 103–36 (W. Ross trans. 1954).
17   *See, e.g.*, L. FULLER, THE MORALITY OF LAW (rev. ed 1969); Fuller, *The Forms and Limits of Adjudication*, 92 HARV. L. REV. 353 (1978); Fuller, *Law as an Instrument of Social Control and Law as a Facilitation of Human Interaction*, 1975 B.Y.U.L. REV. 89; Fuller, *Mediation—Its Forms and Functions*, 44 S. CAL. L. REV. 305 (1971).
18   *See* H. STEINER & D. VAGTS, TRANSNATIONAL LEGAL PROBLEMS 178–82 (2d ed. 1976).
19   *See* T. SCHELLING, THE STRATEGY OF CONFLICT (1960).
20   *Accord, id.* at 300.
21   *See generally* Y. BEN-PORAT, E. HABER & Z. SCHIFF, ENTEBBE RESCUE (1977) [hereinafter cited as ENTEBBE RESCUE]; KYEMBA, *supra* note 13; Y. RABIN, THE RABIN MEMOIRS 282–89 (1979); W. STEVENSON, 90 MINUTES AT ENTEBBE (1976).

22   *See, e.g.*, the authorities collected *supra* note 42 in Part One of this book.

23   *See* STEINER & VAGTS, *supra* note 18, at 258–62. *See generally* A. D'AMATO, THE CONCEPT OF CUSTOM IN INTERNATIONAL LAW (1971).

24   Tokyo Convention on Offenses and Certain Other Acts Committed on Board Aircraft, Sept. 14, 1963, 20 U.S.T. 2941, T.I.A.S. No. 6768.

25   *See* Lissitzyn, *Hijacking, International Law and Human Rights*, in AERIAL PIRACY AND INTERNATIONAL LAW 116, 117–18 (E. McWhinney ed. 1971).

26   Hague Convention for the Suppression of Unlawful Seizure of Aircraft (Hijacking), Dec. 16, 1970, 22 U.S.T. 1641, T.I.A.S. No. 7192.

27   *See also* Ambramovsky, *Multilateral Conventions for the Suppression of Unlawful Seizure and Interference with Aircraft Part I: The Hague Convention*, 13 COLUM. J. TRANSNAT'L L. 381 (1974); Brooks, *Skyjacking and Refugees: The Effect of the Hague Convention Upon Asylum*, 16 HARV. INT'L L.J. 93 (1975); Metsalämpe, *Some Remarks on the Basic Obligations of States in Cases of Unlawful Seizure of Aircraft*, in ESSAYS IN HONOR OF ERIK CASTRÉN 46 (1979); Steelman, *International Terrorism Vis-A-Vis Air-Hijacking*, 9 SW. U.L. REV. 85 (1977).

28   Montreal Convention for the Suppression of Unlawful Acts Against the Safety of Civil Aviation (Sabotage), Sept. 23, 1971, 24 U.S.T. 565, T.I.A.S. No. 7570. *See* Ambramovsky, *Multilateral Conventions for the Suppression of Unlawful Seizure and Interference with Aircraft Part II: The Montreal Convention*, 14 COLUM. J. TRANSNAT'L L. 268, 286–87 (1975).

29   *See* Ambramovsky, *Multilateral Conventions for the Suppression of Unlawful Seizure and Interference with Aircraft Part III: The Legality and Political Feasibility of a Multilateral Air Security Enforcement Convention*, 14 COLUM. J. TRANSNAT'L L. 451, 466–70 (1975).
    In addition, the following resolutions by the appropriate bodies of concerned international organizations were pertinent to the Entebbe crisis:

    1   G.A. Res. 2551, 24 U.N. GAOR Supp. (No. 30) at 108, U.N. Doc. A/7630 (1969), of Dec. 12, on the forcible diversion of civil aircraft in flight;

    2   Res. A 17-1, ICAO Assembly, 17th Sess. (Extraordinary), June 16–30, 1970, *reprinted in* 65 A.J.I.L. 452 (1971), on acts of violence directed against international civil air transport;

    3   S.C. Res. 286, U.N. SCOR, Resolutions and Decisions of the Security Council 16, U.N. Doc. S/INF/25, U.N. Doc. S/RES/286 (1970), of Sept. 9, on the hijacking of aircraft and the release of passengers and crews;

    4   G.A. Res. 2645, 25 U.N. GAOR Supp. (No. 28) at 126, U.N. Doc. A/8028 (1970), of Nov. 25, on aerial hijacking or interference with civil air travel;

    5   Security Council Consensus Decision of June 20, 27 U.N. SCOR Supp. (Apr.-June 1972) at 128, U.N. Doc. S/10705 (1972), condemning hijacking;

    6   G.A. Res. 3034, 27 U.N. GAOR Supp. (No. 30) at 119, U.N. Doc. A/8730 (1972), of Dec. 18, on measures to prevent international terrorism.

30   Geneva Convention on the High Seas, Apr. 29, 1958, art. 15, 13 U.S.T. 2312, 2317, T.I.A.S. No. 5200, 450 U.N.T.S. 11.

31   *See, e.g.*, the comment made by Israeli Ambassador Herzog in the Security Council Entebbe debates: "The act of hijacking can well be regarded as one of piracy." 31 U.N. SCOR (1939th mtg.) at 53–55, U.N. Doc. S/P.V. 1939 (prov. ed. 1976).

32   Fourth Geneva Convention, Aug. 12, 1949, art. 34, 6 U.S.T. 3516, 3540, T.I.A.S. No. 3365, 75 U.N.T.S. 287.

33   *Id.*, art. 147, 6 U.S.T. 3516, 3618, T.I.A.S. No. 3365, 75 U.N.T.S. 287.

34 *Id.*, art. 146, 6 U.S.T. 3516, 3616, T.I.A.S. No. 3365, 75 U.N.T.S. 287.

35 First Geneva Convention, Aug. 12, 1949, art. 3, 6 U.S.T. 3114, 3118, T.I.A.S. No. 3362, 75 U.N.T.S. 31; Second Geneva Convention, Aug. 12, 1949, art. 3, 6 U.S.T. 3217, 3222, T.I.A.S. No. 3363, 75 U.N.T.S. 85; Third Geneva Convention, Aug. 12, 1949, art. 3, 6 U.S.T. 3316, 3320, T.I.A.S. No. 3364, 75 U.N.T.S. 135; Fourth Geneva Convention, Aug. 12, 1949, art. 3, 6 U.S.T. 3516, 3520, T.I.A.S. No. 3365, 75 U.N.T.S. 287.

36 *See also* Note, *The Taking and Killing of Hostages: Coercion and Reprisal in International Law*, 54 NOTRE DAME LAW. 131 (1978).

37 U.N. Charter art. 2, para. 3, provides: "All Members shall settle their international disputes by peaceful means in such a manner that international peace and security, and justice, are not endangered."

38 U.N. Charter art. 33, para. 1, provides: "The parties to any dispute, the continuance of which is likely to endanger the maintenance of international peace and security, shall, first of all, seek a solution by negotiation, enquiry, mediation, conciliation, arbitration, judicial settlement, resort to regional agencies or arrangements, or other peaceful means of their own choice."

39 U.N. Charter art. 2, para. 4, provides: "All Members shall refrain in their international relations from the threat or use of force against the territorial integrity or political independence of any state, or in any other manner inconsistent with the Purposes of the United Nations."

40 U.N. Charter art. 51 states:
Nothing in the present Charter shall impair the inherent right of individual or collective self-defense if an armed attack occurs against a Member of the United Nations, until the Security Council has taken measures necessary to maintain international peace and security. Measures taken by Members in the exercise of this right of self-defense shall be immediately reported to the Security Council and shall not in any way affect the authority and responsibility of the Security Council under the present Charter to take at any time such action as it deems necessary in order to maintain or restore international peace and security.

41 *See, e.g.*, D. BOWETT, SELF-DEFENCE IN INTERNATIONAL LAW 13 (1958).

42 *See The Caroline*, in J. Moore, 2 INTERNATIONAL LAW DIGEST 409, 412 (1906); W. BISHOP, INTERNATIONAL LAW 916–17 (3d ed. 1962). This formulation of the test for self-defense was also argued successfully by Mr. Dallas, for the prosecution in the famous case of *United States v. Holmes*, 26 F. Cas. 360 (C.C.E.D. Pa. 1842) (No. 15,383). *See* L. WEINREB, CRIMINAL LAW: CASES, COMMENT, QUESTIONS 339, 341, 344 (3d ed. 1980).

43 *See* Letter from Myres S. McDougal and Michael Reisman to the New York Times Editor (July 9, 1976), in N.Y. Times, July 16, 1976, at A20, col. 3 [hereinafter cited as McDougal & Reisman Letter]. Yet fifteen years earlier, the doctrine of humanitarian intervention was branded "amorphous" in M. McDOUGAL & F. FELICIANO, LAW AND MINIMUM WORLD PUBLIC ORDER 536 (1961).

44 Judgment in the Corfu Channel Case (U.K. v. Alb.), 1949 I.C.J. 4.

45 *Id.* at 34–35.

46 *Id.* at 108.

47 *Id.* at 47.

48 G.A. Res. 2131, 20 U.N. GAOR Supp. (No. 14) at 11, U.N. Doc. A/6014 (1965). Article 1 states unequivocally:
No State has the right to intervene, directly or indirectly, for any reason whatever,

in the internal or external affairs of any other State. Consequently, armed intervention and all other forms of interference or attempted threats against the personality of the State or against its political, economic and cultural elements, are condemned.

A preambular paragraph in the resolution states: "[A]rmed intervention is synonymous with aggression and, as such, is contrary to the basic principles on which peaceful international co-operation between States should be built. . . ."

49   G.A. Res. 2625, 25 U.N. GAOR Supp. (No. 28) at 121, U.N. Doc. A/8028 (1970). The principles set out in this resolution declare that states shall (1) refrain from the threat or use of force in international relations, (2) settle international disputes peacefully, (3) abstain from intervening for any reason whatever in the internal or external affairs of any other state, (4) cooperate with one another in accordance with the U.N. Charter, (5) promote the realization of the principle of equal rights and self-determination of peoples, (6) recognize the sovereign equality of all other states, and (7) carry out in good faith the obligations assumed by them in accordance with the U.N. Charter.

The following relevant explanatory comments were also made in the text of the Declaration on Friendly Relations: "Every State has the duty to refrain from the threat or use of force to violate the existing international boundaries of another State or as a means of solving international disputes. . . . Armed intervention and all other forms of interference or attempted threats against the personality of the State or against its political, economic, and cultural elements, are in violation of international law. . . . Every State shall refrain from any action aimed at the partial or total disruption of the national unity and territorial integrity of any other State or country. . . . The territorial integrity and political independence of the State are inviolable."

50   G.A. Res. 3314, 29 U.N. GAOR Supp. (No. 31) at 142, U.N. Doc. A/9631 (1974). An examination of the Definition of Aggression reveals the following salient points:

According to article 1, aggression is the use of armed force by a state against the sovereignty, territorial integrity, or political independence of another state.

Article 2 of the Definition provides that the first use of armed force by a state in contravention of the Charter shall constitute prima facie evidence of an act of aggression.

Article 3, paragraph (a) states that the invasion or attack by the armed forces of a state on the territory of another state, or any military occupation, however temporary, resulting from such invasion or attack qualifies as an act of aggression.

Article 3, paragraph (b) of the Definition declares that the use of any weapons by a state against the territory of another state is an act of aggression.

Article 3, paragraph (d) maintains that an attack by the armed forces of a state on the land, sea, or air forces or marine and air fleets of another state is an act of aggression.

Article 3, paragraph (f) adds that the action of a state in allowing its territory, which it has placed at the disposal of another state, to be used by that other state for perpetrating an act of aggression against a third state qualifies as an act of aggression.

Article 5, paragraph (1) of the Definition proclaims most emphatically that no consideration of whatever nature, whether political, economic, military, or otherwise, may serve as a justification for aggression.

And finally, article 5, paragraph (2) states that aggression gives rise to international responsibility.

51 U.N. Charter art. 39 states:
The Security Council shall determine the existence of any threat to the peace, breach of the peace, or act of aggression and shall make recommendations, or decide what measures shall be taken in accordance with Articles 41 and 42, to maintain or restore international peace and security.

52 *See* Akinsanya, *The Entebbe Rescue Mission: A Case of Aggression?*, 9 J. AFRICAN STUD. 46 (1982); Ambramovsky & Greene, *Unilateral Intervention on Behalf of Hijacked American Nationals Held Abroad*, 1979 UTAH L. REV. 231; Margo, *The Legality of the Entebbe Raid in International Law*, 94 S. AFR. L.J. 306 (1977); Murphy, *State Self-Help and Problems of Public International Law*, in LEGAL ASPECTS OF INTERNATIONAL TERRORISM 553 (A. Evans & J. Murphy eds. 1978) [hereinafter this book will be cited as Evans & Murphy]; Paust, *Entebbe and Self-Help: The Israeli Response to Terrorism*, 2 FLETCHER F. 86 (1978); Salter, *Commando Coup at Entebbe: Humanitarian Intervention or Barbaric Aggression?*, 11 INT'L LAW. 331 (1977); Note, *Use of Force for the Protection of Nationals Abroad: The Entebbe Incident*, 9 CASE W. RES. J. INT'L L. 117 (1977).

53 This section is based in substantial part upon an interview with Mr. Gad Yaakobi, Israeli Minister of Transportation during the Entebbe crisis, that was conducted in Boston on October 19, 1977 [hereinafter cited as Yaakobi Interview]. I would like to thank Mr. Yaakobi for his time and cooperation.

54 ENTEBBE RESCUE, *supra* note 21, at 30.

55 *Id*. at viii–ix, 38.

56 Yaakobi Interview.

57 *Id*.

58 *See* Bilder, *The Office of the Legal Adviser: The State Department Lawyer and Foreign Affairs*, 56 A.J.I.L. 633 (1962).

59 For example, during the Cuban missile crisis, Robert Kennedy was a member of the crisis management decision-making team (the Executive Committee) not so much because he was the attorney general but because he was the brother of the president. *See* R. KENNEDY, THIRTEEN DAYS (1971).

60 *See* authorities collected *supra* note 45 in Part One of this book.

61 *See generally* WHO'S WHO IN ISRAEL 401 (I. Ben (Benditer) & M. Grunberg 18th ed. 1978).

62 *See* ENTEBBE RESCUE, *supra* note 21, at 39–40.

63 *Id*. at viii.

64 THE INTERNATIONAL WHO'S WHO 1979–1980, at 55 (Europa Publications Ltd. 43d ed. 1979).

65 ENTEBBE RESCUE, *supra* note 21, at 175.

66 STEVENSON, *supra* note 21, at 28–29.

67 U.N. Secretary-General Kurt Waldheim originally called the Entebbe raid "a serious violation of the sovereignty of a State Member of the United Nations." *See* 31 U.N. SCOR (1939th mtg.) at 7–8, U.N. Doc. S/P.V. 1939 (prov. ed. 1976); U.N. Press Release SG/SM/2343 (July 8, 1976), at 2, para. 9.

68 STEVENSON, *supra* note 21, at 11; Yaakobi Interview.

69 *See* 31 U.N. SCOR (1939th mtg.) at 42–45, U.N. Doc. S/P.V. 1939 (prov. ed. 1976); *Council Fails to Adopt Draft Resolution after Considering Uganda Hijacking Issue*, U.N. CHRONICLE, Aug.–Sept. 1976, at 15, 17–18.

70 Yaakobi Interview.

71 *Id.*; 31 U.N. SCOR (1942d mtg.) at 34–35, U.N. Doc. S/P.V. 1942 (prov. ed. 1976); ENTEBBE RESCUE, *supra* note 21, at 22. This map is currently in the possession of the Israeli government.

72 31 U.N. SCOR (1939th mtg.) at 59–60, U.N. Doc. S/P.V. 1939 (prov. ed. 1976); ENTEBBE RESCUE, *supra* note 21, at 99–100.

73 ENTEBBE RESCUE, *supra* note 21, at 89.

74 STEVENSON, *supra* note 21, at 66–69.

75 Yaakobi Interview.

76 *See* W. LAQUEUR, CONFRONTATION: THE MIDDLE EAST AND WORLD POLITICS 162–63 (1974).

77 31 U.N. SCOR (1939th mtg.) at 16, U.N. Doc. S/P.V. 1939 (prov. ed. 1976); *Council Fails to Adopt Draft Resolution after Considering Uganda Hijacking Issue, supra* note 69, at 15, 16.

78 Yaakobi Interview.

79 STEVENSON, *supra* note 21, at 31.

80 U.N. Charter art. 35, para. 1, states: "Any Member of the United Nations may bring any dispute, or any situation [which might lead to international friction or give rise to a dispute] to the attention of the Security Council or of the General Assembly."

81 STEVENSON, *supra* note 21, at 29.

82 ENTEBBE RESCUE, *supra* note 21, at 265.

83 STEVENSON, *supra* note 21, at 56.

84 Yaakobi Interview.

85 STEVENSON, *supra* note 21, at 82.

86 *Id.* at 30–31.

87 U.N. Charter art. 25 provides: "The Members of the United Nations agree to accept and carry out the decisions of the Security Council in accordance with the present Charter."

88 *Compare* Model Penal Code § 3.02 (Proposed Official Draft 1962): Justification Generally: Choice of Evils.
(1) Conduct which the actor believes to be necessary to avoid a harm or evil to himself or to another is justifiable, provided that:
    (a) the harm or evil sought to be avoided by such conduct is greater than that sought to be prevented by the law defining the offense charged; and
    (b) neither the Code nor other law defining the offense provides exceptions or defenses dealing with the specific situation involved; and
    (c) a legislative purpose to exclude the justification claimed does not otherwise plainly appear.
(2) When the actor was reckless or negligent in bringing about the situation requiring a choice of harms or evils or in appraising the necessity for his conduct, the justification afforded by this Section is unavailable in a prosecution for any offense for which recklessness or negligence, as the case may be, suffices to establish culpability.
See also N. MACHIAVELLI, THE PRINCE 191 (M. Musa trans. & ed. 1964) (the prince must choose the least bad as good).

89 ENTEBBE RESCUE, *supra* note 21, at 253–54.

90 Yaakobi Interview. *Compare* Embassy of Israel, Washington, D.C., Information Background: Legal Aspects of Israel's Rescue Action in Uganda (no date) *with*

Department of State, Briefing Memorandum from Legal Adviser Monroe Leigh to the Secretary of State, Legal Aspects of Entebbe Hijacking Incident (July 8, 1976) (released in 1978 pursuant to a Freedom of Information Act request), *excerpts reprinted in* 73 A.J.I.L. 122–24 (1979).

91 ENTEBBE RESCUE, *supra* note 21, at 290–92; N.Y. Times, July 4, 1976, § 1, at 1, cols. 7–8.
92 Yaakobi Interview.
93 *Id.*; ENTEBBE RESCUE, *supra* note 21, at 269.
94 Yaakobi Interview.
95 *Contra* STEVENSON, *supra* note 21, at 121.
96 *See* ENTEBBE RESCUE, *supra* note 21, at 324.
97 31 U.N. SCOR (1939th mtg.) at 16, U.N. Doc. S/P.V. 1939 (prov. ed. 1976); KYEMBA, *supra* note 13, at 169.
98 N.Y. Times, July 6, 1976, at 4, col. 1.
99 *See Mogadishu Notebook*, WEST AFRICA, June 24, 1974, at 750, 751.
100 AHG/Res. 83/XIII (1976).
101 Charter of the Organization of African Unity (OAU) art. 8.
102 U.N. Charter art. 24, para. 1.
103 *See* 31 U.N. SCOR, Supp. (July–Sept. 1976) at 6, U.N. Doc. S/12126 (1976).
104 *Id.*
105 31 U.N. SCOR (1939th mtg) at 4–5, U.N. Doc. S/P.V. 1939 (prov. ed. 1976).
106 *See, e.g.*, 31 U.N. SCOR (1939th mtg.) at 88, U.N. Doc. S/P.V. 1939 (prov. ed. 1976), where the French delegate stated:
That this tragic affair has been marked by violent and illegal acts cannot be denied. The initial action—that is, the hijacking of a civilian aircraft and the taking of innocent hostages—is in particular an intolerable violation of international morality and of *jus gentium* which could not be justified by any cause and against which the international community has to adopt effective measures and resolve to implement them.
107 *See, e.g.*, the statement of the Libyan representative: "My delegation will oppose any attempt to hijack the debate under the guise of debating the hijacking." 31 U.N. SCOR (1940th mtg.) at 6, U.N. Doc. S/P.V. 1940 (prov. ed. 1976).
108 *See Council Fails to Adopt Draft Resolution After Considering Uganda Hijacking Issue*, *supra* note 69, at 15.
109 31 U.N. SCOR Supp. (July–Sept. 1976) at 15–16, U.N. Doc. S/12139.
110 31 U.N. SCOR Supp. (July–Sept. 1976) at 15, U.N. Doc. S/12138.
111 *Id.*
112 *See* 31 U.N. SCOR (1939th mtg.) at 1, U.N. Doc. S/P.V. 1939 (prov. ed. 1976); 31 U.N. SCOR (1940th mtg.) at 1, U.N. Doc. S/P.V. 1940 (prov. ed. 1976); 31 U.N. SCOR (1941st mtg.) at 1, U.N. Doc. S/P.V. 1941 (prov. ed. 1976); 31 U.N. SCOR (1942nd mtg.) at 1, U.N. Doc. S/P.V. 1942 (prov. ed. 1976); 31 U.N. SCOR (1943d mtg.) at 1, U.N. Doc. S/P.V. 1943 (prov. ed. 1976).
113 *Council Fails to Adopt Draft Resolution After Considering Uganda Hijacking Issue*, *supra* note 69, at 15.
114 *See* 31 U.N. SCOR (1943d mtg.) at 81, U.N. Doc. S/P.V. 1943 (prov. ed. 1976).
115 *Id.*
116 *Id.*
117 *See, e.g.*, 31 U.N. SCOR (1943d mtg.) at 78–80, U.N. Doc. S/P.V. 1943 (prov. ed. 1976), where the representative from Guyana stated:

The subject matter of [the U.S.–U.K. draft resolution]—the problem of hijacking—is not on the agenda of this meeting of the Security Council. What is really before us is the complaint of the current Chairman of the Organization of African Unity, the Prime Minister of Mauritius, concerning the act of aggression of Israel against the Republic of Uganda. . . . Therefore, . . . my delegation will not be participating in the vote on the draft resolution.

118   *See, e.g.*, 31 U.N. SCOR (1942d mtg.) at 13, U.N. Doc. S/P.V. 1942 (prov. ed. 1976), where the Panamanian delegate argued:
There can be no doubt, then, that in the case we are discussing there are two acts of force without legal basis—one committed by a State against another Member State of the United Nations and another carried out by civilians moved by political passions.
If aggression, as defined in General Assembly resolution 3314 (XXIX) is "the use of armed force by a State against the sovereignty, territorial integrity, or political independence of another State, or in any other manner inconsistent with the Charter of the United Nations," it is obvious that the violation of the sovereignty and territorial integrity of Uganda . . . by the Israeli army constituted a use of force not authorized by the United Nations Charter, which only admits of enforcement actions by the United Nations or legitimate individual or collective self-defence against armed attack. Israel was not the victim of an armed attack by Uganda, and therefore its action was not legitimate.

119   Palestinian National Charter art. 8, in 3 THE ARAB-ISRAELI CONFLICT 706 (J. Moore ed. 1974) [hereinafter cited as Moore].

120   31 U.N. SCOR (1939th mtg.) at 36, U.N. Doc. S/P.V. 1939 (prov. ed. 1976).

121   STEVENSON, *supra* note 21, at 4.

122   Palestinian National Charter arts. 2, 15, 22, in 3 Moore, *supra* note 119, at 706, 708–10.

123   *Id.* art 10, in 3 Moore, *supra* note 119, at 707.

124   *See* T. HOBBES, LEVIATHAN (M. Oakeshott ed. 1962).

125   Hobbes asserted that international politics was one of three states of nature. The other two were the mythical state of nature and civil war. All three, however, were tantamount to a state of war. *Id.* at 101.

126   *Id.*

127   *Id.* at 100.

128   *See, e.g.*, N.Y. Times, Jan 11, 1980, at A3, col. 1. *But see* Blum, *The Missing Reversioner: Reflections on the Status of Judea and Samaria*, 3 ISRAEL L. REV. 279 (1968).

129   *See, e.g.*, Bethell, *Incidentally, the U.N. Vote Was Right*, WASH. MONTHLY, May 1980, at 32, 35 (analysis of President Carter's repudiation of U.N. Security Council Resolution 465 (1980) on Jewish settlements).

130   *See, e.g.*, McDOUGAL & FELICIANO, *supra* note 43, at 232–41.

131   *See* 31 U.N. SCOR (1939th mtg.) at 32, U.N. Doc. S/P.V. 1939 (prov. ed. 1976):
From a purely formal point of view, this meeting arises from a complaint brought against the Government of Israel. However, let me make it quite clear that sitting here as the representative . . . of Israel . . . , I am in no way sitting in the dock as the accused party. On the contrary, I stand here as an accuser on behalf of free and decent people in this world.

132   *See* 31 U.N. SCOR (1939th mtg.) at 106, U.N. Doc. S/P.V. 1939 (prov. ed. 1976):
The Zionist representative mentioned Auschwitz, he mentioned Dachau, he men-

tioned Buchenwald. He said that Auschwitz, Dachau and Buchenwald belonged to the past and would never return. I say that Dachau, Auschwitz and Buchenwald are not things of the past; they are still alive . . . , only this time the roles are reversed: those who were the victims—or pretend to be the victims—are now the torturers. The racist and criminal exercises and policies are now being executed against the Palestinian people by the Zionist racists.

133 *See, e.g.*, 31 U.N. SCOR Supp. (July–Sept. 1976) at 14–15, U.N. Doc. S/12136 (1976) (telegram from Siad Barre to Amin circulated as a Security Council document): "The legitimate struggle of the Arab people of Palestine to regain their homeland and the Arab nation to liberate the Zionist occupied territories shall not be stopped by these acts of terrorism and shall continue until final and complete victory is achieved."

134 G.A. Res. 2625, 25 U.N. GAOR Supp. (No. 28) at 121, 123–24, U.N. Doc. A/8028 (1971) (emphasis added), states in relevant part:
The principle of equal rights and self-determination of peoples
By virtue of the principle of equal rights and self-determination of peoples enshrined in the Charter of the United Nations, all peoples have the right freely to determine, without external interference, their political status and to pursue their economic, social and cultural development, and every State has the duty to respect this right in accordance with the provisions of the Charter. . . . Every State has the duty to refrain from any forcible action which deprives peoples referred to above in the elaboration of the present principle of their right to self-determination and freedom and independence. In their actions against, and resistance to, such forcible action in pursuit of the exercise of their right to self-determination such peoples are entitled *to seek and to receive support* in accordance with the purposes and principles of the Charter.

135 G.A. Res. 3314, 29 U.N. GAOR Supp. (No. 31) at 142, 144, U.N. Doc. A/9631 (1975). Article 7 provides (emphasis added):
Nothing in this Definition . . . could in any way prejudice the right to self-determination, freedom and independence, as derived from the Charter, of peoples forcibly deprived of that right and referred to in the Declaration on Principles of International Law concerning Friendly Relations and Co-operation among States in accordance with the Charter of the United Nations, particularly peoples under colonial and racist regimes or other forms of alien domination; nor the right of these peoples to struggle to that end and *to seek and receive support*, in accordance with the principles of the Charter and in conformity with the above-mentioned Declaration.
See Stone, *Hopes and Loopholes in the 1974 Definition of Aggression*, 71 A.J.I.L. 224, 231–39 (1977).

136 The Security Council met eight times between June 9–29, 1976, to consider the Palestinian issue. *See* 31 U.N. SCOR (1924th mtg.) at 1, U.N. Doc. S/P.V. 1924 (prov. ed. 1976); 31 U.N. SCOR (1928th mtg.) at 1, U.N. Doc. S/P.V. 1928 (prov. ed. 1976); 31 U.N. SCOR (1933d mtg.) at 1, U.N. Doc. S/P.V. 1933 (prov. ed. 1976); 31 U.N. SCOR (1934th mtg.) at 1, U.N. Doc. S/P.V. 1934 (prov. ed. 1976); 31 U.N. SCOR (1935th mtg.) at 1, U.N. Doc. S/P.V. 1935 (prov. ed. 1976); 31 U.N. SCOR (1936th mtg.) at 1, U.N. Doc. S/P.V. 1936 (prov. ed. 1976); 31 U.N. SCOR (1937th mtg.) at 1, U.N. Doc. S/P.V. 1937 (prov. ed. 1976); 31 U.N. SCOR (1938th mtg.) at 1, U.N. Doc. S/P.V. 1938 (prov. ed. 1976).

137 31 U.N. SCOR (1938th mtg.) at 62, U.N. Doc. S/P.V. 1938 (prov. ed. 1976). The

text of the draft resolution can be found in 31 U.N. SCOR, Supp. (Apr.–June 1976) at 73, U.N. Doc. S/12119 (1976).

138   *See, e.g.*, 31 U.N. SCOR (1938th mtg.) at 63, U.N. Doc. S/P.V. 1938 (prov. ed. 1976). The U.K. representative explained that his delegation abstained from the vote because the draft proposal did not reconcile the rights of the Palestinians with "the right of all States in the area, including Israel, to live in peace within secure and recognized borders."

139   31 U.N. SCOR (1924th mtg.) at 6–7, U.N. Doc. S/P.V. 1924 (prov. ed. 1976).

140   Provisional Rules of Procedure of the Security Council, Rule 37, U.N. Doc. S/96/Rev. 6 (1974) provides:
Any Member of the United Nations which is not a member of the Security Council may be invited, as the result of a decision of the Security Council, to participate, without vote, in the discussion of any question brought before the Security Council when the Security Council considers that the interests of that Member are specially affected, or when a Member brings a matter to the attention of the Security Council in accordance with Article 35(1) of the Charter.

141   *See Proposal for Israeli Withdrawal from Occupied Territories by June 1977 Fails*, U.N. CHRONICLE, July 1976, at 22.

142   For Uganda's argument that it lived up to the standards of international law in dealing with the hijackers, see 31 U.N. SCOR (1939th mtg.) at 11–25, U.N. Doc. S/P.V. 1939 (prov. ed. 1976). For Israel's argument that Uganda had cooperated with the hijackers/hostage takers see *id.* at 32–50.

143   *Id.* at 13–15, 16.

144   *See also Control of Terrorism in International Life: Cooperation and Self-Help*, 71 AM. SOC. INT'L. L. PROC. 17, 30–31 (1977) (Entebbe raid justified by contract doctrine of "rectification").

145   *Compare with* a New York Times editorial which blithely asserted that in such situations "the ordinary rules of international law simply cannot apply." N.Y. Times, July 6, 1976, at 24, col. 1. In a press conference of July 9, 1976, President Ford drew a parallel between the Entebbe raid and the American intervention into Cambodia to rescue the crew of the *Mayaguez. See* Ford, *Excerpts Relating to Foreign Policy*, 75 DEP'T ST. BULL. 161 (1976). Perhaps somewhat inadvisably he implied that both actions stood or fell on the same legal grounds. *See* Paust, *The Seizure and Recovery of the Mayaguez*, 85 YALE L.J. 774 (1976).

146   *See* ENTEBBE RESCUE, *supra* note 21, at 189–90.

147   *See* N.Y. Times, Dec. 20, 1976, at A1, col. 3; *id.*, Dec. 21, 1976, at 1, col. 6; *id.*, May 18, 1977, at A1, col. 6; *id.*, June 21, 1977, at 1, col. 5. And, of course, religion was a determinative factor in the Iranian hostages crisis. *See* R. KHOMEINI, ISLAMIC GOVERNMENT (1979) (CIA translation of his 1969–1970 lectures on jurisprudence); Mottahedeh, *Iran's Foreign Devils*, FOREIGN POL'Y, Spring 1980, at 19.

148   *See, e.g.*, 31 U.N. SCOR (1941st mtg.) at 41–53, U.N. Doc. S/P.V. 1941 (prov. ed. 1976). The Tanzanian delegate argued that although international law may have recognized in the past the right of a nation to take unilateral action to protect its citizens outside of its borders, this right ceased to exist with the adoption of the U.N. Charter.

149   Support for this absolute interpretation of article 2(4) can be found in its *travaux préparatoires. See* J. STONE, AGGRESSION AND WORLD ORDER 92–103 (1958).

150   31 U.N. SCOR (1941st mtg.) at 23–25, U.N. Doc. S/P.V. 1941 (prov. ed. 1976).

151 G.A. Res. 31/103, 31 U.N. GAOR Supp. (No. 39) at 186, U.N. Doc. A/31/39 (1976); *35-Member Group Established to Draft Convention Against Taking Hostages,* U.N. CHRONICLE, Jan. 1977, at 81.

152 *See Convention Against Hostage-Taking Approved; Call for Appropriate Penalties,* U.N. CHRONICLE, Jan. 1980, at 85.

153 N.Y. Times, July 15, 1976, at 1, col. 1.

154 31 U.N. SCOR (1943d mtg.) at 87, U.N. Doc. S/P.V. 1943 (prov. ed. 1976).

155 31 U.N. SCOR (1943d mtg.) at 76, U.N. Doc. S/P.V. 1943 (prov. ed. 1976).

156 *See, e.g., Security Council Fails to Adopt Resolution Recommending Expulsion of South Africa,* U.N. CHRONICLE, Nov. 1974, at 9 (triple veto by U.S., U.K., and France of proposed Security Council resolution to recommend the expulsion of South Africa from the United Nations).

157 *See generally* KYEMBA, *supra* note 13, at 238–48; Deming, Sullivan & MacPherson, *Idi Amin's Rule of Blood,* NEWSWEEK, Mar. 7, 1977, at 28; Kaufman, *Amin Cuts a Broad but Erratic Swath and People Love Him or Hate Him,* N.Y. Times, July 10, 1976, at 3, col. 1.

158 STEVENSON, *supra* note 21, at 199.

159 *See, e.g.,* KYEMBA, *supra* note 13, at 256 (1976 threat to invade Kenya); N.Y. Times, July 9, 1971, at 3, col. 4; *id.,* Dec. 26, 1971, at 19, col. 1 (threat to attack Tanzania and subsequent border skirmishes); *id.,* Jan. 31, 1971, at 2, col. 3; *id.,* Feb. 1, 1971, at 6, col. 1 (threat to counterattack Sudanese forces after alleging that Sudan was the original aggressor).

160 *An Idi-otic Invasion,* TIME, Nov. 13, 1978, at 51; N.Y. Times, Apr. 12, 1979, at A1, col. 1.

161 *See* STEVENSON, *supra* note 21, at iii.

162 *See, e.g.,* Middleton, *1979 Terrorist Toll Put at a Record 587,* N.Y. Times, May 11, 1980, § 1, at 14, col. 1; Wieseltier, *The Sabbath Ambush,* NEW REPUBLIC, May 24, 1980, at 18. *See also Through the Barrel of a Gun,* MIDDLE EAST, July 1980, at 8, 10–11.

163 In a letter addressed to the president of the Security Council, Amin declared that "Uganda reserves her right to retaliate in whatever way she can to redress the aggression against her." 31 U.N. SCOR Supp. (July–Sept. 1976) at 4–5, U.N. Doc. S/12124 (1976).

164 D. BOWETT, SELF-DEFENCE IN INTERNATIONAL LAW 13 (1958); *Resort to War and Armed Force: Reprisals,* 73 A.J.I.L. 489–92 (1979).

165 *See* KYEMBA, *supra* note 13, at 250; Kaufman, *supra* note 157, at 3, col. 5.

166 For example, during the Cuban missile crisis, legal-moral considerations seemed to play a role more crucial than strategic-military calculations during the Executive Committee's deliberations on whether to launch a surprise preemptive strike against Soviet missile installations in Cuba. *See* KENNEDY, *supra* note 59.

167 Mill, *Utilitarianism,* in THE PHILOSOPHY OF JOHN STUART MILL 321, 370–98 (M. Cohen ed. 1961).

168 For the text of the League of Nations Covenant see BASIC DOCUMENTS OF THE UNITED NATIONS 295 (L. Sohn ed. 1968). League Covenant article 10 was triggered by "external aggression" or "any threat or danger" thereof. *Id.* at 298.

169 *See, e.g.,* Wright, *Some Legal Aspects of the Far Eastern Situation,* 27 A.J.I.L. 509, 510 (1933); Wright, *When Does War Exist?,* 26 A.J.I.L. 362, 365 (1932); League of Nations Assembly Report on the Sino-Japanese Dispute, *reprinted in* 27 A.J.I.L. 119 (Supp. 1932).

170   Charte Des Nations Unies art. 51:
Aucune disposition de la présente Charte ne porte atteinte au droit naturel de
légitime défense, individuelle ou collective, dans le cas où un Membre des
Nations Unies est l'objet d'une agression armée, jusqu'à ce que le Conseil de
Sécurité ait pris les mesures nécessaires pour maintenir la paix et la sécurité
internationales. . . .

171   Kellogg-Briand Pact, Aug. 27, 1928, art. I, 46 Stat. 2343, 2345–46, T.S. No.
796, 94 L.N.T.S. 57, 63, *reprinted in* 1928 (I) FOREIGN RELATIONS OF THE
UNITED STATES 153, 155: "The High Contracting Parties solemnly declare in the
names of their respective peoples that they condemn recourse to war for the
solution of international controversies, and renounce it as an instrument of national
policy in their relations with one another."

172   *See, e.g.*, 1928 (I) FOREIGN RELATIONS OF THE UNITED STATES 15, 17–18
(France); *id.* at 42, 43–44 (Germany); *id.* at 66, 67 (Great Britain). France
unsuccessfully proposed a draft antiwar treaty specifically providing for recognition of the "rights of legitimate self-defense within the framework of existing
treaties." *Id.* at 32, 33. The state right of self-judgment could only be defeated by
the *unanimous* agreement of League Council Members other than representatives of
parties to the dispute. League of Nations Covenant art. 15, para. 7, *reprinted in*
BASIC DOCUMENTS OF THE UNITED NATIONS 295, 300 (L. Sohn ed. 1968).

173   U.N. Charter art. 2, para. 6: "The Organization shall ensure that states which are
not Members of the United Nations act in accordance with these Principles so far
as may be necessary for the maintenance of international peace and security."

174   U.N. Charter art. 2, para. 7:
Nothing contained in the present Charter shall authorize the United Nations to
intervene in matters which are essentially within the domestic jurisdiction of any
state or shall require the Members to submit such matters to settlement under the
present Charter; but this principle shall not prejudice the application of enforcement measures under Chapter VII.

175   U.N. Charter art. 27, para. 3:
Decisions of the Security Council on all other matters shall be made by an
affirmative vote of nine members including the concurring votes of the permanent
members; provided that, in decisions under Chapter VI, and under paragraph 3 of
Article 52, a party to a dispute shall abstain from voting.

176   T. HOBBES, LEVIATHAN 128 (M. Oakeshott ed. 1962).

177   G.A. Res. 377, 5 U.N. GAOR Supp. (No. 20) at 10, U.N. Doc. A/1775 (1950).

178   *See, e.g.*, E. MAY, "LESSONS" OF THE PAST 3–18 (1973); H. MORGENTHAU,
POLITICS AMONG NATIONS 58–59, 97–98 (5th rev. ed. 1978).

179   *See* Camp David Accords, Sept. 17, 1978, *reprinted in* DEP'T STATE BULL., Oct.
1978, at 7. The Camp David Accords include a Framework for Peace in the Middle
East, *reprinted in id.* at 7–9, and a Framework for the Conclusion of a Peace Treaty
Between Egypt and Israel, *reprinted in id.* at 9–10. *See also* Treaty of Peace, Mar.
26, 1979, Egypt-Israel, *reprinted in* 18 I.L.M. 362 (1979).

180   *See generally* Ball, *The Coming Crisis in Israeli-American Relations*, 58 FOREIGN AFF.
231 (1979); Eban, *Camp David—The Unfinished Business*, 57 FOREIGN AFF. 343
(1978); Heller, *Begin's False Autonomy*, FOREIGN POL'Y, Winter 1979–80, at 111;
Khalidi, *Thinking the Unthinkable: A Sovereign Palestinian State*, 56 FOREIGN AFF.
695 (1978); Murphy, *To Bring to an End the State of War: The Egyptian-Israeli Peace
Treaty*, 12 VAND. J. TRANSNAT'L L. 897 (1979); Peres, *A Strategy for Peace in the*

Middle East, 58 FOREIGN AFF. 887 (1980); Ravenal, *Walking on Water in the Middle East*, FOREIGN POL'Y, Winter 1978–79, at 151; Reich, Silberburg & Stein, *The Middle East Peace Process: Sisyphus Reexamined*, 4 SUFFOLK TRANSNAT'L L.J. 17 (1980); Samuelson, *Israeli Expansionism*, HARPER'S, Feb. 1980, at 26; Tucker, *Behind Camp David*, COMMENTARY, Nov. 1978, at 25.

181 Nations known to maintain "antiterrorist" commando units include, inter alia, the U.S., Great Britain, France, West Germany, and Italy. Willenson & Nater, *Getting Tough*, NEWSWEEK, Oct. 31, 1977, at 51.

182 N.Y. Times, Oct. 18, 1977, at 12, col. 1.

183 Two German soldiers were wounded but no hostages were harmed in the raid. *Id.* at 1, col. 6.

184 Cypriot President Spyros Kyprianou, at Larnaca Airport when Egyptian troops arrived, told Egyptian Ambassador Hassan Shash: "This is an independent country and I will hold you personally responsible for any unauthorized action. I order you to hold back your men." Willenson, Jenkins, Schmidt & Clifton, *Debacle in Cyprus*, NEWSWEEK, Mar. 6, 1978, at 33.

185 Fifteen Egyptian soldiers died, though the hostages were released unharmed. The hostage takers had already agreed to surrender prior to the operation. *Id.*

186 *See* 31 U.N. GAOR Annex (Agenda Item 123) at 1, U.N. Doc. A/31/242 (1976).

187 *Id. See also* H. Schmidt, *The 1977 Alastair Buchan Memorial Lecture*, 20 SURVIVAL 2, 9 (1978).

188 *See* U.N. Doc. A/C.6/31/L.10 (1976), *reprinted in* 31 U.N. GAOR Annex (Agenda Item 123) at 2, U.N. Doc. A/31/430 (1976).

189 *See* U.N. Doc. A/C.6/31/L.11 (1976), *reprinted in* 31 U.N. GAOR Annex (Agenda Item 123) at 3, U.N. Doc. A/31/430 (1976).

190 *See* U.N. Doc. A/C.6/31/L.10/Rev. 1 (1976), *reprinted in* 31 U.N. GAOR Annex (Agenda Item 123) at 3–4, U.N. Doc. A/31/430 (1976). *See also* N.Y. Times, Dec. 16, 1976, at 3, col. 3; Grose, *U.N. Assembly's Achievement: A Quiet Session, id.*, Dec. 24, 1976, at A6, col. 1.

191 G.A. Res. 31/103, 31 U.N. GAOR Supp. (No. 39) at 186, U.N. Doc. A/31/39 (1976).

192 *Id.*

193 The complete official title of this resolution is:
Measures to prevent international terrorism which endangers or takes innocent human lives or jeopardizes fundamental freedoms, and study of the underlying causes of those forms of terrorism and acts of violence which lie in misery, frustration, grievance and despair and which cause some people to sacrifice human lives, including their own, in an attempt to effect radical changes.
G.A. Res. 31/102, U.N. GAOR Supp. (No. 39) at 185–86, U.N. Doc. A/31/39 (1976).

194 *35-Member Group Established to Draft Convention Against Taking Hostages*, U.N. CHRONICLE, Jan. 1977, at 81.

195 *Id.*

196 G.A. Res. 3034, 27 U.N. GAOR Supp. (No. 30) at 119, U.N. Doc. A/8730 (1972).

197 *See* 28 U.N. GAOR Supp. (No. 28) at 2, U.N. Doc. A/9028 (1973).

198 *Id.* at 6, paras. 14–17, at 7, paras. 22–24, at 8, para. 24, at 11–12, paras. 35–38, at 13–14, paras. 41–44, at 15, paras. 48–49, at 17, para. 54, at 18, para. 62.

326 WORLD POLITICS AND INTERNATIONAL LAW

199   *See, e.g.*, Draft proposal submitted by the Non-Aligned Group in the Ad Hoc Committee (Algeria, Congo, Democratic Yemen, Guinea, India, Mauritania, Nigeria, Syrian Arab Republic, Tunisia, United Republic of Tanzania, Yemen, Yugoslavia, Zaire, and Zambia), *id.* at 21, para. 3, U.N. Doc. A/9028 (1973).

200   During the Sixth Committee debates over the establishment of the Hostages Committee, the Soviet delegate suggested that it might be preferable to refer the matter of drafting a hostages convention to the Terrorism Committee. This suggestion was, of course, never followed. *See* Nanda, *Progress Report on the United Nations' Attempt to Draft an "International Convention Against the Taking of Hostages,"* 6 OHIO N.U.L. REV. 89, 97 (1979). Moreover, a desire by several Third World countries to have the Hostages Committee first study the causes of international terrorism also bore no fruit. *Id.*

201   28 U.N. GAOR Supp. (No. 28) at 9, para. 29, at 17, para. 56, U.N. Doc. A/9028 (1973). The United States submitted a comprehensive draft convention against international terrorism, but it was not adopted. *Id.* at 28–33, U.N. Doc. A/9028 (1973). *See* Franck & Lockwood, *Preliminary Thoughts Towards an International Convention on Terrorism*, 68 A.J.I.L. 69 (1974). *See also* Evans & Murphy, *supra* note 52; Paust, *Selected Terroristic Claims Arising from the Arab-Israeli Context*, 7 AKRON L. REV. 404 (1974); *Control of Terrorism in International Life: Cooperation and Self-Help*, 71 AM. SOC. INT'L L. PROC. 17 (1977); *Controlling Transnational Terrorism: The Relevance of International Law*, 72 AM. SOC. INT'L L. PROC. 343 (1978); *International Terrorism: Hearing Before the Subcommittee on Foreign Assistance of the Senate Committee on Foreign Relations*, 95th Cong., 1st Sess. (1977).

202   *See, e.g.*, 28 U.N. GAOR Supp. (No. 28) at 9, para. 29, at 14, para. 44, at 17, para. 56, U.N. Doc. A/9028 (1973); Draft proposal submitted by Uruguay, *id.* at 33–34, para. 1, U.N. Doc. A/9028 (1973).

203   *See* N.Y. Times, Aug. 2, 1976, at 4, col. 1; *id.*, Aug. 8, 1976, § 1, at 4, col. 1; *id.*, Feb. 23, 1977, at A2, col. 3. *But see* KYEMBA, *supra* note 13, at 126–27.

204   N.Y. Times, Feb. 25, 1977, at A8, col. 3; *id.*, Feb. 27, 1977, § 4, at 4, col. 5.

205   Four other non-participators were not appointed to the Hostages Committee (Benin, China, Guyana, Pakistan). Nor were the two abstainers from the U.S.–U.K. draft resolution appointed to the Hostages Committee (Panama, Romania). 34 U.N. GAOR Supp. (No. 39) at 2, para. 2, U.N. Doc. A/34/39 (1979).

206   Eight non-members of the Security Council that had participated in the Entebbe debates were not appointed to the Hostages Committee (Uganda, Israel, Mauritius, Cuba, India, Mauritania, Qatar, Cameroon). *See* 31 U.N. SCOR (1943d mtg.) at 2–5, U.N. Doc. S/P.V. 1943 (prov. ed. 1976); 34 U.N. GAOR Supp. (No. 39) at 2, para. 2, U.N. Doc. A/34/39 (1979).

207   Since Byelorussia was appointed to the Hostages Committee, 34 U.N. GAOR Supp. (No. 39) at 2, para. 2, U.N. Doc. A/34/39 (1979), given its special relationship with the Soviet Union, perhaps this number could not unjustifiably be increased to fifteen.

208   They were Algeria, Barbados, Canada, Democratic Yemen, France, Guinea, Iran, Italy, Japan, Nicaragua, Nigeria, Sweden, Syria, Tanzania, U.S.S.R., United Kingdom, U.S.A., Venezuela, and Yugoslavia. *See* 28 U.N. GAOR Supp. (No. 28) at 2, para. 2, U.N. Doc. A/9028 (1973); 34 U.N. GAOR Supp. (No. 39) at 2, para. 2, U.N. Doc. A/34/39 (1979). This number could perhaps not unfairly be increased to twenty since the Ukrainian SSR was a member of the Terrorism Committee, 28 U.N. GAOR Supp. (No. 28) at 2, para. 2, U.N. Doc. A/9028 (1973), while

Byelorussia joined the Hostages Committee. 34 U.N. GAOR Supp. (No. 39) at 2, para. 2, U.N. Doc. A/34/39 (1979). The other fifteen members of the Terrorism Committee were Austria, Congo, Czechoslovakia, Greece, Haiti, Hungary, India, Mauritania, Panama, Tunisia, Turkey, Uruguay, Yemen, Zaire, and Zambia. 28 U.N. GAOR Supp. (No. 28) at 2, para. 2, U.N. Doc. A/9028 (1973). The fifteen members of the Hostages Committee not on the Terrorism Committee were Byelorussia, Chile, Denmark, Egypt, Federal Republic of Germany, Jordan, Kenya, Lesotho, Libya, Mexico, Netherlands, Philippines, Poland, Somalia, and Surinam. *See* 34 U.N. GAOR Supp. (No. 39) at 2, para. 2, U.N. Doc. A/34/39 (1979); 28 U.N. GAOR Supp. (No. 28) at 2, para. 2, U.N. Doc. A/9028 (1973). Bulgaria became the 35th member of the Hostages Committee in 1979. *See* 34 U.N. GAOR Supp. (No. 39) at 2, para. 2 & n.4, U.N. Doc. A/34/39 (1979).

209 *Hostages Committee Recommends That Work Be Continued During 1978*, U.N. CHRONI-CLE, Aug.–Sept. 1977, at 45.

210 U.N. Doc. A/AC.188/L.3 (1977), *reprinted in* 32 U.N. GAOR Supp. (No. 39) at 106–10, U.N. Doc. A/32/39 (1977). For a critique of the German Draft Convention, see Kaye, *The United Nations Effort to Draft a Convention on the Taking of Hostages*, 27 AM. U.L. REV. 433 (1978).

211 32 U.N. GAOR Supp. (No. 39) at 5, U.N. Doc. A/32/39 (1977).

212 Report of the *Ad Hoc* Committee on the Drafting of an International Convention against the Taking of Hostages (8th mtg.) 3, para. 6, U.N. Doc. A/AC.188/SR.8 (1977) [hereinafter cited as First Hostages Report], *reprinted in* 32 U.N. GAOR Supp. (No. 39) at 30, 31, para. 6, U.N. Doc. A/32/39 (1977).

213 U.N. Doc. A/AC.188/L.5 (1977), *reprinted in* 32 U.N. GAOR Supp. (No. 39) at 111, U.N. Doc. A/32/39 (1977).

214 *See* First Hostages Report, *supra* note 212, (14th mtg.) at 3, para. 9, U.N. Doc. A/AC.188/SR.14 (1977), *reprinted in* 32 U.N. GAOR Supp. (No. 39) at 74, 75, para. 9, U.N. Doc. A/32/39 (1977).

215 First Hostages Report, *supra* note 212, (15th mtg.) at 2, para. 5, U.N. Doc. A/AC.188/SR.15 (1977), *reprinted in* 32 U.N. GAOR Supp. (No. 39) at 83, 83–84, para. 5, U.N. Doc. A/32/39 (1977).

216 First Hostages Report, *supra* note 212, (7th mtg.) at 3, para. 5, U.N. Doc. A/AC.188/SR.7 (1977), *reprinted in* 32 U.N. GAOR Supp. (No. 39) at 26, 27, para. 5, U.N. Doc. A/32/39 (1977).

217 First Hostages Report, *supra* note 212, (8th mtg.) at 5, para. 15, U.N. Doc. A/AC.188/SR.8 (1977), *reprinted in* 32 U.N. GAOR Supp. (No. 39) at 32, 32–33, para. 15, U.N. Doc. A/32/39 (1977). *See generally* Brooks, *Skyjacking and Refugees: The Effect of the Hague Convention Upon Asylum*, 16 HARV. INT'L L.J. 93 (1975).

218 *See, e.g.,* First Hostages Report, *supra* note 212, (7th mtg.) at 4–5, para. 12, U.N. Doc. A/AC.188/SR.7 (1977), *reprinted in* 32 U.N. GAOR Supp. (No. 39) at 26, 28, para. 12, U.N. Doc. A/32/39 (1977); First Hostages Report, *supra* note 212, (9th mtg.) at 3, para. 11, U.N. Doc. A/AC.188/SR.9 (1977), *reprinted in* 32 U.N. GAOR Supp. (No. 39) at 38, 39, para. 11, U.N. Doc. A/32/39 (1977); First Hostages Report, *supra* note 212, (11th mtg.) at 10, para. 43, U.N. Doc. A/AC.188/SR.11 (1977), *reprinted in* 32 U.N. GAOR Supp. (No. 39) at 51, 58, para. 43, U.N. Doc. A/32/39 (1977); First Hostages Report, *supra* note 212, (15th mtg.) at 3, para. 6, U.N. Doc. A/AC.188/SR.15 (1977), *reprinted in* 32 U.N. GAOR Supp. (No. 39) at 83, 84, para. 6, U.N. Doc. A/32/39 (1977).

219 First Hostages Report, *supra* note 212, (3d mtg.) at 3, para. 11, U.N. Doc.

A/AC.188/SR.3 (1977), *reprinted in* 32 U.N. GAOR Supp. (No. 39) at 13, 14, para. 11, U.N. Doc. A/32/39 (1977).

220   First Hostages Report, *supra* note 212, (8th mtg.) at 2, para. 2, U.N. Doc. A/AC.188/SR.8 (1977), *reprinted in* 32 U.N. GAOR Supp. (No. 39) at 30, 30, para. 2, U.N. Doc. A/32/39 (1977).

221   First Hostages Report, *supra* note 212, (1st mtg.) at 2, para. 3, U.N. Doc. A/AC.188/SR.1 (1977), *reprinted in* 32 U.N. GAOR Supp. (No. 39) at 10, 10, para. 3, U.N. Doc. A/32/39 (1977); First Hostages Report, *supra* note 212, (5th mtg.) at 3, para. 5, U.N. Doc. A/AC.188/SR.5 (1977), *reprinted with additions in* 32 U.N. GAOR Supp. (No. 39) at 19, 20, para. 5, U.N. Doc. A/32/39 (1977); First Hostages Report, *supra* note 212, (5th mtg.) at 5, para. 12, U.N. Doc. A/AC.188/ SR.5 (1977), *reprinted in* 32 U.N. GAOR Supp. (No. 39) at 19, 22, para. 12, U.N. Doc. A/32/39 (1977).

222   First Hostages Report, *supra* note 212, (8th mtg.) at 5–6, para. 19, U.N. Doc. A/AC.188/SR.8 (1977), *reprinted in* 32 U.N. GAOR Supp. (No. 39) at 30, 33, para. 19, U.N. Doc. A/32/39 (1977).

223   First Hostages Report, *supra* note 212, (12th mtg.) at 4, para. 11, U.N. Doc. A/AC.188/SR.12 (1977), *reprinted in* 32 U.N. GAOR Supp. (No. 39) at 60, 62, para. 11, U.N. Doc. A/32/39 (1977). *See also* First Hostages Report, *supra* note 212, (5th mtg.) at 3, para. 5, U.N. Doc. A/AC.188/SR.5 (1977), *reprinted with additions in* 32 U.N. GAOR Supp. (No. 39) at 19, 20, para. 5, U.N. Doc. A/32/39 (1977).

224   Protocol Additional to the Geneva Conventions of Aug. 12, 1949, and Relating to the Protection of Victims of International Armed Conflicts (Protocol I), *reprinted in* 16 I.L.M. 1391 (1977) [hereinafter cited as Protocol I]; Protocol Additional to the Geneva Conventions of Aug. 12, 1949, and Relating to the Protection of Victims of Non-International Armed Conflicts (Protocol II), *reprinted in* 16 I.L.M. 1442 (1977) [hereinafter cited as Protocol II]. *See* Abi-Saab, *Wars of National Liberation and the Laws of War*, 3 ANNALS INT'L STUD. 93 (1972); Baxter, *Humanitarian Law or Humanitarian Politics? The 1974 Diplomatic Conference on Humanitarian Law*, 16 HARV. INT'L L.J. 1 (1975); De Pue, *The Amended First Article to the First Draft Protocol Additional to the Geneva Conventions of 1949—Its Impact Upon Humanitarian Constraints Governing Armed Conflict*, 75 MIL. L. REV. 71 (1977); Erickson, *Protocol I: A Merging of the Hague and Geneva Law of Armed Conflict*, 19 VA. J. INT'L L. 557 (1979); Forsythe, *Legal Management of Internal War: The 1977 Protocol on Non-International Armed Conflicts*, 72 A.J.I.L. 272 (1978); Gorelick, *Wars of National Liberation: Jus Ad Bellum*, 11 CASE W. RES. J. INT'L L. 71 (1979); O'Brien, *The Jus in Bello in Revolutionary War and Counterinsurgency*, 18 VA. J. INT'L L. 193 (1978); *Protocols Additional to the Geneva Conventions of 1949*, 72 AM. SOC. INT'L L. PROC. 142 (1978); *Revising the Laws of War: Future Developments*, 69 AM. SOC. INT'L L. PROC. 246 (1975). *See generally Changing Rules for Changing Forms of Warfare*, 42 LAW & CONTEMP. PROBS. (Spring 1978).

225   Protocol I, *supra* note 224, art. I:
   1   The High Contracting Parties undertake to respect and to ensure respect for this Protocol in all circumstances.
   2   In cases not covered by this Protocol or by other international agreements, civilians and combatants remain under the protection and authority of the principles of international law derived from established custom, from the principles of humanity and from the dictates of public conscience.

3 This Protocol, which supplements the Geneva Conventions of Aug. 12, 1949 for the protection of war victims, shall apply in the situations referred to in Article 2 common to those Conventions.

4 The situations referred to in the preceding paragraph include armed conflicts in which peoples are fighting against colonial domination and alien occupation and against racist regimes in the exercise of their right of self-determination, as enshrined in the Charter of the United Nations and the Declaration on Principles of International Law concerning Friendly Relations and Co-operation among States in accordance with the Charter of the United Nations.

226 Protocol I, *supra* note 224, art. 75, para. 2: "The following acts are and shall remain prohibited at any time and in any place whatsoever, whether committed by civilian or by military agents: . . . (c) the taking of hostages."

227 Protocol II, *supra* note 224, art. 4:

1 All persons who do not take a direct part or who have ceased to take part in hostilities, whether or not their liberty has been restricted, are entitled to respect for their person, honor and convictions and religious practices. They shall in all circumstances be treated humanely, without any adverse distinction. It is prohibited to order that there shall be no survivors.

2 Without prejudice to the generality of the foregoing, the following acts against the persons referred to in paragraph 1 are and shall remain prohibited at any time and in any place whatsoever: . . . (c) taking of hostages.

228 First Hostages Report, *supra* note 212, (10th mtg.) at 3, para. 8, U.N. Doc. A/AC.188/SR.10 (1977), *reprinted in* 32 U.N. GAOR Supp. (No. 39) at 46, 47, para. 8, U.N. Doc. A/32/39 (1977).

229 First Hostages Report, *supra* note 212, (12th mtg.) at 7, para. 21, U.N. Doc. A/AC.188/SR.12 (1977), *reprinted in* 32 U.N. GAOR Supp. (No. 39) at 60, 64, para. 21, U.N. Doc. A/32/39 (1977).

230 First Hostages Report, *supra* note 212, (16th mtg.) at 4, para. 16, U.N. Doc. A/AC.188/SR.16 (1977), *reprinted in* 32 U.N. GAOR Supp. (No. 39) at 88, 90, para. 16, U.N. Doc. A/32/39 (1977).

231 U.N. Doc. A/AC.188/L.7 (1977), *reprinted in* 32 U.N. GAOR Supp. (No. 39) at 111, U.N. Doc. A/32/39 (1977); U.N. Doc. A/AC.188/L.11 (1977), *reprinted in* 32 U.N. GAOR Supp. (No. 39) at 112, U.N. Doc. A/32/39 (1977).

232 *See* Deming, Pringle, Martin & Collings, *The New War on Terrorism*, NEWSWEEK, Oct. 31, 1977, at 48; *Terror and Triumph at Mogadishu*, TIME, Oct. 31, 1977, at 42.

233 N.Y. Times, Oct. 18, 1977, at 1, col. 6.

234 *New Breed of Commando*, TIME, Oct. 31, 1977, at 44; Willenson & Nater, *supra* note 181, at 51.

235 N.Y. Times, Oct. 18, 1977, at 12, col. 1.

236 N.Y. Times, Oct. 18, 1977, at 1, col. 6.

237 *Terror and Triumph at Mogadishu*, TIME, Oct. 31, 1977, at 42, 43.

238 N.Y. Times, Oct. 18, 1977, at 12, col. 2.

239 *Id.*, Oct. 19, 1977, at A1, col. 6.

240 *Id.*, Oct. 20, 1977, at A17, col. 1.

241 *Final Result on Hijacking Depends on Governments, Says Secretary-General*, U.N. CHRONICLE, Nov. 1977, at 13.

242 *Id.* at 14.

243 G.A. Res. 32/8, 32 U.N. GAOR Supp. (No. 45) at 66, U.N. Doc. A/32/45 (1977).

See Assembly Condemns Acts of Aerial Hijacking, U.N. CHRONICLE, Dec. 1977, at 23.

244　*See* N.Y. Times, Nov. 4, 1977, at A3, col. 1.

245　G.A. Res. 32/147, 32 U.N. GAOR Supp. (No. 45) at 212, U.N. Doc. A/32/45 (1977).

246　*Assembly Asks Continued Study of Causes of International Terrorism*, U.N. CHRONICLE, Jan. 1978, at 100.

247　G.A. Res. 32/148, 32 U.N. GAOR Supp. (No. 45) at 213, U.N. Doc. A/32/45 (1977). *See Assembly Asks Continued Study of Causes of International Terrorism, supra* note 246.

248　*See supra* note 246, at 101. *See* Report of the *Ad Hoc* Committee on International Terrorism, 34 U.N. GAOR Supp. (No. 37), U.N. Doc. A/34/37 (1979). The recommendations contained in this Report were adopted by the General Assembly in G.A. Res. 34/145, 34 U.N. GAOR (105th plen. mtg.) at 1, 19 I.L.M. 533 (1980). *See also* G.A. Res. 36/109, 36 U.N. GAOR (92d plen. mtg.) at 241, U.N. Doc. 36/109 (1981), which took note of Report of the Secretary General, U.N. Doc. No. A/36/425 (1981).

249　33 U.N. GAOR Supp. (No. 39) at 16, para. 57, U.N. Doc. A/33/39 (1978).

250　*Id.* at 3, para. 10.

251　*Id.*

252　*Id.* at 5, para. 15.

253　*Id.* at 5, para. 16.

254　*Id.* at 58, para. 3.

255　*Id. See also id.* at 81, para. 74.

256　First Hostages Report, *supra* note 212, (9th mtg.) at 4, para. 13, U.N. Doc. A/AC.188/SR.9 (1977), *reprinted in* 32 U.N. GAOR Supp. (No. 39) at 38, 40, para. 13, U.N. Doc. A/32/39 (1977).

257　33 U.N. GAOR Supp. (No. 39) at 5, para. 17, U.N. Doc. A/33/39 (1978).

258　First Hostages Report, *supra* note 212, (8th mtg.) at 9, para. 31, U.N. Doc. A/AC.188/SR.8 (1977), *reprinted in* 32 U.N. GAOR Supp. (No. 39) at 30, 36–37, para. 31, U.N. Doc. A/32/39 (1977).

259　U.N. Doc. A/AC.188/L.6 (1977), *reprinted in* 32 U.N. GAOR Supp. (No. 39) at 111, U.N. Doc. A/32/39 (1977).

260　33 U.N. GAOR Supp. (No. 39) at 5–6, para. 19, U.N. Doc. A/33/39 (1978).

261　U.N. Doc. A/AC.188/L.20 (1978), *reprinted in* 33 U.N. GAOR Supp. (No. 39) at 6, para. 20, U.N. Doc. A/33/39 (1978).

262　33 U.N. GAOR Supp. (No. 39) at 63, para. 2, U.N. Doc. A/33/39 (1978).

263　*Id.* at 58, para. 5.

264　*Id.* at 58, para. 6.

265　*Id.* at 57, para. 2. Article 13 of the Strasbourg Convention provides in relevant part: Any State may, at the time of signature or when depositing its instrument of ratification, acceptance or approval, declare that it reserves the right to refuse extradition in respect of any offence mentioned in Article 1 which it considers to be a political offence, an offence connected with a political offence or an offence inspired by political motives, provided that it undertakes to take into due consideration, when evaluating the character of the offence, any particularly serious aspects of the offence, including:

a. that it created a collective danger to the life, physical integrity or liberty of persons; or

b. that it affected persons foreign to the motives behind it; or

c. that cruel or vicious means have been used in the commission of the offence.

European Convention on the Suppression of Terrorism, *opened for signature* Jan. 27, 1977, art. 13, *reprinted in* 15 I.L.M. 1272, 1275 (1976). The Committee of Ministers of the Council of Europe adopted the Convention on November 10, 1976. *Id.* at 1272 n. It entered into force on August 4, 1978. 19 I.L.M. 325 n. (1980). *See also* Agreement Concerning the Application of the European Convention on the Suppression of Terrorism Among the Member States, Dec. 4, 1979, *reprinted in* 19 I.L.M. 325 (1980). The Ministers of Justice of the nine Member States signed the agreement on December 4, 1979. 19 I.L.M. 325 n. (1980). *See also* Bonn Declaration on Hijacking, July 17, 1978, *reprinted in* 73 A.J.I.L. 133 (1979). Parties to the Bonn Declaration were Canada, France, West Germany, Italy, Japan, the United Kingdom, and the United States. *See generally* Fingerman, *Skyjacking and the Bonn Declaration of 1978: Sanctions Applicable to Recalcitrant Nations*, 10 CAL. W. INT'L L.J. 123 (1980); Lodge & Freestone, *The European Community and Terrorism: Political and Legal Aspects*, in TERRORISM IN EUROPE 79 (Y. Alexander & K. Myers eds. 1982).

266   33 U.N. GAOR Supp. (No. 39) at 66, 74, U.N. Doc. A/33/39 (1978).

267   N.Y. Times, Feb. 19, 1978, § 1, at 1, col. 6; *id.*, Feb. 20, 1978, at A1, col. 6.

268   *See, e.g.*, 33 U.N. GAOR Supp. (No. 39) at 82, paras. 78, 79, U.N. Doc. A/33/39 (1978).

269   U.N. Doc. A/RES/33/19 (1978); *News Digest*, U.N. CHRONICLE, Dec. 1978, at 3–4.

270   34 U.N. GAOR Supp. (No. 39) at 2, para. 3, U.N. Doc. A/34/39 (1979).

271   *Id.* at 3, para. 10.

272   *Id.* at 22.

273   *Id.* at 22, para. 89.

274   The Committee adopted the following language:

In so far as the Geneva Conventions of 1949 for the protection of war victims or the Additional Protocols to those Conventions are applicable to a particular act of hostage-taking, and in so far as States Parties to this Convention are bound under those *Conventions* to prosecute or hand over the hostage-taker, the present Convention shall not apply to an act of hostage-taking committed in the course of armed conflicts as defined in the Geneva Conventions of 1949 and the Protocols thereto, including armed conflicts mentioned in article 1, paragraph 4, of Additional Protocol I of 1977, in which peoples are fighting against colonial domination and alien occupation and against racist regimes in the exercise of their right of self-determination as enshrined in the Charter of the United Nations, and the Declaration on Principles of International Law concerning Friendly Relations and Co-operation among States in accordance with the Charter of the United Nations.

Id. at 28, art. 12, para. 1, U.N. Doc. A/34/39 (1979) (emphasis added). In the final version of article 12 adopted by the General Assembly, the word emphasized above is spelled with a lower case "c" so that the phrase now refers to both the 1949 Geneva Conventions and the 1977 Geneva Protocols. *See* Letter from Anthony C.E. Quainton, Director of the State Department's Office for Combating Terrorism, to Israel Singer (Dec. 11, 1979), *reprinted in* 74 A.J.I.L. 420, 421 (1980) [hereinafter cited as Quainton Letter].

275   *See, e.g.*, Quainton Letter, *supra* note 274:

Thus, if for any reason a State Party to the Hostages Convention is not bound to prosecute or extradite an offender under the Geneva Conventions/Geneva Protocols, the prosecute or extradite requirements of the Hostages Convention apply. Accordingly, Article 12(1) does not provide a loophole for members of national liberation movements or anyone else and does not supply a means by which any State Party to the Hostages Convention can escape the prosecute or extradite requirement.

Accord Verwey, *The International Hostages Convention and National Liberation Movements*, 75 A.J.I.L. 69, 84–87 (1981). *See also* American Branch, Int'l L. Ass'n, Report of the Committee on Armed Conflict, 1979–1980 Proceedings and Committee Reports 38, 44.

276   34 U.N. GAOR Supp. (No. 39) at 7–8, para. 22, U.N. Doc. A/34/39 (1978).

277   *Id.* at 15–16, paras. 59–61.

278   *Id.*

279   N.Y. Times, Nov. 5, 1979, at Al, col. 6.

280   U.N. Doc. A/34/819 (1979), at 8, art. 9, para. 1(a).

281   *Id.* at 3–4, para. 14.

282   *Id.* at 3 n.7.

283   *Id.* at 3, para. 14.

284   *See, e.g.*, 34 U.N. GAOR C.6 (14th mtg.) at 8, para. 40, U.N. Doc. A/C.6/34/SR.14 (1979).

285   U.N. Doc. A/34/819 (1979), at 4, para. 16.

286   The U.N. General Assembly adopted the International Convention Against the Taking of Hostages in an annex to resolution 34/146 of Dec. 17, 1979. A text of the Convention, reprinted from Report of the Sixth Committee, U.N. Doc. A/34/819 (1979), at 5, which contains the draft resolution, *id.* at 4, can be found in 74 A.J.I.L. 277–83 (1980) [hereinafter cited as Hostages Convention]. *See Convention Against Hostage-Taking Approved; Call for Appropriate Penalties*, U.N. CHRONICLE, Jan. 1980, at 85.

287   Negative votes were cast by Bulgaria, Byelorussia, Czechoslovakia, East Germany, Hungary, Mongolia, Poland, Ukraine, the U.S.S.R., and Viet Nam. *Id.*

288   *See, e.g.*, 34 U.N. GAOR C.6 (59th mtg.) at 16, para. 79, U.N. Doc. A/C.6/34/SR.59 (1979), where the Spanish delegate mentioned the following unresolved problems: "In the first place, . . . the draft convention did not provide for the regulation of certain important legal questions, such as conflicting requests for extradition, the principles of 'speciality' and *non bis in idem*, and statutory limitation in respect of the offence and the sentence."

289   *See, e.g.*, Rosenstock, *International Convention Against the Taking of Hostages: Another International Community Step Against Terrorism*, 10 DEN. J. INT'L L. & POL'Y 169 (1980).

290   N.Y. Times, July 4, 1976, § 1, at 10, col. 3.

291   Protocol I, *supra* note 224, art. 96, para. 3 states in relevant part: "The authority representing a people engaged against a High Contracting Party in an armed conflict of the type referred to in Article 1, paragraph 4, may undertake to apply the Conventions and this Protocol in relation to that conflict by means of a unilateral declaration addressed to the depository."

292   Hostages Convention, *supra* note 286, art. 5, para. 1, *reprinted in* 74 A.J.I.L. 277, 279 (1980), which provides:
Each State Party shall take such measures as may be necessary to establish its jurisdiction over any of the offences set forth in article 1 which are committed:

(a) in its territory or on board a ship or aircraft registered in that State;

(b) by any of its nationals or, if that State considers it appropriate, by those stateless persons who have their habitual residence in its territory;

(c) in order to compel that State to do or abstain from doing any act; or

(d) with respect to a hostage who is a national of that State, if that State considers it appropriate.

293 U.N. Doc. A/AC.188/L.7 (1977), *reprinted in* 32 U.N. GAOR Supp. (No. 39) at 111, U.N. Doc. A/32/39 (1977); U.N. Doc. A/AC.188/L.11 (1977), *reprinted in* 32 U.N. GAOR Supp. (No. 39) at 112, U.N. Doc. A/32/39 (1977).

294 127 CONG. REC. S8808, 8809 (daily ed. July 30, 1981).

295 *See, e.g.*, Letter of Submittal from Warren Christopher to the President (July 9, 1980), in President's Message to the Senate Transmitting the International Convention Against the Taking of Hostages, 96th Cong., 2d Sess., Senate Executive N, at v, vii (Aug. 4, 1980):

Article 12 ensures that all offenders under the Convention will be subject to prosecution or extradition by States Parties under either the Hostages Convention itself or the Geneva Conventions of 1949 and the 1977 Additional Protocols to those conventions. In short, the prosecute or extradite rule of the Hostages Convention will apply in every case involving an Article 1 offense, unless the Geneva Conventions or Protocols apply to a particular such offense and the concerned State Party to the Hostages Convention is legally bound in that case by the Geneva Conventions and Protocols to prosecute or extradite the alleged offender for offenses also covered by the Hostages Convention. . . . Consensus adoption of this Convention by the representatives of the international community in the UN General Assembly during December, 1979 could hardly have been more timely. Early action by the United States with respect to ratification of this Convention would be equally appropriate, particularly in view of the fact that the United States referred to the Convention in its Memorial to the International Court of Justice in the *Case concerning United States Diplomatic and Consular Staff in Tehran*. The United States should be among the leaders in formally endorsing this agreement for combating international crime and terrorism.

The Department of Justice favors the ratification of this Convention. I hope that the Senate will consider the Convention and give its advice and consent to ratification as soon as possible.

296 *See* 22 I.L.M. 940 (1983).

297 THE COMPLETE WRITINGS OF THUCYDIDES 14 (R. Crawley trans. 1951).

298 In this regard, I would like to thank Professor Herbert Tillema of the Department of Political Science of the University of Missouri at Columbia for describing his preliminary research results to me. Tillema examined 71 cases of foreign military intervention by the great powers between 1946 and mid-1980. Of these, forty-seven interventions (sixty-six percent) were arguably legal under the terms of the United Nations Charter. Nevertheless, seventy instances (ninety-nine percent) complied with pre–World War II standards of international law on the use of force. *See* Tillema & Van Wingen, *Law and Power in Military Intervention*, 26 INT'L STUD. Q. 220 (1982).

299 *See* G. CLARK & L. SOHN, WORLD PEACE THROUGH WORLD LAW (3d ed. 1966).

Notes to Part Three

1   *See* Kissinger, *Hans Morgenthau*, NEW REPUBLIC, Aug. 2 & 9, 1980, at 12.

2   *See* THE COMPLETE WRITINGS OF THUCYDIDES: THE PELOPONNESIAN WAR 331 (Modern Library ed. 1951) (emphasis added) [hereinafter cited as Thucydides]:

For ourselves [Athenians], we shall not trouble you [Melians] with specious pretences—either of how we have a right to our empire because we overthrew the Mede, or are now attacking you because of wrong that you have done us—and make a long speech which would not be believed; and in return we hope that you, instead of thinking to influence us by saying that you did not join the Lacedaemonians, although their colonists, or that you have done us no wrong, will aim at what is feasible, holding in view the real sentiments of us both *since you know as well as we do that right, as the world goes is only in question between equals in power, while the strong do what they can and the weak suffer what they must.*

3   S. Hoffmann, *International Systems and International Law*, in THE STATE OF WAR 88 (1965). *See also* Boyle, *The Law of Power Politics*, 1980 U. ILL. L.F. 915–30 [hereinafter cited as *Power Politics*].

4   *See Power Politics, supra* note 3, at 912–13, 923–24.

5   N. MACHIAVELLI, THE PRINCE 217–25 (M. Musa trans. & ed. 1964).

6   M. KAPLAN, SYSTEM AND PROCESS IN INTERNATIONAL POLITICS 48–50 (1957).

7   *See Power Politics, supra* note 3, at 956–66.

8   *See* M. KAPLAN, *supra* note 6, at 22–36 (six rules for the balance of power system).

9   *See Power Politics, supra* note 3, at 928–29.

10   In a zero-sum game, any player's gains are exactly balanced by the losses of others. 6 INTERNATIONAL ENCYCLOPEDIA OF THE SOCIAL SCIENCES 62–69 (1968).

11   *See* N. MACHIAVELLI, *supra* note 5, at 127:

Now there remains to be seen what ought to be the criteria and actions of a prince in dealing with his subjects and friends. And because I know that many have written about this, I am afraid, by writing about it again, that I shall be thought presumptuous, all the more so for departing, in my discussion of this material, from the procedures of others. But my intention being to write something useful for whoever understands it, it seemed to me more appropriate to pursue the effectual truth of the matter rather than its imagined one. And many have imagined republics and principalities that have never been seen or known to exist in reality; for there is such a gap between how one lives and how one should live that he who neglects what is being done for what should be done will learn his destruction rather than his preservation: for a man who wishes to profess goodness at all times must fall to ruin among so many who are not good. Whereby it is necessary for a prince who wishes to maintain his position to learn how not to be good, and to use it or not according to necessity.

12   *See, e.g.*, Judgment in the Corfu Channel Case (U.K. v. Alb.), 1949 I.C.J. 4, at 34–35 (rejection of intervention, protection, self-help).

13   G.A. Res. 377, 5 U.N. GAOR Supp. (No. 20) at 10, U.N. Doc. A/1775 (1950).

14   *See* PLATO, GORGIAS 53 (Penguin ed. 1960).

15   *See* THE NICOMACHEAN ETHICS OF ARISTOTLE, Book V, at 106–36 (W. Ross trans. 1954).

16   *See* N. MACHIAVELLI, *supra* note 5, at 99.

17   *See id.* at 145 (fighting by means of law).

18   *Cf. id.* at 145–49.

19 *See generally* R. FISHER, POINTS OF CHOICE (1978).

20 *See* N. MACHIAVELLI, *supra* note 5, at 195.

21 *See* Bloom, *The Pahlavi Problem: A Superficial Diagnosis Brought the Shah into the United States*, 207 SCIENCE 282 (1980); N.Y. Times, May 13, 1981, at 1, col. 2. *See also* N.Y. Times, Jan. 27, 1981, at B10, col. 1; *id.*, Mar. 21, 1980, at 26, col. 1; *id.*, May 26, 1981, at C2, col. 5.

22 *See* N.Y. Times, July 21, 1979, at 23, col. 4; *id.*, Nov. 18, 1979, at A1, col. 4; *id.*, Jan. 21, 1981, at A6, col. 1.

23 *See id.*, Nov. 18, 1979, at A1, col. 4.

24 *Id.*, Feb. 16, 1979, at A10, col. 2.

25 For example, the U.N. Ad Hoc Committee on International Terrorism could not even agree on a definition of "terrorism." Report of the Ad Hoc Committee on International Terrorism, 34 U.N. GAOR Supp. (No. 37) at 1, 11, para. 34, U.N. Doc. A/34/37 (1979). Nevertheless, the U.N. General Assembly adopted the recommendations of the Ad Hoc Committee on International Terrorism in G.A. Res. 34/145, 34 U.N. GAOR Supp. (No. 37) at 1, U.N. Doc. A/RES/34/145 (1980).

26 *See, e.g., Terrorism: Dubious Evidence*, ECONOMIST, May 9, 1981, at 28 (C.I.A.'s fatuous redefinition of "terrorism"); *C.I.A.*, ECONOMIST, July 4, 1981, at 26; N.Y. Times, Oct. 18, 1981, at 9, col. 1.

27 *See* N.Y. Times, Nov. 23, 1978, at A1, col. 4.

28 *See* Ledeen & Lewis, *Carter and the Fall of the Shah: The Inside Story*, WASH. Q., Spring 1980, at 3. *Cf.* Wall St. J., Feb. 9, 1979, at 40, col. 1 (Israel's Mossad anticipated fall of Shah since 1977).

29 Richard, *"Unleashing" the Intelligence Community*, 69 A.B.A.J. 906 (1983); American Civil Liberties Union, *Unleashing the Intelligence Agencies*, CIV. LIB. ALERT, Apr. 1981, at 1. *See also* N.Y. Times, Mar. 10, 1981, at 1, col. 1; *id.*, Aug. 25, 1981, at A16, col. 3; *id.*, Oct. 6, 1981, at 1, col. 1.

30 *See, e.g.*, COMMISSION ON C.I.A. ACTIVITIES WITHIN THE UNITED STATES, REPORT TO THE PRESIDENT 101 (illegal mail intercepts), 130 (Operation CHAOS), 152 (infiltration of domestic organizations), 172 (Watergate abuses), 226 (drug testing) (June 1975).

31 1–6 Final Report of the Senate Select Committee to Study Governmental Operations with Respect to Intelligence Activities, S. REP. NO. 755, 94th Cong., 2d Sess. (1976). *See, e.g.*, 1 *id.* at 141 (covert action), 189–203 (use of academic institutions, media, religious groups), 385 (covert drug testing); 2 *id.* at 10–13 (covert action and illegal or improper means).

32 *See* N.Y. Times, Oct. 5, 1981, at B12, col. 1.

33 Intelligence Identities Protection Act of 1982, 50 U.S.C. § 421 (1982).

34 Clark Amendment to the International Security Assistance and Arms Export Control Act of 1976, Pub. L. No. 94–329, 90 Stat. 729, 757 (codified at 22 U.S.C. § 2293 note (1976)):

(a) Notwithstanding any other provision of law, no assistance of any kind may be provided for the purpose, or which would have the effect, of promoting or augmenting, directly or indirectly, the capacity of any nation, group, organization, movement or individual to conduct military or paramilitary operations in Angola unless and until—

(1) the President determines that such assistance should be furnished in the national security interests of the United States;

(2) the President submits to the Committee on Foreign Affairs of the House of

Representatives and the Committee on Foreign Relations of the Senate a report containing—

(A) a description of the amounts and categories of assistance which he recommends be furnished and the identity of the proposed recipients of such assistance; and

(B) a certification that he has determined that the furnishing of such assistance is important to the national security interests of the United States and a detailed statement of the reasons supporting such determination; and

(3) the Congress enacts a joint resolution approving the furnishing of such assistance.

[Subparagraph (b) creates an expedited procedure for consideration of such joint resolution in the House and Senate.]

(c) The prohibition contained in subsection (a) does not apply with respect to assistance which is furnished solely for humanitarian purposes.

(d) The provisions of this section may not be waived under any other provision of law.

35 Continuing Appropriations For Fiscal Year 1983, Pub. L. No. 97–377, § 793, 96 Stat. 1830, 1865 (1982):

None of the funds provided in this Act may be used by the Central Intelligence Agency or the Department of Defense to furnish military equipment, military training or advice, or other support for military activities, to any group or individual, not part of a country's armed forces, for the purpose of overthrowing the Government of Nicaragua or provoking a military exchange between Nicaragua and Honduras.

36 See, e.g., Declaration on the Inadmissibility of Intervention in the Domestic Affairs of States and the Protection of Their Independence and Sovereignty, G.A. Res. 2131, 20 U.N. GAOR Supp. (No. 14) at 11, U.N. Doc. A/6014 (1966); Declaration on Principles of International Law Concerning Friendly Relations and Co-operation Among States in Accordance with the Charter of the United Nations, G.A. Res. 2625, 25 U.N. GAOR Supp. (No. 28) at 121, U.N. Doc. A/8028 (1971).

37 In this regard, another unfortunate consequence of the Iranian hostages crisis was the decision of the Supreme Court in *Haig v. Agee*, 453 U.S. 280 (1981), upholding the authority of the secretary of state to revoke Agee's passport because rumor had it Agee was going to travel to Iran. This case established an unhealthy precedent for the executive to further infringe upon the constitutional right of U.S. citizens to engage in international travel. *See* Farber, *National Security, the Right to Travel, and the Court*, 9 U. CHI. SUP. CT. REV. 263 (1981).

38 *See* Exec. Order No. 12333, 3 C.F.R. 200 (1981), *reprinted in* 50 U.S.C. § 401 note at 840 (Supp. V 1981).

39 *See* Exec. Order No. 12036, 3 C.F.R. 112 (1978), *reprinted in* 50 U.S.C. § 401 note, at 346 (Supp. I 1978). *See also* Note, *The Foreign Intelligence Surveillance Act: Legislating a Judicial Role in National Security Surveillance*, 78 MICH. L. REV. 1116 (1980).

40 *See* Requirements for Maintenance of Status for Nonimmigrant Students from Iran, 8 C.F.R. § 214.5 (1980).

41 *Narenji v. Civiletti*, 617 F.2d 745 (D.C. Cir. 1979), *cert. denied*, 446 U.S. 957 (1980).

42 N.Y. Times, Nov. 9, 1979, at A12, col. 2; *id.*, Nov. 10, 1979, at A6, col. 4.

43   N.Y. Times, Jan. 21, 1981, at A6, col. 1, at A6, col. 3 ("old friend and ally").

44   G.A. Res. 217A,3(1) U.N. GAOR (183d plen. mtg.) at 71, U.N. Doc. A/810 (1948).

45   *See* Final Act of the International Conference on Human Rights, U.N. Doc. A/CONF. 32/41, U.N. Publ. E. 68. XIV. 2 (1968), *endorsed by* G.A. Res. 2442, 23 U.N. GAOR Supp. (No. 18) at 49, U.N. Doc. A/7218 (1968).

46   *See* Falk, *Iran After the Shah: Balance Sheet on Revolution*, 232 NATION 39 (1981); N.Y. Times, Dec. 31, 1978, at A3, col. 4; *id.*, Feb. 16, 1979, at A10, col. 1; Manchester Guardian Weekly, Oct. 21, 1979, at 14, col. 1.

47   P. SALINGER, AMERICA HELD HOSTAGE 116–17 (1981); Kaplan & Halliday, *The Savak-C.I.A. Connection*, 230 NATION 229 (1980).

48   *See, e.g.*, A. SAIKAL, THE RISE AND FALL OF THE SHAH 154–61, 178 (1980) (takeover of Abu Musa, Greater and Lesser Tumbs).

49   U.N. CHARTER art. 2, para. 4, provides: "All Members shall refrain in their international relations from the threat or use of force against the territorial integrity or political independence of any state, or in any other manner inconsistent with the Purposes of the United Nations."

50   *See* R. NIXON, THE MEMOIRS OF RICHARD NIXON 394–97 (1978).

51   *See* authorities collected in note 36 *supra*. *Cf.* U.N. CHARTER art. 2, para. 7.

52   *See* U.N. CHARTER art. 1, para. 2.

53   U.N. CHARTER art. 51 states:
     Nothing in the present Charter shall impair the inherent right of individual or collective self-defense if an armed attack occurs against a Member of the United Nations, until the Security Council has taken measures necessary to maintain international peace and security. Measures taken by Members in the exercise of this right of self-defense shall be immediately reported to the Security Council and shall not in any way affect the authority and responsibility of the Security Council under the present Charter to take at any time such action as it deems necessary in order to maintain or restore international peace and security.

54   *See* Bernstein, *Arms for Afghanistan*, NEW REPUBLIC, July 18, 1981, at 8–10; ECONOMIST, Aug. 8, 1981, at 32–33.

55   Harrison, *A Breakthrough in Afghanistan?*, FOREIGN POL'Y, Summer 1983, at 3.

56   *See* K. ROOSEVELT, COUNTERCOUP (1979); Leigh, *Britain's Role in Restoring the Shah*, Manchester Guardian Weekly, Aug. 3, 1980, at 6, col. 3; Mitgang, *Publisher 'Correcting' Book on C.I.A. Involvement in Iran*, N.Y. Times, Nov. 10, 1979, at 13, col. 1.

57   Sullivan, *Dateline Iran: The Road Not Taken*, FOREIGN POL'Y, Fall 1980, at 175, 186.

58   *Id.* at 183; N.Y. Times, Apr. 20, 1980, at 1, col. 3. *See also* Wash. Post, Aug. 26, 1981, at B18, col. 3 (C.I.A. clandestine operation to bring down Khomeini).

59   D. MCMANUS, FREE AT LAST 241 (1980); P. SALINGER, *supra* note 47, at 237; N.Y. Times, Dec. 2, 1979, at A18, col. 1; N.Y. Times, Jan. 21, 1981, at A6, col. 1. *See generally* Bassiouni, *Protection of Diplomats under Islamic Law*, 74 A.J.I.L. 609 (1980); Mottahedeh, *Iran's Foreign Devils*, FOREIGN POL'Y, Spring 1980, at 19; Perera, *On Diplomatic Immunity*, MIDDLE EAST, July 1980, at 15.

60   *See* Peterzell, *Can Congress Really Check the CIA?*, Wash. Post, Apr. 24, 1983, at C1.

61   U.N. CHARTER art. 2, para. 3, provides: "All Members shall settle their international disputes by peaceful means in such a manner that international peace

and security, and justice, are not endangered."

62   U.N. CHARTER art. 33, para. 1, provides: "The parties to any dispute, the continuance of which is likely to endanger the maintenance of international peace and security, shall, first of all, seek a solution by negotiation, enquiry, mediation, conciliation, arbitration, judicial settlement, resort to regional agencies or arrangements, or other peaceful means of their own choice."

63   Vienna Convention on Diplomatic Relations, Apr. 18, 1961, 23 U.S.T. 3227, T.I.A.S. No. 7502, 596 U.N.T.S. 95.

64   Vienna Convention on Consular Relations, Apr. 24, 1963, 21 U.S.T. 77, T.I.A.S. No. 6820, 596 U.N.T.S. 261.

65   Convention on the Prevention and Punishment of Crimes Against Internationally Protected Persons, Including Diplomatic Agents, Dec. 14, 1973, 28 U.S.T. 1975, T.I.A.S. No. 8532 (entered into force for the United States, Feb. 20, 1977), reprinted in 13 I.L.M. 43 (1974).

66   See The Caroline, in J. Moore, 2 INTERNATIONAL LAW DIGEST 409, 412 (1906); W. BISHOP, INTERNATIONAL LAW 916–19 (3d ed. 1971).

67   Cf. International Law Commission, Draft Article 34 on State Responsibility, reprinted in Schwebel, The Thirty-Second Session of the International Law Commission, 74 A.J.I.L. 961, 963 (1980): "The wrongfulness of an act of a State not in conformity with an international obligation of that State is precluded if the act constitutes a lawful measure of self-defense taken in conformity with the Charter of the United Nations."

68   The United States Supreme Court has held that both domestic and international law preclude the president or his agents from surrendering any person to a foreign government in the absence of an extradition treaty. Valentine v. United States, 299 U.S. 5, 10 (1936).

69   Geneva Convention Relative to the Protection of Civilian Persons in Time of War, Aug. 12, 1949, arts. 3, 146, 147, 6 U.S.T. 3516, 3518, 3616, 3618, T.I.A.S. No. 3365, 75 U.N.T.S. 287, 289, 387, 388.

70   Compare Geneva Conventions Act, 1957, 5 & 6 Eliz. 2, c. 52, § 1.

71   See Vienna Convention on the Law of Treaties, May 22, 1969, art. 27, U.N. Doc. A/CONF. 39/27, at 289 (1969), [1980] Gr. Brit. T.S. No. 58 (Cmd. 7964) (entered into force Jan. 27, 1980), reprinted in 8 I.L.M. 679 (1969).

72   See Franck, The Iran Crisis . . . If We Had Ratified the Genocide Convention, INT'L PRAC. NOTEBOOK, Jan. 1980, at 12 (Am. Branch Int'l. L.A.).

73   See, e.g., N.Y. Times, Nov. 9, 1979, at A3, col. 2; id., Nov. 12, 1979, at A1, col. 5; id., Nov. 13, 1979, at A10, col. 5; id., Nov. 16, 1979, at A16, col. 1; id., Nov. 19, 1979, at A13, col. 1; Wash. Post, Dec. 22, 1979, at A16, col. 1.

74   See, e.g., N.Y. Times, Nov. 5, 1979, at A1, col. 6; id., Nov. 16, 1979, at A1, col. 5; id., Nov. 19, 1979, at A1, col. 6; Wash. Post, Nov. 13, 1979, at A1, col. 5.

75   See, e.g., N.Y. Times, Dec. 5, 1979, at A1, col. 5; id., Dec. 16, 1979, at A1, col. 3; Wash. Post, Nov. 13, 1979, at A10, col. 1; id., Nov. 15, 1979, at A1, col. 3; id., Nov. 18, 1979, at A1, col. 4. Cf. N.Y. Times, Nov. 7, 1979, at A1, col. 6 ("militant Islamic students"); id., Nov. 19, 1979, at A1, col. 6 ("militant students"); Wash. Post, Nov. 13, 1979, at A1, col. 1 ("militant Iranian students").

76   See Peterzell, supra note 60; MIDDLE EAST, Aug. 1980, at 24; N.Y. Times, Sept. 27, 1980, at 4, col. 1; Wall St. J., Sept. 23, 1981, at 1, col. 1; N.Y. Times, May 7, 1982, at 1, col. 3; Wash. Post, Aug. 26, 1981, at B18.

77   See Boston Globe, Oct. 21, 1982, at 1, col. 1; id., Oct. 23, 1982, at 4, col. 1;

Wash. Post, July 27, 1981, at 17; Wash. Post, Mar. 25, 1982, at 20; MIDDLE EAST, Jan. 1982, at 20.

78 N.Y. Times, Nov. 14, 1979, at A1, col. 6; *id.*, Nov. 16, 1979, at A16, col. 1; Wash. Post, Nov. 15, 1979, at A1, col. 5.

79 N.Y. Times, Nov. 14, 1979, at A1, col. 6; *id.*, Nov. 16, 1979, at A16, col. 1; *id.*, Nov. 29, 1979, at A20, col. 1; Wash. Post, Nov. 15, 1979, at A1, col. 5; *id.*, Nov. 18, 1979, at A11, col. 1.

80 Secret negotiations may have been in the offing in mid-November 1979, between Vance and Bani-Sadr, when the then Acting Iranian Foreign Minister was to have visited the U.N. to present the Iranian proposal. Vance had made several secret trips with regard to the release of the hostages during this period. N.Y. Times, Jan. 16, 1980, at A14, col. 1 (interview with Cyrus Vance).

81 *See* P. SALINGER, *supra* note 47, at 43, 104, 107.

82 Bani-Sadr was dismissed as Acting Foreign Minister on Nov. 28, 1979, having only been appointed to that post on Nov. 10, 1979, following the collapse of the Bazargan Government. He retained his post as Minister of Economic and Financial Affairs. Sadegh Ghotbzadeh, Director of State Television, replaced Bani-Sadr as Foreign Minister. N.Y. Times, Nov. 29, 1979, at A1, col. 3; *id.* at A18, col. 5.

83 *See* N.Y. Times, Jan. 26, 1980, at A9, col. 1.

84 S.C. Res. 457, 34 U.N. SCOR (2178th mtg.) at 1, U.N. Doc. S/13677 (Dec. 4, 1979), *reprinted in* 18 I.L.M. 1644 (1979), called on the government of Iran immediately to release all personnel of the U.S. Embassy being held hostage in Teheran and requested the U.N. Secretary-General to lend his good offices for its implementation. Iran's failure to abide by Resolution 457 (1979) precipitated the passage of S.C. Res. 461, 34 U.N. SCOR (2184th mtg.) at 1, U.N. Doc. S/13711/Rev. 1 (Dec. 31, 1979), *reprinted in* 19 I.L.M. 250 (1980), which reaffirmed Resolution 457 and deplored the continued detention of the hostages. It again called on Iran to release immediately all persons of United States nationality being held hostage in Iran and reiterated the earlier request to the Secretary-General to lend his good offices with a view toward achieving the objectives called for therein.

85 *See Concerning United States Diplomatic and Consular Staff in Tehran* (U.S. v. Iran), 1979 I.C.J. 7 (Interim Protection), *reprinted in* 74 A.J.I.L. 258 (1980).

86 *See Concerning United States Diplomatic and Consular Staff in Tehran* (U.S. v. Iran), 1980 I.C.J. 3 (Merits), *reprinted in* DEP'T ST. BULL., July 1980, at 43.

87 *See* R. FISHER, INTERNATIONAL CONFLICT FOR BEGINNERS (1970); Fisher, *Helping the Iranians Change Their Minds*, N.Y. Times, Nov. 10, 1979, at 23, col. 1.

88 *Cf.* C. OSGOOD, AN ALTERNATIVE TO WAR OR SURRENDER 86–134 (1962) (strategy for gradual reduction in tension—GRIT).

89 *See, e.g.*, Hershey, *The Calvo and Drago Doctrines*, 1 A.J.I.L. 26 (1907).

90 *Cf.* Wash. Post, Sept. 19, 1980, at A1, col. 2 (report ordered by Carter).

91 N.Y. Times, Nov. 29, 1979, at A18, col. 5; Wash. Post, Nov. 28, 1979, at A1, col. 3.

92 *See* THUCYDIDES, *supra* note 2, at 335:
Athenians.—". . . You [Melians] will surely not be caught by that idea of disgrace, which in dangers that are disgraceful, and at the same time too plain to be mistaken, proves so fatal to mankind; since in too many cases the very men that have their eyes perfectly open to what they are rushing into, let the thing called disgrace, by the mere influence of a seductive name, lead them on to a point at

which they become so enslaved by the phrase as in fact to fall wilfully into hopeless disaster, and incur disgrace more disgraceful as the companion of error, than when it comes as the result of misfortune."

93   *See* Radway, *The Curse of Free Elections*, FOREIGN POL'Y, Fall 1980, at 61, 67–69. *Compare* N.Y. Times, Apr. 2, 1980, at A8, col. 5 (Carter's pre-Wisconsin primary press conference) *with* H. KISSINGER, WHITE HOUSE YEARS 1399–1400 (1979) ("peace is at hand" speech).

94   N.Y. Times, May 1, 1980, at A1, col. 6. *See* Reston, *Puzzles Along the Potomac, id.*, May 2, 1980, at A27, col. 1; Smith, *Why the President Released 54th Hostage, id.* at B6, col. 1; Wicker, *The Candor Gap, id.* at A27, col. 5.

95   N.Y. Times, Nov. 3, 1980, at A1, col. 6.

96   P. SALINGER, *supra* note 47, at 287.

97   N.Y. Times, Nov. 29, 1979, at A1, col. 6.

98   J. Colins, 6 U.S.-Soviet Military Balance: Far East, Middle East Assessments, CONG. RESEARCH SERV. REP. NO. 80–166 S, at 71 (July 1980).

99   Iranian Assets Control Regulations, Exec. Order Nos. 12,276–84, 3 C.F.R. 104–116 (1982), *reprinted in* 50 U.S.C.A. § 1701, at 225–233 (West Supp. 1983), *repealing* Exec. Order 12,211, 3 C.F.R. 253 (1980), *reprinted in* 50 U.S.C.A. § 1701, at 224 (West Supp. 1983) & Exec. Order 12,170, 3 C.F.R. 457 (1979), *reprinted in* 50 U.S.C. § 1701, at 721 (Supp. 1980). *See* N.Y. Times, Nov. 15, 1979, at A17, col. 1.

100 N.Y. Times, Nov. 11, 1979, at A1, col. 4; *id.*, Nov. 13, 1979, at A8, col. 5; *id.*, Nov. 14, 1979, at A1, col. 6, at A15, col. 3; *id.*, Nov. 17, 1979, at 1, col. 5.

101 N.Y. Times, Dec. 22, 1979, at 1, col. 6; *U.S. Asks Security Council to Impose Sanctions Against Iran*, DEP'T ST. BULL., Feb. 1980, at 67 (Statement of Secretary Vance).

102 N.Y. Times, Jan. 14, 1980, at A1, col. 5; *Soviets Veto Sanctions Against Iran*, DEP'T ST. BULL., Mar. 1980, at 60 (White House Statement).

103 *Additional Sanctions Against Iran*, DEP'T ST. BULL., June 1980, at 43 (President Carter's Message to Congress); Constable, *U.S. Measures to Isolate Iran*, DEP'T ST. BULL., July 1980, at 71.

104 N.Y. Times, Apr. 28, 1980, at A1, col. 4; *Iran Chronology, May 1980*, DEP'T ST. BULL., July 1980, at 72. *But see How Iran Is Getting the Goods Through the Barriers*, MIDDLE EAST, Oct. 1980, at 72. *See generally* Reisman, *The Legal Effect of Vetoed Resolutions*, 74 A.J.I.L. 904 (1980).

105 *See* Nash, *Contemporary Practice of the United States Relating to International Law: Termination of Relations*, 74 A.J.I.L. 657 (1980).

106 *See generally* Cutler, *Negotiating the Iranian Settlement*, 67 A.B.A.J. 996 (1981).

107 *See* P. SALINGER, *supra* note 47, at 105.

108 The Special Operations Review Group, Rescue Mission Report (Aug. 1980) (the Holloway Commission Report), was a ludicrous whitewash. *Compare* Reisman, *Humanitarian Intervention*, 230 NATION 612 (1980) *with* Crown & Fried, *A Legal Disaster, id.* at 613.

109 N.Y. Times, Apr. 28, 1980, at A1, col. 6; Shaplen, *Profiles (David Newsom—pt. 2)*, NEW YORKER, June 9, 1980, at 48, 48–50. *See generally id.* (pts. 1 & 3), NEW YORKER, June 2, 1980, at 43; *id.*, June 16, 1980, at 44.

110 *Compare* N.Y. Times, Apr. 23, 1980, at A1, col. 3 (EEC ministers vote to impose sanctions just before rescue operation) *with id.*, Apr. 28, 1980, at A1, col. 4 (EEC irritation over raid) *and id.*, May 17, 1980, at 6, col. 5 (Britain, France, West

Germany intend to back off) *and id.*, May 19, 1980, at A1, col. 1 (at Naples conference, EEC bans exports to Iran pursuant to contracts signed *after* Nov. 4, 1979, leaving virtually all major European contracts with Iran unaffected) *and id.*, May 23, 1980, at A5, col. 1 (Britain adopts sanctions only with respect to new contracts).

111 *Id.*, May 22, 1980, at A20, col. 1.

112 Shaplen, *Profiles (David Newsom—pt. 2)*, NEW YORKER, June 9, 1980, at 48, 48–50.

113 *Id.*

114 *Id.*

115 *See, e.g.*, Aronson, *The Theory of Cognitive Dissonance: A Current Perspective*, 4 ADVANCES IN EXPERIMENTAL SOC. PSYCH. 1 (L. Berkowitz ed. 1969).

116 *See* Bilder, *The Office of the Legal Adviser: The State Department Lawyer and Foreign Affairs*, 56 A.J.I.L. 633 (1962).

117 *See* 50 U.S.C. § 402 (1976).

118 *See, e.g., Washington Wire*, Wall St. J., Nov. 23, 1979, at 1, col. 5; Wilkie, *Kissinger Threat Alleged*, Boston Globe, Nov. 24, 1979, at 1. *See also* Lewis, *Mr. Kissinger's Role*, N.Y. Times, Nov. 26, 1979, at A21, col. 1; Wicker, *How Super Was Super K?*, Boston Globe, Mar. 2, 1980, at A1; Wilkie, *Was Carter Misled on Shah Visit?*, Boston Globe, Feb. 1, 1981, at 1.

119 *See* N.Y. Times, Nov. 25, 1979, at A19, col. 1, at col. 3. *See generally id.*, Jan. 10, 1979, at A3, col. 3.

120 N.Y. Times, May 27, 1979, § 3, at 1, col. 1, at 11, col. 3. *See also id.*, Nov. 17, 1956, at 23, col. 2.

121 *See generally*, H. KISSINGER, *supra* note 93, at 132, 949, 964, 966, 1117, 1143 & 1255–57.

122 3 *The* SALT II *Treaty: Hearings Before the Committee on Foreign Relations*, 96th Cong., 1st Sess. 151 (1979) (statement of Senator Frank Church).

123 *Id.* at 159.

124 *See* AVIATION WEEK & SPACE TECH., Nov. 3, 1980, at 28.

125 *See* Kissinger, *Nuclear Weapons and the Peace Movement*, WASH Q., Summer 1982, at 31, 37.

126 *See, e.g.*, Wash. Post, Sept. 8, 1979, at A8, col. 1. (Carter speech). *See generally* U.S. DEP'T OF STATE, BUREAU OF PUBLIC AFFAIRS, BACKGROUND ON THE QUESTION OF SOVIET TROOPS IN CUBA, CURRENT POLICY NO. 93 (1979); N.Y. Times, Sept. 6, 1979, at A8, col. 1.

127 *See* N.Y. Times, Aug. 19, 1979, §1, at 26, col. 1; *id.*, Aug. 31, 1979, at A2, col. 3; *id.*, Sept. 1, 1979, at 1, col. 6; *id.*, Sept. 10, 1979, at A1, col. 6; *id.*, Sept. 13, 1979, at A16, col. 4; *id.*, Nov. 3, 1979, at 10, col. 3.

128 KISSINGER, *supra* note 93, at 129–30.

129 Bundy, *The Brigade's My Fault*, N.Y. Times, Oct. 23, 1979, at 23, col. 2.

130 A. CHAYES, T. EHRLICH & A. LOWENFELD, 2 INTERNATIONAL LEGAL PROCESS 1120–49 (1969).

131 Weiss, *Taking Salami Slices in Cuba*, Wall St. J., Sept. 19, 1979, at 20, col. 4.

132 *See* DEP'T ST. BULL., Nov. 1979, at 7.

133 N.Y. Times, Jan. 25, 1977, at 1, col. 6. *See generally* S. TALBOTT, ENDGAME (1980).

134 Stockholm International Peace Research Institute, 1982 Yearbook 269 [hereinafter cited as SIPRI].

135   *See* Joint Statement on Strategic Offensive Arms Issued at Vladivostok Nov. 24, *reprinted in* DEP'T ST. BULL., Dec. 23, 1974, at 879. *See also* Joint Communique Signed at Vladivostok Nov. 24, *reprinted in id.* at 879–81.

136   N.Y. Times, Mar. 31, 1977, at A1, col. 6.

137   News Conference by Secretary of State Cyrus Vance at Geneva (May 21, 1977), *reprinted in* DEP'T ST. BULL., June 13, 1977, at 628; Joint Communique, *reprinted in* DEP'T ST. BULL., June 13, 1977, at 633.

138   *See East Asia: U.S. Normalizes Relations with the People's Republic of China*, DEP'T ST. BULL., Jan. 1979, at 25 (Address by President Carter).

139   U.S. DEP'T OF STATE, BUREAU OF PUBLIC AFFAIRS, SALT II AGREEMENT, SELECTED DOCUMENTS No. 12B (June 18, 1979) [hereinafter cited as SALT II].

140   *See* REPORT OF THE SENATE COMMITTEE ON FOREIGN RELATIONS ON THE SALT II TREATY, EXEC. REP. NO. 14, 96th Cong., 1st Sess. (1979).

141   *See* N.Y. Times, Feb. 1, 1979, at A16, col. 4.

142   *See id.*, Feb. 18, 1979, § 1, at 1, col. 6.

143   *See* Garrity, *The Soviet Military Stake in Afghanistan: 1956–79*, RUSI, Sept. 1980, at 31 (JOURNAL OF THE ROYAL UNITED SERVICES INSTITUTE FOR DEFENCE STUDIES), *reprinted in* DEP'T OF THE AIR FORCE, CURRENT NEWS, SPECIAL EDITION, Feb. 26, 1981, No. 676, at 6.

144   *See* N.Y. Times, June 18, 1981, at A1, col. 2; *id.*, July 2, 1981, at 6, col. 1, at col. 2; U.S. NEWS & WORLD REP., June 29, 1981, at 10; Wash. Post, June 18, 1981, at A34, col. 1; Wash. Post, June 19, 1981, at A10, col. 3.

145   Remarks by Deputy Press Secretary Rex Granum on the President's Decision to Deploy MX, 15 WEEKLY COMP. PRES. DOC. 1016 (June 8, 1979).

146   *MX Missile System*, DEP'T ST. BULL., Nov. 1979, at 25.

147   *See* Feld & Tsipis, *Land-based Intercontinental Ballistic Missiles*, SCIENTIFIC AMERICAN, Nov. 1979, at 51.

148   *Id.* at 58.

149   *See* N.Y. Times, Nov. 23, 1982, at 1, col. 3.

150   *See* REPORT OF THE PRESIDENT'S COMMISSION ON STRATEGIC FORCES 19 (Apr. 6, 1983) [hereinafter cited as Scowcroft Commission].

151   COMMITTEE ON THE PRESENT DANGER, IS AMERICA BECOMING NUMBER 2? (1978). *See generally* Barnet, *The Search for National Security*, NEW YORKER, Apr. 27, 1981, at 50.

152   SALT II, art. 4, para. 9, *supra* note 139, at 24. The Scowcroft Commission Report readily conceded that its proposed Midgetman mobile missile would violate this provision of SALT II. *See* Scowcroft Commission, *supra* note 150, at 24. Hence, it should not be deployed.

153   Mohr, *A Scary Debate Over 'Launch Under Attack,'* N.Y. Times, July 18, 1982, at E4, col. 1.

154   N.Y. Times, Dec. 13, 1979, at A3, col. 1. *See, e.g.*, Lewis, *Intermediate Range Nuclear Weapons*, SCIENTIC AMERICAN, Dec. 1980, at 63–73.

155   Moore, *Theatre Nuclear Forces*, 14 INT'L DEF. REV. 401, 407 (1981) (Pershing 2 can readily be given 4000 km range and MIRved); Wash. Post, Mar. 17, 1982, at A17, col. 1; Christian Sci. Mon., Nov. 16, 1982, at 4 (Pentagon wanted an extra 108 Pershing 2s in West Germany as "spares").

156   SALT II, *supra* note 139, at 42.

157   *U.S. Statement to the North Atlantic Conference, June 29, 1979, reprinted in* DEP'T ST. BULL., Aug. 1979, at 36.

158 N.Y. Times, Nov. 6, 1979, at A7, col. 1.

159 Vienna Convention on the Law of Treaties, *supra* note 71, art 18.

160 N.Y. Times, Sept. 20, 1982, at A1, col. 3.

161 N.Y. Times, Mar. 17, 1982, at 6, col. 2.

162 Agreement on Basic Principles of Relations, May 29, 1972, United States–U.S.S.R., *reprinted in* 11 I.L.M. 756 (1972).

163 *See, e.g.*, N.Y. Times, Feb. 1, 1980, at A27, col. 1 (George Kennan); *id.*, Jan. 8, 1981, at 4, col. 4.

164 *See, e.g.*, Rubin, *How International Law Bolsters the U.S. Hand*, Christian Sci. Mon., Jan. 21, 1980, at 23, col. 1; Rubin, *Guarding the Gulf*, *id.*, Mar. 7, 1980, at 23, col. 1; Rubin, *The Hostages: International Law to the Rescue?*, *id.*, Jan. 9, 1981, at 22, col. 4; Falk, *Comments on International Law and the United States' Response to the Iranian Revolution*, 33 RUTGERS L. REV. 399 (1981).

165 *See, e.g.*, Wall St. J., Mar. 11, 1980, at 39, col. 1; *id.*, June 2, 1980, at 34, col. 6 (Soviets substitute soybean meal); *id.*, July 14, 1980, at 24, col. 6 (Argentina–Soviet grain accord).

166 *Soviet Invasion of Afghanistan*, DEP'T ST. BULL., Jan. 1980, at A (Special) (President's Address).

167 *Id.*

168 *Id.*

169 *See* Proclamation No. 4771, 3 C.F.R. 82 (1981).

170 N.Y. Times, Mar. 22, 1980, at 2, col. 3.

171 *See id.*, Feb. 4, 1980, at A6, col. 4. *See also* Gelb & Ullman, *Keeping Cool at the Khyber Pass*, FOREIGN POL'Y, Spring 1980, at 3.

172 N.Y. Times, Jan. 26, 1980, at 3, col. 1; *id.*, Feb. 4, 1980, at A10, col. 1; *id.*, Feb. 5, 1980, at A14, col. 1; *id.*, Feb. 9, 1980, at 3, col. 4.

173 *Id.*, Feb. 3, 1980, at 13, col. 1.

174 *State of the Union Address*, DEP'T ST. BULL., Feb. 1980, at A (Special), at B: "An attempt by any outside force to gain control of the Persian Gulf region will be regarded as an assault on the vital interests of the United States of America, and such an assault will be repelled by any means necessary, including military force." *See* Wolfe, *The Many Doctrines of Carter*, 231 NATION 1 (1980). *But cf.* Goldman, *Is There a Russian Energy Crisis?*, ATLANTIC, Sept. 1980, at 55 (No!).

175 *See* Koehl & Glick, *The Rapid Deployment Farce*, AM. SPECTATOR, Jan. 1981, at 18–21; Bates, *The Rapid Deployment Force: Fact or Fiction*, RUSI, June 1981, at 23; Record, *The RDF: Is the Pentagon Kidding?*, WASH. Q., Summer 1981, at 41.

176 N.Y. Times, Feb. 2, 1980, at 1, col. 1.

177 *See, e.g.*, Wash. Post, July 17, 1981, at A1, col. 2.

178 *See* Wash. Post, Aug. 7, 1981, at C15, col. 4; *id.*, Oct. 28, 1980, at 1, col. 1.

179 *See* Newsom, *America Engulfed*, FOREIGN POL'Y, Summer 1981, at 17.

180 *See* N.Y. Times, Oct. 2, 1981, at 1, col. 6; Safire, *The Reagan Corollary*, *id.*, Oct. 4, 1981, §E, at 21, col. 5. *See also* Wall St. J., May 1, 1981, at 1, col. 5.

181 War Powers Act of 1973, Pub. L. No. 93-148, 87 Stat. 555.

182 Champaign-Urbana News Gazette, Aug. 18, 1980, at A4, col. 4; *id.*, Aug. 19, 1980, at A4, col. 6; *id.*, Aug. 20, 1980, at A4, col. 4; *id.*, Aug. 21, 1980, at A4, col. 1; *id.*, Aug. 22, 1980, at A4, col. 4; Wash. Post, Sept. 22, 1980, at D13, col. 3; Wash. Star, Sept. 21, 1980, at 6; Anderson, *Why I Tell Secrets*, Wash. Post (Parade), Nov. 30, 1980, at 20–25; Wash. Post, Oct. 23, 1981, at B17; Wash. Post, June 28, 1983, at C15.

183   U.S. Dep't of State, Bureau of Public Affairs, Gist: U.S. Assistance to El Salvador (May 1981); Cong. Q., Aug. 28, 1982, at 2157. *See generally* U.S. Dep't of State, Bureau of Public Affairs, Communist Interference in El Salvador, Special Report No. 80 (Feb. 23, 1981).

184   *Whose Interest?*, Economist, Sept. 27, 1980, at 42; Mansur (pseud.), *The Military in the Persian Gulf: Who Will Guard the Gulf States from Their Guardians?*, Armed Forces J. Int'l, Nov. 1980, at 44; *Dangerous Game*, 231 Nation 395 (1980) (U.S. awacs in Saudi Arabia supplying Iraq with military intelligence); *Who Will Police These Shores?*, Middle East, Oct. 1980, at 26, col. 1, at col. 3; N.Y. Times, Oct. 29, 1981, at 10, col. 1.

185   Treaty of Friendship, Feb. 26, 1921, R.S.F.S.R.-Persia, arts. 5 & 6, 9 L.N.T.S. 383, 403:

Article 5

The two High Contracting Parties undertake:

(1) To prohibit the formation or presence within their respective territories, of any organizations or groups of persons, irrespective of the name by which they are known, whose object is to engage in acts of hostility against Persia or Russia, or against the Allies of Russia.

They will likewise prohibit the formation of troops or armies within their respective territories with the afore-mentioned object.

(2) Not to allow a third Party or any organization, whatever it be called, which is hostile to the other Contracting Party, to import or to convey in transit across their countries material which can be used against the other Party.

(3) To prevent by all means in their power the presence within their territories or within the territories of their Allies of all armies or forces of a third Party in cases in which the presence of such forces would be regarded as a menace to the frontiers, interests or safety of the other Contracting Party.

Article 6

If a third Party should attempt to carry out a policy of usurpation by means of armed intervention in Persia, or if such Power should desire to use Persian territory as a base of operations against Russia, or if a Foreign Power should threaten the frontiers of Federal Russia or those of its Allies, and if the Persian Government should not be able to put a stop to such menace after having been once called upon to do so by Russia, Russia shall have the right to advance her troops into the Persian interior for the purpose of carrying out the military operations necessary for its defense. Russia undertakes, however, to withdraw her troops from Persian territory as soon as the danger has been removed.

Annex II to this Treaty contained a letter from the R.S.F.S.R. Diplomatic Representative further clarifying the Russian government's interpretation of articles 5 and 6 in the following language:

In reply to your letter dated 20th day of Ghows, I have the honour to inform you that Articles 5 and 6 are intended to apply only to cases in which preparations have been made for a considerable armed attack upon Russia or the Soviet Republics allied to her, by the partisans of the regime which has been overthrown or by its supporters among those foreign Powers which are in a position to assist the enemies of the Workers' and Peasants' Republics and at the same time to possess themselves, by force or by underhand methods, of part of the Persian territory, thereby establishing a base of operations for any attacks — made either directly or through the counter-revolutionary forces — which they might meditate against

Russia or the Soviet Republics allied to her. The Articles referred to are therefore in no sense intended to apply to verbal or written attacks directed against the Soviet Government by the various Persian groups, or even by any Russian émigrés in Persia, in so far as such attacks are generally tolerated as between neighbouring Powers animated by sentiments of mutual friendship.

9 L.N.T.S. 383, 413.

186   *See* Reisman, *Termination of the USSR's Treaty Right of Intervention in Iran*, 74 A.J.I.L. 144 (1980). *See also* Hirschfeld, *Moscow and Khomeini: Soviet-Iranian Relations in Historical Perspective*, ORBIS, Summer 1980, at 219.

187   *See generally* Maechling, *An Historic Enmity*, Manchester Guardian Weekly, Oct. 26, 1980, at 16, col. 3; Hardcastle, *The Shatt-al-Arab Saga*, NEW REPUBLIC, Oct. 11, 1980, at 11; *Too Hot to Handle*, MIDDLE EAST, Nov. 1980, at 10; N.Y. Times, Sept. 18, 1980, at A8, col. 1. On the emerging role of Iraq as a Gulf power, see Wright, *Iraq—New Power in the Middle East*, FOREIGN AFF., Winter 1980–81, at 257; Dawisha, *Iraq: The West's Opportunity*, FOREIGN POL'Y, Winter 1980–81, at 134; Kedourie, *The Illusions of Powerlessness*, NEW REPUBLIC, Nov. 29, 1980, at 17.

188   *Iran-Iraq Conflict*, DEP'T ST. BULL., Nov. 1980, at 53, 53–54 (statement of President Carter).

189   *See, e.g.*, Wash. Post, Aug. 27, 1981, at C31, col. 3, col. 4 (C.I.A. will use Egypt and Turkey to mount covert operations against Khomeini); N.Y. Times, Mar. 7, 1982, at 1, col. 3. *See also* MIDDLE EAST, Aug. 1980, at 24; N.Y. Times, July 18, 1983, at 3, col. 1 (U.S. helicopters used for military purposes by Iraq).

190   *See* DEP'T ST. BULL., Dec. 1980, at 46.

191   This inference was confirmed by a conversation this author had in New York City with Leonard Boudin, who was then representing Bank Markazi (Nov. 1980).

192   *See* 50 U.S.C. § 1701, § 1702 (Supp. V 1981), which reads as follows:

§ 1702. Presidential authorities

(a)(1) At the times and to the extent specified in section 1701 of this title, the President may, under such regulations as he may prescribe, by means of instructions, licenses, or otherwise—

(A) Investigate, regulate, or prohibit—

(i) any transactions in foreign exchange,

(ii) transfers of credit or payments between, by, through, or to any banking institution, to the extent that such transfers or payments involve any interest of any foreign country or a national thereof,

(iii) the importing or exporting of currency or securities; and

(B) investigate, regulate, direct and compel, nullify, void, prevent or prohibit, any acquisition, holding, withholding, use, transfer, withdrawal, transportation, importation or exportation of, or dealing in, or exercising any right, power, or privilege with respect to, or transactions involving, any property in which any foreign country or a national thereof has any interest; by any person, or with respect to any property, subject to the jurisdiction of the United States.

193   *See* 22 U.S.C. § 1732 (1976), which provides as follows:

§ 1732. Release of citizens imprisoned by foreign governments

Whenever it is made known to the President that any citizen of the United States has been unjustly deprived of his liberty by or under the authority of any foreign government, it shall be the duty of the President forthwith to demand of that government the reasons of such imprisonment; and if it appears to be wrongful and in violation of the rights of American citizenship, the President shall forthwith demand the release of such citizen, and if the release so demanded is unreasonably delayed or refused, the President shall use such means, not amounting to acts of war, as he may think necessary and proper to obtain or effectuate the release; and all the facts and proceedings relative thereto shall as soon as practicable be communicated by the President to Congress.

194   *See United States v. Pink*, 315 U.S. 203 (1942); *United States v. Belmont*, 301 U.S. 325 (1937).

195   *See generally* STAFF REPORT OF HOUSE COMMITTEE ON BANKING, FINANCE AND URBAN AFFAIRS, 97TH CONG., 1ST SESS., IRAN: THE FINANCIAL ASPECTS OF THE HOSTAGE SETTLEMENT AGREEMENT 3 (Comm. Print 5, July 1981); Winer, *The Iranian Assets Grab*, NATION, Jan. 17, 1981, at 44; ECONOMIST, July 18, 1981, at 63; Manchester Guardian Weekly, Jan. 25, 1981, at 6, col. 2; Norton & Collins, *Reflections on the Iranian Hostage Settlement*, 67 A.B.A.J. 428 (1981); Wall St. J., Jan. 23, 1981, at 1, col. 6; Gordon & Lichtenstein, *The Decision to Block Iranian Assets—Reexamined*, 16 INT'L LAW. 161 (1982); Gordon, *The Blocking of Iranian Assets*, 14 INT'L LAW. 659 (1980); NAT'L CATHOLIC REP., Feb. 29, 1980, at 16; Taylor, *Megabankers, Carter Schemed to Create Iranian Crisis, Freeze Funds*, SPOT-LIGHT, Feb. 9, 1981, at 16; Sherrill, *Big Oil, Big Banks, Big Trouble*, PENTHOUSE, June 1980, at 680; Davis, *Hostages for the Chase Manhattan*, PENTHOUSE, Dec. 1980, at 76; Wright, *Buried Treasure at Chase Manhattan?*, NEW STATESMAN, April 7, 1980, at 12; Ball, *The Unseemly Squabble over Iran's Assets*, FORTUNE, Jan. 28, 1980, at 60; *Legal Repercussions of the Freezing of Iranian Assets and Loans*, INT'L CURRENCY REV., Mar. 1, 1980, at 25.

196   *See* Treas. Reg. 31, § 535.418 (1980).

197   *See* Department Statement (Feb. 18, 1981), in DEP'T ST. BULL., Mar. 1981, at 17. *See also Concerning United States Diplomatic and Consular Staff in Tehran* (U.S. v. Iran) (Order of Discontinuance), *reprinted in* 20 I.L.M. 889 (1981). *But compare* U.N. Doc. S/14338 (Jan. 20, 1981), *reprinted in* 20 I.L.M. 551 (1981) with U.N. Doc. S/1439 (Mar. 5, 1981), *reprinted in* 20 I.L.M. 552 (1981).

198   The Declarations of Algiers consist of (1) the Declaration of the Government of the Democratic and Popular Republic of Algeria; (2) the Declaration of the Government of the Democratic and Popular Republic of Algeria Concerning the Settlement of Claims by the Government of the United States of America and the Government of the Islamic Republic of Iran; (3) the Undertakings of the Government of the United States of America and the Government of the Islamic Republic of Iran with Respect to the Declaration of the Government of the Democratic and Popular Republic of Algeria; (4) an Escrow Agreement; and (5) a Technical Agreement between U.S., U.K., and Algerian Banks. For the full texts of these documents see U.S. DEP'T OF STATE, BUREAU OF PUBLIC AFFAIRS, HOSTAGE AGREEMENTS TRANSMITTED TO CONGRESS, SELECTED DOCUMENTS NO. 19 (Mar. 12, 1981).

199   Vienna Convention on the Law of Treaties, *supra* note 71, art. 52 provides:
Coercion of a State by the threat or use of force
A treaty is void if its conclusion has been procured by the threat or use of force in violation of the principles of international law embodied in the Charter of the United Nations.
See Letter to the Editor by Robert F. Turner (Feb. 23, 1981), in 21 VA. J. INT'L L. 347 (1981).

200 *See supra* note 197.
201 I.C.J. STAT., arts. 36, 53, 59 & 60.
202 *See* L. HENKIN, R. PUGH, O. SCHACHTER & H. SMITH, INTERNATIONAL LAW: CASES AND MATERIALS 580 (1980).
203 *Dames & Moore v. Regan*, 453 U.S. 654 (1981).
204 Settlement of Claims, May 5, 1979, United States-China, 30 U.S.T. 1957, T.I.A.S. No. 9306.
205 *See, e.g.*, H. STEINER & D. VAGTS, TRANSNATIONAL LEGAL PROBLEMS 433 (2d ed. 1976).
206 *See* Wohlstetter, *Meeting the Threat in the Persian Gulf*, SURVEY, Spring 1980, at 109; ECONOMIST, May 9, 1981, at 34, col. 3; Wall St. J., Mar. 5, 1982, at 22, col. 1.
207 *See also* Perlmutter, *American Policy in the Middle East: New Approach for a New Administration*, PARAMETERS, June 1981, at 14; Perlmutter, *Supporting Our Vital Interests in Iran*, Wall St. J., Jan. 23, 1981, at 14, col. 3.
208 Treaty on International Borders and Good Neighborly Relations, June 13, 1975, Iran-Iraq, *reprinted in* 14 I.L.M. 1133 (1975).
209 *India and Pakistan Join in Gulf Game*, MIDDLE EAST, June 1981, at 31.
210 *See, e.g.*, 22 U.S.C. §§ 2302, 2314 (d), 2753(c) & 2754 (1976).
211 *See Together, at Last*, ECONOMIST, Mar. 14, 1981, at 37; *Gulf Security Document*, MIDDLE EAST, Jan. 1981, at 16; *No Secrets on Gulf Security, id.*, Mar. 1981, at 18; *Caution: Building in Progress, id.*, Apr. 1981, at 8; *Gulf Council Shifts into Second Gear, id.*, Oct. 1981, at 25; Wall St. J., Jan. 28, 1982, at 28, col. 3.
212 Interview with Abdullah Bishara, Secretary General of the Gulf Cooperation Council, MIDDLE EAST, Sept. 1981, at 35.
213 *But cf.* Multinational Force and Observers Participation Resolution, Pub. L. No. 97–132, 95 Stat. 1693 (1981). Section 3(a)(3) thereof provides:
   (3) Members of the United States Armed Forces, and United States civilian personnel, who are assigned, detailed, or otherwise provided to the Multinational Force and Observers may perform only those functions or responsibilities which are specified for the United Nations Forces and Observers in the Treaty of Peace and in accordance with the Protocol.
   See Leich, *The Sinai Multinational Force and Observers*, 76 A.J.I.L. 181 (1982); CONG. Q., Dec. 26, 1981, at 2589.
214 *See* Z. SCHIFF & E. YA'ARI, ISRAEL'S LEBANON WAR 62–77 (1984); Schiff, *Green Light, Lebanon*, FOREIGN POL'Y, Spring 1983, at 73; ECONOMIST, June 12, 1982, at 24; MIDDLE EAST, July 1982, at 6; Wash. Post, Aug. 14, 1982, at B7; Wash. Post, Aug. 21, 1982, at 23; Philadelphia Inquirer, Feb. 4, 1983, at 6; Wright, *Israeli Attack No Surprise to Pentagon*, IN THESE TIMES, Sept. 8–14, 1982, at 3.
215 *But cf.* M. JANSEN, THE BATTLE OF BEIRUT 119–30 (1982).
216 Judgment in the Corfu Channel Case (U.K. v. Alb.), 1949 I.C.J. 4, 35:
   The United Kingdom Agent, in his speech in reply, has further classified "Operation Retail" among methods of self-protection or self-help. The Court cannot accept this defence either. Between independent States, respect for territorial sovereignty is an essential foundation of international relations. The Court recognizes that the Albanian Government's complete failure to carry out its duties after the explosions, and the dilatory nature of its diplomatic notes, are extenuating circumstances for the action of the United Kingdom Government. But to ensure respect for international law, of which it is the organ, the Court must

declare that the action of the British Navy constituted a violation of Albanian sovereignty.

217 *Id.* at 18 (emphasis in original).

218 *See* INTERNATIONAL COMMISSION TO ENQUIRE INTO REPORTED VIOLATIONS OF INTERNATIONAL LAW BY ISRAEL DURING ITS INVASION OF LEBANON, ISRAEL IN LEBANON 9 (1983); M. JANSEN, THE BATTLE OF BEIRUT 127–30 (1982). *See also* Report of the Secretary-General on the United Nations Interim Force in Lebanon, U.N. Doc. S/15194/Add. 1 (1982), *reprinted in* 21 I.L.M. 908 (1982) (PLO agreed to ceasefire, while Israel invaded).

219 *See supra* note 66 and accompanying text.

220 Wall St. J., July 9, 1982, at 9, col. 4.

221 N.Y. Times, Aug. 21, 1982, at 6, col. 6. *See also* M. JANSEN, THE BATTLE OF BEIRUT 123–25 (1982).

222 N.Y. Times, July 30, 1982, at 3, col. 5.

223 Geneva Convention Relative to the Treatment of Prisoners of War, Aug. 12, 1949, 6 U.S.T. 3316, T.I.A.S. No. 3364, 75 U.N.T.S. 135.

224 Geneva Convention Relative to the Protection of Civilian Persons in Time of War, Aug. 12, 1949, 6 U.S.T. 3516, T.I.A.S. No. 3365, 75 U.N.T.S. 287.

225 *See, e.g.,* U.S. ARMY FIELD MANUAL 27-10, THE LAW OF LAND WARFARE 138–64 (1956).

226 *But cf.* Comments by Robbie Sabel, Counselor to U.S. Embassy of Israel (Apr. 15, 1983), in 77 AM. SOC. INT'L L. PROC. – – – (1983) (forthcoming).

227 *See, e.g.,* Fourth Geneva Convention, *supra* note 224, art. 1: "The High Contracting Parties undertake to respect and to ensure respect for the present Convention in all circumstances."

228 S.C. Res. 508 (1982), *reprinted in* DEP'T. ST. BULL., Sept. 1982, at 14.

229 S.C. Res. 509 (1982), *reprinted in* DEP'T. ST. BULL., Sept. 1982, at 14.

230 U.N. CHARTER art. 25: "The Members of the United Nations agree to accept and carry out the decisions of the Security Council in accordance with the present Charter."

231 *See* London Agreement, Aug 8, 1945, 59 Stat. 1544, E.A.S. No. 472.

232 G.A. Res. 95(1), U.N. Doc. A/64/Add. 1 (1946).

233 *See Eichmann v. Attorney-General of the Government of Israel,* [1961] 36 I.L.R. 277, 296 (1962).

234 *See, e.g.,* N.Y. Times, Apr. 1, 1983, at 1.

235 *See* The Commission of Inquiry into the Events at the Refugee Camps in Beirut, Final Report (1983).

236 *Application of Yamashita,* 327 U.S. 1 (1946).

237 *See* U.S. ARMY FIELD MANUAL 27–10, THE LAW OF LAND WARFARE, ¶ 501, at 178–79 (1956) (emphasis added).

238 *See* DEP'T OF STATE, BUREAU OF PUBLIC AFFAIRS, LEBANON: PLAN FOR THE PLO EVACUATION FROM WEST BEIRUT, CURRENT POLICY NO. 415, at 8 (Aug. 1982).

239 *See* Sunday Times (London), Jan. 30, 1983, at 1, col. 8.

240 *See* Wash. Post, Nov. 15, 1982, at B25.

241 *See, e.g.,* Fourth Geneva Convention, *supra* note 224, art. 3:
In the case of armed conflict not of an international character occurring in the territory of one of the High Contracting Parties, each Party to the conflict shall be bound to apply, as a minimum, the following provisions:
(1) Persons taking no active part in the hostilities, including members of

armed forces who have laid down their arms and those placed *hors de combat* by sickness, wounds, detention, or any other cause, shall in all circumstances be treated humanely, without any adverse distinction founded on race, colour, religion or faith, sex, birth or wealth, or any other similar criteria.

To this end the following acts are and shall remain prohibited at any time and in any place whatsoever with respect to the above-mentioned persons:

(a) violence to life and person, in particular murder of all kinds, mutilation, cruel treatment and torture;

(b) taking of hostages;

(c) outrages upon personal dignity, in particular humiliating and degrading treatment;

(d) the passing of sentences and the carrying out of executions without previous judgment pronounced by a regularly constituted court, affording all the judicial guarantees which are recognized as indispensable by civilized peoples.

(2) The wounded and sick shall be collected and cared for.

An impartial humanitarian body, such as the International Committee of the Red Cross, may offer its services to the Parties to the conflict.

The Parties to the conflict should further endeavour to bring into force, by means of special agreements, all or part of the other provisions of the present Convention.

The application of the preceding provisions shall not affect the legal status of the Parties to the conflict.

See also ADVISORY COMMITTEE ON HUMAN RIGHTS IN LEBANON, LEBANON: TOWARD LEGAL ORDER AND RESPECT FOR HUMAN RIGHTS (1983).

242 *See* N.Y. Times, Apr. 10, 1976, at 1, col. 6 (Syrian troops intervene); *id.*, June 6, 1976, at 1, col. 8 (Christian leadership endorses Syrian intervention); *id.*, Oct. 19, 1976, at 1, col. 6 (Arab Deterrent Force created).

243 Resolution of the Tenth Meeting of Consultation of the Ministers of Foreign Affairs of the American Republics Establishing an Inter-American Force for the Dominican Republic, May 6, 1965, DEP'T. ST. BULL., May 31, 1965, at 862–63.

244 Dep't of State, Legal Basis For United States Actions in the Dominican Republic (May 17, 1965), 111 CONG. REC. 11119 (1969).

245 Agreement on Troop Withdrawal, May 17, 1983, Israel-Lebanon, *reprinted in* N.Y. Times, May 17, 1983, at 4. *See also* N.Y. Times, May 18, 1983, at 1, col. 3 (U.S.-Israeli secret agreement).

246 *See supra* note 199.

247 *See, e.g.*, Report of the Secretary-General on the United Nations Interim Force in Lebanon (12 Dec. 1980 to 12 June 1981), 36 U.N. SCOR Supp. (Apr.–June 1981) at 1, 11, 21, U.N. Doc. S/14537 (1981); Report of the Secretary-General on the United Nations Interim Force in Lebanon (16 June to 10 Dec. 1981), 37 U.N. SCOR Supp. (Oct.–Dec. 1981) at 1, 9, U.N. Doc. S/14789 (1981).

248 *See* G. ABI-SAAB, U.N. OPERATION IN THE CONGO 1960–1964 (1978).

249 *See supra* note 181.

250 U.N. CHARTER art. 39: "The Security Council shall determine the existence of any threat to the peace, breach of the peace, or act of aggression and shall make recommendations, or decide what measures shall be taken in accordance with Articles 41 and 42, to maintain or restore international peace and security."

251 *See* S.C. Res. 418 (1977), *reprinted in* 16 I.L.M. 1547 (1977).

252 *See supra* note 13.

253 *See* L. SOHN, CASES ON UNITED NATIONS LAW 474–509 (2d ed. 1967).

254 *See* Camp David Accords, Sept. 17, 1978, *reprinted in* DEP'T. ST. BULL., Oct. 1978, at 7. The Camp David Accords include a Framework for Peace in the Middle East, *reprinted in id.* at 7–9, and a Framework for the Conclusion of a Peace Treaty Between Egypt and Israel, *reprinted in id.* at 9–10. *See also* Treaty of Peace, Mar. 26, 1979, Egypt-Israel, *reprinted in* 18 I.L.M. 362 (1979).

255 *See* Kassim, *The Palestine Liberation Organization's Claim to Status: A Juridical Analysis under International Law*, 9 DEN. J. INT'L L. & POL'Y 1, 18–21 (1980).

256 PALESTINIAN NATIONAL CHARTER, arts. 2, 15, 22, *reprinted in* 3 THE ARAB-ISRAELI CONFLICT 706, 708–10 (J. Moore ed. 1974) [hereinafter cited as J. Moore].

257 PALESTINIAN NATIONAL CHARTER, art. 10, *reprinted in* 3 J. Moore, *supra* note 256, at 707.

258 *Deuteronomy* 20:16–17 (King James). To the same effect are *Exodus* 23:23–33, 34:10–24; *Numbers* 33:50–56; and *Joshua* 10:28–43, 24:8–13.

259 *See* Milson, *How to Make Peace with the Palestinians*, COMMENTARY, May 1981, at 25.

260 S.C. Res. 242 (1967), 22 U.N. SCOR (1382d mtg.) at 8–9, U.N. Doc. S/8247 (1967).

261 Address by President Ronald Reagan, *A New Opportunity for Peace in the Middle East*, DEP'T ST. BULL., Sept. 1982, at 23 (Sept. 1, 1982). *But see* Aruri, *The Reagan Mideast Initiative: Short Change and Traps*, PALESTINE CONGRESS OF NORTH AMERICA NEWSLETTER (1983 Supp.).

262 PRESIDENT WILSON'S STATE PAPERS AND ADDRESSES 464–72 (A. Shaw ed. 1918).

263 G.A. Res. 181(II), U.N. Doc. A/519, at 131 (1947).

264 *See* International Convention on the Prevention and Punishment of the Crime of Genocide, *opened for signature* Dec. 9, 1948, 78 U.N.T.S. 277 (1951), art. 2:
In the present Convention, genocide means any of the following acts committed with intent to destroy, in whole or in part, a national, ethnical, racial or religious group as such:
(a) Killing members of the group;
(b) Causing serious bodily or mental harm to members of the group;
(c) Deliberately inflicting on the group conditions of life calculated to bring about its physical destruction in whole or in part;
(d) Imposing measures intended to prevent births within the group;
(e) Forcibly transferring children of the group to another group.
Israel is a party to the Genocide Convention. *See* THE RATIFICATION OF INTERNATIONAL HUMAN RIGHTS TREATIES 10 (1976).

265 *See* NEW REPUBLIC, Oct. 4, 1982, at 13.

266 *See* H. KISSINGER, YEARS OF UPHEAVAL 545–613 (1982).

267 *See, e.g.*, Warnke, *Remarks*, 74 AM. SOC. INT'L L. PROC. 212, 213 (1980).

268 *See Reagan Strategic Arms Policy: No Big Surprises Seen Soon*, 39 CONG. Q. 177 (1981).

269 *Senate Testimony of General Jones on SALT II*, in U.S. DEP'T OF STATE, BUREAU OF PUBLIC AFFAIRS, CURRENT POLICY NO. 72A, at 33, 35–36 (July 9–11, 1979).

270 *Senate Testimony of Secretary Brown on SALT II*, in U.S. DEP'T OF STATE, BUREAU OF

Public Affairs, Current Policy No. 72A, at 9, 15 (July 9–11, 1979).

271 Treaty on the Limitation of Strategic Offensive Arms Interim Agreement and Protocol, May 26, 1972, United States-U.S.S.R., 23 U.S.T. 3462, T.I.A.S. No. 7504.

272 *See* M. Glennon & T. Franck, 1 United States Foreign Relations Law 41–59 (1980).

273 Rostow, *The Case Against* salt ii, in Commentary Report (1979); Rostow, salt ii: A Soft Bargain, A Hard Sell (Committee on Present Danger, 1978).

274 *See, e.g.*, Lens, *A-Bomb Almanac*, Nation, Apr. 4, 1981, at 389; Metcalf, *Missile Accuracy—The Need to Know*, Strategic Review, Summer 1981, at 5; Wicker, *Rethinking the* mx(2), N.Y. Times, Aug. 28, 1981, at A23, col. 5.

275 1 *Military Posture: Hearings Before the House Committee on Armed Services*, 96th Cong., 1st Sess. 1121 (1979) (testimony of Paul Nitze).

276 *See* Newsweek, Jan. 31, 1983, at 20; Chicago Tribune, Mar. 2, 1983, at 8.

277 salt ii, art. 4, paras. 10–13, *supra* note 139, at 26.

278 salt ii, art. 4, para. 8, *supra* note 139, at 22.

279 N.Y. Post, Apr. 3, 1982, at 2.

280 salt ii, *supra* note 139, at 18.

281 salt ii, *supra* note 139, at 30.

282 salt ii, *supra* note 139, at 58.

283 Committee on the Present Danger, Has America Become Number 2? 20 (1982).

284 *Id.* at 18.

285 *Id.* at 35.

286 *See* N.Y. Times, Apr. 2, 1982, at 10, col. 3; Feld & Tsipis, *supra* note 147, at 51.

287 *See* Robinson, *Layered Defense System Pushed to Protect* icbms, Aviation Week & Space Tech., Feb. 9, 1981, at 9; Quirt, *Washington's New Push for Anti-Missiles*, Fortune, Oct. 19, 1981, at 142.

288 Treaty on the Limitation of Anti-Ballistic Missile Systems, May 26, 1972, United States-U.S.S.R., 23 U.S.T. 3435, T.I.A.S. No. 7503, *amended by* Protocol of July 3, 1974, 27 U.S.T. 1645, T.I.A.S. No. 8276.

289 Snow, mx: *Maginot Line of the 1980s*, Bull. Atom. Sci., Nov. 1980, at 22, 25.

290 Feld and Tsipis, *supra* note 147, at 60. *Cf.* Scowcroft Commission, *supra* note 150, at 11, 20.

291 *See* Halperin & Halperin, *The Key West Key*, Foreign Pol'y, Winter 1983–84, at 114, 125–29.

292 N.Y. Times, Oct. 3, 1981, at A9, col. 3; *id.*, Feb. 6, 1983, at 10, col. 6; Defense Daily, Jan. 25, 1983, at 127; F.Y.E.O., Feb. 21, 1983, at 57–2 (*For Your Eyes Only*).

293 N.Y. Times, Apr. 2, 1982, at 10, col. 3.

294 *See, e.g.*, Wash. Post, Mar. 16, 1983, at 19; *id.*, Apr. 19, 1983, at E8; *id.*, May 16, 1983, at 1; *id.*, May 19, 1983, at C19.

295 *See* R. Kennedy, Thirteen Days 9 (1971).

296 *Id.* at 12–17.

297 *Id.* at 26–27, 35.

298 *Id.* at 128.

299 *See* Warnke & Schneider, *A Nuclear War Must Never be Fought*, Across the Board, Mar. 1981, at 14; *PD-59 & Command and Control: Use It or Lose It?*, F.A.S. Pub. Interest Rep., Oct. 1980 (Special Ed.); N.Y. Times, May 30, 1982, at 1;

Arkin, *Why SIOP 6?*, BULL. ATOM. SCI., Apr. 1983, at 9; Nunn, *Termination: The Myth of the Short, Decisive Nuclear War*, PARAMETERS, Dec. 1980, at 36. *Compare* Beres, *Presidential Directive 59: A Critical Assessment*, PARAMETERS, Mar. 1981, at 19, *with* Gray, *Presidential Directive 59: Flawed But Useful, id.* at 28, *and compare* Howard, *On Fighting a Nuclear War*, INT'L SECURITY, Spring 1981, at 3, *with* Slocombe, *The Countervailing Strategy, id.* at 19, *and* Trofimenko, *Counterforce: Illusion of a Panacea, id.* at 29.

300   Wash. Post, Apr. 3, 1983, at D1; Christian Sci. Mon., Apr. 11, 1983, at 23.

301   *See Report on CTB Negotiations*, DEP'T ST. BULL., Nov. 1980, at 47; Caldwell, *CTB: An Effective SALT Substitute*, BULL. ATOM. SCI., Dec. 1980, at 30.

302   N.Y. Times, Nov. 19, 1981, at 1, col. 6. *See* S. TALBOTT, DEADLY GAMBITS (1984).

303   *Special Meeting of Foreign and Defense Ministers Communique*, NATO REVIEW, Feb. 1980, at 25.

304   *See* Eagleburger, *The U.S. Approach to the Negotiations on Intermediate-Range Nuclear Forces*, NATO REVIEW, Feb. 1982, at 7, 10; Wash. Post, Apr. 22, 1983, at 12; NATO Special Consultative Group, INF: PROGRESS REPORT TO MINISTERS (Brussels, Dec. 8, 1983).

305   N.Y. Times, Dec. 22, 1982, at 1, col. 6. *See also id.*, May 4, 1983, at 1, col. 3.

306   North Atlantic Treaty, Sept. 9, 1949, 63 Stat. 2241, T.I.A.S. No. 1964, 34 U.N.T.S. 243.

307   N.Y. Times, June 29, 1982, at 6, col. 5.

308   *See, e.g.*, N.Y. Times, Aug. 1, 1982, at 1; Wash. Post, Aug. 29, 1982, at 9; L.A. Times, Sept. 13, 1982, at 1, col. 2; Aerospace Daily, Oct. 13, 1982, at 226; Wash. Post, July 13, 1983, at 1; N.Y. Times, July 14, 1983, at A1.

309   *See* Comment, *Reagan Changes Course on Non-Proliferation*, 216 SCIENCE 7 (1982). For some indication of what the Reagan administration's non-proliferation policy might be, see L. DUNN, CONTROLLING THE BOMB (1982). Dunn became Special Assistant for Nuclear Affairs at the State Department in the Reagan administration.

310   Treaty on the Non-proliferation of Nuclear Weapons, July 1, 1968, 21 U.S.T. 483, T.I.A.S. No. 6839, 729 U.N.T.S. 161.

311   *See, e.g.*, Hamilton, *To Link or Not to Link*, FOREIGN POL'Y, Fall 1981, at 927. *See also* Selin, *Looking Ahead to SALT III*, INTERNATIONAL SECURITY, Winter 1980–81, at 171; Drell & Wisner, *A New Formula for Nuclear Arms Control, id.* at 186.

312   *See* Comment, *Approval of SALT Agreements by Joint Resolution of Congress*, 21 HARV. INT'L L.J. 421 (1980). *See also* McDougal & Lans, *Treaties and Congress-Executive or Presidential Agreements: Interchangeable Instruments of National Policy*, (pts. 1 & 2) 54 YALE L.J. 181, 534 (1945).

313   Address by Ambassador Jeane J. Kirkpatrick, American Society of International Law Luncheon (April 12, 1984), in 78 AM. SOC. INT'L L. PROC. – – – (1984). *See* N.Y. Times, April 13, 1984, § I, at 3, col. 1.

314   *See generally* Boyle, *American Foreign Policy Toward International Law and Organizations: 1898–1917*, 6 LOY. L.A. INT'L & COMP. L.J. – – – (1983) (forthcoming).

315   Note from Mr. Blaine to Mr. Osborne (Nov. 29, 1881), *reprinted in* U.S. DEP'T OF STATE, 1881–1882 PAPERS RELATING TO THE FOREIGN RELATIONS OF THE UNITED STATES 13. *See* Bastert, *Diplomatic Reversal: Frelinghuysen's Opposition to Blaine's Pan-American Policy in 1882*, 42 MISS. VALLEY HIST. REV. 653 (1956); Wilgus, *James G. Blaine and the Pan-American Movement*, 5 HISPANIC

AM. HIST. REV. 662 (1922).

316   *See* INTER-AMERICAN INSTITUTE OF INTERNATIONAL LEGAL STUDIES, THE INTER-AMERICAN SYSTEM XV–XXXIII (1966).

317   *See* J. RICHARDSON, 1 MESSAGES AND PAPERS OF THE PRESIDENT 205 (Farewell Address) and 776 (Monroe Doctrine) (1911).

318   *See* E. MCCORMAK, JAMES K. POLK: A POLITICAL BIOGRAPHY 690, 698 (1965).

319   *See* Drago, *State Loans in Their Relation to International Policy*, 1 A.J.I.L. 692, 719 (1907); Chandler, *The Pan American Origin of the Monroe Doctrine*, 8 A.J.I.L. 515 (1914) (tracing efforts made by South American countries to formulate a Pan American policy in which the U.S. would have an active role prior to the enunciation of the Monroe Doctrine); Robertson, *Hispanic American Appreciations of the Monroe Doctrine*, 3 HISPANIC AM. HIST. REV. 1 (1920) (while engaged in a dispute with England over title to land Venezuela invoked the Monroe Doctrine in May 1887, and requested the U.S. Secretary of State to promote the settlement of the dispute by arbitration).

320   *See* 9 RICHARDSON, *supra* note 317, at 7024, 7053 (1911): "Chronic wrongdoing, or an impotence which results in a general loosening of the ties of civilized society, may in America, as elsewhere, ultimately require intervention by some civilized nation, and in the Western Hemisphere the adherence of the United States to the Monroe Doctrine may force the United States, however reluctantly, in flagrant cases of such wrongdoing or impotence, to the exercise of an international police power."

321   Drago, *supra* note 319, at 721–22.

322   *See* Olney, *The Development of International Law*, 1 A.J.I.L. 418, 423 (1907); Root, *The Real Monroe Doctrine*, 8 A.J.I.L. 427, 433–37 (1914).

323   *See* D. MUNRO, INTERVENTION AND DOLLAR DIPLOMACY IN THE CARIBBEAN 78–125 (1964).

324   Convention Concerning Customs Revenues, Feb. 8, 1907, United States-Dominican Republic, 35 Stat. 1880, T.S. No. 465. *See* Hollander, *The Convention of 1907 Between the United States and the Dominican Republic*, 1 A.J.I.L. 287 (1907). An earlier 1905 Convention had failed to gain Senate support because the United States undertook the duty of determining the validity of claims against the Dominican Republic. *See* Message to the Senate by President Theodore Roosevelt (Mar. 6, 1905), in 9 RICHARDSON, *supra* note 317, at 7080; Fifth Annual Message to Congress by President Theodore Roosevelt (Dec. 5, 1905), *id.* at 7353, 7377–78. Undaunted, Roosevelt effected a customs agreement on his own accord by the conclusion of a modus vivendi pending the Senate's ratification of the treaty. *See* D. PERKINS, THE MONROE DOCTRINE 1867–1907, at 435 (1966). "The assertion that the United States initiated the receivership by means of military force would be approximately correct." Rippy, *The Initiation of the Customs Receivership in the Dominican Republic*, 17 HISPANIC AM. HIST. REV. 419, 448 (1937).

325   Convention Concerning Customs Revenues, Feb. 8, 1907, United States-Dominican Republic, art. II, 35 Stat. 1880, 1883, T.S. No. 465.

326   *See* Brown, *The Armed Occupation of Santo Domingo*, 11 A.J.I.L. 394, 395–96 (1917).

327   Convention Respecting Customs Revenues, Sept. 24, 1940, United States-Dominican Republic, art. 1, 55 Stat. 1104, 1105, T.S. No. 965.

328   Convention Concerning a Loan, Jan. 10, 1911, United States-Honduras, in 4 UNPERFECTED TREATIES OF THE UNITED STATES OF AMERICA 195 (C. Wiktor ed.

1979), *reprinted in* 5 A.J.I.L. 274 (Supp. 1911). *See* Editorial Comment, *The Proposed Loan Conventions Between the United States and Honduras and the United States and Nicaragua*, 5 A.J.I.L. 1044 (1911). *See also* Baker, *Ideals and Realities in the Wilson Administration's Relations with Honduras*, 21 AMERICAS 3 (1964).

329 Convention Concerning a Loan, June 6, 1911, United States-Nicaragua, in 4 UN-PERFECTED TREATIES, *supra* note 318, at 213, *reprinted in* 5 A.J.I.L. 291 (Supp. 1911).

330 Convention Regarding a Canal Route and Naval Base, Aug. 5, 1914, United States-Nicaragua, 39 Stat. 1661, T.S. No. 624. *See* H. DAVIS, J. FINAN & F. PECK, LATIN AMERICAN DIPLOMATIC HISTORY 160–62 (1977).

331 Treaty Regarding Finances, Economic Development and Tranquility, Sept. 16, 1915, United States-Haiti, 39 Stat. 1654, T.S. No. 623, *reprinted in* 10 A.J.I.L. 234 (Supp. 1916).

332 *See* L. LANGLEY, THE UNITED STATES AND THE CARIBBEAN 1900–1970, at 53–58, 116–25, 149–50 (1980); D. MUNRO, THE UNITED STATES AND THE LATIN AMERICAN REPUBLICS 1921–1933, at 277, 309 (1974) [hereinafter cited as MUNRO, REPUBLICS]; Munro, *Dollar Diplomacy in Nicaragua, 1909–1913*, 38 HISPANIC AM. HIST. REV. 209 (1958).

333 MUNRO, REPUBLICS, *supra* note 332, at 72, 309–41.

334 *Id.* at 139–43. *See also* Baker, *The Woodrow Wilson Administration and Guatemalan Relations*, 27 HISTORIAN 155, 165–66 (1965) (U.S. troops landed in 1920 to protect legation); Wright, *Honduras: A Case Study of United States Support of Free Elections in Central America*, 40 HISPANIC AM. HIST. REV. 212 (1960).

335 *See generally* Adler, *Bryan and Wilsonian Caribbean Penetration*, 20 HISPANIC AM. HIST. REV. 198 (1940).

336 *See, e.g.*, W. KUEHL, SEEKING WORLD ORDER 118 (1969); Alvarez, *Latin America and International Law*, 3 A.J.I.L. 269 (1909) (manner of contribution by Latin American nations to the development of law of nations); Armstrong, *Should the Monroe Policy Be Modified or Abandoned?*, 10 A.J.I.L. 77, 99 (1916); Hughes, *Observations on the Monroe Doctrine*, 17 A.J.I.L. 611 (1923) (historical perspectives and current usefulness of the Monroe Doctrine); Olney, *The Development of International Law*, 1 A.J.I.L. 418, 425–27 (1907); Woolsey, *An American Concept of the Powers*, 45 SCRIBNER'S MAG. 364 (1909) (differences in theory and practice of state equality).

337 *Were American Lives Really in Danger?*, Manchester Guardian Weekly, Nov. 6, 1983, at 15, col. 1; *Grenada and the Rule of Law*, *id.*, Nov. 6, 1983, at 1, col. 1; *School's Chancellor Says Invasion Not Necessary to Save Lives*, N.Y. Times, Oct. 26, 1983, § I, at 20, col. 5; *From Rescued Students, Gratitude and Praise*, N.Y. Times, Oct. 28, 1983, § I, at 1, col. 3; *Ex-Official Cites Ease in Leaving Grenada Day Before Invasion*, N.Y. Times, Oct. 29, 1983, § I, at 7, col. 3. *See also* H. O'SHAUGH-NESSY, GRENADA (1984).

338 *Legal Basis for the Invasion*, N.Y. Times, Oct. 27, 1983, § I, at 22, col. 1. *See* Boyle, *International Law in Time of Crisis: From the Entebbe Raid to the Hostages Convention*, 75 NW. U.L. REV. 769 (1980); Brownlie, *Humanitarian Intervention*, in LAW AND CIVIL WAR IN THE MODERN WORLD 217 (J. N. Moore ed. 1974).

339 *See Text of Reagan's Announcement of Invasion*, N.Y. Times, Oct. 26, 1983, § I, at 16, col. 1; *Legal Basis for the Invasion*, *supra* note 338.

340 *See* Bowett, *Interrelation of Theories of Intervention and Self Defense*, in LAW AND CIVIL WAR IN THE MODERN WORLD 38 (J. N. Moore ed. 1974); Brownlie, *Humanitarian Intervention*, *supra* note 338.

341 *See* D. BOWETT, THE LAW OF INTERNATIONAL INSTITUTIONS 161–68 (4th ed. 1982); A. CHAYES, T. EHRLICH & A. LOWENFELD, 2 INTERNATIONAL LEGAL PROCESS 1077–90 (1968).

342 *Legal Basis for the Invasion, supra* note 338; *Legality of Grenada Attack Disputed,* N.Y. Times, Oct. 26, 1983, § I, at 19, col. 1; *Most OAS Members Assail Action,* N.Y. Times, Oct. 27, 1983, § I, at 19, col. 1; *Transcript of Address by President on Lebanon and Grenada,* N.Y. Times, Oct. 28, 1983, § I, at 10, col. 1.

343 *Britain's Grenada Shut-Out,* ECONOMIST, March 10, 1984, at 32.

344 *Id.* at 34.

345 *Id.*

346 *See, e.g.,* Moore, *Grenada and the International Double Standard,* 78 A.J.I.L. 145 (1984).

347 U.S. DEP'T OF STATE, TREATIES IN FORCE—January 1, 1983, at 267.

348 OAS CHARTER, April 30, 1948, 2 U.S.T. 2394, T.I.A.S. No. 2361, 119 U.N.T.S. 3, *revised by* the Protocol of Buenos Aires, Feb. 27, 1967, 21 U.S.T. 607, T.I.A.S. No. 6847.

349 *See Transcript of Address by President on Lebanon and Grenada, supra* note 342; *Transcript of Schultz's News Conference on Why U.S. Acted,* N.Y. Times, Oct. 26, 1983, § I, at 18, col. 1.

350 CHARTER OF THE ORGANISATION OF EASTERN CARIBBEAN STATES, *opened for signature* June 18, 1981, 20 I.L.M. 1166 (entered into force July 4, 1981).

351 *Transcript of Schultz's News Conference on Why U.S. Acted, supra* note 349.

352 Inter-American Treaty of Reciprocal Assistance (Rio Pact), Sept. 2, 1947, 62 Stat. 1681, T.I.A.S. No. 1838, 21 U.N.T.S. 77.

353 North Atlantic Treaty, April 4, 1949, 63 Stat. 2241, T.I.A.S. No. 1964, 34 U.N.T.S. 243.

354 *See* D. BOWETT, *supra* note 341; 2 A. CHAYES, T. EHRLICH, & A. LOWENFELD, *supra* note 341, at 1077–90; T. FRANCK, *Who Killed Article 2(4)?,* 64 A.J.I.L. 809, 827 (1970).

355 OECS CHARTER art. 8, *supra* note 350.

356 *Legality of Grenada Attack Disputed, supra* note 342.

357 *See id.*

358 *Transcript of Schultz's News Conference on Why U.S. Acted, supra* note 349.

359 *See, e.g.,* L. SOHN, CASES ON UNITED NATIONS LAW 862-1072 (2d ed. 1967).

360 *See* 2 A. CHAYES, T. EHRLICH & A. LOWENFELD, *supra* note 341, at 1057–1149.

361 *Id.* at 1072.

362 *See, e.g.,* Office of the Legal Adviser, Dep't of State, *The Case for U.S. Action on Cuba,* 47 DEP'T ST. BULL. 763 (1962) [hereafter cited as *U.S. Action*].

363 *See* 2 A. CHAYES, T. EHRLICH & A. LOWENFELD, *supra* note 341, at 1150–1233.

364 Resolution of the Council of the O.A.S., April 30, 1965 OEA/Ser.G/V (C–d–1311), 52 DEP'T ST. BULL. 739 (1965).

365 Tenth Meeting of Consultation, Resolution of Mar. 6, 1965, OEA/Ser.F/II.10 Doc. 39, Rev. 2, 52 DEP'T ST. BULL. 862–63 (1965).

366 *See* 2 A. CHAYES, T. EHRLICH & A. LOWENFELD, *supra* note 341, at 1150–1233; 20 U.N. SCOR (1220th mtg.) at 16–17, U.N. Doc. S/P.V. 1220 (1965).

367 OAS CHARTER (rev.) art. 59, *supra* note 348.

368 83 DEP'T ST. BULL. 89 (Dec. 1983).

369 84 DEP'T ST. BULL. 92 (Jan. 1984).

370 1965–I PUBLIC PAPERS OF THE PRESIDENTS OF THE UNITED STATES: LYNDON

B. JOHNSON 469–73.

371   *Quoted in* Schwebel, *The Brezhnev Doctrine Repealed and Peaceful Co-Existence Enacted*, 66 A.J.I.L. 816 (1972).

372   *Compare* L. SOHN, CASES ON UNITED NATIONS LAW 1025-72 (2d ed. 1967) *with* Report of the Security Council, 24 U.N. GAOR Supp. (No. 2) at 66–72, U.N. Doc. A/7602 (1969).

373   N.Y. Times, Jan. 4, 1980, at 1, col. 5; *id.*, Jan. 12, 1980, at 4, col. 5.

374   War Powers Act, 50 U.S.C. §§ 1541–1548 (1976 & Supp. V 1981).

375   Central American Defense Council Pact, Dec. 14, 1963, 517 U.N.T.S. 149. *See* Saxe-Fernandez, *The Central American Defense Council and Pax America*, in LATIN AMERICAN RADICALISM 75 (I. Horowitz, J. de Castro, & J. Gerassi ed. 1969).

376   Clark Amendment to the International Security Assistance and Arms Export Control Act of 1976, Pub. L. No. 94–329, 90 Stat. 729, 757 (current version codified at 22 U.S.C. § 2293 (1982)).

377   N.Y. Times, Jun. 22, 1979, at 1, col. 5; *id.*, Jun. 22, 1979, at 8, col. 2; *id.*, Jun. 23, 1979, at 3, col. 1; *id.*, Jun. 25, 1979, at 11, col. 1.

378   *See generally* L. SOHN, CASES ON UNITED NATIONS LAW (2d ed. 1967); L. SOHN, UNITED NATIONS IN ACTION (1968).

379   Convention Relative to the Laying of Submarine Mines (Hague VIII), Oct. 18, 1907, 36 Stat. 2332, T.S. 541, 3 Martens (3d) at 580.

380   War Powers Act, *supra* note 374.

381   *See, e.g.*, Neutrality Act, 18 U.S.C. §§ 956, 960 (1982).

382   Ethics in Government Act, 28 U.S.C. §§ 591–598 (1982).

383   Continuing Appropriations for Fiscal Year 1983 (Boland Amendment), Pub. L. No. 97-377, § 793, 96 Stat. 1830, 1865 (1982).

384   Accountability for Intelligence Activities Act, 50 U.S.C. § 413 (Supp. V. 1981).

385   *See Military and Paramilitary Activities in and Against Nicaragua* (Nicar. v. U.S.), 1984 I.C.J. – – – (Interim Protection Order of May 10).

386   N.Y. Times, Jan. 23, 1981, at 3, col. 1; *id.*, Mar. 14, 1982, § IV, at 22, col. 1; *id.*, Mar. 6, 1983, § I, at 1, col. 5; *id.*, Apr. 7, 1983, § I, at 1, col. 1.

387   McCartney, *Search for Arms: Proof of Source Elusive in El Salvador*, Wash. Post, Jul. 8, 1984, at 1, col. 1.

388   *See Corfu Channel* (U.K. v. Alb.), 1949 I.C.J. 4, 18 (Judgment of April 9).

389   *See* Greenberger, *Congress Skeptics Balk at Nicaragua Evidence*, Wall St. J., Jun. 15, 1984, at 22; McCartney, *supra* note 387; Taubman, *In From the Cold and Hot for Truth*, N.Y. Times, Jun. 11, 1984, at 14, col. 3; MacMichaels, *Democrats Can Seize Central America Issue*, N.Y. Times, Jul. 17, 1984, § I, at 21, col. 1.

390   Boland Amendment, *supra* note 383.

391   *See, e.g.*, Declaration on the Inadmissibility of Intervention in the Domestic Affairs of States and the Protection of Their Independence and Sovereignty, G.A. Res. 2131, 20 U.N. GAOR Supp. (No. 14) at 11, U.N. Doc. A/6014 (1966); Declaration on the Principles of International Law Concerning Friendly Relations and Co-operation Among States in Accordance with the Charter of the United Nations, G.A. Res. 2625, 25 U.N. GAOR Supp. (No. 28) at 121, U.N. Doc. A/8028 (1971).

392   *See* Lovler, *Training for the Counterrevolution: Cuban Guerrillas in Florida*, 238 NATION 265 (1981).

393   *See* Shneyer & Barta, *The Legality of the U.S. Economic Blockade of Cuba Under International Law*, 13 CASE W. RES. J. INT'L L. 451 (1981). *See also* Dominguez,

Cuban Foreign Policy, FOREIGN AFF., Fall 1978, at 83.

394 Neutrality Act, *supra* note 381.

395 22 U.S.C. § 461 (1982).

396 Res. VI of the Eighth Meeting of Consultation of Ministers of Foreign Affairs, Jan. 31, 1962, OEA/Ser. F/II.8, Doc. 68, at 17–19.

397 *See U.S. Action, supra* note 362, at 765.

398 From May 6 to 13, 1984, this author visited Cuba as part of a five-man delegation of U.S. international law professors at the invitation of the Cuban National Union of Jurists. During that time we conducted extensive interviews with high-level Foreign Ministry officials, Communist Party officials in charge of foreign affairs, and international law professors who serve as consultants to the Foreign Ministry. I will attempt to portray their collective legal-political position as accurately as possible.

399 A. HAIG, CAVEAT 129 (1984).

400 Cuba Trip, *supra* note 398.

401 *Id.*

402 S.C. Res. 435 (1978), *reprinted in* 17 I.L.M. 1563 (1978). *See* U.N. MONTHLY CHRONICLE, Dec. 1978, at 5 (South Africa agrees to cooperate with plan). *See generally* L. SOHN & T. BUERGENTHAL, INTERNATIONAL PROTECTION OF HUMAN RIGHTS 337–504 (1973).

403 N.Y. Times, Feb. 7, 1982, at 4, col. 3; *id.*, July 23, 1982, at 2, col. 3.

404 *See* N.Y. Times, Jan. 14, 1983, § I, at 5, col. 5.

405 Clark Amendment, *supra* note 376.

406 International Convention on the Suppression and Punishment of the Crime of Apartheid, *opened for signature* Nov. 30, 1973, 13 I.L.M. 51 (1974).

Notes to Conclusion

1 *See* N. MACHIAVELLI, THE PRINCE 149 (M. Musa trans. & ed. 1964).

2 *Id.* at 147.

Index

Acheson, Dean, 5, 7
Afghanistan: Soviet invasion of, 213–17, 227
Aircraft, unlawful seizure of, defined, 85
Alabama Claims, 44
Ali, Mohammed, 214
Allison, Graham, 74
Allon, Yigal, 91, 93, 94, 95, 98
American Society of International Law, 48; and founding of *American Journal of International Law*, 23
Amin, Idi, 94, 95, 98, 114, 119, 122–23, 151
Andropov, Yuri, 261–62
Anti-Ballistic Missile Systems Treaty (1972), 255–56, 260
Arab Defense Forces (ADF), 237–38
Austin, John, 18–20
Avineri, Shlomo, 93–95

Bacon, Robert, 23
Bakhtiar, Shahpur, 188
Balance of power: as component of political realism, 8, 173
Bani-Sadr, Abolhassan, 193–94
Barre, Siad, 133, 217
Bazargan, Mehdi, 183
Begin, Menachem, 110, 115, 230, 246
Ben-Elissar, Eliahu, 233
Berlin airlift, 11
Berman, Harold, 5

Bethmann-Hollweg, German Chancellor, 47
Beyond the Nation-State (1964): as statement of functional-integrationist approach, 6
Bishop, Maurice, 274
Blaine, James, 267
Boland Amendment, 185, 283
Brezhnev, Leonid, 208, 278
Brzezinski, Zbigniew, 16, 154, 188, 202, 214, 293, 295
Brown, Harold, 213, 250, 254
Bryan, William Jennings, 23, 40–41, 48

Cambodia: invasion of, 209
Camp David Accords, 132, 245
Caroline, The, 87, 111, 189, 232
Carr, Edward Hallett, 7, 12–13
Carter administration, 204–17; and invasion of Afghanistan, 213–17; and Iran-Iraq War, 218–19; and Iranian Hostages Crisis, 183–92, 219–21; and nuclear arms control, 250, 254, 263–64; and Presidential Directive 59, 259–61
Casablanca Case, 32
Central American Defense Council Pact (CONDECA), 279
Christopher, Warren, 201
Church, Frank, 185, 206
Clark Amendment, 185, 279
Clark, Grenville, 70